WINNING

A RACE DRIVER'S HANDBOOK

George A. Anderson
Guest Authors: Carroll Smith, Bertil Roos, Paul Van Valkenburgh, Danny Collins,
Dennis Eade, Tony Kester, Kathy Maleck, Charlie and Norma Williams

Motorbooks International
Publishers & Wholesalers ®

Acknowledgments

I have seen books with long lists of names in the acknowledgments; now I understand why. I owe thanks to a lot of people for lessons taught, support, suggestions, critique, and information—without which this book may not have happened. Among them are: Bill Bergeron, Dallas Burns, Danny Collins, Paul Dybro, Dennis Eade, Bruce Foss, John Gianelli, Bruce Hanson, Scott Hutchison, Gene Kath, Tony Kester, Kathy Maleck, Kevin Palmer, Paul Pfanner, Bertil Roos, Carroll Smith, Dick Schmidt, Craig Taylor, Charlie and Norma Williams, Bob Witham, Paul Van Valkenburgh, and, finally, my wife Sandie, who has put up with this crazy hobby since her first ride in my three-carb Austin-Healey 3000 in 1968. Thanks to all of them and to the many others whom I have missed in this listing!

First published in 1993 by Motorbooks International Publishers & Wholesalers, PO Box 2, 729 Prospect Avenue, Osceola, WI 54020 USA

Motorbooks International books are also available at discounts in bulk quantity for industrial or sales-promotional use. For details write to Special Sales Manager at the Publisher's address

Library of Congress Cataloging-in-Publication Data

Anderson, George A.
    Winning : a race drivers handbook / George A. Anderson.
        p.   cm.
    Includes index.
    ISBN 0-87938-776-9
    1. Automobile racing.   I. Title.
    GV1029.S53   1993
    796.7'2—dc20   93-25518

On the front cover: Two of the most exciting SCCA racing classes: top, Rookie of the Year Jacques Villeneuve runs at Long Beach in the professional Toyota Atlantic Championship in April 1993; bottom, a Showroom Stock C class Miata leads the pack at the Mid-Ohio National on May 16, 1993. *Geoffrey Hewitt*

Printed and bound in the United States of America

Contents

Introduction

This book is the product of four or five winters spent sitting around, thinking about racing. It began as a four-page handout when, as Competition License Chairman for the Sports Car Club of America (SCCA) Land'O Lakes Region, I found myself answering the same aspiring drivers' questions over and over again. The handout expanded to twenty or thirty pages when I took over as Chief Instructor for the Land'O Lakes Driver School at Brainerd International Raceway in northern Minnesota. It has now expanded into a whole book due to encouragement from Tim Parker of Motorbooks International.

My objective in providing the information has remained the same—to give new racers a help with the logistics of getting started and a grounding in topics that are important to going fast, important to making life simpler, or just fun.

This book is intended to fill a gap in the available racing books. While there are plenty of "car" books and "driving" books currently on the market, there has not been a good "getting started" book since Alan Johnson's *Driving in Competition*, written over twenty years ago. Frankly, I find the books written by big-name drivers to be mostly useless. They're usually ghost-written, tend to be anecdotal rather than tutorial, and are obviously the opinions of individuals who are many years removed from amateur racing. Great for tourists and "wannabe" racers, but not too valuable for someone starting a racing hobby or career.

I have tried to provide two kinds of information in this book. First, I've included facts that are not available elsewhere in any organized form. This includes information specific to club-level amateur racing, both to get started and to run your first few weekends. Second, you'll find introductory-level information on the basics of vehicle dynamics, tires, and cornering.

But you are not done buying books after you have bought this one. Books selling for $20–$30 each are a lot less expensive as learning tools than are race weekends at a $1,000 each. In the past few years, good instructional videotapes have also become available. Make a practice of buying (or borrowing) both kinds of information sources. There are no universal answers to going fast, but exposing yourself to many different ideas will help you find your personal way.

By the way, please study this book's section on eye technique before you spend much time with racing videos. The camera operators do not usually understand eye technique and thus do not show you, the driver, what you need to be looking at. Don't let them teach you tunnel vision.

The opinions and facts in this book come from more than twelve years of racing Formula Fords, along with a few rentals in other classes, and a prior five years or so of autocrossing (now called Solo II) in a Lotus Elan and a 289 Cobra roadster. Over that period of time, I've won a few races, lost more, and DNFed and crashed a few times. I've also had two stints at Bertil Roos' driving school. I've been teaching aspiring race drivers for the past ten years at the Land'O Lakes region driver school, have been Chief Instructor for Land'O Lakes for the past three, and have served as an Instructor for the SCCA National Racing School.

I'm an engineer by training (and it probably shows in the book). About ten years ago, I developed and marketed a computer suspension-analysis service. For a few years, I ran a mail-order racing parts business called The Book. The business became the basis for what is now Donnybrooke Motor Racing Equipment, our local race shop and Spec Racer outlet. The business gave me a lot of practice answering novice drivers' questions. I hope that's made this a better book.

GUEST AUTHORS

During my years of racing, I've been fortunate to meet and get to know many people who know more than I do about the sport. Later on, I will tell you about camaraderie among racers. There's no stronger evidence of that than the number of friends who have agreed to help me with this book. Supplementing my opinions, you will find additional comments from a number of knowledgeable people:

Danny Collins has been racing for thirty-nine (!) years, beginning with a supercharged 1500cc Alfa Romeo in 1953. His racing resume includes Ferraris in the United States, Corvettes and Formula Juniors in Europe, and recently, winning Midwest Division races in a homemade Formula Continental. The people he's run against are a "who's who" of worldwide sports car racing.

Danny has been teaching aspiring racers since his days as SCCA's first Director of Driver Training in 1972. He also created and ran SCCA Enterprises' National Racing School, active from 1988 to 1990. By Danny's estimate, he has taught over 3,000 aspiring drivers.

Dennis Eade has been taking care of race cars for more than twenty years. He began crewing on a friend's Formula Vee in 1971, leaving the real world to go racing full time (mostly Formula Fords and Sports 2000s) in 1975. In 1981, he started Competition Preparations (Comprep), which, in its first full year of operation, prepared the SCCA national Formula Atlantic champion. Of 1983, the first year of pro Sports

2000, Dennis says: "We won all the races." Simple as that. The next few years saw two East Coast Formula Atlantic championships, and in 1990–1991, Comprep was responsible for the US factory Reynard Formula Atlantic effort. Now, in 1992, he is building a brand-new Atlantic car, designated the XFR92XS.

Tony Kester has competed in hundreds of races, in cars ranging from small sedans to International Motor Sports Association (IMSA) Camel Lights. He has also done thousands of miles of testing for manufacturers such as Hoosier and Goodyear, Oldsmobile, and Lola Cars, and for dozens of independent teams.

Tony was a divisional SCCA champion, 1990 Formula Ford national champion, and 1991 Olds Pro Series champion (winning a record six races of nine, five of them in a row). He holds and has held numerous track records.

Through his Datasport consulting business, Tony has coached scores of drivers with many wins and championships to their credit.

Kathy Maleck has been throwing flags at racers for sixteen years and has worked races all over the world. These races have included Formula One (forty-five of them), twenty-four-hour enduros, Formula Ford Festivals in England, and club events all over the United States. She's also the current SCCA National Administrator of Flagging and Communications, and has served as a race chair for twelve years as well as holding various regional offices. In the real world, Kathy's an accountant. The text on flags has benefitted from her professional attention to detail.

Bertil Roos' racing career began with a homemade Formula Vee in Sweden in 1967, and progressed to include six major championships and experience in rallying, ice racing, sports racing classes, Can-Am, IndyCars, and most Formula classes, including Formula One. For the last sixteen years, he's been teaching aspiring racers at his school in the Poconos, north of Philadelphia.

Carroll Smith has, I think, been racing since wheel spokes were made from wood. He raced in Fords at Le Mans in the 1960s, and most recently with son Chris in Formula Atlantic. You'll be buying at least two of his books, so you can read all about his background there.

Paul Van Valkenburgh is a professional racing engineer and author whose career began in the 1960s and includes extensive work with Mark Donohue in the original Trans-Am series. You'll be buying Paul's book *Race Car Engineering* too, so you can read about him later as well.

Charlie Williams and **Norma Williams** have been involved in SCCA racing for over twenty-five years. Charlie began building engines and preparing race cars in 1968 and has done engines for everything from Formula Vee to Formula 5000. His engines have won three national championships and currently hold at least seven lap records around the country. His first national championship came in 1978, when Dan Gurney chose Charlie's engines to power David Loring in the then-revolutionary Eagle Formula Ford. Most recently, Charlie powered Craig Taylor to the 1991 United States Automobile Club (USAC) Formula 2000 title, also receiving USAC's Western Series Engine Builder of the Year award.

In addition to taking care of her two racing sons, Brian and Keith, Norma is unofficial mother to half the paddock. Norma runs the Williams racing team while allowing Charlie and the boys to believe that they are in charge. To find Charlie and Norma, look for a big black trailer behind a motor home with plastic geraniums decorating its steps.

Throughout the book, all of these experts will provide additional information, whether it's a real-life example, or to expand on a point I've made. In some cases, however, they disagree with me or with each other and will tell you why.

Pay special attention to these areas of disagreement. You will learn that there is no one solution that works for everybody. The process of learning to race involves taking in a lot of often contradictory information and, finally, finding your own best way.

THE APPENDICES

There are, of course, many subjects that I cannot cover in depth or even touch on. Space is too short and, at this stage of your career, much of the available technical information is superfluous anyway. In the Appendices, I have included a list of the books that I have found most useful in learning about racing and understanding how the cars work. You can sail into them as you're ready. Throughout the text, I will be referring to these authors; for example, "Paul Frère says…" and so on. Where you see such an author reference, you will find the book listed in the Publications section of the Appendices.

I have also included a glossary of terminology in the Appendices. If you see a term you don't understand, hopefully you will find it there. Also, the Glossary contains a few bits of information that didn't fit anywhere else. I encourage you to at least skim through it.

Finally, by special arrangement with the publisher of *Sports Car* magazine, I have been able to reprint their series of "Hot Laps" articles. These articles, included as an appendix, give you specific information on how to drive most of the SCCA tracks across the country. Their expert authors are also a resource for you in considering how the book's somewhat theoretical discussions of cornering can be applied to real racetracks.

A FEW CAUTIONS

I will not be telling you anything about front-drive cars. There are two reasons for this. First, I do not have any competition experience in such cars. Second, front-wheel-drive is a totally inappropriate configuration for a car that is to be driven fast.

Front-drive cars have been popularized for three reasons: they are cheap and easy to manufacture, they are inherently lighter weight than rear-wheel-drive cars (hence, better fuel economy) and they feature huge understeer in almost any situation, which is preferred in cars designed for low-performance, untrained drivers.

(None of the above is intended to demean those who race front-drive cars. To me, racing one of these cars is a little like choosing to compete in a three-legged sack race. You can have a lot of fun, but it is not the configuration for maximum performance.)

Tony Kester: "I also feel that front-wheel drive is not the choice for high performance. But after seeing many Showroom Stock FWD drivers go on to successful careers—due to factory connections—I feel that it is an important area of expertise for an aspiring professional."

Danny Collins: "You can learn to go fast in anything. Just don't try to make your street car over into a race car unless it falls into a Showroom Stock or Improved Touring car class. It's too expensive and the cost-time-benefit ratio isn't worth the bother."

I will also not be telling you much about car tuning, about suspensions, or about engines. Two reasons for this: First, there's plenty to cover in this book without poaching on subjects that have been well covered by others; and second, you shouldn't be concentrating on the car's performance during your first year anyway. You, the driver, are where investment of time and money will pay off best.

A word about finances: This book would be incomplete without a discussion of racing costs, so I have included some numbers in 1992 dollars. If you are reading the book some time after its publication, please mentally adjust the cost figures to reflect inflation. Racing costs never go up at *less* than inflation!

One final comment paraphrases the disclaimer provided in Carroll Smith's *Tune to Win*: "Racing is dangerous. You can be injured or killed doing it. The information, ideas, and techniques provided herein apply to a properly-prepared, responsibly-driven racing car participating in a controlled and sanctioned racing event. I do not recommend your exploring the limit under any other circumstances. In any event, exploring the limit inevitably involves exceeding it once in a while. Your decision to conduct the exploration is yours, as are the consequences. I disclaim responsibility for your actions—and your accidents."

TWO OTHER MANDATORY BOOKS

Two books need to be mentioned up front: *Prepare to Win* and *Tune to Win,* both written by Carroll Smith in 1975 and 1978, respectively, and published by Aero Publishers. If you are serious about going racing, you will buy these two books. Period. All other books are optional.

Prepare to Win is a short course in mechanical engineering as applied to race cars. You will learn about hardware, tools, and techniques. More important than the specific technical information, though, is the philosophy: prevention, thoroughness, and attention to detail. Read and believe.

Tune to Win builds on *Prepare to Win* by teaching you how to make your car go faster. Again, thoroughness and attention to detail are the keys. A tenth of a second here, a tenth there, and fifteen laps later you have a significant advantage.

Even if you are going to pay others to prepare and tune your car, your performance (and your life) depends on the work being done properly. Buy the books, study them, and be an educated consumer. There isn't a *competent* race mechanic in the world who doesn't want his customers to understand what he's doing.

Charlie Williams: "The more a customer knows, the easier it makes my job. If you have a problem, I can talk you through it. The more you get involved, the more my work is appreciated."

These books should be available from your local race parts supplier. Racing businesses are pretty marginal undertakings, usually run by knowledgeable and helpful people. You need to know such people. They need you as a customer. You may also call Classic Motorbooks at 1-800-826-6600, with your Master Card or Visa number handy. (You will quickly learn that there are three essential cards in a driver's wallet: club membership, racing license, and credit card.)

Danny Collins: "Today, an ever-increasing number of enthusiasts is becoming involved in one facet or another of motorsports, whether it be 'run-what-you-brung' parking lot autocrosses, speed events with marque clubs such as the Porsche Club of America, Ferrari clubs, BMW clubs, or other clubs conducting informal speed events on racetracks.

"Many of these drivers have followed racing for years and have reached a point in their lives where they want to fulfill their fantasies of driving a race car in competition...whether it be with SCCA or with the many regional and vintage sports car clubs located throughout the country.

"This book will help prospective participants gain a deeper understanding of the sport they are considering entering. Or it can offer more insight to those already competing in the sport.

"One cautionary note: Don't be overwhelmed by the detailed information. You don't have to memorize or comprehend all of this vast store of data to get started in racing. All racing instructors are so enthusiastic to share their vast storehouse of tricks, that it's easy for them to overlook the fact that they successfully started with a fraction of the experience and knowledge they try to cram down the throats of novices.

"Every prospective racer is different. They bring to a racing school widely differing backgrounds and experiences. By the end of two to four days, you can become amazingly proficient. We all manage to become successful by enthusiastic determination and practice.

"In 1962, I had the privilege of racing against three future World Champions in England in the three-hour 'Tourist Trophy.' The three, Jimmy Clark, Graham Hill, and John Surtees, all displayed different driving techniques. Jimmy Clark was wild, colorful, and flamboyant. John Surtees, then eight-time World Motorcycle Champion, drove so smoothly, as you might expect from a bike rider, you hardly knew he was on the racetrack. Graham Hill drove a more mechanical, 'by-the-book' technique. Despite these widely differing techniques, all three soon became World Formula 1 Champions.

"It's been my long observation that with proper motivation and practice, we can all become quite proficient. But first, we must try it!

"In the Appendices, George lists a number of professional schools devoted to fulfilling your dreams without your having to invest in a race car. Today you have broad choices, whereas in the old days you had to commit to buying a car, preparing it, and forging your way through a maze of rules and requirements on your own. Many novices today rent a variety of cars for one or two seasons before actually committing to the purchase of a car for racing.

"The hardest part of racing is making the decision to start and then following through.

"This book should whet your appetite with insight and knowledge. However, you have to follow up by taking advantage of the opportunities herein offered so you can shift your butt from that sofa to the bucket seat of a race car!"

Chapter 1

Getting Started

WHAT *IS* CLUB RACING?

Club racing is the grassroots of American sports car racing. Thousands of racers gather at road racing tracks across the country on most summer weekends, competing with each other for the fun of it, with no prize money involved. These are usually closed events where spectators are not allowed. Most of these racers never go on to professional series, such as IndyCars, but rather remain forever amateurs, balancing family and career with one of the most consuming hobbies in the world.

There is no money and little glory—but lots of fun. The satisfaction and enjoyment are internal and are very hard to explain to anyone who has not tried it. The closest you can get in a book is probably Peter Scott's description of on-track sessions in his book *Racing! The Drivers Handbook*, Part 4: "Race Weekend," beginning with "1:20PM Saturday."

Most club racing in the United States is sanctioned by the Sports Car Club of America, although there are several smaller sanctioning bodies as well. These organizations define the classes for racing cars and the rules of racing. The members of the clubs comprise the volunteer workers who manage the race weekends. All are nonprofit organizations. (With the clubs, unprofitable status is a matter of legal choice. With racers and the tracks, it's just the way things seem to turn out.)

Since nobody makes any money at club racing, there's little publicity. As a potential participant, you will have to work a bit to locate contacts, and you will probably find the volunteer membership and licensing bureaucracy to be a bit of a challenge. In the end, though, these clubs offer fun and camaraderie that is hard to match anywhere else.

SCCA has two levels of club racing, National and Regional. National races are points events, leading to the annual SCCA National Championship Race, referred to by everyone as the Runoffs (In fact, it's now legally an SCCA trademark). Regional races are, at least theoretically, a lower-pressure environment where everybody is running for fun. In practice, the main difference between Regionals and Nationals is that speeds and the level of equipment tend to be somewhat higher at Nationals. Most SCCA drivers have National racing licenses and run both types of events.

Participation is wide open; there are doctors, lawyers, and preachers. There are also sheet-metal workers, bureaucrats, and farmers. The only requirement is a dedication to the hobby—dedication at a level that few of us understood when we began.

As a racing driver or aspiring driver, you will be the minority in club membership. (In SCCA, you're about 15%. Of 55,000 members, drivers are 7,000–9,000.) Most participants in club racing are not drivers, they are the workers and officials who crew on the cars and who staff and manage the racing. In fact, most drivers get started in club racing as crew members or by "working a weekend" as a race official.

WHAT IT'S LIKE

You should understand what you're getting into.

Racing is a selfish sport. If you become a serious racer, you will give it more physical and mental energy, more time, and more money than you ever expected. This will be energy, time, and money that would otherwise be expended in other important areas of your life, like your family and your career. Don't say I didn't warn you.

So why do we do it? You can probably get a hundred different answers to that question. My theory is that there is some kind of physical mechanism, like the runner's "endorphin high," at work. It is absolutely impossible to describe the feeling of driving a car in high-speed competition, particularly the intensity of the experience. It is emotionally, if not physically, addicting. Again, I warned you.

IS IT DANGEROUS?

Club racing is not a particularly dangerous sport. Your life insurance company, for example, won't ask about it

Most racetrack paddocks feature ample space for teams to set up and spread out. Often there's grass, but sometimes just sand and dirt. There is hardly ever any significant amount of shade.

Used tires, properly placed and anchored, can absorb a terrific amount of energy, providing valuable protection for drivers, as with this H-Production MG Midget/Austin-Healey Sprite. Randy McKee

when you apply for coverage. They do, however, often ask whether you're a skydiver or a private pilot.

Why is the reality of racing so different from the public and newspaper "image" of the sport?

First, all club racing organizations place a tremendous emphasis on safety. It is difficult, though not impossible, for a driver to get an unsafe car onto the racetrack. Cars are inspected at least annually, and there are strict requirements on safety items like roll structures and fuel cells. There are similarly strict requirements on driver safety gear, like suits and helmets.

Second, club racing tracks are safe. Both the track owners and the sanctioning organizations work hard at this. In contrast to the walls at Indianapolis, most club circuits feature large runoff areas and good "tire wall" padding where there *are* walls and other hard objects.

Here's a car coming in after a typical club racing crash. This Formula 440 has "lost a corner" (of the car). The number of damaged corners is the usual measure of crash severity for Formula cars.

The physiology of getting seriously hurt is basically an issue of too-sudden deceleration. Lengthening the time spent crashing reduces peak accelerations and minimizes injuries. Runoff areas and tire walls are terrific crash lengtheners.

Finally, almost all club racing drivers understand that this is for fun, not for money. You get the occasional crazy driver, and national-level racing certainly approaches pro racing in intensity, but most of us will still back out when it gets too dangerous. Most of us are old enough to know we're not going to live forever. And most of us also have to finance and fix what gets broken. It makes a difference.

Charlie Williams: "Don't forget that it takes two to tangle. You can always back off!"

All of that being said, it is still true that there is danger. I was once bumped by the son of a famous IndyCar driver, my right front tire against his left rear as he passed me at 130mph. He was either phenomenally good, or phenomenally lucky. Had he been an inch or two farther over, he would have been launched into an airborne tumble that could well have made him the ex-son of a famous driver. It wasn't fun.

I have also crashed a couple of times, including one time at well over 100mph. My most embarrassing memory is screwing up a pass, touching tires, and launching a friend of mine into an airborne flip resulting in more than $2,000 worth of damage to his car. His only injuries were strap bruises. So this sport really is pretty safe.

By the way, you pay for your own crash damage. There's no easily available insurance and, if there were, it would be prohibitively expensive. Crashes are "no fault," and each driver pays for his or her own repairs regardless of who caused the accident. (In this litigious society, club racing is somewhat unusual. I have never heard of anyone contesting the "no-fault" arrangement or seeking damages from another racer.)

DO YOU HAVE WHAT IT TAKES?

The short answer to this question is: "You won't know until you're out there." Every year, there are drivers who attend all or part of a school and just don't come back. The majority of people who make it to a school, however, do continue on to get their licenses. From that point, they usually drop out only because they can't or won't make the financial, emotional, and time commitments that are required. Everyone underestimates these commitments; so will you.

If you do not do well at long-term projects, then racing probably isn't for you. Like all new drivers that went before you (myself included), you will arrive at your first driver school confidently expecting to stand out as the class star. After all, you've been driving fast all your life, you've watched a lot of racing, and you just know that it's going to be easy.

It *isn't* easy and you are not going to be fast right away. You will probably go for a year or longer before you can realistically assess your abilities and potential.

Paul Van Valkenburgh: "I devoted a whole chapter in my book about what it takes to win. I never considered the driver who just wants to get out there and drive fast—legally. If that's your goal, you might as well just run solo events."

If you do not get along fairly well with people, it will be harder for you. There is a lot of camaraderie among drivers, lots of exchanging information, lots of helping each other, and lots of loaning of tools and parts. To the extent you can join this group, things will be easier. Also, it is difficult to race without one or two friends as crew people. Keeping them coming back is critical to your success. We'll talk more about that later.

You should have at least a moderate level of mechanical aptitude and interest in automobile mechanics. To some extent, the importance of this is inversely proportional to the amount of money you have available to purchase the expertise that you lack. This is especially true with respect to the car's engine.

The chassis, however, is another matter. You will be the only one in the car when you're on the racetrack. Thus, only *you* can gather the information necessary to tune the car's suspension. If you don't understand how the suspension works, tuning will be difficult or impossible. At a minimum, you have to communicate effectively with someone who has the responsibility for adjusting the car. More likely, you will have to do it yourself.

Dennis Eade: "To excel in driving, one needs to be a student of driving tactics, vehicle dynamics, and basic mechanics. A well-rounded knowledge of all three is wonderful, but not always necessary. If you are lacking in an area, be prepared to acquire the assistance of someone with the skills you lack."

Tony Kester: "The driver-mechanic relationship requires that you *communicate* to get the most out of your crew-driver-car combination. To communicate, the driver must have at least a *basic* understanding of race cars."

If you're married or otherwise committed, you should have an understanding spouse or friend. The classiest case of spouse involvement I've ever seen was a couple who used to tow an old Formula Ford to the track behind a beautiful 1930s Rolls-Royce hearse. Their double bed fit neatly in the glassed-in back of the tow car!

There are always exceptions. One was a friend of mine who always painted his race cars the same color so his wife wouldn't know when he spent the money for a new one. He also tended to work on the cars on Sunday mornings when she was in church, thinking (I guess) that he was at home.

Finally, you should have the financial ability to spend several thousand dollars a year on your racing, plus come up with the cash ($5,000–$15,000) for your chosen equipment.

Racing is not cheap. There are people out there who race cars bought with borrowed money. There are also people out there who are spending the rent money on tires. If these are your choices, OK, but I don't advise going about it this way.

You will also see some nice, but expensive setups. The lift gate on this transporter makes a great place to work on the car, and there is living space in the front of the box.

HOW MUCH *DOES* IT COST?

More than you ever expected.

Most beginning racers underestimate the costs. Depending on your financial resources, this can be an annoyance, a family issue, or even a safety hazard. In this section we'll talk about estimating costs, and about where and where not to save money. There are basically three categories of costs: weekend cash expenses, prorated operating costs for the car, and capital costs for the car, tools, and equipment.

WEEKEND CASH EXPENSES

Weekend expenses start with the entry fee. Figure $125–$150, these days. Next, you have to get there, so estimate your tow vehicle gas. Depending on what you're towing with and how far you go, this can be a significant item. Add motel costs or camping fees. Food. Wine or beer on Friday night if you're so inclined (Saturday, too, if the usual free beer party is not enough). Crew expenses are negotiable between the (normally unpaid) crew and the driver—often the driver picks up the food and housing expenses for the crew,

You will see some clever and economical camping setups, particularly at regional races. Here's an open race car trailer that also carries a pop-up truck camper.

An enclosed trailer is nice for hauling the essentials to the racetrack. Of course, the definition of "essentials" tends to expand to fill whatever you're using as a hauler. It's a good thing that this team still has a little room for their car!

but packing everybody into one motel room is pretty common. Your total expenses for the entry, the tow, food, and housing will add up to $300–$500 pretty easily.

Now estimate the consumables for the race car, gas, oil, brake pads, and so on. If you're realistic you'll probably quickly exceed $100 per weekend, especially if you're planning to run something that requires lots of high-octane racing gasoline.

Tire expenses are a major cost variable. For a beginner it's crazy to be putting on new tires ($400–$500) every weekend, but if you expect to do this, figure accordingly.

PRORATED CAR OPERATING COSTS

Now look at how much it costs to operate the race car for the weekend. The biggest item (excluding crash damage) is probably the engine. To get a per-weekend cost, estimate your rebuild cost and divide by the number of weekends between rebuilds. This is a minimum figure assuming you don't blow an engine. For my Formula Ford 1600 and friendly prices from Charlie Williams, I used to figure $150–$200 per weekend. Using a local machine shop and doing your own

assembly, you could easily run for half this figure, but it isn't zero!

Don't forget the cost of "improving" the car during the season, and of the winter chassis rebuild: new seatbelts, paint, U-joints, whatever. If you don't have a car yet, talk to someone who has one similar to what you're considering. Assume their estimates are low; none of us is comfortable with what this stuff costs. If you're the type who just has to have the latest go-fast unobtanium parts, estimate accordingly. Prorate these costs over the number of race weekends you intend to run.

CAPITAL EXPENSES

There are some Truths about buying a race car. The First Truth is that you will not save money by buying a low-priced, clapped-out, and/or obsolete car. The low price will be accompanied by low reliability, expensive items needing replacement, (often) unobtainable parts, and headaches. It will also probably be unsafe.

The Second Truth about car prices is that it does not cost more to race a more expensive car. Parts prices are the

Sample Racing Budget

Tow Vehicle/Camper	250 miles @ 10 MPG	$30
Entry Fee		$125
Food for Driver & Crew	(Camp at race track)	$40
Beer/Wine for Crew		$15
Race Car Consumables	Brake pads, oil, etc.	$100
Race Gas	15 gallons aviation gas @$1.75	$26
Tires	3 weekends @ $450/set	$150
	Total Variable Cost/Weekend	$486
Annual Engine Costs	Rebuild/no major damage	$1,500
Annual Race Car	Maintenance & Improvements	$1,000
Tow Vehicle & Trailer	Insurance & Maintenance	$1,000
		$3,500
	divide by 7 race weekends	$500
	Total Race Weekend Cost	$986

same or lower, per-weekend costs are unchanged, and (assuming you paid a fair price) a quality car won't depreciate much more than a junker.

So pick a class in which you can afford to buy a good mid-priced car. If the tradeoff is between the beater Sports 2000 or the clean Formula Ford 1600, go for the Ford. If you can afford a *good* S2000, fine, go for it. Don't worry about a few hundred dollars one way or another to get a quality car; you won't notice it as much as you will notice being parked in the grass because your junker let you down again.

Tony Kester: "Look for a well-maintained, well-set-up car driven by a competent but middle-of-the-pack driver. The fast guys tend to use cars up."

Also take a hard look at other capital expenses. They can be significant. First, there's the trailer. An enclosed trailer is really nice and a used trailer bought right won't depreciate much. (Often, a car seller will sell the car with the trailer—usually, you can't do better than to buy it.) Second, there's the tools. It's easy to spend over $1,000 in tools if you're working on the car yourself. Finally, you'll need miscellaneous items like a tire gauge, air tank, jack, jack stands, and on and on. Sit down and add them up.

Don't overlook the cost of your personal safety equipment (helmet, suit, underwear, and so forth). We'll talk later about what to buy. For budgeting purposes, assume that it will run you another $700–$1,000.

Tony Kester: "Safety equipment is the *most important part* of your racing budget. How much is your skin worth?"

Norma Williams: "A full set of safety equipment can easily run $1,000–$1,200. This includes suit, underwear, shoes, socks, gloves, hood, helmet, and helmet skirt. Open-car drivers should add the cost of arm restraints.

"A lot of my customers need custom-made suits (more expensive); they are too tall, too short, or too much tummy!

"I realize that this sounds like a lot of money, but if you buy good equipment the first time and take care of it, it should last several years."

Your total capital expense to get started will probably be in the $5,000–$15,000 range. With some luck, you will be able to recoup at least two-thirds of this when you decide to liquidate. At least, that's a good thing to tell your spouse. Don't admit that selling the race car is the only liquidation most of us ever do, and that it is normally associated with buying a newer, more expensive one.

THE TOTAL

A sample racing budget, including prorated one-time expenses, is shown in the table. As you can see, $1,000 per weekend does not include extras like test days.

While working on this book, I was discussing costs with Vic Brunamonti, a successful Improved Touring driver from Indiana. It turned out that Vic had been keeping detailed records of his costs over six years of racing an RX-7, and he kindly agreed to share the information.

"Deadbone Platoon Racing" ITA Mazda RX-7 Budget

	1985	1986	1987	1988	1989	1990	Totals
Car-related Expenses, including tires, fluids, and all maintenance	$1,680	$2,090	$1,980	$1,040	$2,170	$370	$9,330
Driver Safety Gear		$350					$350
Weekend Expenses	$330	$1,620	$2,410	$1,530	$1,940	$220	$8,050
	$2,010	$4,060	$4,390	$2,570	$4,110	$590	$17,730
# of Race Weekends	1	6	9	6	9	1	32
Cost per Weekend	$2,010	$677	$488	$428	$457	$590	$554

Bought Prepared Car & Spares	-$2,800	
Bought Parts Car (1987)	-$250	
Sold Car & Spares in 1990	$5,000	
"Profit" on equipment	$1,950	Per Race Cost after Car Sale $493

Note that Vic has been racing economically. He's been flat-towing the car to races, staying with friends and camping out, and, most important, exercising a lot of restraint in what he spends on the car. Including the purchase and sale of the car, Vic ran for an average of $500 per weekend. (No, I don't know what "Deadbone Platoon" means; Vic is a civilian employee of the US Navy—maybe it's Navy lingo.)

Even at this low level of expenditure, Vic managed twenty wins, seventeen pole-position starts, and five second places in thirty-two races. With this record, he was able to win $2,800 in contingency money from Bridgestone, reducing his average costs still further, to $400 per race. I didn't include these winnings in the table, though, because most drivers will not be able to equal Vic's success.

My guess is that your early racing experience will run you $500–$1,000 per weekend, plus capital expenses. Most drivers are spending this and more; $1,000–$2,000 per weekend is common for a serious team running Nationals. Many spend more.

(It can get worse—lots worse. Jim Derhaag, a regular SCCA Trans-Am pro racer, recently told me that he figures his racing costs $50 a mile. That's $4,000–$6,000 per hour!)

HOW TO BEGIN

Getting started may be the hardest part about club racing. *You* have to do all the work—finding people, asking questions, learning.... There's only one shortcut, which we'll discuss in a minute. First, we'll talk about the way in which most people first get involved in racing: going to the track as a spectator, worker, or crew member.

We'll proceed as if you are starting with SCCA, as most drivers do. Other club racing organization contacts are listed in the Appendices. While their procedures will be similar to SCCA's, you should contact them for details.

To begin with, you should join SCCA (call (800)255-5550 or (303)694-7222 with your Visa or Master card ready). Tell them you're interested in racing, would like to join, and want a copy of the SCCA *General Competition Rules* (hereafter referred to as the *GCR*). If you are interested in a particular class of car, order the rulebook for that class as well. Joining SCCA will get you *Sports Car* magazine and a number of benefits including personal injury insurance at the racetrack. Plus, you can't get a racing license without being a member.

If you plan to get a racing license, you might as well also ask Denver (that's how we usually refer to club headquarters) to send you a copy of the standard SCCA Driver Medical Form when you call for your membership and *GCR*.

The SCCA is divided into eight geographic divisions and each division is divided into regions. While you're on the phone, verify the SCCA region that you live in and get some

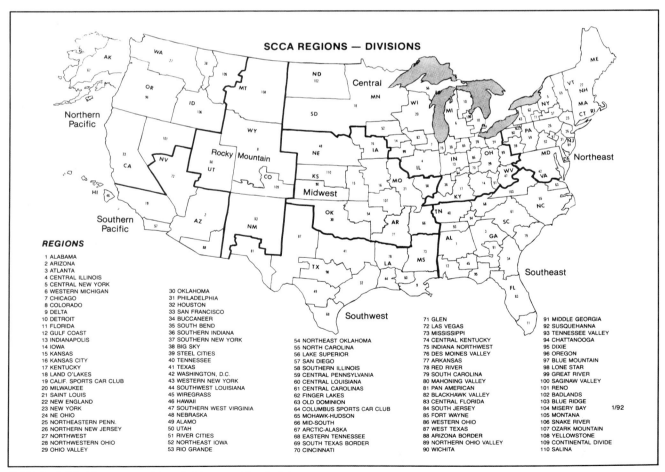

SCCA REGIONS — DIVISIONS

REGIONS

1 ALABAMA
2 ARIZONA
3 ATLANTA
4 CENTRAL ILLINOIS
5 CENTRAL NEW YORK
6 WESTERN MICHIGAN
7 CHICAGO
8 COLORADO
9 DELTA
10 DETROIT
11 FLORIDA
12 GULF COAST
13 INDIANAPOLIS
14 IOWA
15 KANSAS
16 KANSAS CITY
17 KENTUCKY
18 LAND O'LAKES
19 CALIF. SPORTS CAR CLUB
20 MILWAUKEE
21 SAINT LOUIS
22 NEW ENGLAND
23 NEW YORK
24 NE OHIO
25 NORTHEASTERN PENN.
26 NORTHERN NEW JERSEY
27 NORTHWEST
28 NORTHWESTERN OHIO
29 OHIO VALLEY

30 OKLAHOMA
31 PHILADELPHIA
32 HOUSTON
33 SAN FRANCISCO
34 BUCCANEER
35 SOUTH BEND
36 SOUTHERN INDIANA
37 SOUTHERN NEW YORK
38 BIG SKY
39 STEEL CITIES
40 TENNESSEE
41 TEXAS
42 WASHINGTON, D.C.
43 WESTERN NEW YORK
44 SOUTHWEST LOUISIANA
45 WIREGRASS
46 HAWAII
47 SOUTHERN WEST VIRGINIA
48 NEBRASKA
49 ALAMO
50 UTAH
51 RIVER CITIES
52 NORTHEAST IOWA
53 RIO GRANDE

54 NORTHEAST OKLAHOMA
55 NORTH CAROLINA
56 LAKE SUPERIOR
57 SAN DIEGO
58 SOUTHERN ILLINOIS
59 CENTRAL PENNSYLVANIA
60 CENTRAL LOUISIANA
61 CENTRAL CAROLINAS
62 FINGER LAKES
63 OLD DOMINION
64 COLUMBUS SPORTS CAR CLUB
65 MOHAWK-HUDSON
66 MID-SOUTH
67 ARCTIC-ALASKA
68 EASTERN TENNESSEE
69 SOUTH TEXAS BORDER
70 CINCINNATI

71 GLEN
72 LAS VEGAS
73 MISSISSIPPI
74 CENTRAL KENTUCKY
75 INDIANA NORTHWEST
76 DES MOINES VALLEY
77 ARKANSAS
78 RED RIVER
79 SOUTH CAROLINA
80 MAHONING VALLEY
81 PAN AMERICAN
82 BLACKHAWK VALLEY
83 CENTRAL FLORIDA
84 SOUTH JERSEY
85 FORT WAYNE
86 WESTERN OHIO
87 WEST TEXAS
88 ARIZONA BORDER
89 NORTHERN OHIO VALLEY
90 WICHITA

91 MIDDLE GEORGIA
92 SUSQUEHANNA
93 TENNESSEE VALLEY
94 CHATTANOOGA
95 DIXIE
96 OREGON
97 BLUE MOUNTAIN
98 LONE STAR
99 GREAT RIVER
100 SAGINAW VALLEY
101 RENO
102 BADLANDS
103 BLUE RIDGE
104 MISERY BAY   1/92
105 MONTANA
106 SNAKE RIVER
107 OZARK MOUNTAIN
108 YELLOWSTONE
109 CONTINENTAL DIVIDE
110 SALINA

SCCA is divided into competition divisions and local club regions. SCCA

contact names and telephone numbers. One contact should be the Regional Executive, which is SCCA's name for the local club president.

The next step is to arrange to go to a race as a worker or as a crew member for someone. The workers are the people who make the race happen—they flag on the corners, time the cars, direct the traffic, and much more. (A good beginning driver's resolution should be: "Though they make mistakes and jack me around, I shall not criticize the workers, for without them I could not race.")

If you have no strong preference, I'd suggest contacting your regional chief and volunteering as a tech inspector. As a tech inspector (officially, a scrutineer) you'll have the opportunity to look at a lot of race cars, plus you'll have a fairly flexible schedule that will allow you the opportunity to talk to drivers.

An alternative is to volunteer as a corner worker (officially, Flagging and Communications). Working a corner is pretty exciting as far as watching the racing, but you don't get close to the cars and you won't have much chance to wander around during the day. Try your Regional Executive for other worker jobs.

Another alternative is to contact the Regional Competition Chairman and ask if he or she knows of any good drivers who would like some crew help. Don't worry about not having experience, most at-track crew work is easy—gassing the car, setting the tire pressures, drinking the beer, and so forth. If you have a car class preference, try to hook up with someone in that class. Call the driver and explain that you're a potential driver and want to learn what it's about before you take the plunge. Volunteer to help both at the track and between races. Chances are he or she will be flattered to be sought after as a teacher, plus be ecstatic at having the extra help.

Now for the shortcut I mentioned earlier: You can "rent a ride" either from an individual or from a racing shop. Cost for this can range from $800 up, with $1,500+ being quite common for a driver's school weekend. If you go this route, you can skip the worker-crew weekends since part of what you are paying for is the expertise of the car supplier. The Competition Chairman may be able to put you in touch with a few potential rides.

THE RACETRACKS

Every racetrack is unique, but each will include most of the features shown in the figure. Your weekend will begin at the Registration building, you'll park your race car and tow rig in the paddock, and run the track as shown. As drawn, the "typical" racetrack would be a tough place to run—no real racetrack would have a chicane, a hairpin, *and* a carousel turn.

You will read about most of the other common racetrack features later in this book. They're shown here to give you a context for those discussions.

THE RULES

The weekend rules that you will be required to live by are contained in the *GCR*. There is no help for it; you must read and understand the *GCR* as it pertains to you, the driver, and to you, the car entrant. You can skip the stuff on how many fire extinguishers are required per corner.

(There are many places in this book where I state authoritatively that "the *GCR* says...." While these statements may be true as this book is being written, they may not be true as it is being read. Keep up to date on rule changes; it will do no good to cite *this* book as an authority in discussions with SCCA officialdom.)

Most people begin at the bottom. This crewman at least has the good fortune to be lying on a paved surface. Usually, it's done in the dirt!

The car preparation rules that you will live by are contained in whichever book pertains to your particular class: Production Car Specifications; GT Category Specifications; Showroom Stock Specifications; Improved Touring Specifications; Sports Racer and Formula Car Specifications. You may wish to order one or two of these, depending on your interests, when you make your membership call to Denver.

The theory is that these specification books are definitive, comprehensive, and to be followed without question. The facts are somewhat different, and highly dependent on the class. For example, you will probably not be disqualified for having out-of-spec tailpipe height. Before you go crazy trying to exploit and/or follow the rulebook, get some racing experience. Learn, for your class, what's important and what's not; also learn what's enforced and what's not.

DRIVER LICENSING: NOVICE PERMIT

All sanctioning bodies require that drivers undergo some form of training and that they be licensed. The purpose of this training and licensing is, obviously, to ensure that we are out there among drivers with at least a minimum competence level.

The first step in SCCA is issuance of a Novice Permit. This document, normally referred to as a "logbook," is actually a little booklet with pages for recording your driver schools and first races. You obtain your logbook from your region's Regional Executive, his or her Competition Licensing designee, or from the SCCA national office. If possible, get yours from your regional office; they get to keep a portion of the fee (currently $45), and they can always use the money.

In addition to the fee, you must present a properly filled-out medical physical form, proof that you're at least eighteen, and a couple of passport-sized pictures. The physical form is available from your region or from Denver.

In a previous incarnation as our region's Competition License Chairman, my pet peeve was improperly filled-out

Most at-track maintenance is minor: gassing the car, checking valve clearances, and so on. Once in a while, though, you might get to do some real work, like helping change a clutch. On this FF 2000 car, it's relatively easy. The bellhousing, gearbox, and rear suspension separate from the rest of the car at the rear of the engine block.

physical forms. Over half had to be sent back for correction. It is *your* problem, not the doctor's, if your form is incomplete. Review it carefully before you leave your doctor's office.

To compete in a Regional race, you must successfully complete two SCCA driver schools with six hours total track time, or one accredited "pro" school and one SCCA school. In the Appendices, I have included a list of schools that have appeared on the SCCA-approved list at one time or another, together with some descriptive information. The approved list changes frequently, so be sure to inquire about a school's current approval status before signing up. *Sports Car* magazine periodically publishes a current list, and the information is always available via a call to Denver.

(Your evidence that you have completed an accredited school should be in the form of your *original* graduation certificate. Some Chief Stewards will not accept copies; it is too easy to temporarily alter the name on an original, then copy it.)

There is a place in your logbook for the Chief Steward to sign off, indicating "Driver School Requirements Completed." Normally, this will occur after your second school. Be sure to verify this signoff before you leave the racetrack; it sometimes gets overlooked.

It is possible for a Chief Steward to waive your second school if you have "prior racing experience." Please note that it cannot be waived because you are a nice guy or gal, because it is a long time until the next school, because your mother is coming tomorrow to watch you race, or because you did a great job in your first school.

If you are going to ask that your second school be waived, it is important that you contact the Chief Steward and the Chief Instructor *prior to showing up* at your first school. (Their names will be on the race entry form, but their phone numbers will probably not be provided. Call the Registrar for help.) Outline your reasons for making the request, and seek clarification of their waiver requirements.

Regardless of your experience, it is extremely unlikely that you will get your second school waived if your first school was an accredited "pro" school rather than an SCCA

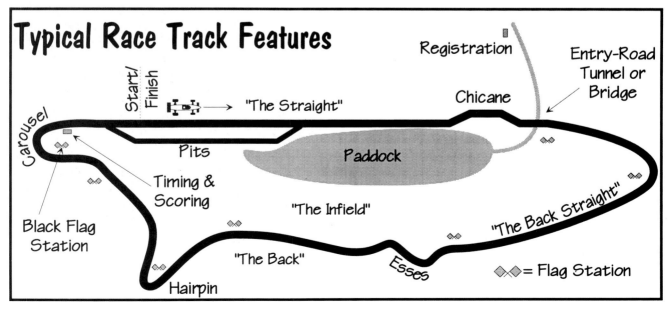

Typical Race Track Features

Registration

Entry-Road Tunnel or Bridge

Start/ Finish

Carousel

"The Straight"

Chicane

Pits

Paddock

Timing & Scoring

"The Infield"

"The Back Straight"

Black Flag Station

"The Back"

Esses

◇◇ = Flag Station

Hairpin

school. This is not due to professional jealousy or to some kind of revenue-raising policy. The pro school environment is radically different from the on-track environment at an SCCA event. You need the experience of one SCCA school before actually going out there and trying to run a club race.

If your second school is a pro school, then you will not have your logbook signed off prior to showing up for your first Regional race weekend. This situation can cause great difficulty in Registration. Call the Chief Steward ahead of time, and seek his or her advice on how to proceed.

The fact that you have completed two schools does not mean that you have completed your "driver education." Try to attend one or two more schools, even during the season following your novice year. At this stage of your racing, you need seat time. You will also continue to benefit from the instruction, though you may get a bit tired of the flags briefing.

If you are already licensed, be sure to contact the Chief Instructor or Chief Steward prior to entering a school. Some schools must restrict attendance due to overcrowding. If this is not an issue, though, and you promise not to be out there dive-bombing the *real* students, you will probably be granted permission to enter. Skip the driver school "race," though. Let the real novices have their fun and let one of them have the thrill of a "first win."

REGIONAL COMPETITION

You will complete your first two regional races "under observation" and your conduct will be recorded in your novice logbook. If you receive satisfactory ratings, you can send your logbook to Denver together with an Application for Upgrade to a Regional Competition License. (If you are really aggressive, you will have requested this last bit of paper when you called Denver to join the club. If not, call them again or see if someone in your region's officialdom has copies.)

By the way, keep copies of everything you send to Denver. They are good people, but they get a lot of mail and sometimes they get a bit behind. If you have not received your new license prior to your next race, you have two options: First, advise the Registrar by telephone on Wednesday night. Seek his or her help in verifying your status with Denver. Registrars regularly call Denver on Thursday night or Friday afternoon. Or second, take the aforementioned copies of your paperwork with you to Registration.

Here is some advice that you probably will not follow: Keep your logbook until it is ready to expire or until you have completed an additional four Regionals. At that time, you can upgrade directly to a National Competition License. By doing this, you avoid the hassle of an unnecessary administrative transaction. Your logbook is every bit as good as a regional license as far as Registration is concerned. The reason you will not do this is that you will be too eager to get your first "real racing license," as I was.

You can retain your regional license by being a finisher in at least two races (Regionals or Nationals) during each one-year license term.

NATIONAL COMPETITION

Finish four Regionals and you can apply for a National Competition License. Yes, it is quite feasible to get a National license in your first year. Keep your National by finishing four Regionals or two Nationals plus one other race each year. Most of us have National licenses, whether we run primarily Regionals or not.

LICENSE MISCELLANY

A race does not count toward license requirements unless you are a "finisher." This means that you must complete at least half as many laps as the overall race winner (not your class winner). If you are having trouble but can maintain reasonable speed, by all means make sure that you stay out there until you can be classed as a finisher. If you are just limping along under protection of a white flag, please park it. Your fellow competitors do not deserve to be put at risk simply because you are trying to get a finish.

If, after amassing several years of experience, a year comes when you do not meet license renewal requirements, it is possible to get them waived by your divisional (not regional) licensing administrator or by Denver. You will need evidence, however. Keep all old grid sheets and race results sheets. Keep your old licenses. You will probably be asked for copies if you ever need to apply for a renewal waiver.

THE RACE ENTRY FORM

Once you are licensed, you will automatically receive entry forms. These are mailed by the race-sponsoring regions using labels bought from Denver. Typically, a region will mail to all licensed drivers in its division. Sometimes, you will even get out-of-division race entry forms. (The Florida regions used to mail to Minnesota for their January races. I don't know if they were just gloating or if they actually generated some entries!)

Be sure to post the weekend schedule so everyone on the crew knows when the car has to be ready. An easily visible clock is a good idea, too. The signboard arrangement in the photo may be unnecessarily elaborate, but you can be sure that everyone knows what happens and when.

15

Race control, a place few drivers see, is where the "other" action is. Stop by sometime; the staff will be glad to show you what's going on. Note the track map (just to the left of the picture's center); magnets with flag symbols, emergency vehicle symbols, and car numbers are used to maintain a pictorial track status at all times.

There is quite a bit of lag time in the entry-mailing system, however. This means that, as a novice, you will have to work a bit to get entry forms. Watch *Sports Car* for a list of driver's schools and regional races. Registrars' phone numbers are often included; phone them and ask to be includedin the mailing. Your local region's Chief Registrar will also have other Registrars' phone numbers, and your Regional Executive will often have received extra entry forms from nearby regions. You should be able to get what you need from one of these sources.

SUPPLEMENTAL REGULATIONS

Although the *GCR* is the principal body of rules that govern your racing, each race entry form includes Supplemental Regulations, usually called "the Supps." These are

Unsung heroes, the registrars can't even see the racing. Be patient, be appreciative. Also, take time to read the notices stuck to the wall. You may find schedule changes or other critical information.

read by fewer drivers than you might think, but they should be read by you.

The Supps will tell you about limits on crew and guest list sizes, fees for passes, rules at that particular track and event, and so on. Sometimes, certain classes of cars must receive tech inspection regardless of whether they have received annual tech. This will be stated in the Supps. Once in a great while, you will find something like the following: "If you have read this far, you get an extra crew pass. Ask at Registration."

Read the Supps. Nothing bad will happen if you do; something bad could well happen if you do not.

WEEKEND SCHEDULES

A normal club racing weekend will consist of five or six race groups, each with practice and qualifying on Saturday and a warm-up and races on Sunday. Race groups usually include multiple classes, though popular classes like Spec Racers and Formula Fords often are in one-class groups. Total available track time will be in the neighborhood of 1 1/2 hours.

Practice and Qualifying are usually around 1/2 hour each. The only real difference between the sessions is that your lap times are recorded during Qualifying and used to place you on the starting grid. The cars are gridded from fastest to slowest, regardless of class. It is quite normal to see cars from a "slower" class gridded ahead of those from a supposedly faster class.

The Sunday "warm-up" sessions are usually quite short, ten or fifteen minutes. Often, too, there are only two sessions with the race groups divided between them; this results in huge speed disparities and a crowded racetrack. Sunday morning is a good time to bed brake pads or to verify that everything is OK after some emergency maintenance. It is not much good as extra practice time, however.

Tony Kester: "If you're in the first race group and intend to go out for the warm-up, remember that your race will start *immediately* after the warm-up sessions are over."

The schedule for the weekend will be included as part of the entry form. Study it carefully, underlining your race group's sessions. Check for unusual scheduling; sometimes there will be two qualifying sessions, for example. I usually mail a marked copy to each of my crew ahead of the race weekend. This reminds them that I am counting on them, and it lets them know when to arrive on Saturday morning.

Another thing to watch is the hours that Registration is open. There is little point in arriving too early on Friday night. Also, if you have guests or visitors coming during the weekend, they will not be able to get into the track if Registration is closed. It sounds dumb, but I still forget to advise guests about Registration hours from time to time.

Frequently, you will get a revised weekend schedule at Registration. These revisions are usually due to race grouping changes which result in more balanced group sizes. If you *do* get a revised schedule, take care to destroy all copies of the old one.

Tape the final schedule to the side of the trailer or tow vehicle where everyone can see it. Take one to the motel, too.

SPECTATOR RACES

The race entry form will tell you whether or not the event is a "spectator" race, with tickets sold to the general public. Early in your career, you will probably be running Regionals, which are almost never spectator events. Some Nationals, like the famous June Sprints at Elkhart Lake, are spectator events though, requiring special preparation on your part.

Cars in popular classes, like these Formula Fords, often run in one-class groups. Classes with normally light turnouts will be run together; often four or five classes per group.

TECHNICAL AND SAFETY INSPECTION FORM
SPORTS CAR CLUB OF AMERICA, INC.

EVENT _____ DATE _____ ENG. SIZE _____ CC

ENTRANT _____ MAKE & MODEL _____ YR ____

DRIVER _____ REGION OF RECORD _____

CAR NO. _____ CLASS _____ COLOR _____ LOG BOOK NO. _____

ALL ITEMS MUST BE MARKED INDIVIDUALLY WHERE APPLICABLE

VEHICLE ___ WAS ___ WAS NOT INSPECTED

ANNUAL TECH : DATE _____

REGION _____

SPEC BOOK PAGE _____
(SS, GT, Prod Only)

DRIVER SAFETY EQUIPMENT	Appr.	Rej.
helmet, medical info.		
goggles or visor		
suit of approved material		
underwear		
shoes		
socks		
gloves		
mask		

VEHICLE INTERIOR		
window net/arm restraint		
roll bar/roll cage		
driver seat		
restraint harness		
head restraint		
fire extinguisher		
mirror(s)		
firewall and floor		
interior trim		
conform to regulations		
steering lock		
passenger seat		

FUEL TANK COMPARTMENT		
fuel tank		
filler cap or dry break		
vent or dry break		
check valves		
battery		
firewall		

ENGINE COMPARTMENT	Appr.	Rej.
clean		
carburetion/fuel injection		
fuel pump, lines & fittings		
oil supply tank, oil lines		
oil cooler(s), catch tank		
radiator, hoses		
coolant catch tank		
battery		
wiring		
exhaust manifold		
firewall		
scattershield		

VEHICLE EXTERIOR		
SCCA emblems		
neat and clean		
numbers & class letters		
body panels secure		
windshield & windows		
headlights		
brake & tail lights		
exhaust system		
doors		
top		
fenders		
exterior mirrors		
master switch (OFF)		
exterior modifications		
hubcaps removed		

SUSPENSION — RUNNING GEAR		
steering linkage		
suspension & shocks		
wheel bearings		
wheels & tires		
brakes & hoses		
fluid levels		
spherical rod ends		

COMMENTS _____

Approved for competition _____

_____ Scrutineer   _____ Chief Scrutineer

Sticker issued (Date) _____

This tech card shows the items that will be inspected on your car. Note that the emphasis is on safety items. SCCA

At least once a year, the tech inspectors will look your car over to make sure it meets all safety requirements. If serious violations are found, you may not be allowed to run the car. Minor ones will be noted in the logbook as "fix before next event."

Generally, your crew and vehicle passes will be strictly limited at a spectator event. Read the Supps carefully and plan accordingly. Also, you should expect that spectators will be in and around your paddock space. Plan some kind of "fence" to keep them from getting underfoot. Strings of colored vinyl flags bought from a party supply store or provided as a promotional item by a tire or oil company make good fences.

Unfortunately, you need to protect your belongings from theft at a spectator race. Make sure there is someone watching your paddock space during your sessions, and lock up your wallet and credit cards.

Finally, if you're not busy and a little kid comes by—let him sit in the race car! Wouldn't that have been a thrill for you when you were six years old?

WORKERS AND RACE OPERATION

At the racetrack you will be dealing 100% with volunteers. These are people who are giving their time, talents,

Here, the tech inspectors are getting ready to weigh a GT-1 car after a qualifying session. They are using portable electronic scales. More commonly, you will be weighed on a whole-car mechanical platform scale or with a pair of small platform scales under first the front, then the rear tires.

and money to be around racing. They do not get paid for anything that they do, including any personal expenses like food and camping or motel costs.

Workers come from all walks of life. You'll find a large percentage of professionals: engineers and computer folk, accountants, managers, doctors and other medical people, but you will also find service workers, trades people, and homemakers. They all look the same on the weekend and, from your viewpoint, they are all there to help you.

By the way, most workers are officially called "marshals" and "officials" by the SCCA rulebooks, but *only* by the SCCA rulebooks; everybody else refers to them as workers. (There *are* a few Stewards, however, who prefer to be called "Sir." Ah, bureaucracy.) Here is a brief overview of some of the specialties:

REGISTRARS

The first people you will meet at the racetrack are the Registrars. Registration is usually located in a little building near the entrance to the racetrack, though sometimes the entrance that you will use as a club racing participant is not the big, fancy one used when the track runs its professional races.

To register, you will have to show your club membership card and your license or logbook. You will have to list your crew and guests in your driver's folder, come up with any unpaid fees, and sign the insurance waiver. After these tasks are accomplished, you will receive your track entry credentials, plus a wad of paper that includes late changes to rules and schedules, an entry list, and other incidental information.

Of all the workers, I think I most appreciate the Registrars. Their job is to get several hundred drivers, crew, and workers properly equipped with credentials after having reviewed each individual's licenses and membership status, and having protected the club by ensuring that each individual sign the insurance waiver. Their reward for all this is to be able to sit alone in the Registration building for most of the time that the racing is going on. Thanks, folks!

As in most administrative encounters, the person charged with enforcing the rules is not responsible for creating them and does not have the power to change them. There are always a few people who do not understand this fact and who choose to make the Registrars' lives miserable. Don't be one of them.

Norma Williams: "From my experience in working Registration, I can tell you that it really helps if the driver sends the entry forms in early. This keeps the lines at Registration moving, because the driver file is already made up. If you don't know who is going to crew when you mail your entry, you can always add or delete when you get to the track."

TECH INSPECTORS

Next, you will meet the tech inspectors. As mentioned, officially, SCCA calls these people scrutineers, but the *GCR* is the only place you will find this term used. It is Tech's responsibility to ensure that all cars and all driver gear meet minimum safety requirements. In addition, it is Tech that is called upon to inspect cars for suspected or alleged violation of preparation rules.

Generally, cars will receive annual inspection, re-inspections after any serious on-track incidents, and additional inspections at the discretion of the race officials. These inspections are recorded in the vehicle logbook issued for every SCCA car. Each car is assigned an identity number when its logbook is issued; this number is permanently stamped on the car's roll bar. The identity number and the logbook remain with the car for the duration of its racing career.

(Be aware that "logbook" can refer to either your Novice Permit or to your "vehicle logbook." I once ordered novice logbooks from Denver and received car logbooks. Make sure you are clear on which is called for in a given context. The car logbook is required at Tech, the driver logbook at Registration.)

Up until a few years ago, cars received tech inspections before every race. This rule was changed, though, and now it is only necessary for the driver to present the car logbook and his or her personal safety equipment (helmet, suit, and other items) for inspection at each race. (Ask about Tech's location at Registration; it's usually called the "Tech Barn.") Tech will review the logbook for any previous problems, note the race entry on a new page of the logbook, and verify that the safety equipment is in compliance.

You may have also received a "Tech Card" at Registration (see sample in figure). If you did, then you should fill out the car and entrant information at the top of the card and take it to Tech as well.

After passing Tech, you will receive a sticker attesting to that fact. This sticker goes on the front of your car to show that it is approved to be on the racetrack. Clean the bodywork carefully with solvent (bug and tar remover is OK and safe on paint) before putting the sticker in place. Press it down well; they have a tendency to blow off at speed.

Tech may also make spot inspections during the race weekend, noting any problems in the car logbooks. In addition, they will instantly appear following an on-track incident, and will record any damage in your car logbook so that proper repairs can be verified by tech inspectors before your next race.

Tech is also responsible for weighing cars to ensure that they meet their specified minimum weight. There will usually be posted hours when they staff the scales. In addition, you may be directed to the scales after your qualifying session or after the race.

GRID WORKERS

Another class of worker that is important to you is the grid worker. When your practice or race group is preparing to go onto the track, these workers are responsible for properly placing you at "pre-grid" and for signaling you onto the

As you move your car onto the grid for a race, the grid workers will signal you into proper position. These cars are Formula Atlantics.

track. As you near the pre-grid area, one of these people will point to your car, then to the place where you are to put it.

Generally, practice and qualifying sessions are pretty laid-back, but there are strict requirements for pre-race grids. If you are not on time or don't follow instructions, the grid workers have the power to put you at the back of the grid. As a beginner, take the time to understand what is required of you, and take pains to comply.

PIT WORKERS

In the pits, cars are managed by pit workers. These folks look out for your safety and the safety of your crew by managing the race car traffic from its entry into the pits to its exit into the paddock or back onto the racetrack.

In the pits, workers manage traffic to keep everybody safe. The worker at the pit exit, shown here, blends pit traffic into the racing traffic. He's looking back down the main straight, signaling this Formula Ford onto the track.

Watch the grid workers carefully; if you're not ready, you end up in the back! Here, a grid worker is holding up a not-very-legible five-minute warning sign.

When you come into the pits, a worker near the pit entrance will usually blow an air horn or a whistle to warn people in the pits that a car is coming. When you pull into your pit, another worker will position himself or herself in front of your car, ready to merge you back into the pit lane traffic when you are ready to go.

As you approach pit exit, you will have a choice of entering the paddock or reentering the racetrack. If your choice is the latter, you will again receive the help of a pit worker. He or she will be positioned with a good view of oncoming traffic and will use hand signals ("slow down," "stop," or "go!") to blend you safely into the racing traffic.

Tony Kester: "Always signal your intentions to the worker at pit exit; point to the track or to the paddock. The sooner the worker knows your intentions, the sooner he or she will be able to find you a hole in traffic."

Do not try to second-guess the pit workers. You cannot possibly see as much from your mirrors as they can by looking behind you. Have faith. And obey.

FLAGGING AND COMMUNICATIONS WORKERS

Corner workers, distinctively attired in white, are the people you will see the most of during your racing career. (Twenty to fifty of them, once per lap.)

Generally, corner stations are set up with personnel sufficient to cover all aspects of the turn. The staff includes the

A pair of flaggers. The blue flagger (on the right) is looking toward the oncoming cars, ready to advise drivers of overtaking traffic. The yellow flagger (on the left) is watching the corner for incidents and the corner captain for instructions. When she is directed to use her flag, the two flaggers will reverse positions and the man will watch for the captain's instructions, relaying them to the yellow flagger.

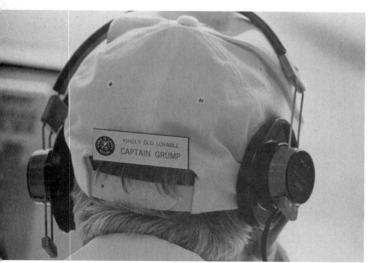

Some stewards take themselves quite seriously, even to the point of cultivating reputations as grouches. Others, though, have a more laid-back attitude.

Here's the black flag station in the pits, staffed by one or two of the operating stewards. You do not want to make the acquaintance of the stewards as a result of getting a black flag. The beer party is a far better place to do it.

Corner Captain, flagger(s), communicator, and first-intervention safety people. As volunteer worker turnout permits, additional workers will be placed in positions to provide rapid assistance to spun, stuck, crashed, or parked race vehicles.

Early on in your career, you should spend some time "working" a corner to understand things from the corner workers' perspective. Some club schools, in fact, require this as part of the school. Regardless of requirements, talk to the chief flag marshal and arrange it; you'll find the experience to be valuable.

STEWARDS

There are always many Stewards around. These individuals fall into two categories: the Chief Steward and his or her assistants, and the Stewards of the Meeting (SOMs). The Chief Steward and the deputies have the responsibility for managing the weekend's activity. The SOMs are "primarily in a judicial capacity" (per the *GCR*) and have the responsibility for resolving the inevitable protests and disagreements.

You could race for several years without meeting a Steward in an official capacity. In fact, that should be your objective. It is, however, a good idea to cultivate their friendship at the Saturday night beer party. You may need it someday.

To better understand the roles of the Stewards and the many other worker specialties, spend some time reading your *GCR*.

TIMING AND SCORING

You will find Timing and Scoring located in a building on the last turn or on the straight near the starting bridge. These folks use a combination of hand stopwatches and

The course marshals bring you home when you've had a problem. This Formula Vee is "coming in on the hook," probably due to an engine problem.

electronic timing equipment to keep track of lap times. They also keep "lap charts," which document the progress of the race. Each column of a lap chart shows all car numbers, in order, for one lap. The left-hand column is in starting grid order and the rightmost column shows the finishing order. The official lap chart is important when a race must be stopped and restarted. It also makes for interesting reading after the race.

OTHER SPECIALTIES

There are many other specialties, all of which are critical to the conduct of a successful weekend. These include (alphabetically) communication tech, course marshals, fire and rescue, medical, paddock marshals, race chairman, and sound control. All of these people are essential to your being able to race. With full knowledge that I am repetitious on this subject, I say again: Be grateful.

Medical is not just for drivers of crashed cars. They will be happy to help with everything from small cuts and splin-

A lap chart shows the order of the cars on each lap of the race. This lap chart will be posted after the race; they usually make interesting reading. You can easily see how your race position changes from lap to lap.

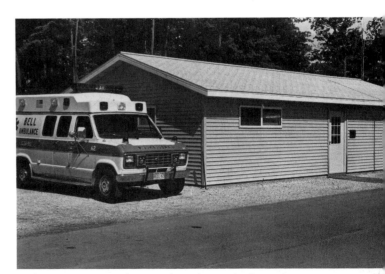

Make sure your crew knows where the medical services are located. The folks in Medical will be happy to help with off-track injuries and problems as well. It's usually pretty boring in there. And a good thing, too!

ters to major paddock injuries. In Medical, it's usually quiet to the point of boredom; they'll be glad to see you.

Worker Licensing

It is not just the drivers who are licensed. All sanctioning bodies have systems to ensure that the races are staffed with trained, competent people. Within SCCA, there is a regional-divisional-national licensing sequence for each worker specialty. It has training and participation requirements similar to those for drivers. The time and energy that these folks contribute to racing go beyond just showing up on the weekends.

Workers are licensed by specialty. A nationally licensed grid worker, for instance, cannot work in a flagging and communications position that requires a National license in F and C. Many enthusiastic workers, however, have licenses in multiple specialties.

CARS AND CLASSES

Let's talk briefly about cars and classes. Frankly, this is not a topic that is well suited to being studied in a book. You will learn more, and learn it more quickly, by spending a couple of hours wandering the racing paddock and asking questions. Thus, this section is included primarily for completeness; how could there be a racing book that doesn't talk about cars? At a minimum, I'll try to give you some observations that may help in your selection of a car class for your racing.

First, you should understand that there are *lots* of classes. The table shows twenty-three 1991 national racing classes. In addition, there are many regional-only classes, including the Improved Touring groups. The total number of classes is currently around thirty-five. There are two reasons for

this. First, SCCA has long-standing policies that an owner will always have a class in which to race his car and that classes will be set up in a way that everyone has at least a theoretical chance to win. Second, club management has historically tended to add classes much more frequently than it has consolidated them. The result is that many classes will have few or no cars entered on any given race weekend.

There are many ways to differentiate racing classes. I'll walk you through them here as a means of highlighting the tradeoffs in selecting a class.

The traditional way that race cars are differentiated is as "closed-wheel" and "open-wheel" types. You will often see this on race schedules, particularly as a way to split the cars between two brief Sunday morning practice sessions. The idea of separating cars this way is that a driver in an open-wheel car is quite vulnerable to a closed-wheel driver who is used to leaning on people in corners.

Open-wheel cars are considered by many to be "more dangerous" than closed-wheel cars. The reason for this is that contact between exposed, rotating tires can cause one of the cars to be "launched" into the air. (Think about the forces involved when the tread surface of an overtaking car's left front tire hits the tread surface of the right rear tire of the car he is trying to pass.)

Launches can be quite spectacular, with six feet of air instantly appearing between the car and the ground. They are, however, quite rare and injuries are usually limited to strap bruises.

In my opinion, the danger of open-wheel cars is overrated. Drivers in open-wheel classes are aware and careful to avoid tire contact. In fact, I have been leaned on harder and

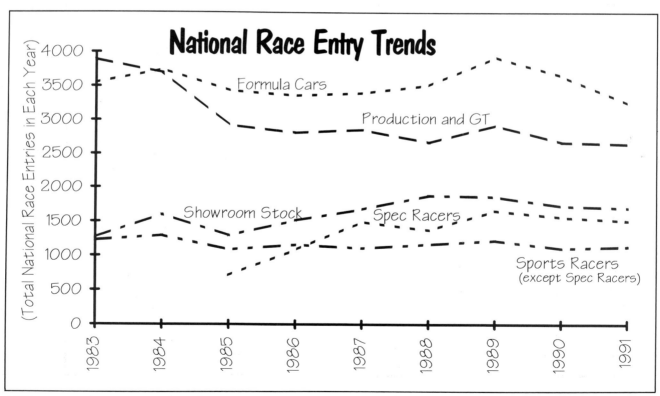

SCCA entry trends 1983–1991. This information is normally published in Sports Car *magazine each fall.*

forced onto the grass more frequently when running closed-wheel cars. The protection of all that bodywork seems to give drivers a feeling of invulnerability.

Danny Collins: "The safety difference between open- and closed-wheel cars depends more on a driver's knowledge of what causes accidents than on the difference in the type of car driven. See the section on passing in chapter 4, especially regarding passing on the entry to corners."

Kathy Maleck: "From a worker's standpoint, we are always concerned about open-wheel cars making tire-to-tire contact. As with most incidents, the danger depends on the car speeds and the impact/contact. Wheels may touch and both cars may continue, or wheels may touch and both cars may go airborne. In most cases the driver walks away angry and a little hurt in the bank account, but still physically intact."

Tony Kester: "Open-wheel cars, especially FF and FV [Formula Ford and Formula Vee] (due to their lack of side pods and large area between the wheels), are without doubt inherently more apt to give you "airborne ranger" experience than are those with fenders. But only if you hook wheels in just the right situation. These situations are obviously to be avoided at all costs and are fairly uncommon.

The most dangerous class I've ever driven is [closed-wheel] S2000, which is populated with numerous drivers who feel that body slamming a competitor into the middle of next week and flagrantly blocking passing attempts are the marks of a good driver. The odds of a flip in these cars is negligible, but crashes are extremely common."

Carroll Smith: "Avoid the 'Doctor-Lawyer' classes— mainly affluent self-made drivers who 'Could have been F1 drivers but family/business prevented it.' They tend to live in S2000 and they hit each other a lot."

Getting back to differentiation among cars, another useful way to differentiate among cars is by tire type: racing tires and street tires. Almost any car on racing tires is faster in the corners than almost any car on street tires. As a result, mixing cars on race tires with those on street tires leads to problems in the corners. We tend to separate car groups on this basis in our driver school at Brainerd.

Another useful differentiation is between purpose-built race cars and cars that were originally manufactured for

Class	Southeast	Northeast	Central	Midwest	Rocky Mountain	Southwest	Southern Pacific	Northern Pacific	National Averages
Spec Racer	23.4	20.3	27.1	21.6	13.2	18.5	18.7	13.3	20.5
Formula Vee	10.0	15.0	19.1	12.1	6.2	13.1	7.1	17.9	13.1
Formula Ford	6.8	11.2	18.3	9.0	11.5	14.8	10.1	9.3	11.5
Formula C	12.3	12.0	14.1	5.7	2.5	3.1	6.4	4.4	8.6
Sports 2000	7.8	9.1	13.6	6.6	7.2	2.4	5.3	11.4	8.3
SS C	10.2	9.2	9.7	4.2	5.0	6.0	5.9	3.3	7.2
GT1	4.8	10.8	13.0	5.2	2.5	3.8	2.7	6.9	6.9
SS GT	5.9	10.1	7.7	3.3	2.0	2.0	8.7	5.4	6.0
Formula Atlantic	4.1	8.2	11.3	5.5	1.0	2.5	4.9	4.1	5.8
GT3	4.7	7.3	5.8	6.1	1.8	4.4	5.9	6.9	5.5
SS A	4.4	8.0	6.3	5.0	1.2	3.6	6.3	4.3	5.2
Formula 440	11.3	5.4	3.8	3.6	1.0	5.1	2.7	3.9	5.1
SS B	5.7	5.3	4.5	4.7	2.3	2.3	6.4	4.6	4.6
GT4	4.8	5.3	5.3	2.3	3.5	3.8	3.1	4.1	4.2
F Production	4.5	4.9	4.8	4.4	0.3	3.8	1.4	3.6	3.8
E Production	3.8	5.3	4.3	3.5	2.0	1.6	3.4	4.7	3.8
GT2	3.5	6.7	3.8	2.2	0.3	0.5	5.0	4.3	3.5
G Production	2.9	5.6	5.7	2.6	0.3	0.5	3.1	1.6	3.2
H Production	5.2	3.0	4.1	3.4	0.3	2.3	0.9	2.6	3.0
D Sports Racing	2.3	1.8	4.7	2.8	0.5	2.8	2.6	4.1	2.8
Shelby Can Am	2.6	3.3	2.8	1.9	1.8	1.4	3.4	0.0	2.3
GT5	1.9	4.3	2.1	1.8	0.0	0.6	1.7	3.6	2.1
C Sports Racing	1.7	3.2	2.2	1.2	0.0	3.1	2.3	2.3	2.1
Totals	145	175	194	119	67	102	118	126	139

1991 SCCA Divisions' Average Entries by Class, All National Races, Sorted From Largest To Smallest Fields

When open-wheel cars (these are Formula Fords) touch tires, it is possible for one of the cars to get "launched." Though it happens rarely, the possibility makes many people consider open-wheel cars to be more dangerous than cars with closed-in wheels. (The white car wasn't damaged.) Jim Casey

street use. Purpose-built cars tend to be smaller, lighter, and to have better suspensions. They are also easier to work on, but chassis and body parts are expensive because they are manufactured in tiny quantities. Most purpose-built racing cars run in classes where engine modifications are strictly controlled.

Converted street cars present greater opportunity for engineering creativity and for creative rule interpretation. Usually, too, performance parts are readily available and not too expensive. This is especially true for street car models that are of interest to circle-track and drag racers. Converted street cars tend to be less expensive to buy as well. Over the long term, however, I don't think they're really any cheaper to race.

Finally, one can differentiate between professional classes and amateur classes. Pro classes involve cars that are the same as or similar to cars that run in professional racing series like International Motorsports Association (IMSA), Formula Atlantic, and SCCA's Trans-Am.

A new driver should stay away from a professional type of car. The speeds, expense, and technology are just too much. A few years ago, a new driver in our region bought a professional GT-1 Corvette (we are talking here about a 180mph car that will not corner worth a damn). It terrified him and he quickly sold it; I think his total number of laps could have been counted on one hand.

SCCA CLASSES: PRODUCTION AND GT CLASSES

Production cars, based on production sports cars, are the historical backbone of SCCA racing. In the 1950s, a driver just took his MG to the track and raced it. Over the years, various levels of modifications were permitted, but it is only in the past ten years or so that the rule against "gutting" an interior was eliminated. In my opinion, the factory teams of the late 1960s and the 1970s were the turning point in Production racing. There is little "production" equipment left in Production race cars.

GT cars, a class introduced in the 1980s, are based on mass-produced sports sedans. In this class you will find a mixture of "retired" cars from professional series and cars built specifically for club racing.

SCCA tried to keep its last vestige of purity through most of the 1980s by insisting that a Production or GT car actually include the chassis produced by its nominal manufacturer. This tenacity produced a "ship-in-a-bottle" syndrome wherein a stiff, capable chassis had to be created inside the nominal manufacturer's body and chassis. These chassis were euphemistically called "roll cages." In 1990, SCCA finally gave up and now permits tube-frame chassis in the GT class.

Interest in Production and GT cars seems to be waning. Except in the pro classes (primarily GT-1), there is little manufacturer interest and there seem to be few innovations. This situation may present an opportunity for a beginning driver. A good, reliable Production or GT car with a garage full of spares can be had fairly cheaply.

SHOWROOM STOCK CLASS

The idea of Showroom Stock (SS) is quite literal. You take a car off the showroom floor, put some safety equipment in it, and off you go racing. There are four classes of Showroom Stock: SSGT, SSA, SSB, and SSC. Cars are classed

The manufacturer would never recognize this chassis, but tube-frame cars are what's needed to be competitive in serious GT-car racing.

But not all of the Production-type cars that you will see are high tech. Here's a neat and tidy example of an E-Production car.

by the SCCA according to their potential, and class assignments are frequently adjusted to equalize competition. Cars running Nationals must be no older than four years; for Regional competition, it's six years.

Showroom Stock cars must be raced exactly as they originally came from their makers. A car that finishes a race without an inconsequential engine drive belt (power steering, for example) will be disqualified. Even the brake pads must be factory issue. One recent controversy involved a car that had been manufactured with a sunroof, but the owner had puttied and painted it over on the outside and installed a new headliner. Outcome: Disqualification. (A sunroof car is at a disadvantage because the rules say that it must run with the sunroof open, an aerodynamic no-no.)

Showroom Stock seems to attract two types of drivers. The larger group is *fun* racers who buy into the spirit of the class, often drive their cars on the street during the week, and sometimes even drive them to the racetrack. The other group is *serious* racers who are in it for other reasons. Serious Showroom Stock cars have had expensive, "stock" engine rebuilds and are never driven on the street. Entrants in this latter group can include car manufacturers. Peugeot is said to have once manufactured a group of cars that were just a bit special in the performance department—exclusively available to serious SCCA Showroom Stock (SSB) racers.

Unfortunately, serious SS racing has become an area where cheating is common. A car with solid suspension bushings hidden inside the stock-looking rubber bushings will corner just a bit better. A car with the (heavy) inner bumper structures removed can be brought back to required weight with some ballast hidden inside its frame; it will then have a lower center of gravity and will roll less in corners. A fuel-control computer memory chip can be changed to have a slightly different program in it, producing more horsepower.

Cheating has a snowball effect; if most people are doing it, then everybody else almost has to cheat to be competitive.

Improved Touring cars offer low entry costs and good fun per dollar. Here's an older Datsun and a VW Rabbit. Note the class designations. The ITB Rabbit is, at least theoretically, faster than the ITC Datsun.

SCCA is trying hard to eliminate cheating in Showroom Stock. Teardowns are becoming more frequent and more thorough. I think it's getting better, but with the manufacturers' huge financial motivation to be successful and the fan-

Most Sports Racers, like the ones in the background, look like doorstops. Once in a while, though, someone tries a new approach. Note that the air is ducted to the inside of the enclosed rear tires on this Sports 2000 Tiga. Theoretically, this should reduce drag by helping to fill in the low-pressure area behind the car.

Race on Sunday, drive to work on Monday? This SSB Toyota's color scheme may be a little wild for daily commuting, but under all the colored film, it's a street car.

Spec Racers (nee Sports Renault) are SCCA's most popular class. Here's a crowd of them on the pace lap at New Hampshire International. Kim Sanders

tastically complicated nature of today's production cars, I am skeptical that cheating can be effectively eliminated.

Carroll Smith: "Eliminate Showroom Stock cheating? Good luck!"

Buy a Showroom Stocker if you want to go out and have fun. Understand, however, that you will be looking at the tailpipes of the serious racers. A new driver does not have much of a chance in this league.

IMPROVED TOURING CLASS

Improved Touring, or IT, is intended to be an inexpensive, entry-level class where outdated Showroom Stock cars and other, similar cars can be raced with stock engines and on street tires. By and large, it is successful at achieving this objective. The preparation rules are more liberal than in Showroom Stock, so pressure to cheat is reduced but not eliminated.

Basically, an IT car is a street car with minor suspension improvements.

IT is becoming one of SCCA's most popular groups. It's almost déjà vu from SCCA Production racing in the 1950s and early 1960s. Street cars are raced with minimal modifications—no gutting, for example.

It is quite popular, too, with new racers. Often it is a situation where an aspiring racer already has a Volkswagen Rabbit, a Mazda RX-7, or whatever, and decides to convert it and go racing. I don't advise that approach (see the section below on how to select a car), but many people are doing it and having a lot of fun.

SPORTS RACING CLASS

A Sports Racer is a purpose-built race car with a full body covering its wheels. Classes are established primarily by engine specifications, with other characteristics of the car being relatively unrestricted.

In the old days, Sports Racers were beautiful, intuitively streamlined vehicles with many complex curves and sometimes even tail fins. These days, they all look like doorstops: aerodynamically sound, but unattractive from an aesthetic viewpoint.

Back in the heyday of Sports Racers, we had classes from ASR to DSR. The A-cars were the fastest cars that ever ran in club racing: big, V-8 powered, and easily capable of doing 200mph. The club racing cars were usually hand-me-downs from the SCCA's Canadian-American (Can-Am) series, where drivers like Mark Donohue were kings. There

were also BSR cars, running twin-cam 1600cc Cosworths and hitting 160mph. Both are seen only on the vintage circuit nowadays.

There are a few DSR cars still around, now often running snowmobile (well, "two-stroke") engines. There is also a small band of zealots, headed by two guys with lots of money, who are trying to keep CSR alive. You may go several years without even seeing such a car.

The big event in recent sports racing history was the arrival of Sports Renault (SRen). This is a standardized class based on cars manufactured by an SCCA subsidiary, SCCA Enterprises. They are purpose-built cars running Renault engines and a specified brand and model of street tire.

The primary objective of the class is to eliminate equipment differences from the performance equation, leaving only driver skill. A secondary objective is to attract new drivers by providing a low-cost entry class where advanced mechanical skills are not required.

The Sports Renault class has been renamed Spec Racer (SR) due to Renault's withdrawal of financial support. Over 600 of these cars now exist and they comprise the most successful class in club racing.

The underpinning of the class is SCCA's determination to make it a "driver" class where all cars are made as equal as possible. Engines, for example, come sealed from the official engine builder. You cannot open them, much less screw around with them. The rulebook can be accurately paraphrased as follows: (1) Everything that is not permitted is prohibited; (2) you can paint the car and wheels any color you like; and (3) there are no other rules.

As a race car, a Spec Racer is a success. They are quite responsive and fun to drive, though burdened with a heavy chassis (which means lots of driver protection). They are reasonably fast, exceeding 100mph on a long straight, and they are economical. Dedicated SR drivers include people who started in the cars as novices, plus many who have switched from other more expensive, or more technically difficult, classes.

If you are considering buying a Spec Racer, you should know that during 1993–1996, this class is undergoing a change of driveline. The original Renault engines and four-speed transaxles are being replaced by Ford 1.9 liter units and Mazda five-speeds. This changeover, scheduled to be completed in 1997, means that cars with Renault drivelines will be good, cheap rides but will be obsolete unless upgraded with the newer (and noticeably faster) hardware. Your choice of driveline will depend on your economic circumstances and your ability to do the eventually required upgrade yourself.

Danny Collins: "Over 600 Spec Racers have been built, purchased, and raced. After the original tires were changed over to a softer compound spec-tire in 1990, the cars handled much better and behaved more like race cars on 'slicks.' After one to three years in a Spec Racer, a competitive driver in this class can hold their own in any race car! I've personally rented them for twelve races between 1988 and 1992 even though I was also racing my own Formula 2000 [Formula Continental]. Because it's easy to 'flick' them into a four-wheel drift, I think they're a real kick in the butt!"

Carroll Smith: "Right on!"

FORMULA CLASS

There are those who say: "If you can't see the tires, then it isn't a real race car." If you adhere to this theory, then a Formula car is in your future.

Formula cars are primarily differentiated by engine regulations, but significant chassis regulations exist in some classes. Aerodynamic downforce devices (such as wings) are also closely regulated.

Formula racing consists of two groups of cars: Pro cars from the Formula Atlantic and (now-defunct) Formula Super Vee series, and amateur cars such as Formula Ford 1600s and 2000s, Formula Vees, and Formula 440s. (One could dispute my placement of FF 2000 cars in the latter group; there are several pro series for these cars. From a speed and technology viewpoint, however, I think they are quite accessible to beginning drivers.)

Two of the most popular classes in club racing are Formula Ford and Formula Vee. Fords feature pure racing chassis and 1600cc Cortina engines in near-stock form. FFs are further divided between newer cars and "Club Fords," which are typically pre-1985 designs. Formula Vee chassis are restricted to using Volkswagen suspension components and near-stock 1200cc air-cooled VW engines.

HOW TO SELECT A CLASS

So far, I've ducked the question of what class of car a beginner should buy. There's good reason for that: There's hardly any question so subjective and on which you're going to get so many firmly held opinions. Most drivers will tell you that their class is the best. Question them some more, and you will usually find out that they've never raced in any other class!

Go to the track, hang around, crew for people, see what's available, and make your own decision. As I have already said, the only thing I would recommend staying away from are the pro-class cars like Formula Atlantic, Formula Super Vee, and GT-1/Trans-Am. Even if you can deal with the financial and technical aspects of these cars, they represent a huge step up from zero. Start with something smaller.

Charlie Williams: "Another thing to consider in selecting a class is the degree of engine modification involved. Pro class engines are expensive and fragile.

"I do not recommend highly modified engines for amateur racers unless this is your thing and you like building engines more than having track time. A carefully maintained semi-stock or slightly modified engine will last most club racers a season."

In making your selection, consider carefully the popularity of the various classes. Study a current table of National race entries (published annually in a fall issue of *Sports Car*), concentrating on your SCCA division. (Popularity of classes varies quite a bit across the country.) If you want to win a lot of relatively meaningless trophies, select a class that is not popular.

If, on the other hand, you really want to compete, I suggest selecting a class with an average of at least five or six starters per race. Another reason to select a popular class is that your race car will be easier to sell when you are ready to move up (or on).

If your interest is in a regional class such as IT, the information on race starters is a little harder to get. Call your regional Chief Registrar and see if you can borrow copies of race entry lists from recent events at nearby tracks.

Dennis Eade: "Choose a chassis that you can *afford* to run. Don't be swayed by what you would someday *like* to run or by the most *glamorous* class. A good Club Ford that you can run is much more fun than an old worn-out Atlantic car that you can't afford to buy parts for."

HOW TO SELECT THE RIGHT CAR

This is an easy one. Select means "buy," not "build." You buy a good used race car to begin your career.

Why buy a used car instead of converting the street car you already own? First, it takes a lot of time and money to build a race car from scratch. Everything you need has to be bought new and the total cost will be a lot more than you expect. When you buy a used car, somebody else has paid the new price—it's virtually guaranteed that you'll save money. The same thing applies to the work involved: it takes a lot of work to build a car, none of which you're compensated for when you sell it.

Formula cars comprise SCCA's fastest classes. The Formula Atlantic class is the top of the league and a traditional stepping stone to IndyCar racing. These cars feature front and rear wings, plus ground effects tunnels on each side of the driver. Brian Nooney

Formula 440s are the other end of the Formula car spectrum. These low-cost racers feature two-cycle engines, belt drive, and virtually no suspension. They are faster in a straight line than Formula Vees, but usually slower in the corners. (No, I don't know how he's steering the car!)

An SSGT Camaro, a good entry-level car for the novice.

On the other hand, this GT-1 tube-frame Chevrolet Beretta is too much car for a new driver.

Second and more important, unless you have been around SCCA racing for some time, you do not know how to build a competitive car. The rulebooks can give you the minimums, but you won't know what else to do or to not do. The result of your money and work is likely to be an uncompetitive car at best, an unfinished and frustrating project at worst.

If you're going to ignore my advice and build your own race car anyway, do not, repeat, do not ignore the following: Contact your local Chief of Tech, explain what you are doing, and seek advice. Get the car inspected and the car logbook issued well before your first weekend. It is not uncommon for a novice to show up at driver's school with a car that can't be raced due to serious technical or safety violations. Don't let it be you.

OK, now that we've dispensed with building your own car, what about buying a new one? With the possible exception of a Spec Racer, there are a couple of reasons to avoid a new car. First, you don't need to spend the money. Your first season or two of racing should be dedicated to learning to race; you need a car that will consistently finish races, not one that an experienced driver could win with. Race cars depreciate—you might as well take advantage of that by buying a car from someone who *does* want or need the newest thing.

The second reason for not buying a new car is that new cars come with a varying quantity of problems that need to be solved by the owner. They often need to be assembled and aligned and there are usually design and fabrication problems that need to be fixed. First, as a new driver you probably don't have the tools and skills to deal with a new

car and, second, why buy the grief? A good used car will have most of the bugs worked out before you get it.

So, you're convinced and are going to buy a used car. What should you look for? The first thing you want to find is an honest, competent, and helpful seller. This won't be as difficult as you might think; racers are usually honest, helpful, and competent as well. It isn't like going to Crazy Sam's Home-of-the-Good-Deal used car lot.

Stick with a local car if you can. You're a lot less likely to get a snow job from someone who knows they will see you at the racetrack. Ask him or her to help you at your first driver's school. A weekend of knowledgeable help is invaluable to a beginner in an unfamiliar car.

As far as the car itself is concerned, you're looking for neatness, cleanliness, and attention to detail. If you haven't yet read Carroll Smith's *Prepare to Win*, do so before you go car shopping. The neat, well-prepared example will be obvious to you after you've looked at a few cars. Look at each car's logbook—usually there's not much there, but major crashes and so on will be noted. If there are repeated entries noting things to be fixed, *caveat emptor!*

Look at the seller's shop, too. Is it neat, well-equipped? If it looks like poverty city, then he may have had to cut corners on the car, too.

Dennis Eade: "The most important part of this is remembering that you are doing it to have fun. Quite frequently this gets lost in the madness. To have fun, you first must have a race car that will provide you with solid reliability.

"If you cannot or do not want to rebuild the chassis yourself, choose a chassis that is in good condition. Beware of the deal that is too good to be true. It always is!

"If you are not knowledgeable yet, find a friend who is or approach your local race shop for assistance. More than likely they are familiar with the car and its owner and can give you good, sound advice. If they don't know the car, you should pay them to inspect the chassis. This could save you a tremendous amount of money and aggravation in the future months."

Most cars come equipped with "valuable spares"; if the seller says they are worth X-amount of dollars, see if he or she will keep them and knock X-amount of dollars off the price of the car. If the owner keeps the spares, you will probably be able to buy them from him or her as needed.

Carroll Smith: "Beware; the 'valuable spares' are usually worn out and worthless."

Don't be too concerned with the car's win record. A car that has consistent finishes, hence good reliability, is what

Spec Racers are popular and cost-effective rentals. Here's a lineup outside a race shop trailer.

you need. A race winner has usually led a much harder life than a mid-pack finisher.

The engine is another matter: If you're buying a car with a prepared engine (other that Showroom Stock or Spec Racer, for example), don't pay much unless it is verifiably from a "name" national builder. Home-built engines usually are uncompetitive from a power standpoint and often are of dubious reliability and legality. Talk to people who know the class, ideally to someone who knows the car. Call the engine builder. The engine is basically a pig in a poke, so do as much research as you can.

Charlie Williams: "Don't count on getting a good engine in a used race car. Save some money for the engine builder.

"If you *are* investing money in an engine, *be sure* to talk to its builder. I have found that a Williams sticker on the engine doesn't always mean that it is one of mine. The best approach is to not pay any more than the car is worth to you without an engine. Then if you get an engine that is rebuildable or usable, you get a bonus."

Tony Kester: "The engine is absolutely the most important place, next to safety equipment, to spend your money."

RENTING A CAR

If you are going to rent a car, the selection criteria are similar to buying but you can cut a few corners. A misjudgment will only ruin your weekend rather than becoming a permanent resident of your garage. Safety is an exception, however. You can be hurt by an unsafe rental just as surely as by an unsafe purchase.

Your first choice in renting is whether to deal with a professional race shop or with an individual. Each situation has its pros and cons.

PRO RACE SHOP RENTALS

At a professional racing shop, your choice of car class will be limited. Often, a Spec Racer will be the only thing available. If you just want to race something, these cars are a good choice. If you want to try a specific class, however, the pro rental may not work for you.

Pro rentals are expensive. This is not because it is a hugely profitable business—it isn't. It is because the race shop must recover its expenses and overhead, including the wages, lodging, and food of the crew person assigned to your car. In exchange, you get an arrive-and-drive situation and (usually) excellent equipment.

Carroll Smith: "Pro rentals only *look* expensive. Usually they are a good value."

Normally, a pro rental price will be all-inclusive except for your personal safety equipment and the event entry fee. The rental will include the car, delivery to the track, fuel, crew support, and so forth. The only variable is likely to be whether the deal includes new tires or not.

If you are going to be renting from a shop that you don't know well, ask for the names and telephone numbers of two or three people who have recently rented from them. Call them and ask how things went. Was the equipment reliable? Was the preparation thorough and on-time? Would they rent again? It also won't hurt to ask what they paid—maybe you'll find that there is some dickering room in the quoted price.

INDIVIDUAL RENTALS

Your first problem in renting from an individual will be finding him or her. Check the classified ads in your regional newsletter. Get on the telephone with local drivers. Tell them what you're looking for and ask if they can give you

You can sometimes find private rental deals by wandering the paddock. This S2000 would be suitable for a novice rental. The S2000's extra expense and speed, though, are probably not worth it to a new driver.

any leads. Keep following leads until you finally find something that works.

Your search for an individual rental will be made easier if you are flexible about what weekend you run, and if you are making the calls well ahead of the race date.

Before you make a commitment, though, go to the lessor's shop and look at the car. You are interested first in safety, second in reliability, and third in performance. Ask about the car's finishing record. Any recent DNFs? What were the causes? Look over the roll bar and safety harnesses. Cast your eyes around the shop. Mentally pretend that you are thinking about buying the car. If you're uncertain, check the lessor's reputation with other drivers that you trust.

The individual "deal" is highly flexible. You may simply pick up the car on Thursday and return it on Sunday night. More likely, the lessor will want to be at the track with you—you're an unknown quantity to him. Again, tires will be a variable. He'll usually throw a used set into the deal, but new ones will be on you. If you do pop for the new tires, be clear about who owns them at the end of the weekend. They will have residual value.

RENTAL AGREEMENTS

Generally, the terms of a rental are that you must return the car to the lessor in the same condition that you received it. If you hurt it, you fix it. If somebody else hurts it, you fix it. If the engine blows, you fix it. If you get hurt, that's your problem too. It's exactly as if you owned the car: you bear all the risk.

If you rent from a pro shop, you will be required to sign a multipage agreement that absolves them from responsibility for virtually everything while promising you, the renter, as little as possible. You will probably also not be able to negotiate changes to this agreement, since the person you are dealing with will not understand the agreement and will not be interested in paying his lawyer to evaluate your suggestions. One feature of the agreement will be that the lessor will do all damage repair, charging you his regular shop rates.

The reality of club racing sponsorship: Here's a typical amateur sponsorship deal on a two-liter Ford Formula Continental car. The driver's last name and the name of the sponsoring company are the same. Brian Nooney

If you rent from an individual, the agreement is subject to a lot of negotiation. He or she may have some kind of contract that you can begin with, or you can begin with a clean sheet of paper. In this situation, I suggest that you adopt the philosophy that "Good fences make good neighbors." Try to anticipate and agree ahead of time on major areas of potential dispute. These include the amount of support you will receive at the track, whether you can fix crash damage yourself, and other details. The language doesn't have to be fancy, but you should try to cover as much ground as possible.

One area for serious discussion (in either type of rental) is the engine. My belief is that the lessor should be responsible for all engine damage unless the engine has been seriously overrevved. An alternative would be an agreement to split the costs of a catastrophic engine failure. I don't think that a renter should have sole responsibility for a blown en-

Aspiring drivers never want to sit still for the classroom stuff, but it's important. Take good notes. Bob Bondurant School of High Performance Driving

gine; most of the causes are not under the driver's control. You may well find that your lessor does not share this philosophy. It's worth a try, though.

Costs? In 1992 dollars, figure anywhere from $800–$1,500 for an individual rental depending on the car, the included services, and the hunger of the lessor. For a pro shop's Spec Racer, figure $1,300–$1,800. The low side would be for a single race weekend. The high side would be for a double-race weekend or a driver school, where there are more on-track hours to wear out the car. You won't be doing it, but a Formula Atlantic weekend rental is about $8,000.

You will be required to post a damage deposit, usually in the form of a personal check to be held by the lessor. A typical number is $3,000. Don't get too hung up on the amount. It really doesn't matter, since you are on the hook for the *actual* cost of damages anyway.

Dennis Eade: "Formula Atlantic rentals currently range from $18,000–$35,000 for a pro race weekend with a test day. We are charging $20,515 in 1992.

"For an SCCA National weekend and a test day, the range is $7,000–$13,000. Our price is $8,000. Expect to provide a $25,000 damage deposit, too."

SPONSORSHIP

Forget about getting any significant sponsorship.

The only reason that I am even including this topic in the "Getting Started" section of the book is that an amazing number of aspiring drivers ask about it.

The vast majority of "sponsor" lettering on amateur race cars is put there because the driver has some connection with the sponsor. Usually the sponsor is the driver's company or the driver's daddy's company. These folks are generally writing off their racing expenses as advertising, but do not get or expect a business benefit that is in any way commensurate with the cost of the sponsorship.

Carroll Smith: "All successful racing drivers' initial sponsorship proposals start with the same word: 'Dad?'"

The economics of advertising are not complicated. Basically, a manufacturer, distributor, or merchant will budget a varying percentage of product sales for advertising. In mass-market consumer items like cosmetics, a manufacturer might spend 30% or more. You are not likely to be of interest to someone with this kind of budget. More relevant to amateur racing, a small retailer might budget 3–5% of total sales.

Even being generous and using the 5% figure, this means that your local tire dealer or restaurant must get *twenty times* its sponsorship money back in sales in order for you to be a break-even investment. A free set of tires must generate sales of twenty sets, and so on. No beginner can generate that kind of business for a sponsor.

It is even rare for a pro-level sponsor to be into racing strictly as a business proposition. Usually, the sponsor's decision makers have some personal interest. A good illustration of this occurred a few years ago when a large home vacuum cleaner manufacturer was a major sponsor of Mario Andretti's IndyCar. Do you think the homemakers of America ran out to buy vacuum cleaners when they saw Mario on TV? I doubt it. Do you think the president of the vacuum cleaner company liked being pictured in the magazine ads with Mario's arm around him?

If you want to take a run at a potential sponsor, check with SCCA on the availability of their "sponsor kit." This kit, created in 1992, includes a color brochure describing club racing plus some demographic information, and a nice presentation folder into which you put your sponsorship pitch.

DRIVER SCHOOL

The way most drivers get started in racing is by going to a local club school. These schools, run by the SCCA regions or regional sanctioning organization, are about the most basic introduction to racing that there is. You are responsible for providing your own car and equipment at a club school.

Carroll Smith: "Actually, Step #1 is to drive a stick-shift car on the street and learn how to shift and use the gearbox. It is not instinctive, it is important, and you don't need to waste expensive school time learning it. The same goes for 'lines.'"

Alternatively, you could begin by attending a professional school. There are a number of significant differences between a pro school and a club school. Pro schools are an arrive-and-drive proposition, supplying the cars, the driver gear, everything that you need. Consistency of instruction quality is high. They are expensive, but not out of sight compared to a realistic total of the costs involved for a club school weekend.

Which type of school should you start with?

If you're not sure whether you *want* to go racing, a pro school is a good place to find out. If racing is not for you, you'll have found out before you invest a lot of time and money. Renting a car for an SCCA school is an alternate way to experiment, but the costs of an SCCA school in a rented car can easily equal a pro school and the quality of training is nowhere near equal.

If you're certain that racing *is* for you, then I'd suggest postponing attendance at a pro school until you've learned the basics of dealing with your car and the racing environment. In my view, a novice at a pro school is so overwhelmed by the newness of it all that he or she cannot possibly take full advantage of the instruction. Better to learn the shifting, braking, and the feel of the car in the somewhat less expensive SCCA environment, then go to the pros for the winning edge. (The counterargument to this position says that a pro school can more easily teach you good habits if you have not already developed bad ones. You'll have to make your own decision.)

Danny Collins: "I differ on the order. Develop self-confidence on proper car driving techniques in a pro school before you get out to mix it up with rank novices in a club school. As a novice, you have enough anxiety without trying to learn everything about controlling what is often a strange car in the wheel-to-wheel racing atmosphere of the club school. It's like throwing a kid into the deep end of the pool and yelling instructions on how to swim! Glub! Glub! I call shoving a novice out into heavy club traffic without prior coaching 'The Trial and Error School of Motor Racing.' Some manage, but it's doing it the hard way!"

Carroll Smith: "I agree with Danny. I strongly suggest a three-day pro school. The level of instruction and on-track time are orders of magnitude above SCCA. So is the cost, but it's a cheap way to find out if you *really* want to race."

PREPARATION: BEFORE YOU GO

As is true for most of life's experiences, what you get out of a school depends on what you put into it. You should devote some time to preparing, whether you're going to a pro school or to an SCCA school.

Get and study some (more) books on driving and on racing. Regardless of whether you are going to a pro school or to a club school, you are going to be paying a large amount of money for the training, probably $50–$100 per hour. This is an expensive way to learn the basic vocabulary, the concepts of cornering, of heel-and-toe downshifting, and

so on. I learned to race before the days of home videotapes, but it seems to me that a few hours spent vicariously "in-car" would be helpful as well.

Prepare yourself medically. Go ahead and get a racing physical even if you are going to a pro school that doesn't require it. You need to verify that your vision is OK, and that you are in generally good physical condition. Racing, even in a school, is stressful and you should make sure that you are ready for it. Also, if you cannot pass the physical, you will probably not be able to proceed in SCCA racing anyway. Not good news, but probably best found out before you make the investment in a pro school.

If there is any question about your vision, see your eye doctor and tell him or her what you are planning to do. Follow the resulting advice. Remember that not all glasses frames will fit through the openings in full-face helmets. If you wear a larger-than-average frame style, you should make sure that you can get them on when wearing the helmet you will use at school. If there's any doubt, buy a set of glasses in a smaller frame style.

(Incidentally, if you do have a medical or a vision situation that is outside the standard SCCA limits, do not automatically assume that you cannot race. Contact your division's medical director for advice.)

GETTING THE MOST OUT OF A SCHOOL

You should try to optimize your school experience by "tuning" your individual instructional situation.

Try to hook up with another student (or two) with similar experience, capability, and aspirations. You will both (or all) benefit from comparing notes and helping one another. There is usually a little "milling-around" time at the beginning of a school; this is the time to meet the other students and establish relationships.

Also, do a little research ahead of time on which of the school's instructors are the best. Talk to previous graduates. Ask the pro school staff if they have any instructors with several years' experience racing in your chosen car class. If you're going to an SCCA school, find out who are the top drivers for your class of car; call one of them ahead of time and ask if he or she will agree to be your instructor.

Then, go to the school's Chief Instructor at the beginning of the first day and request a specific individual instructor and specific student partner(s). Odds are that you will get your requests.

RECORD KEEPING

Get organized right away. During the course of your career, you will need to keep voluminous records of the racetracks you run, the car settings that worked (and didn't work), and of your qualifying and finishing positions. This is best done in one or more large three-ring binders.

Before you go to your first school, buy a three-ring binder and a notebook with punched pages that can be transferred to the binder. Plan to take notes both during the classroom sessions and between on-track sessions. These notes, and the school handouts, go into the binder as the beginning of your career records.

WHAT TO EXPECT

A racing school is generally not a slick, glamorous place. You will begin with some kind of lecture from a senior instructor. Because the experience level in the class will be highly varied, you (who are well prepared, right?) will find much of this material to be quite basic. Pay attention anyway. You have nothing better to do and, guaranteed, you will learn something of value. Among the gems will be specific information on the racetrack, and logistical information on the conduct of the school. Take notes; remember that you are paying a lot for this experience and want to get the maximum from it.

Following the first classroom session, you will be assigned to an individual instructor. Usually this instructor will have more than one student, but he will have few enough that he can devote time to each individual's problems.

PROFESSIONAL SCHOOLS

Before you pick a pro school, do some research. Make a list of candidates, call for literature and study it, then call back with a list of questions.

Usually, you won't be taught personally by the "famous name" owner—but ask. The most critical factor in your receiving value from a school is the quality of the instructors. If you are being lectured to and trained by people with limited club racing experience, it will be difficult for you to get what you need. Such instructors may be fine for the "wannabes" and dreamers who comprise a significant portion of schools' customers, but these instructors' expertise is likely to be derived from the school curriculum itself rather than being from firsthand experience.

Thus, in talking to schools, I suggest that you try to get specific information on the chief and the individual instructors who will staff the dates that you plan to attend. They can't guarantee any specific individual, of course, but the credentials of the planned staff should give you a good idea of how the school compares to others.

A few other things to ask about include: What does the classroom instruction cover? Some schools don't cover SCCA material like flags, and so on. How many hours of classroom time will you get? What's the school's policy on car damage? If you bonk one, who pays? If you'll be using their personal safety equipment (suit and helmet, for instance), does it meet SCCA standards? Will you be able to practice passing under braking? Will there be practice starts and races?

One item that comes up in connection with pro schools is rev limits. Some schools pace your training by setting progressively higher rpm limits for each race car session, finally allowing you to reach redline. Other schools proudly advertise: "No artificial rev limits!" It probably doesn't matter much.

Your first sessions at a pro school will usually be in a street sedan of some sort. Typically, you will be paired with a "partner" with whom you will share a car. Your training will begin with you, your partner, and an instructor going out onto the school's course to learn some basics. These will include driving position, steering and braking techniques, and controlling the car at its limit in corners or on a skid pad. Your partner will ride in the back seat while you are driving, and vice versa. Don't be surprised if your instructor grabs the steering wheel to make a point.

(At some schools, you and your partner alternate between classroom and car sessions. When you are in the classroom, your partner is in the car, and vice versa. This approach, I think, makes more efficient use of your time by eliminating time spent as an observer.)

The first segment of the school's curriculum will be organized to teach you specific topics in car control and driving. Depending on the school's philosophy, particular topics may be emphasized. Bondurant, for example, is strong on trail braking. Roos believes that eye technique is paramount. Regardless of where you go, they will preach smoothness.

Most of the larger schools feature some kind of specialized training equipment. You might be put into a skid car, a slide car, or an accident simulator. While it is certainly true that these are intended as marketing differentiators for the schools, each has intrinsic value as well. The objective is to create training situations that cannot be easily duplicated in a normal car on the racetrack. Take full advantage of the opportunity.

In between your on-track sessions, you will get classroom lectures on various aspects of driving and racing. Typically, these are concentrated on lines and technique. In some schools, race operations and flags are covered in depth as well.

After you have completed your "basic training," you will move into the school's race cars. These are usually small Formula cars on street tires, loosely based on Formula Fords. After being fitted in the car, you will be sent out to practice shifting, double-clutching, and to generally get the feel of the car.

From here you will have several more race car sessions, each with specific lesson objectives.

One thing that you will *not* get, however, is any significant amount of wheel-to-wheel racing time. Passing will usually be restricted to the straightaways, and allowed only in the later on-track sessions. At the end, there may be a short race, but—face it—the schools cannot afford to have their equipment getting torn up in crashes, no matter who pays. For this reason, as I mentioned earlier, it's required that you get wheel-to-wheel experience by attending at least one club racing school before you compete.

One more note: School cars aren't as equal as you might think. If you can strike up a conversation with one of the school mechanics, you might be able to find out which have the strongest motors. Try to stand near one of those cars when the assignments are being made! Cars are assigned primarily by students' body size (for example, there are "tall" and "short" car setups), but you might get lucky.

CLUB SCHOOLS

The main objective of an SCCA school is to get you at least three hours of safe, on-track time. They generally start you out with a classroom session and a written test. You should prepare for the school by carefully reading your *GCR*, with concentration on the flags and on the on-course and in-the-pits rules. Also study the jobs of the various race officials; trick questions about the Stewards and the Stewards of the Meeting are popular.

You have to show up with an SCCA-legal race car to run the school. If at all possible, get the car's technical inspection completed before the weekend. Many regions have a pre-race tech session during the week. Sometimes you can coax your friendly neighborhood Chief of Tech to make a special visit to your garage. Pre-race tech is absolutely imperative if you have a new, never-raced car that needs a logbook. You do not need tech inspection problems on your driver school weekend.

Most SCCA schools are one-day events. This makes for a busy day—you need to bring some crew help: your spouse, an available teenager, or a friend. You'll be in the car for a half hour, out of the car talking to your instructor, then back in the car. Usually seven times! This is all new, it's exciting, your adrenaline is high, and it's easy to forget something like gasoline, tire pressure, or tightening the lug nuts. Your objective for the school is to run every session in its entirety. This means you must be ready when the session begins and the car must stay intact and running until it's over. Use a checklist.

In some areas of the country, two-day schools are the

At a pro school, you'll run with nearly identical cars. Here's a row of Bondurant's Formula Fords, with Bob himself talking to the students. Bob Bondurant School of High Performance Driving

An SCCA school is a bit more eclectic than a pro school. Here's a grid that includes Formula Fords, Vees, and 440s, plus a gaggle of Spec Racers! Bill Bergeron

norm. I think this is a preferable situation for the novice, just because the time pressure factor is diminished. The earlier comments about crew and checklists still apply, however.

Your SCCA instructor will be an experienced driver, usually in your class or type of car. His or her racing skill will be anywhere from superb to abysmal, and teaching ability ditto. You will have to form your own opinion and act accordingly.

(Once in a while, you will get a bad instructor or one you can't get along with. Schools try hard to prevent this, but it happens. If you are having a problem, make sure the Chief Instructor knows about it. If at all possible, you will be assigned another instructor.)

Be cautious, work up to things at your own rate, and don't try to be the fastest student on the track. Even if you're the next Mario, there is probably someone more aggressive (read foolish) or someone with a faster car. Your program should be smoothness, not speed. Concentration on consistency and smoothness from lap to lap will automatically produce steadily quicker times. Most schools' grading criteria emphasize consistent, slowly declining lap times. Schools do not give good marks to a student whose lap times are all over the place, even if the student manages a good one once in a while.

Do not, repeat, do not disobey or argue with the workers, even if you think they are wrong. There are two reasons for this. First, they are volunteers without whom we couldn't go racing. Be grateful. Second, a serious altercation with a worker will almost certainly cause the Chief Steward to fail you for the school. If you have a problem, talk to the Chief Instructor or the Chief Steward—politely and calmly.

That's about it for SCCA schools. Attendance at one, at least, is required. Your other required school can be another SCCA school or an SCCA-approved pro school.

Chapter 2

Basic Physics

You do not have to be a physicist to drive a race car, but it will be easier to discuss some of the things that you should know if we start with a bit of physics in the form of some definitions.

SPEED, MASS, AND ACCELERATION

Velocity is the speed and direction that the car is traveling. As racers, we are not rigorous in the use of the term velocity; thus it is important to remember that when we talk about speed and changing speed, we are often really talking about velocity.

Acceleration is a change in velocity. It is produced by some force acting on the car. Forces that can accelerate a race car include those generated through the tires, by aerodynamic drag, and by contact with objects moving at a different velocity. Generally, we prefer to avoid this last class of forces.

Mass, for our purposes, is equivalent to weight. The amount of force required to change the velocity of (or accelerate) an object depends on its mass. In physics terms, the equations that relate these terms are:

Acceleration = Force ÷ Mass
Velocity = Acceleration x Time

Mass you can't do anything about once you are on the racetrack, so you are left to manage the forces and the times. To make the car do something that it is not now doing, you must exert forces on it through the tire contact patches, which we'll talk about in the next chapter.

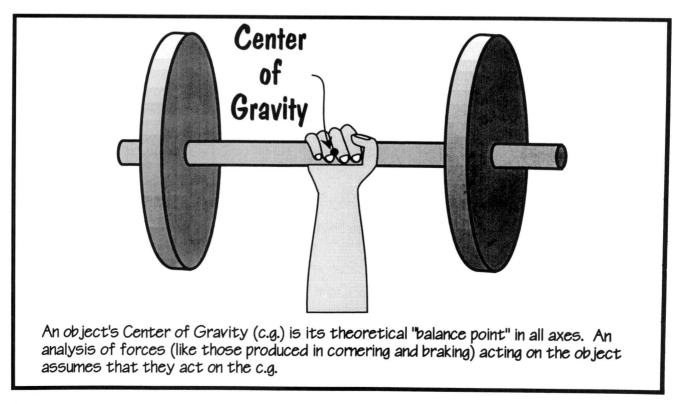

An object's Center of Gravity (c.g.) is its theoretical "balance point" in all axes. An analysis of forces (like those produced in cornering and braking) acting on the object assumes that they act on the c.g.

High Polar Moment of Inertia

This weight bar has a high polar moment around the indicated axis because the weights are out towards the ends of the bar. You could visualize one weight as being the engine and one as being the gas tank & rear axle of a car like a Mustang.

Low Polar Moment of Inertia

This weight bar has a low polar moment around the indicated axis because the weights are near the center of the bar. You could visualize the one weight as being the engine and one as being the gas tank & driver of a sports racer or a formula car.

Center of gravity (c.g.) of an object is the average position of its mass. For example, the center of gravity of two children on a level teeter-totter is at the pivot, probably almost exactly centered left-to-right on the board. Another way to think about c.g. is that it's the "balance point" of the car. If you could hook a rope to the c.g., the car would be exactly balanced left-to-right and front-to-back.

Center of gravity is important to us as racers because all forces acting on the car can be considered to be acting on its c.g.

The car's c.g. is normally close to the car's centerline, but will be slightly off due to asymmetric positioning of some objects in the car (such as the battery) and due to any off-center positioning of the driver, who is an appreciable component of the car's mass. The car's c.g. height and fore-and-aft position are highly dependent on the car design.

The optimum c.g. height is zero inches above the track surface (for minimum weight transfer under the various accelerations that the car experiences). The optimum lateral location is on the centerline of the car (for symmetric handling). Optimum fore-and-aft position depends on the tires on the car and on which end is being driven by the engine.

Polar moment of inertia refers to the difficulty of spinning an object on an axis drawn through its center of gravity. Back to the children on the teeter-totter for an example: The difficulty you would have in rocking the teeter-totter would depend not only on the weight of the children, but also on their distance from the center. If they sat close to the pivot, the board would be easier to move than if they sat way out at the end.

The figures illustrate this concept using a weight-lifting bar. As you can see, objects having the same mass and the same center of gravity can have quite different polar moments of inertia. (Also, polar moments are different for different axes of rotation. The polar moment of the weight bar along the axis of the bar is much smaller than its polar moment for an axis perpendicular to the bar.)

A car actually has two relevant polar moments. One is for an axis perpendicular to the road surface. This *yaw moment* is the one that affects turn-in to corners. The second is

About 20 square inches of front contact patch - that's all!

Here's the contact patch of a Spec Racer's right front tire, pasted onto a 1/2" grid. You can estimate the contact area by counting the number of squares it covers, then dividing by four. Note that it's heavier on the inside edge due to the wheel's negative camber setting.

for an axis perpendicular to the direction of travel; this *pitch moment* is the one that resists dive under braking. (The third polar moment is *roll* along the car's longitudinal axis. You do not want to learn about this one.)

Carroll Smith: "You do not want to learn about roll—but you will!"

Due to the way cars are designed, the yaw and pitch moments will tend to have similar values. Thus, we refer to a car's polar moment as if it had only one.

The responsiveness of a car is primarily determined by its polar moment of inertia. A car with a high polar moment will be harder to get turned into a corner and it will tend to keep turning after you want it to be done. It will also assume a nose-down attitude under braking a bit more slowly. This is not a big problem, but when the nose is stopped by the springs or bump stops, the rear will not immediately stop moving; it will tend to keep rising. This can lead to transient rear-tire lockup.

TRACTION AND TIRE DYNAMICS

You can get along without learning about many technical aspects of racing. You can do well without understanding bump steer, without knowing how your engine makes its horsepower, and without knowing how to change the brake pads. You cannot do well, however, without understanding how your tires work.

Four small patches of rubber connect your race car to the road. For example, a 3,000lb car with 30lb per sq-in (psi) of tire pressure has about 100sq-in of contact patch. Distributed evenly, this is approximately the area of a 4x6in index card at each tire. An 1,100lb Formula Ford with average 15psi tire pressure has only about 75sq-in of contact patch: two 3x5 cards and two 4x6s.

Every force that affects your car on the racetrack is transmitted through these tiny contact patches. Thus, it's important to understand as much as possible about them.

Danny Collins: "The main point is that tire patch! Making it work to the max."

ADHESION

All other things being equal (which they never are), a tire can transmit a roughly constant amount of thrust between the wheel and the road. That thrust can be used laterally for cornering, or fore and aft for braking or accelerating.

At the rear, about 22 square inches does the job.

Here's the contact patch of the right rear tire on the same Spec Racer. Note that it's more evenly loaded than the front, due to a near-zero camber setting..

The total of the lateral and fore-and-aft thrust is a constant, however. You can use 100% of the available thrust for cornering, 100% for braking, or some for each, but you cannot have more than 100% in total.

This phenomenon is easy to feel when adding a little throttle in a maximum side-force turn. The added acceleration will take cornering power from the tires, causing them to slide outward. In a front-wheel-drive car, this means *understeer* ("push"); on the rear wheels, *oversteer* ("loose").

Carroll Smith: "This is a bit of an oversimplification. You will get push from rear-wheel-drive cars, too, if they're set up with a lot of understeer."

On a street-type tire, the total available thrust is about 0.7–0.9g. This means that for each 100lb of weight the tire is carrying, it can generate 70–90lb of thrust. On a racing tire, the available thrust is about 1.2–1.4g.

Unlike the friction in your classical physics textbook, the g coefficient of a tire is diminished as the weight on the tire increases. Thus, a car with equal tires on all corners should have exactly 25% of its weight on each tire for maximum thrust. Easy to say, but hard to do since we are talking about both the *static* weight due to the mass of the car and the *dynamic* weight transferred due to the very thrust that we are trying to optimize.

Breakaway

When a tire is asked for more thrust than it can provide, it begins to break away and deliver less, not more, thrust. Everyone has experienced this on the street in the rain. A little too much throttle leaves you with spinning tires, going nowhere.

Street tires break away more gently than do race tires. This means that the edge is sharper on race tires; street tires are more forgiving, more tolerant of mistakes.

The slower breakaway characteristics of street tires make them an excellent choice for driving schools. Students can explore the limits of adhesion more completely, with less downside risk. This does not mean that you should run street tires on a car not designed for them, but it does explain why the pro schools run almost exclusively on street tires. (Yes, they're cheaper, too. A handy convergence of economic and pedagogical motivations.)

Bertil Roos: "I agree that street tires are an excellent choice for driving schools. One of the reasons is that students can explore the limit at much lower speeds than they

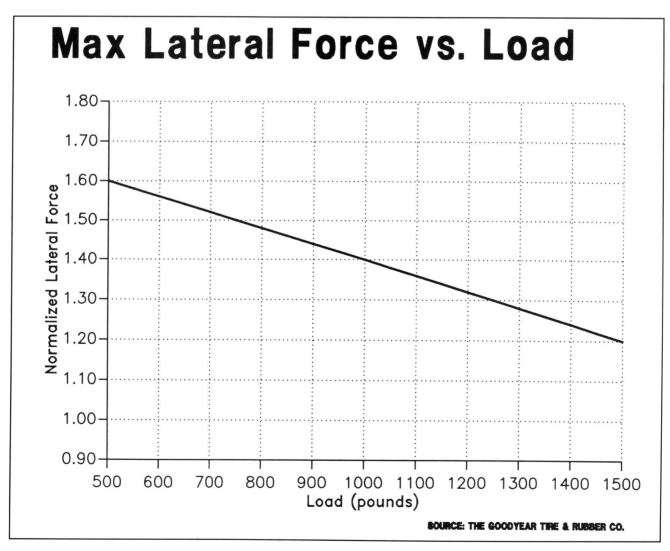

Max Lateral Force vs. Load

SOURCE: THE GOODYEAR TIRE & RUBBER CO.

can on race tires. My experience with street tires is that with 13in wheels and 70 Series street tires, high sidewalls made the cars [FF 2000s] unpredictable and unstable. But since we equipped our cars with 15in rims, 7in wide, and 50 Series tires, we have a street tire combination that is absolutely fantastic. Of course, it helps that they are less expensive.

"Most important is that the cars are driving and sliding so that the students can experience understeering and oversteering. If we put slicks on, they hold so well that a beginner can drive however he or she wants on the racetrack. The car will do anything the driver wants but, suddenly, when the slicks let go, the student will not know what hit him and he will not be able to learn from it.

"I think it would be a good idea for a beginning driver with a 1600 Formula Ford or even a Formula Ford 2000 to go testing with a good set of street tires. It makes the testing so much less expensive, it's going to hone your car control techniques enormously, and it's going to make it very, very easy to drive the car when you get on slicks later on."

Tony Kester: "Hard compound racing slicks also are a good configuration for driving practice (as opposed to testing)."

Carroll Smith: "I disagree with Bertil on the street tire idea. The chances of finding a set of street tires with characteristics that would make a *racing* car driveable are slim indeed! As usual, Tony is right on!"

Slip

Before beginning a discussion of several important topics (like oversteer and understeer), it is necessary to talk about tire slip. I approach this with some trepidation, as it is a difficult subject to explain and there's quite a bit of misinformation around.

Slip is a result of the rubber in the tire's contact patch area *stretching* as it transmits thrust between the tire carcass and the racetrack surface.

As the tire turns, each little molecule of rubber at the leading edge of the contact patch gets a chance to grab hold of the track. Of course, each of these molecules is also linked to its brothers in a network going all the way back to

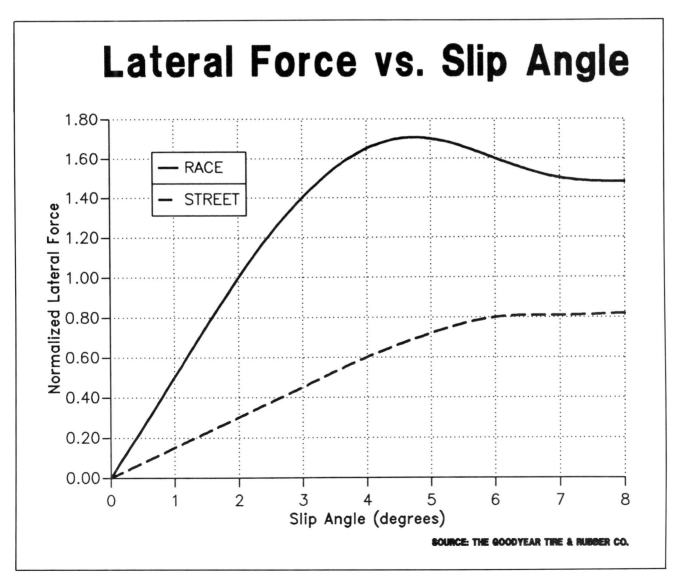

Lateral Force vs. Slip Angle

SOURCE: THE GOODYEAR TIRE & RUBBER CO.

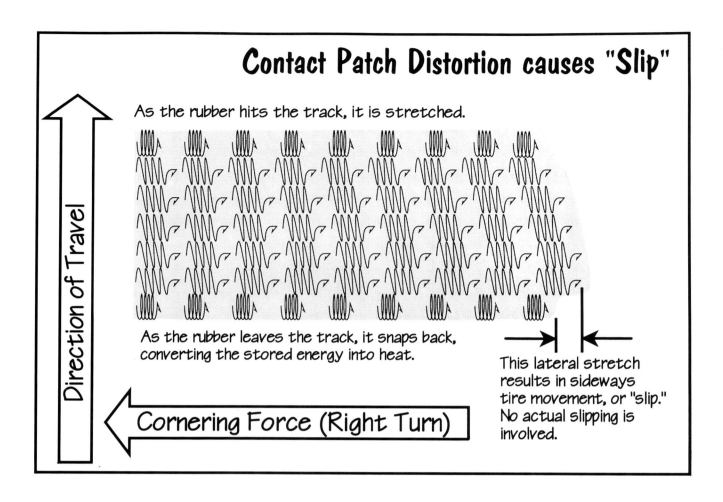

Contact Patch Distortion causes "Slip"

Direction of Travel

As the rubber hits the track, it is stretched.

As the rubber leaves the track, it snaps back, converting the stored energy into heat.

Cornering Force (Right Turn)

This lateral stretch results in sideways tire movement, or "slip." No actual slipping is involved.

the cords in the tire. Immediately after grabbing the track, this chain of linked rubber molecules begins to stretch in the direction of the tire thrust. As long as the bottom molecule can retain its grip on the road (the tire is not skidding), this rubber network remains stretched. When the molecule is picked off the track at the rearward edge of the contact patch, then the rubber snaps back into place.

(If you think about these little rubber molecules grabbing the track, it may be easier to see why the tire's thrust is roughly constant regardless of direction. Once the molecule

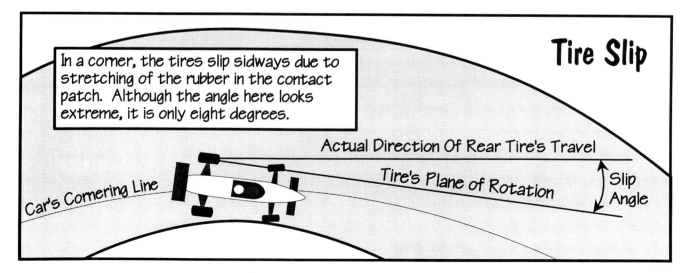

Tire Slip

In a corner, the tires slip sideways due to stretching of the rubber in the contact patch. Although the angle here looks extreme, it is only eight degrees.

Actual Direction Of Rear Tire's Travel

Tire's Plane of Rotation

Slip Angle

Car's Cornering Line

hits the track, all it can know is that it's being pulled on by its brother molecules. It doesn't know which way the tire is rotating, or whether it's accelerating, braking, or cornering. Regardless of the direction of the thrust, all that molecule on the track can do is hang on.)

Obviously, if the rubber is stretching, something has to be moving. Also obviously, it isn't the rubber molecule that has firmly grabbed the track surface. It can only be the other end of the "rubber band": the tire carcass. Thus, the stretching of the contact patch causes the *tire* to move relative to the track surface. Whenever a tire is transmitting a thrust, there is a slip. Going to the grocery store, the slips are small. On the racetrack, they're larger.

If the tire is transmitting an acceleration or braking thrust, it will actually be turning slightly faster or slower due to slip. This is expressed as a percentage. Fore-and-aft percentage slip may be of interest to drag racers; it is not of much interest to us.

Paul Van Valkenburgh: "Except in braking! Longitudinal slip is terribly important in braking, especially if you are buying the tires. It can take a lot of practice to ride that fine line between ultimate braking traction and a set of flatspotted tires."

When the thrust is a cornering thrust, however, we are very interested. When cornering, the tire appears to be slipping sideways due to the stretching of the rubber. It's not really slipping, however, it's simply moving over as the rubber between the road and the tire carcass is stretched. This apparent slipping is expressed as a *slip angle*. The slip angle is the angle between the apparent direction of the wheel (a vertical plane through its center) and the actual line of travel. We are talking about numbers in the 5–10 degree range.

When the little rubber molecules lose their grip, the slip becomes a slide. Adhesion is *decreased*, and the slip-slide angle is *increased*. A tire's maximum cornering force is developed just before slip turns to slide. As your racing career progresses, you will become increasingly familiar with the feel of this transition. Or you will be slow.

OVERSTEER AND UNDERSTEER

Steering is a dynamic situation. Once the car is turned into the corner and slip angles develop, there are two distinct factors that steer the car. One is the difference between front and rear slip angles. The second is the steering angles of the front (and, possibly, the rear) wheels. The car's trajectory is determined by the net effect of the slip angles and the steering angles.

If the front and rear slip angles are the same, we have a "neutral" car whose trajectory is determined primarily by the steering angles.

Oversteer occurs when the rear tires have larger slip angles than the fronts. You will frequently see an oversteering car go through a corner with the front wheels pointed almost straight ahead. All of the required turning is accomplished through the differing front and rear slip angles. When the tail is "hung out," the difference in slip angles is so extreme that we have to *subtract* from the slip-induced turn by turning the steering in the *opposite* direction. An oversteering car is often referred to as being "loose."

Understeer is the reverse; the fronts are slipping at a larger angle than the rears. To make the turn, then, we must turn the steering wheel by the amount we wish to turn *plus* an amount sufficient to compensate for the fact that the front slip angles are larger than those at the rear. An understeering car is often referred to as having a lot of "push," or as "pushing."

When a car is in an extreme understeering situation, it often feels as if the front tires "wash out" and just cannot produce enough turning force. You have probably felt this in your street car on an icy or wet road. Steering washout occurs because adding steering angle to compensate understeer causes additional front slip, hence more understeer. The added understeer in turn requires yet more steering to compensate. So you crank in more steering, producing more understeer, requiring more steering. This tail chasing can sometimes end at the point where the tires start actually skidding and steering inputs don't matter anymore.

WHY TIRES GET HOT—AND WHY IT'S IMPORTANT

Tire slip is the principal reason that racing tires get hot. When the rubber molecules are picked off the track at the trailing edge of the contact patch, the stretched rubber snaps back. The energy that was stored in the stretched rubber then has to go somewhere. It becomes heat and it goes into the tire. The more slip, the more heat.

Why do we want heat? The "stickiness" of a tire depends on its temperature. A purpose-built racing tire has a design operating temperature somewhere in the range of

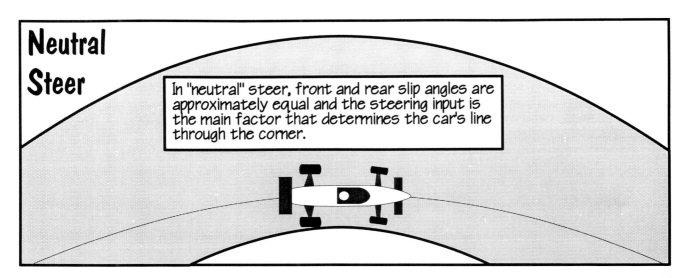

Neutral Steer

In "neutral" steer, front and rear slip angles are approximately equal and the steering input is the main factor that determines the car's line through the corner.

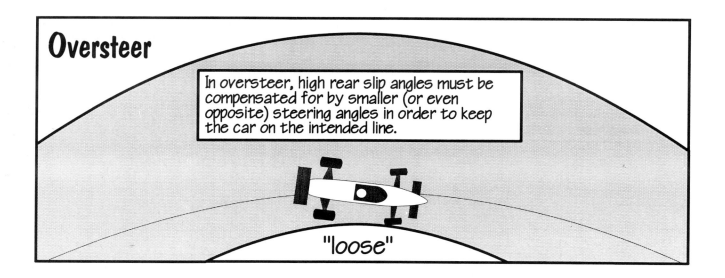

190–250 degrees Fahrenheit. Sports car tires are designed for the lower part of this range; stock car tires are designed for the higher temperatures. A street tire, too, has a design temperature range, though it is lower. A tire is best when operated in its design range; it is not as sticky above and below this optimum.

When we want to heat the tires, we need to develop tire slip. On a road-racing track we throw the car frantically from side to side during the pace lap. Drag racers accomplish the same thing by doing "burnouts." In neither case is the heat due to friction between the tires and the track; it is due to the stored energy in the stretched rubber being dissipated into the tire.

"SCRUBBING OFF" SPEED

The only sources of energy in the race car are the engine and the kinetic energy of the car's motion. The kinetic energy is, of course, a stored form of engine-supplied energy.

Now you can guess where the heat energy in the tires must come from. It comes from the engine. It is wasted energy that must necessarily slow the car down. The more tire slip, the more wasted energy.

So, when cornering we want the minimum tire slip that gets the job done, but no more. This is particularly important to understand in a long, fast turn where you can drive many different lines. The minimum-thrust, minimum-slip line is the one to take. This is the line that will give you maximum rpm at the end of the corner.

Danny Collins: "[Regarding corner entry and tire scrub], the object in all cases is to quickly capture that drift angle for each tire. A 15-degree angle for old-fashioned bias-ply tires, 6–12 degrees on radial street tires, 4–6 degrees on bias-ply race tires, and 2 degrees for racing radials!

"Once the front (understeer) or the rear (oversteer) exceeds the ideal drift angle, that end of the car is *impeding the progress of the car with *excess tire scrub.*"

TIRE PRESSURES

The first variable to be considered in managing the contact patches is tire pressure. Optimum pressure is determined by the weight on the tire and by its construction. Too little pressure, and the weight of the car will be carried disproportionately on the sidewalls and the outer edges of the contact

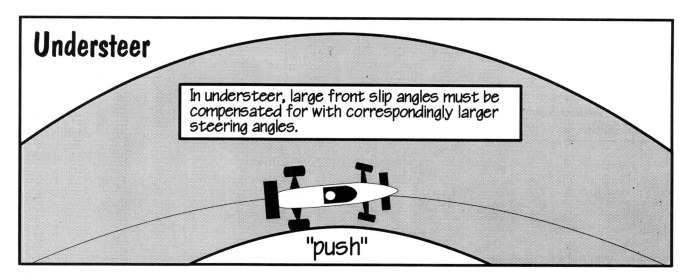

patch. Too much, and the weight will be carried in the center of the contact patch.

Rather than embarking on a long series of experiments, consult your tire supplier or your fellow competitors for advice on tire pressures. Use the consensus as a starting point, then tune using temperatures.

Carroll Smith: "True, except if your tire is Japanese, in which case the tire supplier won't have a clue!"

One rough-tuning technique that is especially popular on street tires is to chalk or paint a radial white mark where the shoulder of the tread meets the sidewall. After a few laps, the mark will be worn away where it contacted the track and you will know whether the tire is rolling too far onto the sidewall. If so, add air pressure. If, however, there is still some white on the tread, you are running too much pressure.

Tony Kester: "Don't get carried away with pressure accuracy just because you have a tire gauge that reads in tenths—setting to the nearest half pound is fine."

Carroll Smith: "Yes!"

Paul Van Valkenburgh: "Forget this business about chalk on the sidewalls. It can show you how bad things are, but keeping your sidewalls neat is the *last* thing you want to change pressures for."

TIRE TEMPERATURE

Tire temperature is of interest primarily as a *relative* thing.

A properly inflated tire will wear off the mark to the edge of the tread, but not any farther.

Optimum tire pressure can be roughly determined by marking the sidewall and tread shoulder, then running a few laps. (White shoe polish or chalk will work fine.)

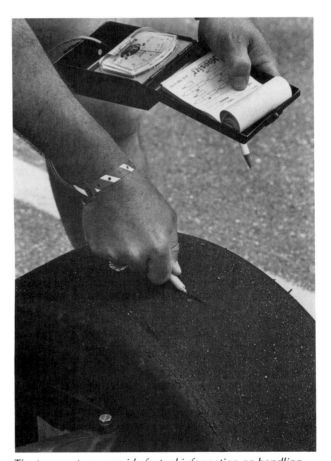

Tire temperatures provide factual information on handling. Open wheels are a real convenience for this job. Note that the needle end of the sensor has been pushed well into the tread, but at an angle—this minimizes the likelihood that the tire will be punctured.

On a closed-wheel car it's necessary to grovel a bit to get the tire temps, as this Goodyear engineer demonstrates.

First, the temperature of your tires *relative* to the temperature of similar tires being used by your competition. If you're running cooler temperatures, you are not driving as hard as your competition and are almost certainly slower.

Carroll Smith states in his book: "It usually means that the driver is not going hard enough. Seldom, if ever, will this be due to intent.... The only cure is an honest appraisal of the situation, more car time, and a really serious effort to improve."

Old, hard tires will not get as hot as new ones. The reason is that the rubber stretches less and, hence, absorbs less energy. We are talking maybe a 10–20 degrees difference, though, so be careful not to use it as an excuse.

Second, the temperature of your front tires *relative* to the rears. Remember that heat comes from tire slip. The hot end is the one that's slipping the most. (For example, if the rears are hotter, the car is generally oversteering.) Tire engineers will tell you that looking at the tire temps is more accurate in assessing oversteer and understeer than is talking to the driver.

Third, the *relative* temperature laterally across the tread. The temperature need not be even, but it should be smoothly increasing from one side to the other. Usually from outside to inside. If the center temperature is higher or lower than the edges, the tire is over- or underinflated.

Carroll Smith: "*May* be over- or underinflated, not necessarily *is*."

Beyond that, it's hard to generalize. My experience is that a flat profile is not always the best. You'll have to experiment with suspension settings to determine optimum handling, then get a temperature profile that can be used for reference in future setups.

Absolute tire temperature is determined by the tires, the track, and the weather. You do not have to worry much about it. If you are running in a pro series with a choice of compounds, you will have access to tire engineers who will

Hoosier's Tips for Monitoring Tire Performance

(This section was contributed by Bruce Foss, who has been Hoosier's Road Racing Product manager since 1984. His efforts have supported wins and national championships in a wide range of amateur and pro series.)

Today we see a wide range of racing car configurations, but the one thing they share is the four tires that connect them to the racing surface. The ability to monitor and analyze tire performance is a key factor for proper chassis set-up and superior handling.

Tire Temperature

The most common procedure is to take tire temperature reading in three places, near the outside and inside edges of the tread, and at the center. To ensure the accuracy of these readings, it is important for the driver to maintain his pace on the lap prior to entering the pits. The temperatures should then be read immediately.

Start with the most loaded tire and move around the car, finishing with the least loaded tire. Most road courses have predominantly right-hand corners, so you would want to start with the left-side tires.

Insert the needle into the tread rubber at approximately a 45 degree angle. Move the probe with a slight in-and-out motion to ensure that you are reading peak temperature at that point. Allow the probe to rest in the rubber until the reading on the display stabilizes. Then move to the next point on the tire.

Tire readings should be taken first on the inside, then in the middle, then on the outside of the tread area.

Always read the tires in exactly the same order or your readings will not be comparable from session to session. For the same reason, always use the same pyrometer.

If you're concerned about the accuracy of your tire pyrometer, check it in some boiling water.

Tire Pressures

Tire pressures should be checked regularly; about 5 minutes before you go out on the track is about right. These "cold" pressures are your beginning point for finding the right tire operating pressure.

Your tire manufacturer will usually have a recommended "hot" operating pressure for you to use. Starting pressures to achieve this goal will vary with conditions. For example, a tire manufacturer may recommend operating pressure of 18psi front and 20psi rear. The easiest way to establish the starting pressure is to start approximately 4psi below these goals. When the car comes into the pits, immediately check the tire pressures. If the pressures are too high, bleed to the proper pressure. Check the pressures again after the tires have cooled (about an hour). These are your starting pressures.

To ensure consistency, always use the same pressure gauge for your readings. Mechanical gauges can easily vary by a pound or two. To make sure that your gauge is within this tolerance, borrow two or three gauges from other teams in the paddock and read the same tire. If they are all pretty close, you can be confident that your gauge is good.

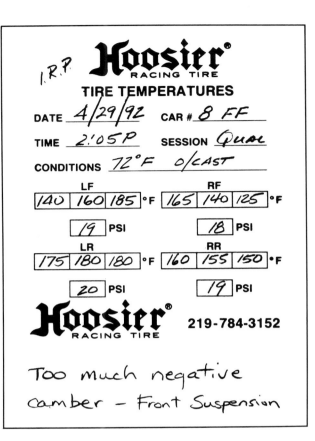

I.R.P.

Hoosier® RACING TIRE

TIRE TEMPERATURES

DATE _4/29/92_ CAR # _8 FF_

TIME _2:05P_ SESSION _Qual_

CONDITIONS _72°F O/CAST_

LF				RF			
140	160	185	°F	165	140	125	°F

19 PSI		18 PSI

LR				RR			
175	180	180	°F	160	155	150	°F

20 PSI		19 PSI

Hoosier® RACING TIRE   219-784-3152

Too much negative
camber – Front Suspension

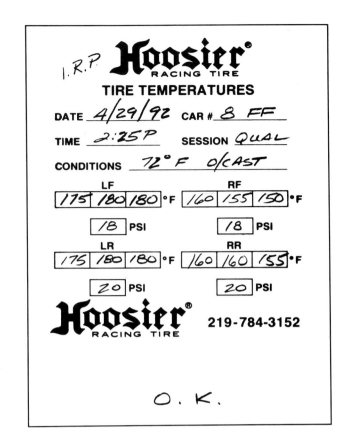

I.R.P.

Hoosier® RACING TIRE

TIRE TEMPERATURES

DATE _4/29/92_ CAR # _8 FF_

TIME _2:25P_ SESSION _Qual_

CONDITIONS _72°F O/CAST_

LF				RF			
175	180	180	°F	160	155	150	°F

18 PSI		18 PSI

LR				RR			
175	180	180	°F	160	160	155	°F

20 PSI		20 PSI

Hoosier® RACING TIRE   219-784-3152

O. K.

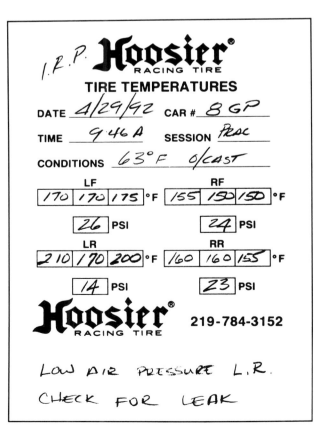

I.R.P.

Hoosier® RACING TIRE

TIRE TEMPERATURES

DATE _4/29/92_ CAR # _8 GP_

TIME _9:46A_ SESSION _Prac_

CONDITIONS _63°F O/CAST_

LF				RF			
170	170	175	°F	155	150	150	°F

26 PSI		24 PSI

LR				RR			
210	170	200	°F	160	160	155	°F

14 PSI		23 PSI

Hoosier® RACING TIRE   219-784-3152

LOW AIR PRESSURE L.R.
CHECK FOR LEAK

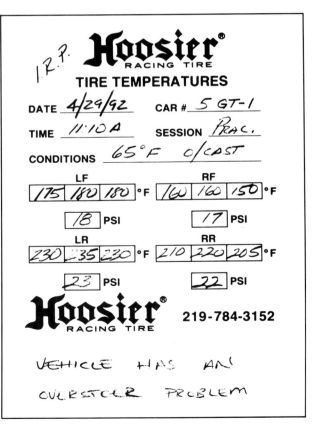

I.R.P.

Hoosier® RACING TIRE

TIRE TEMPERATURES

DATE _4/29/92_ CAR # _5 GT-1_

TIME _11:10A_ SESSION _Prac._

CONDITIONS _65°F O/CAST_

LF				RF			
175	180	180	°F	160	160	150	°F

18 PSI		17 PSI

LR				RR			
230	235	230	°F	210	220	205	°F

23 PSI		22 PSI

Hoosier® RACING TIRE   219-784-3152

VEHICLE HAS AN
OVERSTEER PROBLEM

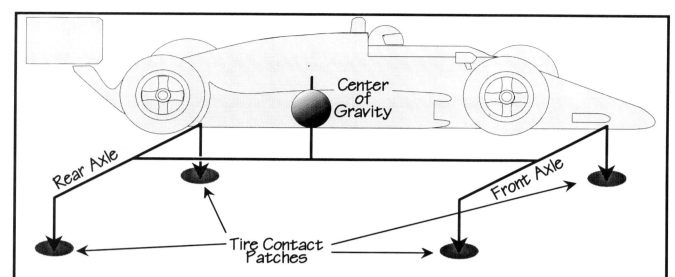

This simple wire-frame model can be used to understand dynamic weight transfer during cornering, braking and acceleration. The reaction of the c.g. to these forces changes the loads on the tires, affecting the amount of force they can generate.

worry about it. In club racing, you will have little or no choice of compounds, so again, nothing to worry about.

Finally, tire temperature is a dynamic thing. Measuring it in the pits gets you only a long-term average. The tires most recently used give you the most accurate temperatures. Don't worry about left-to-right absolute differences. At Brainerd, for example, right-side tire temps in the pits are useless because they are almost a mile old. If you are interested in temperature dynamics, read Chapter 2 of Paul Van Valkenburgh's *Race Car Engineering and Mechanics*.

Carroll Smith: "It's important to realize how quickly the *surface* of the tire heats up and cools down. You must take the core temperature of the tread. The trick surface-reading electronic pyrometers are a badge of ignorance."

Tony Kester: "A lot depends, too, on how fast you did the last lap before pitting. If you're doing temps, try to come in as 'hot' as possible, then *slow down* at pit entrance. Remember—club racing pits are full of moms and friends, not professional crews."

Paul Van Valkenburgh: "Tire temp is actually much more complex than you might conclude from the basics discussed here. For example, on Showroom Stock production tires, the guy who can keep his temperatures down by driving more smoothly is probably going to be faster. Also, on treaded tires, the tread depth will play a critical role."

VEHICLE DYNAMICS

Now that we have covered the tires, it's time to talk about the way the car uses them. Specifically, we will discuss the dynamic weight transfers that occur as the car is accelerated laterally in corners and longitudinally in braking and under engine acceleration.

(In the following discussion, we're going to gloss over, ignore, or simplify many things. These include the distinction between mass and weight, the behavior of the suspension, and all numerical calculations. The objective is to under-

stand intuitively why the car does what it does, not to understand the physics. Physicists, please restrain yourselves.)

For purposes of weight transfer discussions, we will use a wire frame model of the car shown in the figure. The sphere represents the car's center of gravity. The wire frame itself represents the car's chassis and suspension. The shaded areas under the arrowheads represent the tire contact patches.

There are two main forces that the car exerts on its tires during cornering and braking. Static forces are due to the intrinsic weight distribution of the car. These are represented by the equal-sized contact patches in the first wire frame drawing.

Along with static forces, we have dynamic forces due to the cornering and braking itself. These are due to the fact that the car's center of gravity is up in the air somewhere, instead of being on the track like the contact patches are. Carroll Smith shows you the calculations in Chapter 3 of *Tune to Win*.

BRAKING FORCES

When you're on the brakes, the nose of the car goes down due to the dynamic transfer of weight from the rear to the front. The transfer might amount to a 40% increase in front tire load. This weight transfer increases the size of the front contact patches and reduces the size of the rear patches.

Remembering that the thrust available from the tire depends on its load, what would you conclude about braking thrust? The fronts can generate a lot of thrust and the rears can't generate much. This is shown by the relative size of the thrust vectors.

Thus (assuming no wings or ground effects), the fronts are called upon to do most of the braking. That's why the front brakes are always bigger and why the brake bias on the car *always* favors the front.

Braking

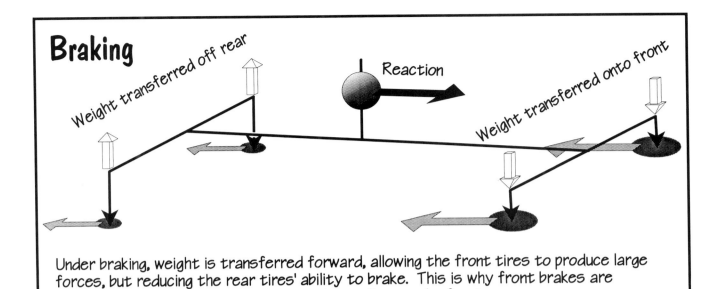

Under braking, weight is transferred forward, allowing the front tires to produce large forces, but reducing the rear tires' ability to brake. This is why front brakes are always larger, and why the brake bias always favors the fronts.

Tony Kester: "The harder you brake, the more front bias you're going to need. Often the track will change during a race or session, requiring a bias adjustment."

Carroll Smith: "With aerodynamic download [downforce], the more skilled the driver is, the more rear bias he can use and the more total braking force he can develop."

In the rain, the tires can't generate as much braking thrust, hence there's not as much forward weight transfer. Guess what? *Less* front brake bias is needed.

Engine Acceleration

When the car is accelerating, the weight transfer and thrust vector situation is reversed. Weight is transferred to the rears, which can then generate the required forces. This weight transfer is one of the reasons that front-wheel drive is not used in serious race cars. Rearward weight transfer limits the available front tire thrust to a low value.

Cornering Forces

Weight also transfers to the outside tires during cornering just as it transfers to the front under braking. Except more

Acceleration

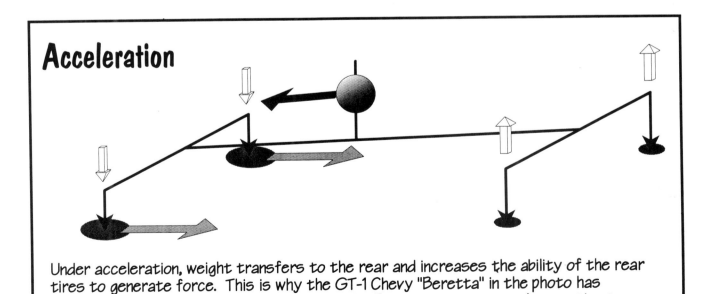

Under acceleration, weight transfers to the rear and increases the ability of the rear tires to generate force. This is why the GT-1 Chevy "Beretta" in the photo has rear-wheel drive, not front-wheel drive like the Beretta street car. Attempting to transmit high torque through the fronts would produce only wheelspin.

This Chevy Beretta GT-1 car is front-engine, rear drive. Front-wheel drive just won't do it when a large amount of torque has to be transferred.

A right-hand-drive car, like this H-Production MG, has a weight-transfer advantage on clockwise circuits. The driver's weight is on the inside for most corners.

gets transferred: 80% of the total axle weight or more. In fact, the inside tires do little work in a corner.

So what? Well, it means that your principal concern in cornering should be with the outside tires. The inside tires can be in the dirt, on the grass, whatever.

Bertil Roos: "Note that George's earlier figures show braking and accelerating in a straight line. This one, that illustrates cornering, has no acceleration—which is uncommon in racing.

"Imagine how the contact patches look the minute you turn in, just before you go off the brake but after you have started to turn. The outside front tire has the greatest load. Then imagine how the contact patches look, in the turn, once you get off the brake and get back on the accelerator, transferring weight also. Here, the load is on the outside

rear. These load patterns are the ones you'll have while turning on the racetrack."

Regarding putting the inside tires in the dirt, Paul Frère observes: "The fact that dust and stones are also raised and thrown in the face of the man behind is an incidental, but admittedly worthwhile, advantage...."

Carroll Smith: "Paul is an honest man, but in his driving days tires were tougher and not subject to stone cuts. Be careful."

Remember that the tires work best when they carry equal weight? That's why the drivers of two-seater cars like to be on the inside in a turn. The driver weight tends to make the inside tires work harder and increases the total cornering power of the car. For most American clockwise tracks, this means right-hand drive.

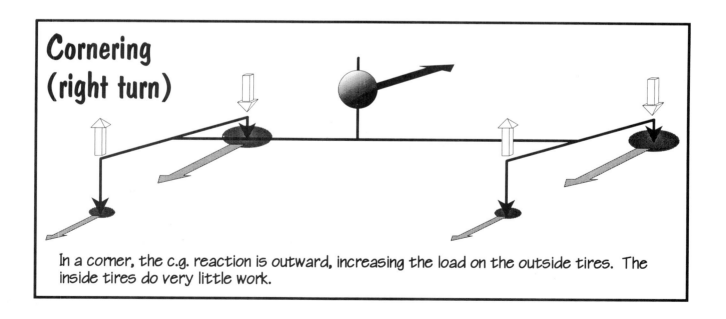

Cornering (right turn)

In a corner, the c.g. reaction is outward, increasing the load on the outside tires. The inside tires do very little work.

Chapter 3

Basic Driving Techniques

Now that you have been introduced to the way your tires work and the way in which weight is transferred among them, it's time to talk about actually driving the car. There's not much to be said about driving in a straight line. Cornering, however, is a subject that you'll never stop learning about.

Bertil Roos: "I object a little to the sentence, 'Cornering, however, is a subject that you'll never stop learning about.' It doesn't really agree with me. It might seem that way to a lot of drivers—that they never stop learning in corners. But the reason for that is that they never got the basic theoretical understanding of what they are trying to accom-

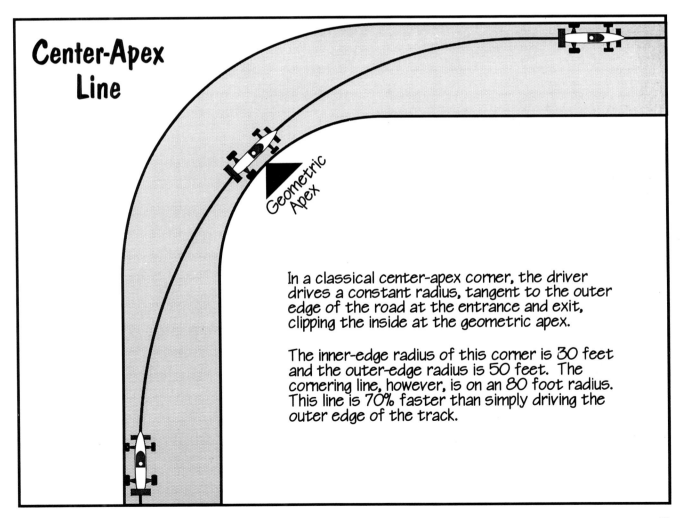

Center-Apex Line

Geometric Apex

In a classical center-apex corner, the driver drives a constant radius, tangent to the outer edge of the road at the entrance and exit, clipping the inside at the geometric apex.

The inner-edge radius of this corner is 30 feet and the outer-edge radius is 50 feet. The cornering line, however, is on an 80 foot radius. This line is 70% faster than simply driving the outer edge of the track.

plish in a corner. There are ways to explain it where it's easy to understand. I work with a corner backwards and figure out any corner, wherever you can imagine in the whole world, in three or four laps."

Author comment: "Maybe that's one of the differences between a Formula One driver and us club racers."

BASIC PRINCIPLE OF RACING CORNERS

The underlying theory of fast cornering is simple. One simply drives the car through the corner on the largest possible radius. This radius is tangent to the outside of the road at the entrance and exit, and touches or *clips* the inside of the road at the center of the turn. This inside clipping point is called the *apex* of the turn. The point where the car leaves the edge of the road at the entrance is called the *turn-in* point.

Paul Van Valkenburgh: "I think that 'constant radius' is an interesting concept, but would point out that it is both a practical and a theoretical impossibility. Due to the finite time required for steering and tire response, a vehicle cannot instantaneously go from traveling in a straight line to cornering at its maximum lateral acceleration. There will always be some rise time as the radius changes from infinite to the minimum."

The radius shown in the figure is the fastest line through the corner and it requires that the car go at a constant speed.

The two key phrases in the previous sentence are *constant speed* and *through the corner*. Let's talk about them.

First, you will almost never be cornering at a constant speed. There are many reasons for this. Cornering itself involves dissipation of energy into the tires; this loss of energy slows the car. Speed involves aerodynamic drag that is proportional to the square of velocity. And you will have your foot on the accelerator. The closest you will come to a constant-velocity turn will be a high-speed, flat-out sweeper. Even there, you will exit the corner at a lower speed than you will enter it (due to tire scrub). At the opposite extreme in a low-speed corner, you will accelerate and exit at a much higher speed than you will enter.

Second, the objective of the exercise is not to get through the corner at the maximum speed. It is to get around the racetrack at the maximum speed. The situation is quite analogous to drag racing, where the car with the fastest trap speed is often not the one with the lowest elapsed time. It's not just having the speed, it's having the speed in the right places. The corners are often not the right places.

If you travel through a 60mph corner and accelerate to the end of a 1,500ft straight, you will spend about one-fourth of your time in the corner and three-fourths of your time on the straight. Now, suppose you could trade 2mph of slower average cornering speed for 1mph of higher average speed

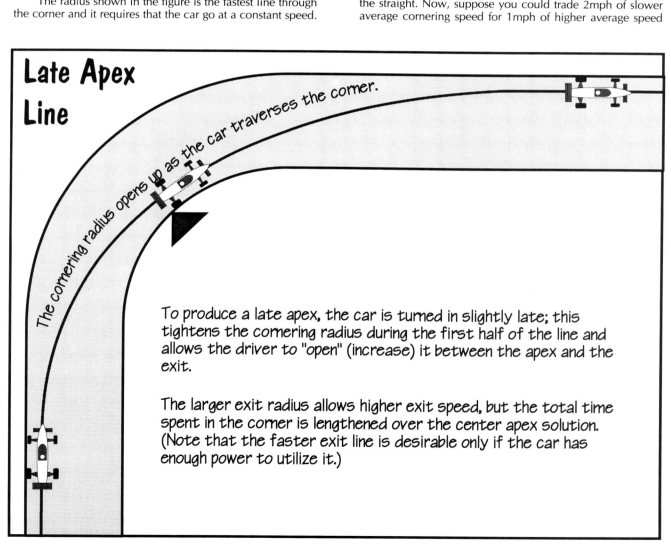

Late Apex Line

The cornering radius opens up as the car traverses the corner.

To produce a late apex, the car is turned in slightly late; this tightens the cornering radius during the first half of the line and allows the driver to "open" (increase) it between the apex and the exit.

The larger exit radius allows higher exit speed, but the total time spent in the corner is lengthened over the center apex solution. (Note that the faster exit line is desirable only if the car has enough power to utilize it.)

down the straight. That trade would cost you about 0.2 second in the corner and would gain you about 0.3 second down the straight. Net: 0.1 second.

A tenth of a second? No big deal, you say?

At the end of that straight, you're probably going 100mph. That's about 150ft per second. A tenth of that is 15ft, more than a car length. Enough to break a following car's draft (if you're lucky), enough to move you several places up in a competitive grid, or enough to create a 200ft lead during an average 12–18-lap race. If you don't want it, I'll take it.

Thus, the basic principle of racing corners is that you must optimize your speed for the race course, not just maximize it for the corners.

CENTER APEX CORNER

The center apex line is the constant-radius, maximum speed line shown in the previous figure. Nothing fancy about it. When you begin learning to race, you should concentrate on taking center apex lines through most turns. This is the easiest training line because most tracks have the geometric center of each turn marketed with paint and/or a pylon. Once you can consistently drive at the limit and exactly clip that apex on every lap, you can begin modifying your line with confidence.

Bertil Roos: "George says: 'You should concentrate on taking center apex lines through most turns. This line is the easiest....'

"I don't agree with that. Definitely not. In corners, where you are always trying to go fast, the main trouble is to stay on the road coming out. The main problem is to make the car turn enough while at maximum speed. It's easy to run off the road. And because of that, we must take late apexes—so we can come off the corners fast without dropping our wheels off. So now, if we are a beginner, and we are encouraged to use earlier apexes, that is really going to complicate the exit for us. We will come off of the corners, drop our wheels off, run off the road, scare the hell out of ourselves, and become really timid about how we exit the corners.

"If you take a too-early apex you cannot exit the turn under full power, and if you cannot be on full power it is not realistic—you cannot learn the right things. Therefore, the opposite is what I suggest to my students. If you are a beginner, or if you are not familiar with the track yet, *create late apexes.* You can come off the corners—really blasting off the corners—and at maximum speed see that you can clear exit the edge. As you gain experience, that's when you can make the apex a little earlier, and a little earlier, until you get it to that point where you come off the corner under full gas and you have to use up every inch of the

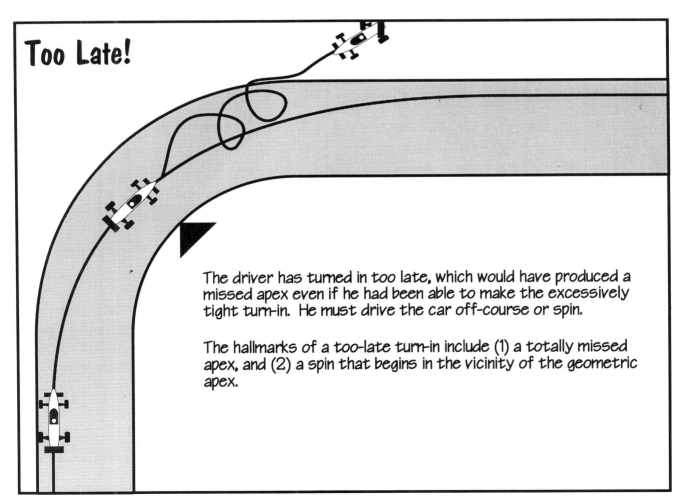

Too Late!

The driver has turned in too late, which would have produced a missed apex even if he had been able to make the excessively tight turn-in. He must drive the car off-course or spin.

The hallmarks of a too-late turn-in include (1) a totally missed apex, and (2) a spin that begins in the vicinity of the geometric apex.

road. I think it's really dumb to encourage students to run with early apexes."

Author comment: "I didn't say *early* apexes. I think a beginning driver must first learn to place his or her car *consistently* on a corner, hitting absolutely the same apex point each time, before he or she begins trying to move the apex around. The painted apex marker makes a good target for this consistency practice. In your first few weekends, make a point of working on this consistency whether you use the painted apex marker or you follow Bertil's advice and work with later apexes. Find some physical reference and learn to hit it, over and over and over again."

Carroll Smith: "I agree with Bertil—I have never seen a corner in which the fast line is a center apex, *especially* for beginners."

LATE APEXES

The late apex line is characterized by a radius that *increases* slightly as the car progresses through the corner. The car is turned more tightly at the beginning, then the corner is opened up as the car exits. Given constant available cornering power, then, the car can be driven progressively faster as it traverses the corner. (Of course, you have to have enough engine power to take advantage of this larger radius.) Near the exit you can be traveling faster than a driver who is fol-

lowing a constant-radius, center apex line. Is that a long straight ahead? Which driver will be ahead going into the next corner?

You establish a late apex line by turning in slightly later than for a center apex turn. Many, possibly most, racetrack turns are best driven with a slightly late apex line.

Danny Collins: "The 'late apex' theory is often taught to prevent overly eager novices from early apexing into the weeds—in the process screwing up an opportunity to exit the turn at a decent speed. Since exit speed is so important, most instructors employ the old European style of 'enter slow, so you can exit fast,' putting far too much emphasis on the straightaway.

"However, this ignores [the fact] that elapsed time lost in entering the turn at an artificially low speed also adds to overall lap times! I prefer a 'Fast In, Fast Out' technique, which is what good, experienced racers do when they are in a hurry and not teaching students!"

Bertil Roos: "Regarding Danny's comment about the straightaway: We're not really emphasizing the long straight. It's only that you must always use an apex that is late enough so that you can keep the gas pedal to the floor coming out of corners and still stay on the road. In the long run, your goal is to adjust this late apex to be as early as

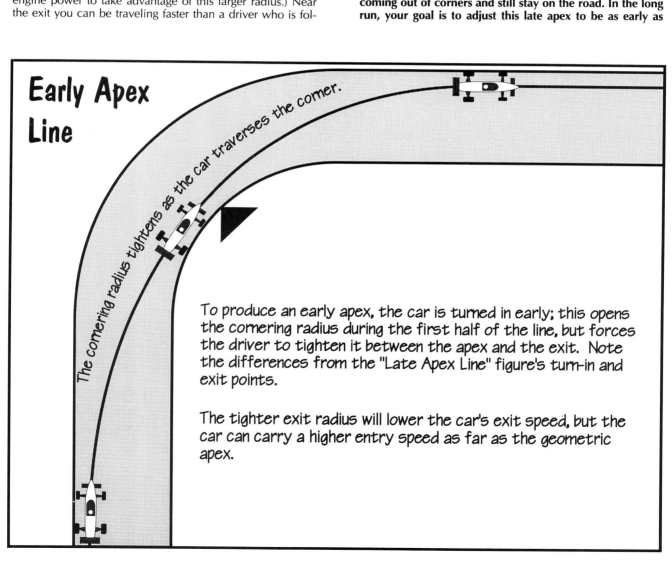

Early Apex Line

The cornering radius tightens as the car traverses the corner.

To produce an early apex, the car is turned in early; this opens the cornering radius during the first half of the line, but forces the driver to tighten it between the apex and the exit. Note the differences from the "Late Apex Line" figure's turn-in and exit points.

The tighter exit radius will lower the car's exit speed, but the car can carry a higher entry speed as far as the geometric apex.

possible, because you don't want to come off the corners too easy. Because the later apex you take, the more time you waste in entry.

"I don't think we should make a big deal about turning in too late, because turning in too late (not too-too late) is a good way when you're inexperienced and you're unfamiliar with the track. The too-late apex is when you come out of the corner and it is a little too easy for the car.

"Anyway, the simple answer to everything is: *Whatever keeps the gas pedal on the floor longer is better.*"

Of course, it's possible to overdo it. When you turn in too late, you will find that you need to turn onto an impossibly tight line in order to clip an apex. At this point of impending disaster, you have quite a bit of racetrack between you and the weeds. To recover, straighten the car and get back onto the brakes. (If you don't straighten the car before braking, you'll spin.) This maneuver needs to be done quickly. Good luck!

Bertil Roos: "George talks about 'an impossibly tight line.' It's not an impossible thing; if you accidentally turn in too late, you have to pay for it—not by crashing the car on the exit, but simply by staying longer on the brake. As you turn into the tighter corner, you stay on the brake until the car points up enough to clip the apex and then you release the brake and nail the gas. If you go wide because you turned in too late, that means that you released the brake too early and went on the gas too early, ending up way too wide."

"I don't think it is a good idea to encourage people to brake in the middle of corners."

Author comment: "Bertil's advice may again testify to the difference between a club driver and a Formula One driver. Trust me, dear reader, it is possible to turn in so late that there is no hope of seeing an apex. Straightening out the car and braking is a desperation move, not a recommendation."

EARLY APEXES

An early apex line is the opposite of a late apex line; in the early apex line, the radius *decreases* slightly through the corner. Guess what? Lower exit speed.

Bertil Roos: "'Guess what? Lower exit speed.' That's true of course, but I prefer to say—'Guess what? Drive off the road.' That's a little stronger.

"Turning in too early is the most common thing for the beginner. They turn in too early, making the first half of the corner easy, and therefore making the second half too difficult.

"To me, a perfect apex happens when you clip it and you manage to just barely stay on the road as you leave the corner under full gas. Any apex earlier than that will make you drop the wheels off on the exit, have extra strain on the car coming out, and have difficulties."

Danny Collins: "Early apexing—the 'In Fast, Out Slow' method."

Carroll Smith: "Danny and Bertil are right. Although Bertil carries the late apex theory a little far, it's all a compromise."

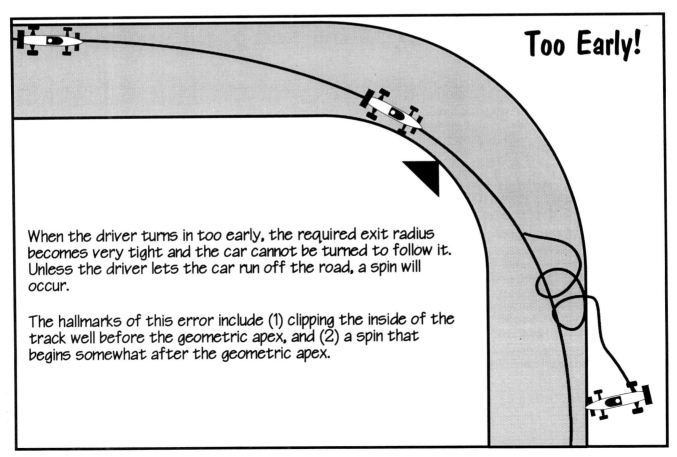

Too Early!

When the driver turns in too early, the required exit radius becomes very tight and the car cannot be turned to follow it. Unless the driver lets the car run off the road, a spin will occur.

The hallmarks of this error include (1) clipping the inside of the track well before the geometric apex, and (2) a spin that begins somewhat after the geometric apex.

Alan Johnson argues that a late apex line allows you to carry your speed a bit further into the turn, and that this is useful at the *end* of a straight. While this may be theoretically true, a car spends so little time in this phase of the corner that it is hard for me to see that any significant benefit could accrue. Early apex lines are seldom useful—usually only in cases where the turn itself has a diminishing radius or is a partial turn that leads directly to another, more important turn.

If you turn too early, you will find yourself trying to turn onto an impossibly tight line as you pass the geometric apex of the corner. When you can't make the turn, try to recognize it early enough to drive off rather than spinning. (The straighten-and-brake maneuver mentioned probably won't work. You don't have enough racetrack to complete it before you get to the weeds.)

Too-early apexes are a common novice driving problem. One reason is probably that they begin with a false sense of security. The gentle entry radius doesn't make the car feel uncomfortable. It is only when you find that you just can't finish the turn that you will figure out you have turned too early.

The need to crank in additional steering after your clipping point is a reliable indicator that you have early apexed.

Carroll Smith: "If, on the exit side of any corner (after the clipping point), the driver is doing anything with the steering wheel other than unwinding lock, chances are that his line is wrong."

Tony Kester: "The most common cause of early *apexing* is early *braking*. The driver brakes too early, turns in when his brain tells him that he's going slow enough, and he's still ten feet from the correct turn-in point.

"The best cure for early apexing is later braking. If you brake *late* enough, you *can't* early apex."

THROWAWAY LINES

Most racetracks have at least one pair of turns that are too close together to constitute completely separable cornering problems. A fast line through the first turn puts you in the wrong place to take a fast line through the second. As you can see in the figure, exiting the first turn on *its* optimum line will put you several car widths away from the proper entry to the second.

In virtually all of these cases, the correct approach is to throw away the first corner in order to be properly set up for the second. The reason, of course, is that some kind of straight section follows the second corner—you need to optimize your speed going onto this straight even at the cost of a slower line through the first corner.

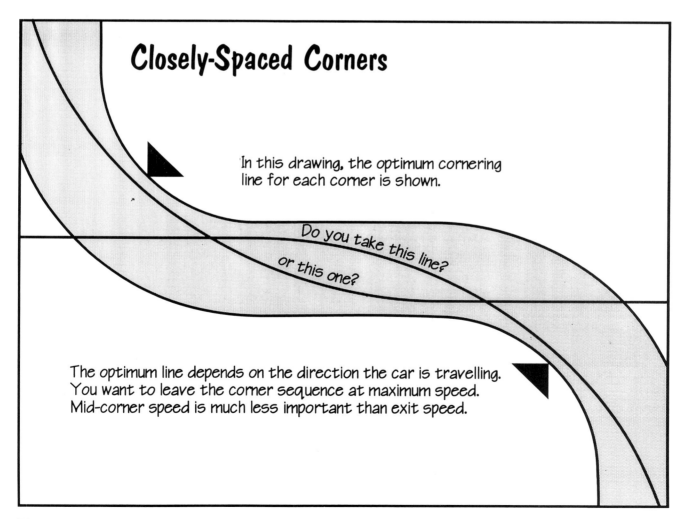

Closely-Spaced Corners

In this drawing, the optimum cornering line for each corner is shown.

Do you take this line? or this one?

The optimum line depends on the direction the car is travelling. You want to leave the corner sequence at maximum speed. Mid-corner speed is much less important than exit speed.

Danny Collins: "I don't like that word 'throwaway.' You need to keep those tire patches hooked up, but on a line giving you leverage and angles for good exits. Throwaway seems to imply that you can waste valuable elapsed time by 'pussy-footing' along until you can gain an advantage somewhere else. The stopwatch won't tolerate 'throwing away' valuable time."

Bertil Roos: "It's not really a good phrase, 'throwing away a corner,' because we're never throwing away a corner. In an S-turn like the figure shows, as I approach corner number 1, I am braking, downshifting, and looking into the corner. My intention is to place my car up against the left side, a little ahead of the car in the illustration. That is what I visualize as I enter the corner and, if I can get the car to that point, Turn 2 will be easy for me. So I'm not really throwing Turn 1 away. I only pinpoint what I want to accomplish with the corner and then I try to accomplish it in the fastest possible way."

Carroll Smith: "I use the term 'throwaway' all the time, but don't like it either. Let's find a better word."

The second and third figures illustrate this throwaway line through the first of two turns. (Note that coupled turns don't have to involve a change of direction. A carousel or hairpin can be usefully considered to be a pair of coupled turns as well.)

Danny Collins: "After many years of teaching, I've found that oval-shaped turns offer the best opportunity to learn a lot about basic racing technique, particularly if they link two straights.

"The entry is difficult because you must brake hard, downshift well, turn in, and quickly transfer weight to max g-force using those tire patches to do so. You must blend all this together using the 'gyroscope-balance bar' between your ears in concert with forward vision...all the while coordinating the feedback from those tire patches transmitted through the palms and fingers of your hands, the balls of your feet, and those sensors located somewhere in the seat of your driving suit. It takes plenty of practice and patience in the beginning. But once these delicate shifts of balance are smoothly mastered, you can become an excellent race driver."

If you encounter three (or more) closely connected corners, the approach is the same. Work out the line through the last corner to optimize your straight-entry speed. In the preceding corners, then, do what is necessary to enter the last corner in the optimum position. We'll talk later about walking the racetrack to learn it. Track-walking is particularly important where connected corners are involved. One walk around the track will show you the consensus line. It

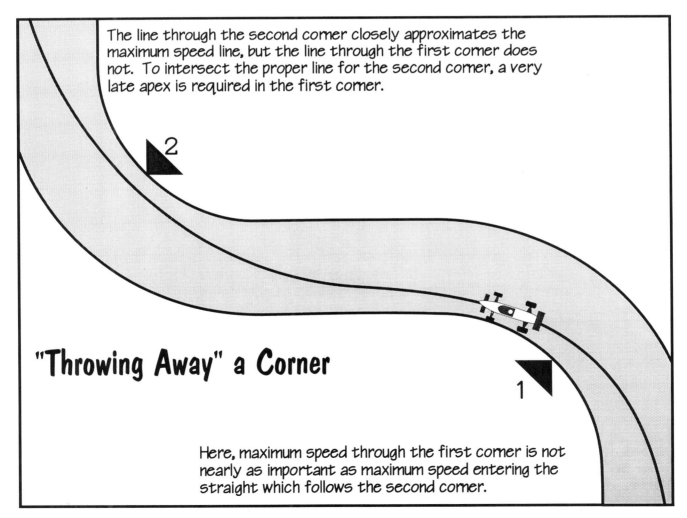

The line through the second corner closely approximates the maximum speed line, but the line through the first corner does not. To intersect the proper line for the second corner, a very late apex is required in the first corner.

"Throwing Away" a Corner

Here, maximum speed through the first corner is not nearly as important as maximum speed entering the straight which follows the second corner.

may not be the best line for you, but it is a good place to start.

Paul Van Valkenburgh: "The consensus line is probably the best place to *finish* a corner. Even if you were to predict the absolutely 'best' line using a computer simulation, if everyone else was taking a significantly different one, you would be in big trouble. Where the majority goes is where the best rubber is laid down for traction and where there is the least loose contamination. Here is where observation and experimentation is better than the best theory."

Two Separate Decisions: Brake Point and Turn-in Point

I have found that it's easiest to manage cornering lines by considering them to be established by two, separate decisions: Where is the brake point? Where is the turn-in point? (For now, you can assume that the turn-in point is also the point where your braking ends. We'll talk more about that in a few pages.)

Your choice of brake point determines your speed at your turn-in point. That's pretty straightforward. But why would this decision be separate from the turn-in decision? The reason is that the speed that you should have at your turn-in point varies as you move it.

If you decide that you want to make a later apex, you will choose a later turn-in point and will (necessarily) be turning onto a tighter initial radius. With a fixed brake point, then, you will be on the brakes longer and thus will automat-

ically have the lower speed required to establish the tighter entry radius.

If you decide that you want to make an earlier apex, the opposite is true. You will turn earlier, having spent less time on the brakes, and you will carry more speed into the larger-radius entry arc.

If you like your line, but find that it's too easy to drive, you are not going fast enough. Delay your brake point by a few feet, but leave your turn-in point alone. You'll find yourself on approximately the same line, but going faster.

Paul Van Valkenburgh: "Regarding your brake point, also remember that it will change with your maximum speed in the preceding straight. Say you get a better exit out of the last corner, or get a draft, and are going 5mph faster when you reach your regular brake point. You could be in big trouble!"

REAL CORNERS

Corners printed on the pages of racing books are lovely things. They are flat and their surface is homogeneous and smooth. Their edges are well defined and they are the same width at the exit as they are at the entrance. One can confidently assume that the car's adhesion is a constant. Not only that, one can evaluate alternative lines clearly in plan (aerial) view. None of these things are true in the real world.

In the real world, corner surfaces vary a lot. The racing line is worn differently than the surface off the line. There are

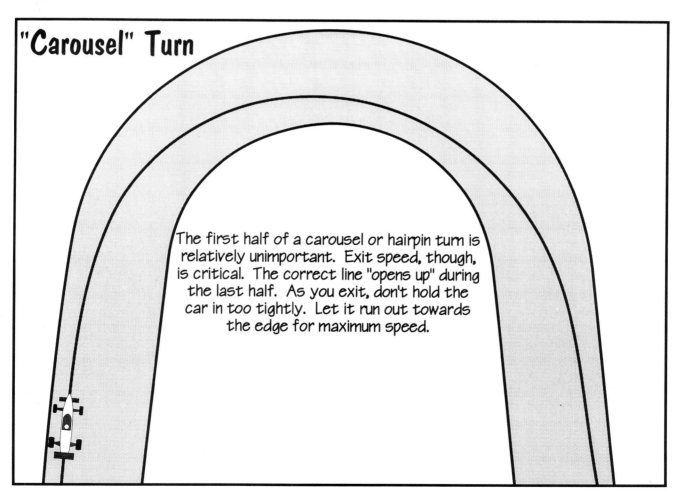

"Carousel" Turn

The first half of a carousel or hairpin turn is relatively unimportant. Exit speed, though, is critical. The correct line "opens up" during the last half. As you exit, don't hold the car in too tightly. Let it run out towards the edge for maximum speed.

patched sections, ripples, bumps, and hollows. If that isn't enough, corners can also be deliberately crowned for drainage or banked for speed.

The edges of real-world corners vary a lot, too. Some are broken asphalt dropping off to sand that has been driven on by thousands of cars. Some have "FIA curbs," which serve to keep drivers from getting too aggressive about widening the track. Some have asphalt structures variously referred to as "dragon's teeth," "rumpltey-bumps," and "speed bumps." These, too, are intended to keep drivers from wearing out the edge of the track.

Real corners usually aren't 90 degrees and they usually aren't truly constant radius.

Finally, the world is not as flat as the page of a book. There are hills. You will find real-world racetrack corners going up hills, at the top of hills, and coming down hills.

When you go to a new track, the only way you can learn its reality is to walk around it. Study the surfaces of the corners, the crowning and banking of the road. Consider the effects that these features will have on your car's behavior. Take some notes if you have a poor memory.

While walking, look at the racing line. It will be fairly obvious, darkened by thousands of racing tires. You should plan to drive this consensus line as you begin to learn the track. Also look at the marks that spinning cars have made on the track surface, on the grass, and (unfortunately) on off-track obstacles like guard rails and walls. These marks are evidence of common mistakes—try to figure out what must have happened to cause them. Learn from it.

As you gain experience, these track walks will become increasingly valuable.

DRIVING LINES THROUGH REAL CORNERS

Remember that you must make two, separate decisions: selecting your brake point and selecting your turn-in point. The length of time you are on the brakes determines your corner entry speed. Your turn-in point determines your line.

During the time you are on the brakes, you must be braking at the absolute maximum capability of the car. In

An FIA curb is designed to keep you from widening the curve by driving on the grass at the apex or the exit. It has a slight slope upward, then a flat top. At a minimum, hitting the curb will upset the car. Some are smooth enough to cause spins. If you have to drive straight off for some reason, you will find that an FIA curb is a marvelous launching ramp.

The real-world surface is slightly different than the page of a book. This one is actually pretty flat and even, as real-world corners go. Note, though, that it slopes toward the "dragon's teeth" bumps at the apex. Also, this is the first of a pair of corners—adjust your line accordingly.

You can see that these two Formula Atlantic cars are following the darkened consensus line through this sequence of turns at Road Atlanta. You'll easily see the consensus line when you walk the track. It's a good starting point for learning a new track. Tim Suddard/GrassRoots Motorsports

most cases, this is determined by the lockup point of the tires. In a car with inadequate brakes (such as a Showroom Stocker), it will be determined by how hard you can brake and still have the brakes last the length of the session.

Regardless of the line that you select, you must be cornering *at the limit all the way through*. The difference between slow drivers and fast drivers is not that the slow drivers take the wrong lines. It's that the slow drivers are not consistently going through *all* the corners at the limit. Variations in lines differentiate the fast drivers from the extremely fast drivers.

Paul Van Valkenburgh: "The previous paragraph should be in *bold!* This is a most important point. For the first few thousand racing miles, learning the feel of the limit is far more important than fine-tuning the line."

So, learning to drive at the limit is the first step.

How can you tell when you're at the limit? If you were literally driving on the page of a book, it would be easy. Watch the author's shaded line on the drawing. If it is physically possible for you to drive inside it, you are going too slow. If it is physically impossible for you to keep the car

Here's a real corner being negotiated by two Formula Continentals. Note the repair patch toward the bottom center of the picture. It's the reference point for the corner exit. A perfect exit involves running over this patch with the two outside tires. Note that the first car is running on a line that will accomplish this objective. The other car is not. Guess who won the race?

from sliding wide of the line, you are going too fast and you are going to run out of racetrack.

In the real world, there's no shaded guide line drawn through the corners. Fortunately, there are many other cars to watch. You should be able to pick out initial reference points for your brake point, for your turn-in point, for the apex, and for your exit fairly quickly.

Tony Kester: "Ask a good driver (not just someone who thinks he's good) if you can follow him around for a few laps. There are guys who will do this for you, and it's the *most effective* way to learn the line.

"Seeing is believing and when you actually see how the line should be driven, your mind will more easily accept that it can be done just that way."

Carroll Smith: "It also helps to *watch* the good drivers from the spectators' viewpoints, but *only* the good ones."

Speaking of reference points, avoid selecting points that move. This sounds obvious, but it is tempting to use the numbered brake markers, tufts of grass, and even corner workers as references. Brake markers and grass tufts get driven over and knocked down quite frequently. Brake markers also may not be placed consistently from weekend to weekend. Corner workers have been known to walk around. The best reference points are permanent features of the track surface: pavement changes, chunks and holes at the track edge, and paint marks.

If you are driving your line smoothly, consistently, and the car feels solid, you are slow. Remember the real world? Each little bit of track surface that you cover has its own limit. If you are at the limit on some of them, you will be past the limit on others and you will be making steering and throttle adjustments to correct the line of the car. The car will not feel comfortable and solid; it will feel uncomfortable and busy—because it *will be* uncomfortable and busy.

If the car feels busy at the entry to the corner, but you can exit in the middle of the track, then you are turning in too late. You are creating a late apex corner, but you do not have the horsepower to get the speed to utilize the larger-radius exit line. Turning late and coming out slow is a common driving error. Turn in earlier. Note that you may well be able to turn in earlier *without* moving your brake point. This will have the effect of increasing your entry speed, but you will also be increasing your cornering radius at the entry. Hence, you can go into the corner faster and you will come out faster.

Conversely, if you do OK between your turn-in point and the apex, but find yourself running out of road at the exit, you are making an early apex corner. Nothing good will come of it. Turn in later. In this case, you may also have to move your brake point slightly later.

Tony Kester: "Less-experienced drivers invariably brake earlier than necessary—causing an early turn-in and apex. Braking *later* usually cures this."

It's relatively easy to drive a race car around the track on good-looking lines—slowly. As you are working on the corners, be honest with yourself. If at any point you feel that you could turn the car onto a tighter radius, then you are not at the limit at that point. Only the welder can know whether a good-*looking* weld is really a good weld; similarly, only the driver can know whether a good-*looking* line is really being traversed at the limit. Only the driver and the stopwatch, that is.

If you are really driving at the limit, you will have spins and near-spins occasionally. If this is not happening then, again, you are fooling yourself about being at the limit.

Tony Kester: "The most important part of going fast is learning when you are at your (and/or your car's) limit. Spins are not a good way to find out. If you almost spin, back off a little next time and try again. If it happens again, change your line. If it keeps happening every time you sneak up on the limit, *that is as fast as you can go through that corner, in that car, on that day*. Period.

"Successful drivers use their brains more than their courage."

Carroll Smith: "Fast head, slow hands, does it."

FULL THROTTLE IN THE CORNERS

You should be back on full throttle as soon as possible after your foot leaves the brakes. Surprisingly, this move stabilizes the car. The net effect of the dynamic weight transfer gives the rear tires the ability to transmit the acceleration thrust. The fronts do not seem to lose enough thrust capability to matter.

Danny Collins: "The 'European' schools have long subscribed to the 'full throttle as soon as your foot leaves the brakes.' This is a dangerous *oversimplification* if you take the statement literally.

"Example: If you are turning into a hairpin-shaped turn and slam on full throttle, you lift the nose inducing gross understeer as you plow straight off into the weeds...another reason I spend a lot of time with students on tight turns. You must reserve some power/balance to be able to shift direction, coordinating the shape of the exit of the turn with the steering and the correct amount of throttle pressure."

Bertil Roos: "Racing is all about keeping the gas pedal to the floor. The longer the time, the better.

"Our goal, one of the many, many goals we have as a race car driver, is: 'I want to learn this damned track so I can drive around here either with full gas or with full brake. Nothing in between.' That is a goal we must have. We might not always accomplish it, but we must always have this goal and must always try to come as close to it as we possibly can.

"I don't like Danny's comment, especially for beginners who are driving smaller cars. No, the gas pedal should be on the floor. That is so important, that goal: Full Gas, Full Brake. As you are practicing, trying to fine tune your lines, how do you know what is better? What is better is what keeps your gas to the floor longer and what shortens the time you spend on the brake. Those things are better.

"And this is important advice also: As you go around and listen to various people, to all the BS, it can be useful to keep this rule in your mind: Everything which keeps the gas pedal to the floor longer and uses less brake—that is information that should be considered and evaluated. And if it doesn't—forget about spending time on it."

Tony Kester: "Immediate full throttle is possibly true in low-horsepower cars, but in Formula Fords or bigger, not necessarily so.

"If your entry speed is near the optimum, the outside rear tire is already hanging on by its fingernails and [rearward] weight transfer probably won't quite counteract the effect of your slam dance onto the throttle. A better way to approach this issue is to say that you should give the car as much throttle as it will possibly take, as soon as possible after you get off the brakes."

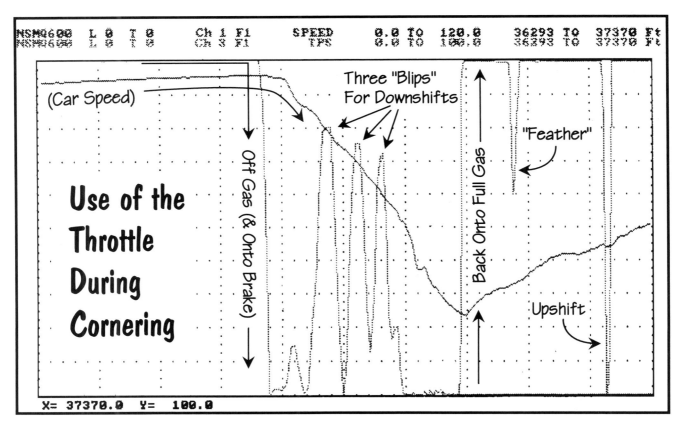

"This might mean full throttle and it might mean modulating the throttle for a second or two. If the car gets squirrelly, ease off a little. If not, hammer down!"

Carroll Smith: "Danny is a conservative person—so is his approach to driving. Bertil is an outrageous person and so is *his* approach to driving. Tony is a thoughtfully aggressive person and a truly outstanding driver who has spent most of his career in bad equipment. His approach to this throttle debate is, to my way of thinking, the correct one.

"It is all a question of *balance*. The slam-bang sideways approach has *never* worked, neither does the conservative 'don't upset things' approach. There is a time for finesse and a time for you to pick the car up by the scruff of its neck and force it to do what you want it to do—often on the same lap!

"The car, like a good lover, will tell you what it wants. (Actually, the footprints will.) Keep your receptors open and listen!"

HILLS AND VALLEYS

At the top and bottom of hills, you will quickly become aware that the car's vertical momentum becomes a factor. At the top of a hill, the car will get light. This means *less* adhesion for turning and braking. At the bottom of the hill, the reverse is true. More adhesion.

These adhesion changes are, however, transitory things and demand a great deal of finesse if you are to exploit them. As you walk the track on your Friday-night survey, carefully consider the car's likely behavior through each vertical acceleration change.

Tony Kester: "A turn at the top of a hill is deceptive. As you approach the turn, the slope allows you to increase braking because of added adhesion. Then as the car turns along the hill the track is effectively banked, making your cornering much faster than it first appears."

Bertil Roos: "That is what is really fun in racing—lots of hills and valleys and jumps and crazy things. That's what really makes things exciting. Unfortunately, in this country there is not too much of it. The track which comes to mind when you're talking about hills and valleys and jumps is the old Nürburgring in Germany. There were some unbelievable things, which I've never seen elsewhere in the world. Places like the Carousel, which you jump into and jump out of. Corners that had a crest on the apex, where you jumped from the apex to the exit edge. Many places where you got totally airborne. Those things are fun, and I really miss them.

"You're trying here to learn how to deal with hills and valleys, how to anticipate the car's behavior and how to

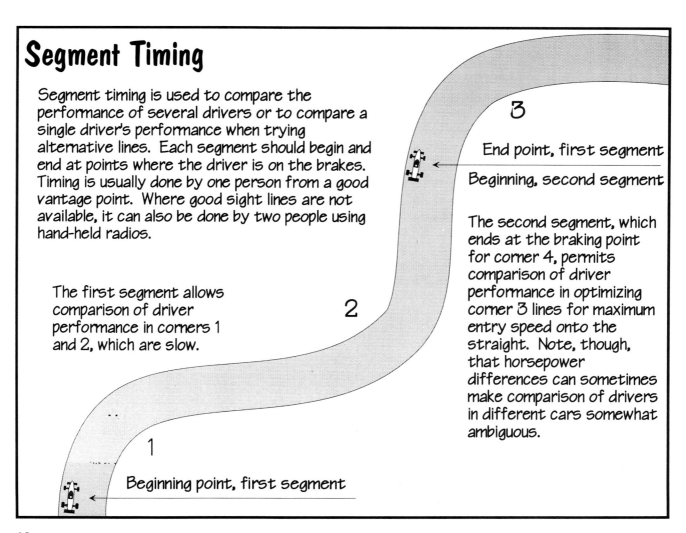

Segment Timing

Segment timing is used to compare the performance of several drivers or to compare a single driver's performance when trying alternative lines. Each segment should begin and end at points where the driver is on the brakes. Timing is usually done by one person from a good vantage point. Where good sight lines are not available, it can also be done by two people using hand-held radios.

3

End point, first segment

Beginning, second segment

The second segment, which ends at the braking point for corner 4, permits comparison of driver performance in optimizing corner 3 lines for maximum entry speed onto the straight. Note, though, that horsepower differences can sometimes make comparison of drivers in different cars somewhat ambiguous.

The first segment allows comparison of driver performance in corners 1 and 2, which are slow.

2

1

Beginning point, first segment

deal with it. Again, just like on the level, you must set a specific goal for how you want to end each corner. And if you set a specific goal, it's easy to find the steps to accomplish it."

Author comment: "Well, maybe for some people it's easy! My guess is that you'll find it's damned hard work."

Carroll Smith: "For once, I agree with Bertil. Bumps and hills are challenging and fun!"

WHICH CORNERS TO WORK ON?

You figure out which corners to work on by segment timing the car. There is no other really effective way. Segments will ideally begin at the entry to one corner and end at the entry to the next. Send your crew out with a couple of stopwatches and a clipboard. Have them compare your elapsed time through various track segments with the ETs of faster competitors. Have them note others' lines and brake points as they compare to yours. Work with them to analyze your situation and to prioritize your efforts.

Bertil Roos: "If you cannot take a corner perfectly from start to finish, then change your strategy and only focus on making the *second* half of the corner right. Enter sensibly, turn in gently, come up, place yourself correctly in the middle phase of the corner, nail it, and have full gas in the second half, out of the corner. When you can do that, then start working on the first half. That's how we should practice.

"And you know, if you follow that advice and you keep practicing that way, you're going to soon learn to get your car right, having confidence earlier and earlier. You will be able to get on full gas earlier and earlier, until you finally learn what it takes to go on full gas right after you release the brake."

If you are running in a class where the cars have brake lights, your crew should note your brake points, as well as those of the other drivers.

BRAKING TECHNIQUES

Braking on the racetrack is not appreciably different from braking on the street, except that you are not going to be as gentle about it. Your objective is to balance the car as quickly as possible at the absolute edge of tire lockup. Maintaining your braking at this point is sometimes referred to as "threshold" braking.

You have probably read that the brakes should not be applied suddenly, rather that they should be applied slowly, but firmly. The argument is that this will keep you from upsetting the car. It will, but this is not a totally accurate assessment of the situation.

You should apply the brakes as quickly as possible, up to the point where your sudden braking upsets the car. This upset point varies quite a bit between car types.

A larger, softly sprung car like a Showroom Stocker requires a moderately slow brake application. The reason is that the transition to a braking attitude requires a fair amount of suspension travel; the high center of gravity tries to pivot forward, the nose goes down 2–3in, and the tail comes up by a similar amount. If you attempt to achieve this travel too quickly, the car will overshoot (high polar moment of inertia, remember?), the rear tires will become unloaded, and they will lock up. Once they are locked, you cannot unlock them without reducing brake pressure. At best, this ruins the corner. At worst, it loops you into the weeds.

At the other extreme, a small Formula car or Sports Racer requires almost no finesse at all. The car c.g. is low and the polar moment is low. The car will respond quickly with no "dive overshoot" or other unacceptable behavior.

Bertil Roos: "Regarding 'almost no finesse at all.' That's a little optimistic—low center of gravity and all that. Braking is one of the most difficult things on the racetrack to do."

Tony Kester: "It's easier to utilize a large percentage of the braking ability of a small Formula or sports racing car, but *maximizing* braking takes finesse in whatever type of car you drive. The quicker reacting the car is, the quicker and more precise must be the driver's corrections."

Now that we've talked about applying the brakes, when should you get off them? Unless you're trail braking (see below), you will get off the brakes approximately at your turn-in point. You will turn the wheel, releasing the brakes as you do so. At that instant, the car will begin to transfer weight from the inside tires to the outside, and from the front to the rear. If the car is well set up, this technique will cause the turn-in to begin nicely without continuing on to become a spin.

Carroll Smith: "Bertil and Tony are right—one of the last things that the outstanding driver learns to do right is braking. The *very* last thing that he learns to do right is to take his foot *off* the pedal properly."

The other important thing to know about braking is that new brake pads must be "bedded" before being relied upon for maximum performance. This process is described in chapter 6.

BRAKING WHILE CORNERING

When cornering anywhere near the limit, braking spells instant disaster. Here's why:

In a stable cornering attitude, at the limit, both the front and the rear tires are working to their maximum. They are *just* capable of enough lateral thrust to carry the static and laterally transferred weight, and are at the edge of breakaway.

When you hit the brakes, weight is transferred from rear to front. This makes the front tires happy, since they get additional weight and can generate additional thrust. The rears, however, lose weight, can no longer generate the required *lateral* thrust (to say nothing about the small braking thrust they are being asked to deliver), and they let go. Spin.

Once in a while, you will encounter a corner-entry situation that demands that you brake while you are doing some turning. Typically, this will occur in a diminishing-radius corner like a hairpin or a carousel.

Do what's necessary, but be careful to blend the braking and the cornering so that you don't exceed the total thrust available from the *rear* tires.

TRAIL BRAKING

The idea of trail braking is that the turn-in is begun well before the car's brakes are released. One professional school teaches students to complete 70% of their braking in a straight line, *beginning* to reduce braking at the turn-in, but carrying the last braking until the car is pointed at the apex.

This is a dicey business in a well-balanced car for the reasons cited previously. It makes the front tires stick, and the rears tend to come loose. In an inherently understeering car, it can help the turn-in if used in small doses. The physics of the situation in a normal corner, however, dictates that large doses of trail braking can be safely administered only if the car is not at the limit or poorly set up.

A convincing "traction circle" argument is sometimes made for trail braking in all corners. The idea is that you make a gradual transition between braking and cornering, keeping the tire at its limit during the entire process. (In the *Drive to Win* video, Gilbert Pednault gives an excellent

The shining brake lights on this Camaro indicate that the driver is trail braking into this ninety-degree corner.

This Nissan driver is off the brakes much earlier than the Camaro driver (no brake lights are showing). The Nissan probably does not understeer as much as the Camaro.

chalk-talk explanation of the traction circle model.)

Basically, the idea is to look at a tire's cornering capability as a thrust vector drawn from the center of the contact patch. The length of this vector is limited by a circle. The circle represents the 100% capability of the tire as it is used in cornering, braking, and engine acceleration. The position of the vector in the traction circle is determined by which of these thrusts are being generated.

The traction circle argument for trail braking is that a driver can maximize total thrust by blending the end of braking past the turn-in and into the first part of the corner. If this blending is done properly, the point of the thrust vector moves smoothly around the circle, maintaining maximum length (thrust) at all times.

The argument, in my opinion, could only be valid for a fraction of a second (maybe 200 milliseconds) as you enter a normal turn. (At 60mph, or 90ft per second, 200 milliseconds is 18ft. The turn-in phase doesn't last any longer than that.) Out of 200 milliseconds, how much could you save? Five?

The trail braking argument is also inherently flawed in that it does not recognize that there is more to the car than the contact patch of the outside front tire. Trail braking is a sometimes-useful tool for getting a car to turn in, but I do not believe that it has any practical advantage in normal cornering.

Thinking about the diminishing-radius situation, though, you can see that the turn-in phase could be quite long—maybe a second or two. In this case, blending the turning and the braking is going to be advantageous.

In a diminishing-radius entry, you are tightening the steering as you get into the turn, and it becomes *necessary* to combine braking and turning. The alternative, braking in a straight line, would force you to enter too slowly. This situation arises both in turns that have decreasing-radius layouts and in turns, such as carousels, where you must enter on a decreasing radius in order to get a good exit shot.

On a more quantitative note, Paul Van Valkenburgh reports in his book that there was hard data collected by Mark

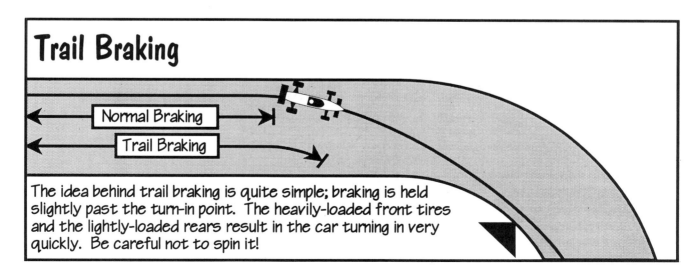

Trail Braking

Normal Braking

Trail Braking

The idea behind trail braking is quite simple; braking is held slightly past the turn-in point. The heavily-loaded front tires and the lightly-loaded rears result in the car turning in very quickly. Be careful not to spin it!

Donohue to prove that managing the braking-to-cornering transition is an effective way to reduce lap times. (The data was taken on a late-sixties Trans-Am Camaro, though, a mechanical assembly that probably would have required moderate trail braking in order to get turned in at all!)

Danny Collins: "Fast corners such as at Brainerd are great fun and perhaps my favorites, but the drastic weight transfer encountered entering tight hairpins does offer trail braking opportunities or necessities.

"Every technique offers some advantage that can be overused."

Bertil Roos: "Here is confusion—trail braking, no trail braking, and so on. Trail braking, as I understand it from Donohue's book [*The Unfair Advantage*], is to have the intention to put on your brakes and not be finished with the braking before you are quite a bit into the corner. That is what I understand is trail braking. To use the brake for a fraction in the initial turn-in to make the car respond to the initial steering input, that is not really trail braking. Trail braking is something you do in an understeering car because you must stay on the brake longer to make the car turn in enough.

"Let's take that again. I think trail braking is planning to brake far into the corner—to have your slowest point of speed one-third or even later into the corner. The way I teach and the way I drive is that your slowest point of speed is just at the initial turn-in. In most corners, I turn in a little on the late side to get a late enough apex, and I want a crisp steering response to make the turn-in. That's why I stay on the brake momentarily: the car turns in more easily. Then it's off the brake and onto the gas.

Carroll Smith: "'Slowest...at the initial turn-in....' Bertil is the only person in the world who believes this! Is it possible that Moss, Clark, Stewart, Lauda, Jones, Andretti, Senna, et. al., are wrong?"

Bertil Roos: "Now, if you could measure exactly what I was doing with the brake pedal entering the corner, you would find out that the slower the corner was, the later I would be turning in. The slower the corner was, too, the longer I would be keeping my foot on the brake after I initially turned the steering wheel. The faster the corner is, the earlier I would go off the brake.

"Now, with the same car and the same racetrack, if we screw around with the car and make the car more understeering, then you send me out, you will find that, in every place around the track, I am staying on the brake longer. And the reason is, the car is understeering more, the car turns more sluggishly, and therefore it needs to be helped by the brake pedal longer to get the job done. Trail braking is necessary if the car is understeering. You can't drive an understeering car if you don't trail brake well into the corners.

"If you have an understeering car, trail braking is the desirable driving technique. But people can misunderstand this. They say, 'Trail braking is the only way to get this car around the track, so that must be the right way to drive.' No, that is the wrong way to reason. What they should say is: 'Dammit, this car turns so sluggishly I have to stay on the brake all day. Let's make the car turn a little more eagerly. Let's make the car less understeering because if we do that, I can go off the brake earlier and go on the gas earlier.'"

Carroll Smith: "There are no absolutes in trail braking. In some cars in some corners, it is the fast way. In some cars in the same corners, it is not. Every driver trail brakes sometimes. It is not new, it is natural and again, if your re-

ceptors are open, the footprints will tell you."

Tony Kester: "In medium- to high-speed corners, trail braking is the absolute fastest way to enter a turn! Granted, it's not easy and the car must be set up well. But if racing was easy, I'd rather play golf!

"Also, if some braking can be done in the corner, the actual braking point can be later, making the straightaway longer. In that way, a significant additional portion of the track can be covered at a higher speed."

Paul Van Valkenburgh: "Lines and trail braking are so controversial that I refuse to get drawn into the debate. On these subjects, I hear a lot of egos and absolute statements and generalities that ignore the incredible variations in different car and tire configurations, different setups, different speeds, different corner types, and so on. Your top professional drivers don't sit around debating the theoretically best technique—they simply go out there and *find* approximately the fastest way around for each unique set of conditions. They then hone that line so that they can duplicate it at the limit, within a few hundredths of a second, on every single lap."

As a new driver, you may already be aware that trail braking is a controversial subject. (If you weren't, the views above should give you a clue!) Most of the debate is probably semantic—does holding the brakes a tenth of a second into the turn-in constitute trail braking or not?

As far as the traction circle model is concerned, there is little controversy. It is a useful way to think about things.

Bertil Roos: "The traction circle is only theory. If you talk about the traction circle, that only represents one wheel. We must take into consideration that we have four of them. One for each tire contact patch.

"In a right-hand corner maybe you can really get some good figures on the left front tire, but if you're trail braking—what people forget is that your right rear wheel is up in the air. You can play with your inside front tire traction circle, but you must not forget that the friction circles on the rest of the wheels are extremely small. There's not much bite left on the diagonal, the inside rear wheel.

"The same thing goes when you're under full gas in the corner: the weight is shifted to the outside rear wheel, making the inside front wheel ineffective."

Author comment: "When I say that the traction circle is a good model, I am thinking about it as a representation of the whole car's performance rather than as the performance of a single tire. Bertil is reiterating my point that the traction circle is not a good reason to argue for trail braking into all corners."

Carroll Smith: "One would have to be a fool to visualize the traction circle as one tire. We feel it as four contact patches (well, OK, sometimes three) and, if we are going to visualize it at all, we must also visualize the load transfers."

DRIVING TECHNIQUES: USING YOUR MIRRORS

As a new driver, learning to use your mirrors is one of your most important tasks. You are going to be passed and you are going to be passed a *lot*. You are going to be passed by other novice drivers who will do it carefully. However, you are also going to be passed aggressively by experienced drivers in faster cars. Although it is theoretically their responsibility to pass safely, that fact will not get your car (or your body!) repaired if you do something stupid because you are not aware of overtaking traffic.

True confessions time: When I am on the Brainerd racetrack with students, one of my amusements is startling them in one of several fairly safe corner entry sections. I'll late

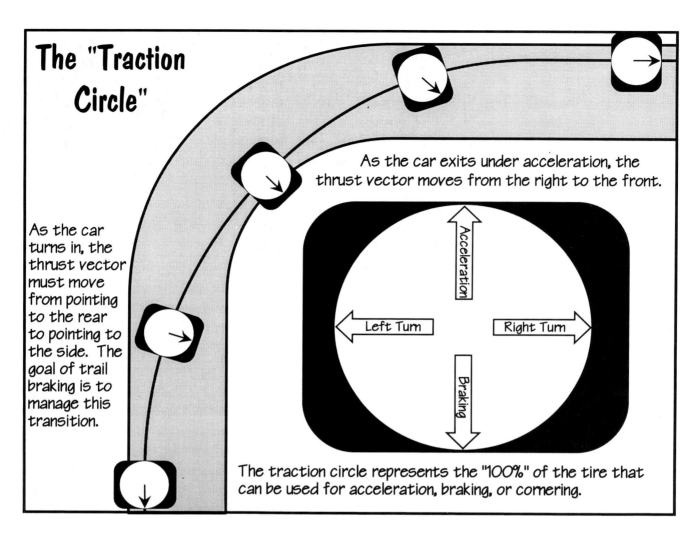

The "Traction Circle"

As the car turns in, the thrust vector must move from pointing to the rear to pointing to the side. The goal of trail braking is to manage this transition.

As the car exits under acceleration, the thrust vector moves from the right to the front.

Acceleration

Left Turn

Right Turn

Braking

The traction circle represents the "100%" of the tire that can be used for acceleration, braking, or cornering.

Just like your high-school driving instructor told you: hands at ten o'clock and two o'clock. There's plenty of room in this Spec Racer cockpit. On the far left are the fire system release handle and the ignition switch. The ignition has a military-type cover on it—just push on the cover to kill the ignition if the throttle sticks or you're engaged in crashing the car. The tach has a "tell-tale" which will show the highest rpm that the driver reaches during the session. The starter button is on the far right.

brake them, suddenly appearing alongside and very close. It's not uncommon to see their cars jump sideways 6in or so! I rationalize this fairly irresponsible behavior by arguing that it's good mirror training.

Before you go out, make sure that your mirrors are correctly adjusted. Make this a part of your on-the-grid checklist; mirrors get bumped out of position with predictable regularity as the car is attended to in the paddock.

On the track, develop some regular mirror-looking habits. Check before your brake point on each corner; this will show you the presence of any car that is in a position to outbrake you. Check again as you exit the corner but before you come back from the edge of the track; this will show you if anyone has come through, inside your line. Finally, check fairly frequently as you travel the straights. In mixed-class sessions, overtaking speed differentials of 30–50mph can exist. Since 50mph is 75ft per second, you can be caught fairly quickly.

Tony Kester: "Just as on the street, *always* know what is around and behind your car. After years of doing this, I have found that I can't drive on a racetrack comfortably (even alone) without effective rearview mirrors.

"The mirrors should be part of your visual scan, easily as important as the instruments."

STEERING

Both hands on the wheel, above the spokes at 10

o'clock and 2 o'clock. It isn't hard. Your position in the car should allow you to turn the wheel through almost 180 degrees without changing your grip. You should develop the habit of gripping the wheel with a moderate *unvarying* pressure, even in tight situations.

EYE TECHNIQUE

The way I teach proper eye technique is to give the following simple advice: *Look where you're going.*

An obvious statement? Not really. To understand its application to racing, you have to think about it carefully.

The first common misunderstanding is to confuse the direction in which the car is pointing with where you're going. When you are braking for a corner, your car is pointed straight ahead. Where it is going, however, is into the corner. Thus, your eyes must be looking at the apex of the corner *well before you turn the wheel*. This involves a conscious turn of the head.

The second misunderstanding is to look ahead, but too close to the car. At 100mph, you are traveling about 150ft per second. Your reaction time is 0.25–0.50 second and your car's response to whatever you try to do is probably another 0.25 second. The first 100ft or so in front of the car isn't where you are going. For all practical purposes, you are already there.

Thus, looking where you're going involves looking 1–2 seconds ahead of the car and often *not* where the car is pointing.

Bertil Roos: "I think it is better to say, 'Look where you want to go.' That is the problem with people in racing and in street driving: they look where they're going and where they're going is too often wrong. They should look where they want to go.

"Regarding '... your eyes must be looking at the apex of the corner...' That's not always literally correct; there are many corners where you have to turn in and travel quite a distance through the corner before you can reach the apex with your eyes."

Carroll Smith: "I agree with Bertil about looking *where you want the car to go.* You should look at the apex only until you are sure where you are going to clip—then you had better be looking far, far, beyond it."

A feeling that things are happening too fast is really an

This eye technique business is not exactly a new idea. Here's Dan Gurney at Spa. He's on the brakes, front wheels straight. Dan's head, though, is turned toward the corner—he's looking where he's going. (He's hard enough on the brakes that the right front wheel has just locked up. Note the absence of tire smoke, which would indicate that it had been locked up more than momentarily.) All American Racers

indication that you aren't looking far enough ahead of the car.

Eye technique can be practiced on the street and it will improve the safety of your driving. Consciously turn your head before turning corners. Look where you're going, not where the car is pointed. You'll know that you have it when you find that the windshield pillar is constantly in your way when traversing a twisty road. Experiment with look-points on the freeway to see what happens when your look-point is too close to the car. Things will feel rushed and you will find yourself making many small, unnecessary steering corrections. Move your look-point back out and see how smoothly and slowly things move.

This eye technique was, for me, difficult to learn. It also dropped my lap times by between 1–2 seconds. Really.

Danny Collins: "My contention is that if you look well

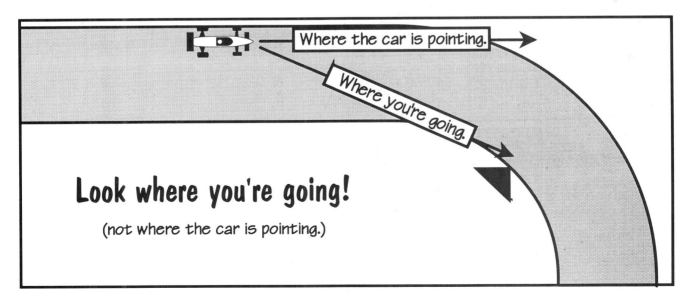

Where the car is pointing.

Where you're going.

Look where you're going!

(not where the car is pointing.)

ahead, whether you can actually see the 'target' or not, you've greatly improved your sense of balance, which increases your ability to maintain a 'smooth balance' of the car, or really maintaining a more consistent slip angle to all four tire patches.

"I discovered by experimentation, in the mid-1960s, that if a driver allows his eyes to linger too long concentrating on the late braking zone, that driver lost an average of 0.2 second per turn (times 10 turns, equals your 2 seconds per lap). Once a driver stares too long at his braking zone, he delays refocusing his eyes on the... apex-area of a turn, and, as a consequence, often *misses* the target."

Bertil Roos: "Danny basically is saying that if you don't have eye technique, you're not going to go fast. That is paramount in what we're talking about here."

Tony Kester: "When learning a new track, I try to establish four points of reference: brake point, turn-in point, apex, and exit. Until I have many laps at a track and these points become second nature, they are my main focus while driving and they always remain my main *visual* focus.

"Using these points is the best way I've found to run *consistent* lap times. Remember, the winner of a race is the driver with the *lowest average lap time* for the distance, not the driver with the *fastest lap*. Consistency counts!

BRAKE...LOOK...TURN

We talked earlier about making two decisions in a corner: brake point and turn-in point. Now I'll add a third event and give you your cornering mantra: *brake, look, turn*. If you learn nothing else from this book, remember that this is your cornering sequence. (Yes, this means that you will recognize your turn-in point with your peripheral vision. Your eyes will be focused on the apex.)

Proper eye technique will allow you to overcome another common driver problem: becoming fixated on the rear end of a car that you are following. Once, before I learned this technique, I was trying (in my Formula Ford) to get by a poorly driven Formula Continental car. He was holding me up badly in the corners, but I couldn't get by him on the straight. I resolved to force him into a mistake by sticking right on his gearbox (we'll talk about "putting on pressure" later in the book). I became so fixated that I began driving his lines, the problem being that he had wings for downforce and I did not. The result was a big-time spin, leaving me crosswise on the track with the rest of the pack diving onto the grass on both sides to get around me.

So, if you find yourself focused on the car in front of you as it goes through the turn, you are not using your eyes properly. Another way I have heard this said is: *You first race the track, then you race the competition.*

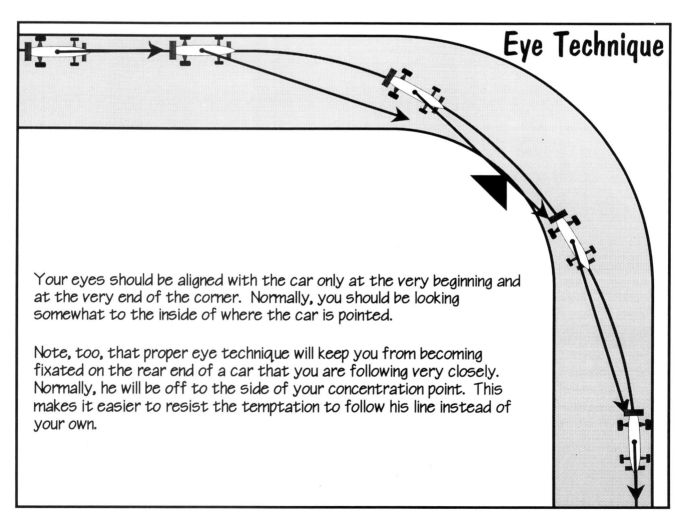

Eye Technique

Your eyes should be aligned with the car only at the very beginning and at the very end of the corner. Normally, you should be looking somewhat to the inside of where the car is pointed.

Note, too, that proper eye technique will keep you from becoming fixated on the rear end of a car that you are following very closely. Normally, he will be off to the side of your concentration point. This makes it easier to resist the temptation to follow his line instead of your own.

UNDERSTEER AND OVERSTEER

In *Tune to Win*, Carroll Smith says: "First of all, neutral steer is a rare and transient condition..." That about says it. A well set up car will understeer, oversteer, and neutral steer every lap depending on track conditions, driver inputs, and even the wind.

So when we talk about a car being set up for oversteer (or understeer), we are talking about a bias toward the selected condition, not an absolute refusal to do anything else.

A slight preference toward oversteer is best. Understeer is a stable, comfortable situation and, as such, is instinctively preferred by the novice driver. It is, however, not optimum for a number of reasons.

A slightly oversteering car is easier to turn into a corner. This is particularly true in tight corners. When releasing the brakes and turning, the car will inherently want to turn in.

Surprisingly, Bertil also argues that an oversteering car is safer to drive. According to his experience, understeering cars tend to let go and spin quite suddenly. An oversteering car, he says, is more predictable and smooth when pressed to the limit.

Bertil Roos: "Let's try to make some sense out of this here. First, I never talk about what is safer. My business is race car driving; my only concern is what is faster. What George heard me talk about is why people have such poor car control. The reason is that they have not practiced sliding. The reason they have not practiced sliding is that they are driving understeering cars. An understeering car sticks too much in the back end and will not slide.

"An understeering setup allows the driver to be sloppy. He doesn't have to be precise with the steering wheel. He doesn't have to have precise timing in his footwork—when to release the brake, exactly when to hit the gas pedal, and so on. People who are driving understeering cars tend to become sloppy and imprecise because they can manhandle the car a lot and throw the car around and be brutal to the car.

"But even if the car is understeering, you can abuse the car to the point where the rear end will finally let go. If you come up to a corner with your brakes on and the rear end light, then crank the steering wheel, you can still knock the rear end loose. If you knock the rear end loose, it snaps away so quickly that you cannot control it. It's going to be a terrible slide. I myself cannot even control that. It's going to be too much slide or too little, and it's going to be a mess.

"If the car is set up with less understeer, more toward neutral, the rear end comes around more of itself. When the rear slips away, it happens much more slowly and gradually. Now it is controllable. I can plant the rear end with the gas pedal and stop it from sliding further, whenever I want. So be sure you don't have an understeering car if you want to learn to slide, because you can not slide if the car is past a certain point in its bias toward understeering."

Carroll Smith: "Here we go again! I agree with Bertil that oversteer teaches car control and that a strongly understeering car is liable to 'snap' into oversteer and be difficult to drive (and slow). I also agree that the successful racing driver must have excellent car control. *But*, I also feel that he should seldom use it.

"Consider this: In order for a car to accelerate while still turning, there must be excess tractive capacity to the driving wheels. This means that *some* amount of corner entry understeer *must* be present. Admittedly longitudinal and transverse load transfers take care of some of the equation, but the basic understeer requirement remains.

"If a driver has learned in a bad car and has never been able to apply vehicle dynamics to optimize vehicle behavior, the fast way is as Bertil suggests. It can become a habit, however, which must be broken in order to succeed in the upper levels of racing."

Another reason you do not want understeer is that it can cause significant amounts of drag. In *Tune to Win* Carroll provides an analysis showing that an understeering Formula Ford can lose 8% of its available power to understeer drag. (Remember that the heat in your hot tires comes at the expense of speed.)

Besides, oversteer is more fun! With the tail slightly out, you can use the throttle *and* the steering to control the car's attitude. You don't have to trail brake to get the thing turned in, and the car will be lively and responsive. None of this is true in an understeering car.

In fast corners, the car should be as neutral as possible. It is not fun to have the back end wanting to come around at 150mph. This high-speed neutral steer is accomplished, where legal, by tuning the aerodynamics. The raised lip on the rear of a Sports Racer or a Formula Ford has the effect of creating downforce at high speeds, allowing the low-speed setup to be biased toward oversteer. The wings allowed in other classes like DSR, FC, and FA just make the setup easier to do. If you have no aerodynamic options to create high-speed neutral steer, you'll have to get it some other way and live with the consequences.

Chassis tuning is beyond the scope of this book. Carroll Smith and Paul Van Valkenburgh can help you on that subject.

TENSION

The car will not go any faster if you pull on the steering wheel as you try to pass. Your driving will not benefit from this, nor will you benefit by holding the wheel with the grip of death. When you are doing these things, you cannot feel what the car is telling you. You cannot feel the subtle changes in steering feedback as the front tires near their breakaway point. You cannot feel the rear trying to slip out. When you cannot feel these conditions, you cannot approach them as closely as the driver who can. And close to the limits is what speed is all about.

I had an extremely bad case of death-grip early in my racing career. I would get out of the car with aching hands! I finally broke the habit by driving street cars using only my fingertips for six months during an off-season. When I got back in the race car, I discovered that the steering wheel had all sorts of information for me. I was about 1 second quicker everywhere I went, and received my region's Most Improved Driver award for the year.

SHIFTING: CLUTCH ADJUSTMENT

Before you begin to worry about shifting, make sure that your clutch pedal travel is optimized. This means that there should be a minimum amount of travel before you reach the release point *and* a minimum amount of travel afterwards. Excess travel wastes time and can damage the clutch plate springs.

Prerelease travel is usually easy to adjust by changing the length of the clutch cable or of the slave-cylinder actuation rod. Overtravel is adjusted in a purpose-built race chassis by setting the pedal stop. On a street car or a converted street car, you may have to add a pedal stop of some kind.

UPSHIFTS

Upshifting is basically the same as you would do it on the street. Resist the urge to slam the gear lever around. It will not make the car go any faster and it could (literally) cause the gear lever to break off in your hand. We'll talk later about selecting shift points. As a beginner, you should choose one of the following: (1) what your engine builder recommends; (2) 200–300rpm below what others in similar cars claim to be using; and (3) 200–300rpm below the indicated redline (in Showroom Stock).

Some drivers talk about "power shifting," which involves making the upshift without lifting your foot off the throttle. I don't recommend this. The technique is extremely hard on the entire driveline due to the shock loads involved, and you run serious risk of overrevving the engine. Also, it cannot possibly have much effect on lap times due to the extremely short time interval spent making an upshift, power-on or not.

HEEL AND TOE

Ahh...heel and toe. The perennial topic of racing books. Before we sail into this classic discussion, let's talk about how gearboxes work.

All modern gearboxes are "constant mesh," meaning that all the paired gears that create the ratios are in constant rotation against one another. We don't actually shift gears. What we do is select one of the ratios to be connected to the gearbox output shaft. This selection is accomplished by mov-

ing a hub or ring, internally splined onto the output shaft, into side engagement with one of the output gears in the box.

(Street boxes typically accomplish one of the ratios by directly connecting the input shaft to the output shaft, so technically no gear is involved. This 1:1 ratio is normally used for top gear or next-to-top gear. You still move a hub or ring, though, to engage the two shafts.)

The gearbox output shaft and the shift hubs spin as determined by the car's road speed and rear axle ratio. The gears spin as determined by the speed of the input shaft. The highest gear (fourth or fifth) spins the fastest, and first gear spins slowest. The task in shifting, then, is to match the speeds of the shift hub on the output shaft and the gear being selected. Since road speed determines the shift hub speed, we are left with managing the speed of the gear.

In an upshift, this is not difficult. The new gear being selected is, at the moment the clutch is released, spinning much faster than its corresponding hub on the output shaft. When the lower-gear hub is disengaged, then, the gear sets lose drive force and their rotation begins to slow due to internal drag. The new gear quickly slows to near the speed of the corresponding hub, and engagement is relatively easy.

Downshifting, however, is another matter. Here the gear you want to select is already turning more slowly than its corresponding hub. Waiting while the gear sets slow down

In a purpose-built race car the pedal area is a bit tight, but you can adjust pedal heights to make your heel-and-toe maneuver easy. Note how the brake master cylinders extend out ahead of the front bulkhead. They'll be the first to go in a crash. Most cars have some kind of protective structure around front-mounted master cylinders.

In a Showroom Stocker, you have to have heel and toe, too. The pedal setup in this Mazda Miata is pretty good right from the factory. In other cars, you might have to make a few "slight" adjustments—be careful you don't go too far or your car may be judged in violation of the rules.

will only make things worse. You must somehow accelerate the slower gear to match the hub speed before they will easily engage. In street gearboxes, this is done with "synchro rings" that are actually small, conical clutches between the shift hubs and the gear. These clutches are engaged as you move the hub toward the gear, and they speed up the gear before allowing the hub to engage it. You can feel the synchro rings resisting your shift when you downshift; there is more resistance when the speed mismatch is greater.

Street synchro rings slow your downshifts and, if used hard, will eventually wear to the point of uselessness. Racing boxes have no synchromesh. Thus, with either type of box in a race car, you have to use the engine to speed the new gear up to the hub speed. It's easy; just release the clutch pedal after putting the box in neutral and rev the engine to approximately the speed it will reach after the downshift is completed. Then push the clutch in, make the shift, and release it again.

This is called *double-clutching*. The clutch is used twice: once to make the shift into neutral, then again to make the shift from neutral to the new, lower gear. While the car is in neutral (clutch out), the throttle is blipped to speed up the gears.

The reason we talk about heel and toe is that you have to accomplish the double-clutching during braking and before turning into a corner. The ball of your right foot is hard on the brakes while you use the side of your foot (not really your heel) to rev the engine during the middle phase of the double-clutching exercise.

You may have to modify pedal heights to make the heel-and-toe maneuver possible. Taking the time to do it is worthwhile, though usually not a great deal of fun.

Just like the diagrams! The second of these Formula Vees is moving up on his victim. Just after this photo was snapped, he moved out to his right and made the pass. Yes, you do have to run this close!

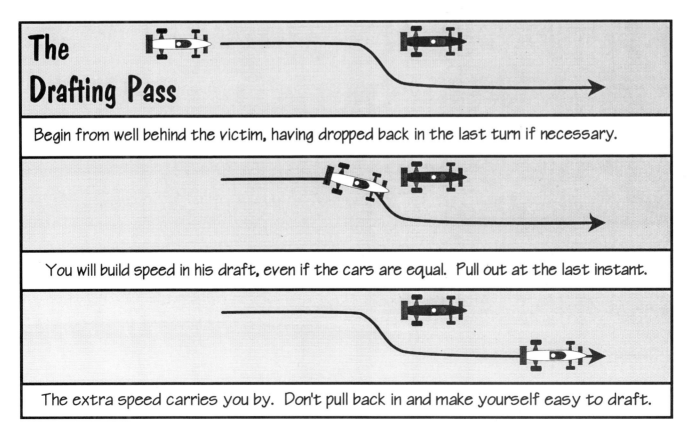

The Drafting Pass

Begin from well behind the victim, having dropped back in the last turn if necessary.

You will build speed in his draft, even if the cars are equal. Pull out at the last instant.

The extra speed carries you by. Don't pull back in and make yourself easy to draft.

DOWNSHIFTS

In bygone days, racing drivers would downshift through each of the gears, carefully using engine deceleration to supplement weak brakes. With modern equipment, we go for the gear that's needed in the corner. There isn't time for such fooling around, and the bursts of engine deceleration would upset your carefully adjusted brake bias anyway.

The downshift sequence during corner entry, then, simply involves braking at the limit while making a heel-and-toe, double-clutch selection of the gear to be used in the corner. Right? Well, almost. You also have to delay engagement of the new gear until the car has been slowed to the point where its speed will not overrev the engine.

In some cases, typically involving a short braking period and a one-gear downshift, you can skip the double-clutch exercise. Just make the shift as quickly as possible. Although you'll be forcing your gearshift, in exchange, you get an extra split-second of undivided concentration on the corner. This works best with a (nonsynchro) racing box.

You can force almost any racing box downshift without double-clutching, but you will end the weekend with many metal chips inside the box. In the *Drive to Win* video, you are advised that double-clutching is not necessary. That is certainly true, particularly if you are driving someone else's car. Webster and Hewland, too, will tell you that omitting the double-clutch step is acceptable, even desirable. They sell gears and dog rings.

If you are not double-clutching, it is probably a good idea to examine the dog rings after qualifying, while checklisting the car before the race. If you have beaten up the shift dogs, you run the risk of missed shifts and consequent buzzing of the motor. Change them.

Tony Kester: "All nonsynchro (Hewland, Staffs, and so on) gearboxes must be double-clutched to downshift smoothly and efficiently. Eliminating this step destroys gears, dog rings, and shift fingers. It can also upset the car by causing a momentary lockup of the rear wheels as the lower gear is engaged. Anyone who recommends any kind of 'ramrodding' technique is *wrong*.

"That being said, you might find yourself without a clutch someday. Put the lever into neutral, then blip the throttle and 'gently force' the lever into the new gear. This is effectively the same as double-clutching."

Carroll Smith: "Semantics again—If one learns to synchronize the revs properly, there is no need to double-clutch or, indeed, to use the clutch at all."

PASSING

As a novice, you will be getting passed a lot more than you will be doing the passing. The technique for getting passed is important enough that I'll reiterate it: Use your mirrors, don't get surprised. Don't change your line, and signal the overtaking driver. Point where you want *him or her* to go.

Following are some tips for situations where you are the perpetrator instead of the victim.

PASSING BETWEEN CORNERS

The safest place to pass is between corners, especially on long straights. Stay directly behind your victim, building momentum in his draft until the last possible minute, check your mirrors, and pull out smoothly. Wherever possible, pick the side that puts you on the inside at the next corner. Be sure you can be beside him and clearly visible before the turn-in point for that corner.

The first reason to avoid an outside pass is that you need to be beside your victim and clearly visible before he moves to the outside for the corner. This move is made well before the actual turn-in point, hence your choosing the outside line shortens the available time to make the pass. The second reason is that putting him on the inside makes it easy for him to re-pass at the corner.

Here's the mid-phase of a drafting pass, this time with Formula Fords. Car #66 is making his move.

The Vee on the left used to occupy the space behind the third car in line. In making his pass, he's moved well over so he isn't giving any draft to the fifth car in the pack. The third car is in position to make his move, too. If his timing is good, he'll snap over behind car #86 and maybe draft by him, too. The front car here is a Formula 440. They are faster than Vees in a straight line, but give up a lot in the corners due to poor suspension.

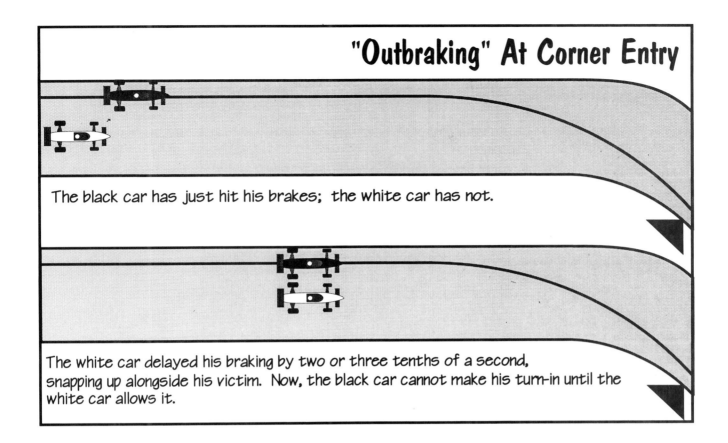

"Outbraking" At Corner Entry

The black car has just hit his brakes; the white car has not.

The white car delayed his braking by two or three tenths of a second, snapping up alongside his victim. Now, the black car cannot make his turn-in until the white car allows it.

You should never begin a straightaway pass from directly behind your victim unless you have a massive horsepower advantage. Drop back a little in the last corner, then use his draft to accelerate on him. Done correctly, you will have enough speed to get by him before the air resistance slows you down again.

Sometimes you will find yourself able to draft up to beside a competitor, but unable to complete the pass due to a shortage of horsepower. When this happens, don't slow yourself and him down by repeatedly learning this lesson. Take a lesson, instead, from the National Association for Stock Car Automobile Racing (NASCAR) stockers and stay in his draft. You'll both go faster.

PASSING IN CORNERS

Bertil Roos teaches that "you can't pass unless you're on the brakes." This may be a little strong, but if you and your intended victim are about equal in hardware and ability, it's damned hard to pass anywhere else.

Passing on corner entry is difficult, dangerous, and required to win races. Thus, I will spend some time illustrating the technique—and how it can go wrong.

Passing on corner entry is easy to describe. You position your car to the inside of your intended victim, no more than a few feet behind him. He brakes, you delay your braking by a heartbeat, and suddenly you're beside him. You are now blocking his turn-in and are in control of the corner.

You'll have to brake for somewhat longer than your normal distance, since you'll be taking a smaller radius than normal, but there's not much he can do about it. You're also forcing him into taking a smaller radius (he can't turn in yet because you're in the way), so he must stay on his brakes too.

Tony Kester: "Stay directly behind the leading car until the last possible instant. The longer you can wait to pull to the inside position for the pass, the less chance there is for the other driver to take action to block your move."

Note that "outbraking" is really a misnomer. What we are talking about here is "late braking" a competitor. It can be done successfully when the two cars have equal brakes, as long as the overtaking car does not shoot so far past the victim that he does not maintain control of the corner. Superior brakes (or braking control), though, are certainly an asset to the overtaking car. If the overtaking car has *poorer* brakes than the intended victim, attempting this maneuver is probably hopeless.

Though easy to describe, an outbraking pass is not that easy to do. The problem is that the overtaking car must brake late enough to get beside the intended victim, then must maintain this position so that the victim cannot turn into the corner.

If the braking is not late enough or is not hard enough, the overtaking car can end up inside of the victim, but not alongside. In this event, the victim will not realize what has happened. He will make his normal turn-in and will be hit by the car attempting the pass.

PASSING DURING PRACTICE

You have two objectives while passing cars in practice: first, to get by safely, and second, to observe the behavior of the cars that you're passing.

There is absolutely no reason to take chances while

Controlling the Corner Entry

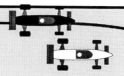

The white car necessarily moves ahead and must delay his turn-in because he began his braking later than the black car. The black car can't turn in either, though, because white is in control of the corner.

As white re-intersects the racing line, black has no choice but to turn in behind him. Note that the maneuver has slowed both cars, to the advantage of any following traffic.

Here, the Rabbit driver has attempted to make a late-braking pass, but has gotten it wrong. (That's not dust coming from the left front tire—it's smoke!) The innocent Bimmer driver is about to receive a crinkled door as a result. Craig Bryant

passing during a practice session. Your lap times don't matter and you aren't proving anything to anybody. Be cautious, give the car you're passing plenty of time to see you, and avoid "at the limit" passes in corners.

While passing cars in practice, note carefully the behavior of the individual drivers. These are likely to be the drivers you'll be passing in the race and it is important for you to know how they behave. All good drivers are aware of their mirrors and take predictable lines in corners. As a practical matter, these are the drivers you're *least* likely to be passing. No mirrors and unpredictable driving seem to go together; practice is the time to find these people and note carefully what they look like from the rear. (Fortunately, these drivers usually brake early. By taking advantage of this, you can be by them cleanly and safely without losing too much time.)

Similarly, there is no reason to behave competitively when you are being passed in practice. The old "I was bedding some pads" excuse can be applied as ego salve, even if you were driving your tail off.

Passing During Qualifying

There is little reason to take chances when passing during a qualifying session. This may not sound logical when you're shooting for a fast lap, but it's true.

In a tight grid, qualifying times are separated by tenths of a second. Any pass (except a clean one on a straight) involves throwing away this much time or more. Thus, your lap time is blown and you might as well blow it big time by being careful.

Overdoing It

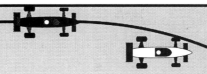

If the white car has braked too late or his brakes are not as good as those of his intended victim, he will shoot by and will still be going too fast to turn in.

As white desperately tries to stay on the track, black will simply take a normal line, laughing all the way. He will go inside of white and be gone, even if white stays out of the weeds. White is effectively taking a too-late apex line.

Crashing At Corner Entry

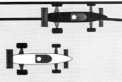

The white car has screwed up the pass and is not far enough forward to be seen by the other driver.

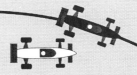

The unsuspecting victim makes his normal turn-in. The white car, already braking at the maximum, cannot avoid hitting him. At this point, the best that black can hope for is that he will not be launched by tangling tires with white. White may also be making things worse by locking his brakes, trying to avoid the inevitable.

The only exception to this is if you're an erratic driver who happens to be on an exceptionally quick lap. A smooth, consistent driver has few reasons to take chances while passing during a qualifying session.

So why do the Formula One racers take big chances (and have big crashes) during qualifying? Qualifying tires, good for about two laps, force them to do so. You aren't on qualifying tires, so don't take chances.

Passing in the Race

There is little to be said about cautious passing during a race. If we were by nature cautious individuals, we wouldn't be doing this at all.

It is important to remember that it is not possible to win the race in the first turn of the first lap. However, it *is* possible to lose it there. This is demonstrated frequently, hopefully not by you.

Being Passed

If you are constantly being surprised by cars passing you, you should do one of three things: (1) fix your mirrors so that you can see, (2) learn to use the perfectly good mirrors you have, or (3) quit racing.

Carroll Smith: "Right on! This should be in red capital letters!"

Your behavior while being passed says a lot about your judgment. Unless you are dicing with the other driver (*really* dicing!), it is *always* a good idea to make his pass as easy as possible.

You want to go fast, right? Holding someone up will slow you down by reducing your concentration on going fast. Letting him by will give you someone to draft, however briefly, and may result in your learning some new techniques as you follow him. As they say in the human relations business, it's a win-win situation.

There are a few drivers who get an ego boost from hold-ing up someone who's obviously faster. Unfortunately, not few enough.

GOING FAST (FINALLY!)

Going fast is a lot like walking sideways along a crumbling rock cliff with your toes hanging over the edge. If you're hanging out and going fast, you'll be constantly shifting balance and reacting as the cliff tries to crumble away underneath you. Really fast drivers have their toes hung out a long, long way.

Said another way, if you are comfortable and solid in the corners, you are not going fast enough. At the limit, your tires are changing their traction (and slip angles) every second, a situation that requires a constant stream of small corrections on the steering and (sometimes) the throttle.

If you are truly testing the edge of the cliff, sometimes you will fall off. If you stand back from the edge, corners will be smooth, comfortable places and you will be slow.

A BRIEF REVIEW

I've thrown a lot at you in this chapter. Here are some of the main points to remember:

• Look where you're going, not where the car happens to be pointed.

• If things are happening too fast, you're probably not looking far enough ahead of the car.

• The objective in selecting a cornering line is to maximize your average speed around the track, not your speed through the corner.

• Your corner entry sequence is: brake, look, turn.

• If you have to crank in more steering after your clipping point, you have clipped a too-early apex.

• If you exit the corner in the middle of the track, your apex was too late.

• Check your mirrors just before you brake for a turn, as you exit the turn, and frequently on the straights.

Chapter 4

Basic Driver Information

SAFETY EQUIPMENT

One of the helmet companies used to suggest: "If you've got a cheap head, buy a cheap helmet." Resist the temptation to save money on helmets or on other safety equipment.

Resist the temptation, too, to look at your Showroom Stock or Improved Touring car as being relatively safe from fire. You will be carrying gas in a tank not intended for racing or for racing impacts. You will be sitting in an interior that is filled with flammable fabrics and plastics. Your car has a relatively high center of gravity and is thus quite prone to roll over during an off-course excursion. When it is upside down, there are no check valves to prevent gasoline leaks. In my view, SS and IT drivers should be especially careful to equip themselves with good safety equipment.

HELMETS

Department of Transportation (DOT) sticker helmets are junk. Regardless of your particular club requirements, your helmet must have a Snell Foundation approval sticker indicating it meets the Special Applications (SA) test specification. Don't choose less than maximum protection. The 90SA is the latest Special Applications Snell approval, written in 1990. Basically, Special Applications means racing. There is a 90M spec, as well, for motorcycles. However, motorcycle helmets are not designed for multiple impacts, they do not have fireproof linings, and they are deficient in other areas.

Buy a full-face helmet even if you're going to be driving a closed car. This safety precaution is worth the minor discomfort. I suggest using a visor as well, even if you keep it tilted up. It can be snapped down to protect your eyes in a fire.

Structurally, a helmet consists of a hard shell, usually made of fiberglass, and a crushable foam lining. Lately, manufacturers have been making a big deal out of helmet weight savings through use of exotic materials like Kevlar or carbon fiber in the shell. This is fine for IndyCar drivers who spend a lot of time cornering at 4g, but a club racer will see maybe 1.4g and then only briefly. I would not spend the extra money if I were you.

The purpose of the crushable foam lining is to reduce the peak g-acceleration that your head gets in an impact, by permanently absorbing energy. (Resilient foam is not used because its force/displacement curve produces a higher peak. Also, all the absorbed energy is put right back into your head as the foam rebounds.) The condition of the crushable foam helmet liner is critical to your safety.

The first thing to realize is that crushing of the foam is a one-time deal. If you take an impact in the helmet, send it back to the manufacturer for examination and relining as necessary. The second thing is that the foam is subject to damage by paint solvents, sunlight, and heat. You can paint your helmet, but get it into fresh air as quickly as possible. Do not leave it in the sun or store it in places where it can get hot. Finally, the foam stiffens as it ages. This means that you will have to get a new helmet or a new lining every few years. Unfortunately, the manufacturer, with an obvious conflict of interest, is the only place you can go for advice on need for replacement. If no manufacturer recommendation is available, the Snell Foundation recommends that you use a helmet for no longer than five years.

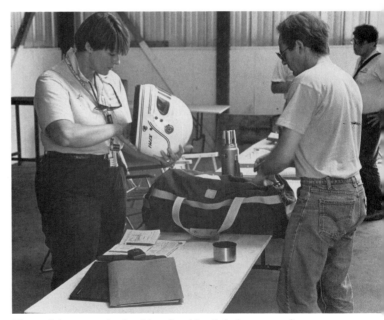

The tech inspector is checking the driver's helmet to make sure it has the required Snell sticker. Next, she will look at the driver's suit, underwear, gloves, and shoes. Although Tech checks for the minimum, consider carefully before stopping at that point.

Snell 90SA Helmet Standard

Here, excerpted with permission, is the introduction to the Snell SA90 helmet specification. In brackets, I have added some additional information from other parts of the Standard. Hopefully, this will help you understand why you are wearing one of these helmets:

Introduction

This Standard addresses the problem of protecting the head from direct impact with surfaces or objects that might be encountered in a racing accident. The Standard prescribes direct measures of several factors bearing on a helmet's ability to protect the head as well as its general serviceability as automotive racing headgear. Thus, this Standard is directed toward the kinds of performance bearing on head protection that may not readily be discernible by even knowledgeable consumers at the time of purchase.

A racing helmet consists generally of a rigid head covering and a retention system composed of flexible straps and hardware. The rigid covering consists of a stiff outer shell surrounding a crushable liner. The stiff outer shell protects by its capacity to spread a concentrated load at its outer surface over a larger area of the liner and the wearer's head. The crushable liner protects the head from direct impact by its capacity to manage impact energy.

The retention system holds the headgear in position throughout normal usage and especially during accidents. This Standard tests the strength of the retention but does not address whether it will hold the headgear in position on a particular wearer's head. *The manufacturer must provide suitable guidance to the wearer so that he will be able to satisfy himself of the quality of fit and the positional stability of a particular helmet before using it.*

The capacity for impact protection is determined by direct measurement of the shock delivered through the helmet to a headform when the helmeted headform is dropped [6.5kg dropped weight, from 3m] in a specified manner onto each of three unyielding [135kg] anvils [flat, hemispherical, edge]. A fourth anvil [steel bar] is used to test impact protection for repeated strikes against a roll cage assembly.

The strength of the retention system is tested by placing the helmet on a headform and shock loading [38kg, dropped 120mm] the strap with a mechanical structure simulating the human jaw.

Most racing helmets are intended to accommodate a range of head sizes and shapes. Various thicknesses of resilient lining material are sometimes placed within otherwise identical helmets during production or during fitting to configure the helmet to several different ranges of head size. This resilient padding does not significantly affect the way the helmet absorbs and attenuates impact and is not directly addressed by this Standard; however such padding may degrade the positional stability of the helmet.

The helmet must also resist penetration by projectiles such as parts of exploding engines or other damaged mechanical assemblies. This capacity is tested by placing the helmet on a headform and dropping a metal cone of specified mass and geometry onto the shell [3kg, dropped from 3m, 60deg angled point]. The tip of this cone must not penetrate the headform.

Similarly, the helmets must resist chemical attack by solvents and petrochemicals associated with motorsports. This capacity may be tested by applying a solvent mix before further conditioning and testing.

Since race drivers are frequently unable to escape quickly from accident involved vehicles, their helmets must also provide some measure of protection against fire. Helmet components are tested separately for flame resistance by exposing them to a direct propane flame of a specified temperature [790deg C] for specified periods of time [30sec for the helmet shell itself]. When the flame is withdrawn, each of these components must self-extinguish within a specified time limit. Furthermore, when the helmet shell is tested, the temperature of the lining material within the helmet that would presumably touch the wearer's head must not exceed 70° C.

The chin strap must also be flame resistant [15sec]. The chin strap will be tested similarly to other helmet components. It must not melt and must self-extinguish within the allowed time.

Full face helmets provide a measure of facial protection in addition to the impact protection generally sought. The principal feature of a full face helmet is a chin bar that extends forward to cover the jaw area converting the facial opening into a visual port. Frequently a face shield is provided so that the wearer's face is fully covered.

In order to be considered a full face helmet the chin bar must be an integral part of the helmet structure. The Standard then tests the rigidity of the chin bar by dropping a [5kg] weight onto it at a specified velocity [3.5m/sec] so as to attempt to force the chin bar toward the interior of the helmet. The chin bar must not deflect more than a specified amount.

If a face shield is provided with a full face helmet, then this face shield must resist penetration by small particles. A sharp lead pellet of a specified weight is directed into the face shield at a specified velocity [1gm, 5.5mm diameter lead pellet, traveling about 300mph]. The pellet must not penetrate into the helmet interior.

This face shield must also withstand a flammability test [45sec of propane flame]. As for other components, the face shield must be self extinguishing within an allotted time. Furthermore, the face shield must not melt down allowing flame to reach the interior of the helmet.

Finally, this face shield must have a positive "hold down." Since inadvertent displacement of the face shield during racing could have disastrous consequences, the only way to remove or raise the face shield from its normal operating position must involve the deliberate disengagement of some catch mechanism. Friction mechanisms will not satisfy this requirement.

Ventilation and frequently, forced air ventilation, are important considerations for automotive racing. This Standard does not limit the diameter of ventilation holes into the helmet but makes specific mention of the kinds of ports and fittings appropriate for forced air ventilation. However, there are no direct demands on either the quantity or quality of air flow to the wearer.

Other general features of racing helmets may include eyeshades and accommodations for goggles. These features deal with matters of safety and comfort that are not directly addressed in this Standard but which merit the consideration of wearers as well as manufacturers.

Although helmet use has been shown to reduce the risk of head injuries significantly, there are limits to a helmet's protective capability. No helmet can protect the wearer against all foreseeable accidents. Therefore injury may occur in accidents which exceed the protective capability of any helmet including even those helmets meeting the requirements of this Standard.

A helmet's protective capability may be exhausted protecting the wearer in an accident. Helmets are constructed so that the energy of a blow is managed by the helmet, causing its partial destruction. The damage may not be readily apparent and the Foundation strongly recommends that a helmet involved in an accident be returned to its manufacturer for complete inspection. If it is not possible to do so, the helmet should always be destroyed and replaced.

Finally, the protective capability may diminish over time. Some helmets are made of materials which deteriorate with age and therefore have a limited life span. At the present time, the Foundation recommends that the helmets be replaced after five (5) years, or less if the manufacturer so recommends.

The Snell Memorial Foundation is a nonprofit organization that tests various types of helmets and certifies them for use. It was founded by friends of driver Pete Snell, who died of massive head injuries in a racing accident during the mid-1950s. Additional information and copies of the full specification are available by writing: Snell Memorial Foundation, Inc.. PO Box 493, St. James, NY 11780

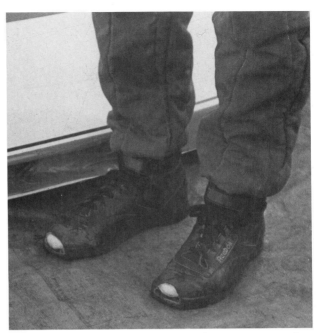

These leather running shoes work fine for racing, except that a bit of trimming had to be done for clearance in a tight footwell. Do what's necessary, but don't forget the Nomex socks!

Your helmet should fit somewhat snugly. It should not slide over your skin when pulled left and right. Gaps between your head and the foam are highly undesirable; in an impact, this is space that will allow your head to accelerate before hitting the foam. Bad.

For obvious reasons, you should not be able to get the helmet off with the chin strap fastened. Be sure to check this.

Carroll Smith: "Also, check the chin strap attachment points regularly."

If you wear glasses, be sure that you can put them on through the helmet opening.

There are various aerodynamic and ventilation claims made for helmet designs. I have had three or four helmets in

the last fifteen years, some ventilated and some unventilated. None have worked well in the rain, and they have been indistinguishable in the dry. If your helmet fits properly, there is no place for internal airflow anyway.

DRIVING SUIT

Buy a name-brand suit, two or three layers. The theory of racing suits is that fireproof or fire resistant materials are not the insulation. They simply stay around during a fire to maintain a trapped layer of air, which *is* the insulation. This is why more layers are better and it is also the reason you need to own and wear a full set of underwear, socks, and a head sock (aka balaclava).

Various claims of comfort are made for the alternative suit fabrics. In my experience, they're all hot to wear. Even hotter with the underwear, which you will also be wearing. Solve this problem as necessary by putting ice in your pockets, down the crotch, and down your neck after you're in the car. Installed liberally, there will still be some ice left at the end of a half hour session or race.

I have had both Nomex and PBI suits. These fabrics (and probably all other fire-resistant materials) wear poorly, with cuffs and other wear points going bad after a couple of years. I would advise wearing your suit only during on-track sessions. Wearing it between sessions will inevitably result in it being stained with flammable oil and grease, plus it will wear out much faster. If you must cruise the paddock all day in your hero-driver suit, at least understand that it is costing you money.

Proban (which is a treated cotton) underwear is cooler and more comfortable than Nomex. It is also somewhat hard to find and does not retain its whiteness after multiple washings. PBI underwear is the only truly fireproof type but it is very expensive and does not hold its shape well. Nomex, which you will probably end up with, is just fine. You might want to consider buying two sets. A clean set is nice to have on the second day of a hot weekend.

GLOVES

Gloves should consist of two or three layers of material. Given the downside risk of burned hands, I wear only three-layer gloves, even though they are a bit more expensive and harder to find. For the same reason, I recommend the long gauntlet style. The long overlap between the glove cuff and your suit virtually guarantees no gaps that could expose your skin to fire.

I was surprised to see a recent *Sports Car* advertisement for "thin" one-layer gloves, apparently Air Force surplus. Dumb. When you crash an F-16, gloves probably don't matter much. In a gasoline fire, though, one layer won't provide any significant level of protection.

You will be doing a lot of signaling with your hands. Fist up on the grid, at the pit entrance, and so forth. Give the people who must see these signals a break: buy bright orange gloves. This is not the place to color-coordinate your ensemble.

SHOES

If anything is optional in the safety line, I'd nominate racing shoes. Many of us wear leather running shoes (always with Nomex or other fire-resistant socks).

Depending on your car, you will have to pay more or less attention to the width of the shoe soles. I suggest avoiding the wide wedge edges that are featured on some running-shoe styles. Don't buy them in the first place, or if you already own a pair, cut off the edges with a coarse hacksaw blade. Nothing good will come from catching your shoe sole behind the edge of a pedal.

Norma Williams: "This is expensive equipment; take care of it! Our boys both wear two-layer PBI racing suits. After each session, they change out of the safety clothing and I hang up the suit and underwear on the trailer tent railing to air. I organize all of their other safety equipment and put it in one spot. I also clean the helmet visor. When they are ready to go out again, so is their gear."

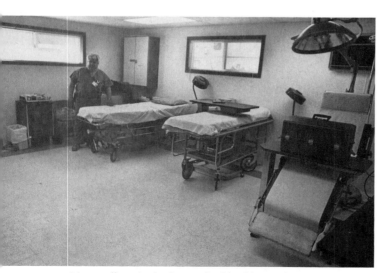

It's usually quiet in the medical building, often called the "quack shack." This smiling doctor is a great guy, but try not to see him in a professional capacity. You only want to meet the medical folks at the beer party, too!

MEDICAL ADVICE

Most of the major things you should and shouldn't do are things that you already know.

The most obvious is also so important that it must be said: No alcohol or drugs. Period.

You should be in top physical condition when you climb into the race car. Besides whatever training activity you choose, this also means you should be well rested and *not* hung-over. Let the spectators, workers, and crew party hearty; you came for another kind of fun.

Tony Kester: "No athlete would start a game without warming up first. The fact that most racers *aren't* in top shape is all the more reason for them to loosen up before getting into the car. Take a few minutes to stretch all the muscles that you will use (and that includes almost all the muscles in your body!) and try to work up a sweat. You'll get up to speed faster on the track, and you'll have fewer aches and pains the next day."

The consensus of medical opinion says that you should eat lightly, if at all, before a race. The meal should lean toward more sugar and carbohydrates, and away from fats. Medical advice bulletins that I have received over the years uniformly point out that it is unpleasant and unproductive to

It's important to fit yourself carefully into the seat; here, the driver is using some blankets to adjust the seat in a car he's using only for the weekend. Some closed-cell foam, anchored with race tape, would provide a more secure seating position. With the belts tightened up, though, he won't be moving around much in any case.

vomit inside your helmet. Apparently this happens. Don't let it be you.

Dehydration and heat exhaustion are real risks. On extremely hot weekends, there are always reports of drivers keeling over when they get out of their cars. Your performance suffers long before you're at the passing-out stage. Start each session ahead of the game by drinking plain water or an electrolyte solution like Gatorade. On hot days, especially, it's hard to overdo this preventive step.

Stop by the bathroom on the way to the grid. To quote the *SCCA Medical Safety Manual*: "the pressure of the seatbelt against a distended bladder can cause rupture [in a crash, presumably]. A ruptured bladder is a major medical emergency and can be fatal. The same reasoning applies to a full colon and stomach."

The medical consensus also advises us to remove jewelry such as rings, watches, and anything around the neck. There are two arguments for this: First, metal objects can be heated and make things worse in a fire. Second, they can catch on things during a crash. One bulletin mentions that "a ring can cause amputation of a finger." Neither of these risks seems significant to me, but then there's no reason to wear jewelry under your driver suit, either.

You do not want anything blocking your windpipe before, during, or after a crash. This means no gum, and no false teeth or bridges. You also do not want the items in your pockets to poke holes in you. This is most easily avoided by not putting anything in your pockets. If you need to carry some kind of tool, tape it to the roll bar or to another convenient part of the car.

GETTING FITTED INTO THE CAR

On the racetrack, you will experience an intensity of concentration that probably exceeds anything you have ever felt. This concentration *must* be focused on the car's behavior, the track, and on other competitors. To the extent it is not, you will be a menace to yourself and to others. Also, you will be slow.

Thus, you must carefully fit yourself into the car to minimize distractions due to discomfort and due to inconvenient control and/or instrument locations.

Your objective in fitting yourself to the car is to achieve a position where you can be relaxed while operating the pedals, shifter, and steering without extending your arms or legs to the point where the joints are locked.

Position and Seating

The first step in fitting is to make sure that you can be belted tightly into the seat with absolutely no freedom of movement. In a padded seat, this is relatively easy. You just haul on the belts until you are thoroughly pressed into the padding. In a racing shell, you may have to use some foam and some duct tape to make things snug.

Use semi-rigid closed-cell foam for padding a shell-type seat. A couple of years ago, I was running one of my crew members through a driver school as a reward for loyal service. In preparation we carefully converted my (lard-ass model) seat into a jockey-sized repository for him, using open-cell upholstery foam and a few hundred yards of duct tape. It looked great and felt great. When he pushed the clutch pedal, he moved neatly rearward into the soft foam and the pedal did not budge. Live and learn.

Dennis Eade: "Before a newcomer can early *or* late apex, he or she must be able to see the apexes and be comfortable in the car. This is something that is neglected by many drivers. Spend time in the chassis to fit to your seat. If you don't fit, make yourself a seat from flotation foam. This foam is readily available in any boat shop as a two-part kit. The two cans of liquid, when mixed, produce a foam that expands and hardens within 15 minutes or so.

"The procedure is simple. Sit in the car on top of a large, heavy-duty plastic garbage bag. Have a helper mix a small amount of foam, and pour it into the bag so that it can expand to fill the voids between your body and the chassis. Fill the areas between the sides of your legs and the chassis, at the small of your back, and between your shoulders and the chassis. Work slowly. It is much easier to pour more foam in the bag than it is to clean the overflowing excess out of your hair, suit, chassis, and garage. Sit there until the foam sets; then you can cut or sand it to whatever final shape you need.

"Once your seat is done, adjust the pedals so you can use them to their full extension. Set the brake and throttle so you can comfortably roll your foot onto the throttle while still maintaining good brake pressure."

Next, you should position the seat so that the pedals and steering wheel distances are as correct as possible. You

Here's a nicely foamed backrest and shoulder support in the new Piper Formula Ford.

should be able to completely depress the gas and clutch pedals without fully straightening your legs. You should be able to reach the top of the steering wheel without fully extending your arm. At full extension of your arm, you should be able to lay your wrist on the top of the steering wheel without leaning forward. You should also be able to make your two-three shift (or to reach the top rightmost gear if it is not third) without fully straightening your arm.

(If the seat is padded, you will have to tightly cinch the belts before checking the previous items. Tight belts might move you rearward by a couple of inches or more.)

Now comes the fun part. Adjust the seat position, the pedals, the steering wheel location, and the shift linkage as necessary (and as feasible) to optimize your driving position. This is tedious and requires patience, since the adjustments interact. An on-track session or two will probably be required before you get it right. Invest the time; it will come back to you in faster laps.

(You might as well get used to tail-chasing because of interacting adjustments; it happens all the time in racing. Car alignment is a particular joy in this respect.)

If you are renting a car or using a pro school car, "fitting" will usually consist of placing the seat to suit your leg length, then stuffing some foam behind you to suit your upper body and arm length.

To get properly fitted into a car owned by someone else, you may have to make a nuisance of yourself with the school mechanics or rental car owner. Do it. You are paying a lot of money and you should be able to operate the car comfortably and effectively. If it is a rented car, try to arrange to get fitted in the lessor's shop, prior to the race weekend. If it must be done at the track, do it *immediately* upon arrival. This is especially important if you are unusually large or small, or if your legs are unusually long or short. I once watched a 6ft, 3in 225lb student miss most of his first pro school session because the seatbelts couldn't be made long enough to accommodate him. They didn't try him in the car until 5 minutes before he was due to go out. Don't let this happen to you.

Roll bar height can be an issue for taller drivers in open cars. The *GCR* specifies that the top of the roll bar must be 2in above the top of the driver's helmet. If you cannot arrange yourself to meet this requirement, the race officials will not allow you to drive the car. Even if you manage to sneak onto the racetrack, the corners will call the problem in to Race Control and you will be black-flagged.

If there is any risk that you will be too tall for your rental car, check it out early—like before you sign a contract or fork over any money.

Sometimes you can adjust the gauges to the optimum. Note that the gauges in this GT-3 car are easily visible and have been rotated so that "normal" readings are at the top. All the driver needs to do is to make a quick scan for "all needles vertical." The light at the top center of the "dashboard" is probably an oil pressure warning light.

(The steering wheel has been taken off the hex-shaped hub. The two double gauges on the right show the four individual cylinders' exhaust gas temperatures; these are used for tuning only, so there's no reason to turn them in any particular way.)

INSTRUMENTS

If you are in someone else's car, you will have to live with the instrument positions. In your own car, you should optimize things to the extent the rules allow it.

The standard racing configuration is for gauge needles to point straight up when the reading is in the normal range. This allows a quick scan with little expenditure of brain power. Don't worry about reading the numbers. You are not going to have time. The tach, too, should be rotated so that the redline is straight up.

In some cars, you will be happy to just get the gauges turned so that you can *see* the needles. Do what's necessary.

BELTS AND ARM RESTRAINTS

There are two important considerations in fitting the belts. First, the lap belt must capture your pelvis by going across the hip bone area. It absolutely must *not* ride so high that it ends up cutting into your stomach area above your hip bones. If you think about it for maybe a tenth of a second, you can visualize the damage that would occur from a too-high belt in a collision. Everything between it and the spine gets crushed. If you have any questions about lap belt location, study the drawing in the "Driver's Restraint System" section of the *GCR*.

The second belt-adjustment consideration is helmet clearance. In an open car, there is the 2in clearance rule. In a closed car, you want a reasonable clearance from the roof or you are going to be pounding on your spine with the top of your head in a rollover. Not recommended. While major problems with head clearance must be dealt with through seat modifications, minor clearance increases can be had by pulling yourself down with the shoulder belts.

The fitting sequence is as follows:

1. Seat yourself so that you have enough helmet clearance. (Yes, wear the helmet.) If you find yourself having to slouch quite a bit for clearance, you may have to readjust your seat and controls locations.

2. Establish a lap belt buckle location that ensures proper capture of your pelvis.

3. Set the crotch belt(s) length so that when the crotch belt is pulled tight by the shoulder belts, the lap belt buckle is in the proper position. (The length of the crotch belt establishes the length of the shoulder belts. You loosen the shoulder belts prior to buckling up, then tighten them against the crotch belt when everything is assembled and latched.)

4. Verify the whole mess by hooking up and tightening all the belts. You may have to go through the cycle a couple of times to get things right, especially if the seat is padded.

Don't be too concerned if you cannot fasten and tighten the belts without help. This is pretty common in cramped cockpits—your crew will be available on the grid to help you anyway. (In a pro school situation, you will have a "partner" with whom you share the car. One of the partner's jobs is helping you with your belts.) Make sure, however, that you have no problem *releasing* the belts without help.

If you are buying belts, I strongly recommend the style with lap belt length adjusters next to the buckle. It is a lot easier to hook up with loose belts, and then tighten them. If the adjuster is on the floor, you will be stuck with fixed-length lap belts.

How tight to wear the belts? As tight as you can get them. Their purpose is to keep you from moving around in a crash; any slack creates the risk that you will move far enough to bang into something. Also, the belts keep you from moving around while racing, allowing you to concen-trate on the business at hand rather than on staying in your seat.

Once the belts are right, you can begin on the arm restraints. Your first problem is to anchor the strap ends to your seatbelt buckle without compromising the buckle's quick release. The way you do this will vary with the belt system and the restraints, but test your final assembly order several times to make sure you can get out of the car quickly if you have to.

The length of the arm restraint straps should allow easy steering and shifting, and should allow you to give clear hand signals to overtaking drivers. This latter requirement will usually determine the strap length.

MIRRORS

Sit in the race car and have one of your crew members move around behind you to establish the mirror field of view. In many cars, perhaps a majority, this field of view is inadequate. In your car, it should not be.

It is vitally important that your mirrors enable you to see

Sometimes, like in this Swift, you're lucky to be able to see the gauges. Here, they are turned so that the driver can see the normal needle positions and the tach's redline through the steering wheel. The F and counterclockwise arrow are to remind the driver which way to turn the cockpit brake bias adjustment. Note, too, the T-handle fire system release mounted up high where a corner worker can easily find it. The hitch-pin safety will be removed during final preparations on the grid. It would be less-easily forgotten if the driver had attached a red streamer ribbon to it.

a car that is directly behind you. It is amazing to me how many race cars are delivered with mirrors that cannot accomplish this task. Remedy this problem on your car by moving the mirror mounts farther out, or by putting the mirrors on extensions of some sort.

It is equally important that you be able to see out to the sides so that a competitor cannot be in a "blind quarter." Even though it's theoretically his responsibility as the overtaking car to avoid contact, you do not want to be turning into him because you cannot see him. The first remedy to a blind-spot problem is to move the mirrors farther forward. The second, less desirable, remedy is to use convex mirrors. This latter cure is only slightly less unpleasant than the disease, since it screws up your depth perception. Unfortunately, convex glass is often the only answer.

At the racetrack, you will see some cars with Wink brand multi-panel panoramic mirrors. These cars are driven by racers who understand the value of mirrors and do not care about cosmetics. The Wink design gives almost 180 degrees of rear view using flat, nondistorting glass. They are most common in Production and GT cars, but I have seen them on Sports Racers. In about 1975, I was told by an MG driver that, if I once tried one I would never want to be without it. He was right. I finally tried one and now I've been using them on my street cars ever since. Their consummate ugliness is exceeded only by their effectiveness.

RACING FLAGS

It is important that you, as a beginner, thoroughly understand the flags before you get out on the racetrack. They are the workers' and Operating Stewards' sole means of communicating with you. You will have enough new things to learn without also having to learn the flags the hard way.

It is also important that you learn to *look* for the flag signals. On your first lap at a new track, locate all of the corner stations. From then on, your eyes should check each station as you exit the preceding turn. It's not as hard as it sounds *and* it's important.

The corner workers and flags are the operating stewards' means of communicating with drivers. This mixed-class warmup group is being shown a stationary yellow. Note, too, the medical crew and the tow truck on the far side of the track. Race organizers will often locate emergency vehicles in two or more places on a long racetrack.

The *GCR* states: "The flag signals...shall be obeyed immediately and without question." While experienced drivers may choose to read some equivocation into this statement, you should not.

GREEN

This is the easiest flag; you can even ignore it if you like. It is used to indicate that "the course is open" during practice and qualifying sessions, and to start each race. It is normally displayed only at start-finish.

YELLOW

This is the most important flag, and the one you will see most often. It indicates a hazardous situation ahead and mandates that you "slow down, refrain from passing, and drive with caution." "Slow down" does not mean "nail the brakes." In serious competition, it usually means nothing—unfortunate, but true.

You will normally see a yellow at the corner just before the incident, and sometimes one or two corners before that one as well.

In some stationary yellow situations, the corner will drop the flag after a couple of laps even if the hazard (typically, a parked car that they can't move for some reason) is still there. You are supposed to be smart enough to remember this incident on your own. This allows them to "reuse" the yellow later on. So if you see it again, expect something new.

STATIONARY YELLOW

You will see a stationary (officially, "standing") yellow in a couple of different cases. It usually will mean that there is something happening ahead, but off of the racing surface. For example, something has occurred in the runoff area or at the edge of the track. It may also be displayed for a worker who is in an unprotected area (maybe returning from assisting a driver or moving a car). Finally, it may be displayed to "lead" or "back up" another flag that you will see at the next station, giving you more warning of the situation at that station.

Kathy Maleck: "The SCCA Competition Board is considering adopting FIA flag rules, which differ slightly from our current rules. If you begin crossing borders to run Canadian series or run some professional series later in your career, you will need to be knowledgeable about FIA [Fédération Internationale de l'Automobile] procedures.

"In races where the FIA flagging procedures are used, you will see a stationary yellow used to back up all waving yellows. Additionally, you will see two stationary yellows used to back up a double-waving-yellow situation. At some circuits in the United States, it is standard procedure to back up waving yellows. My best suggestion to drivers visiting tracks that are new to them is to ask about the local procedure."

WAVED YELLOW

A waved yellow is the most serious warning (short of stopping the race) that the corner can give you per the *GCR*. In addition to "slow down," the *GCR* requires that you "prepare to stop." You may arrive at the incident and find the track blocked, a multiple car crash, or worse. There will usually be corner workers exposed to danger.

In addition to the waving yellow, you will often get hand signals from a corner worker to indicate which side of the track is clear. For example, you might be "pushed" over to the outside of the track or "pulled" to the inside. These signals are particularly valuable when the corner is blind.

SERIOUSLY WAVED YELLOW

There is another yellow flag signal, not included in the

GCR, that you will receive from the corner workers. Loosely translated it means, "Waving yellow, no s#@t!" It consists of a corner worker standing on tiptoe waving the yellow high in the air at arms' length, accompanied by one or two other workers who are also waving their arms. This one, you obey. Slow down and prepare to stop, no s#@t! You are almost certainly going to encounter a blocked track, probably with corner workers exposed to serious danger. No "hot lap" or race position is important enough to justify ignoring this flag. It is unambiguous; you will know when you are getting it.

BLUE WITH DIAGONAL YELLOW STRIPE

This is an advisory flag that indicates that you are being followed closely by another car. You are under no regulatory obligation to do anything in particular in response to a blue flag.

As a beginner, this flag is important to you. If you see it and do not already know that someone is on your tail, you have learned the lesson that you are not watching your mirrors enough. If you see it at all, particularly if it is waved, you should give way. You will learn much more by following a faster car than you will when worrying about him running up your tailpipe. Give way as quickly as possible, or he will probably pass you in a place that you wish he wouldn't.

The blue flag's meaning will vary with the flagger's attitude and expertise. Most often, a waved blue flag will mean that you *are* being overtaken.

A furled black flag, displayed with your car number, is a message from the stewards that you have been bad. If you continue to be bad, they will probably pull you in with a full black flag.

YELLOW WITH VERTICAL RED STRIPE

This is the "surface flag," normally called the slippery flag or the oil flag. It is used to indicate a change in track surface condition or deterioration of adhesion. In addition to warning of an oil- or rain-slicked corner, I have seen it used to warn of bodywork pieces, gravel, and even paper on the track. (The latter incident was mine; we left a clipboard on the rear deck of the car. It scattered sheets of paper for about 100 yards when it blew off at speed.)

As a beginner, you should slow down unquestioningly when you see this flag. It *could* be oil, and I can assure you from personal experience that you do not want to hit the oil at speed. It is like hitting ball bearings.

An oil spill and a coolant spill produce indistinguishable sheens on the track; the coolant, however, will be gone in a lap or two if it is on the racing line. The oil will not.

After a couple of laps, the corner will normally drop the slippery flag *whether or not the track is still slippery*. Just as in the case of the stationary yellow, they expect you to be familiar with the corner condition and they would like to have the flag available in case it is needed again.

When you *do* get the flag again, expect something new in addition to the problem you know about.

One additional note: Don't blame the corner workers if you hit an oil patch without warning. The cruel reality is that they do not know that the track is slippery until they see one or two spins. Instead of being angry, just pray that they get the flag up quickly enough to protect *you* from getting hit by the *next* driver who finds the oil.

Kathy Maleck: "At large racetracks, you may encounter a situation where it is raining on some parts while others are dry and possibly sunny. If a flagger displays a surface flag in this case, it is to warn you of the wet turn. If it's raining everywhere, you will not get this flag—you are expected to know that it's slippery."

WHITE

In SCCA racing, a white flag is used to indicate that there is a slow vehicle on the racetrack. It is generally thought of as an emergency vehicle flag, to indicate the presence of an ambulance or a wrecker. Just as often, however, the flag will be used to indicate the presence of a semi-disabled car limping its way to the pits.

The white flag normally will be shown at the two corner stations before you encounter the slow vehicle. Many tracks will display a waving white at the station immediately before the vehicle.

(Note: White flag or no, it is stupid to be driving your limping car to the pits or to be limping around the track to get "a finish." It is dangerous for you and for the others on the racetrack. Pull it safely off-course and wait to be flat-towed at the end of the session.)

The white flag is advisory only. You are instructed to "take care." Every year in our driver school we have some novice who forgets this and pulls in behind the fire truck or wrecker, holding the entire field behind him in a confused jumble. Pass the moving obstacle safely but expeditiously. It is in everybody's best interest.

(In oval-track racing, the white flag means something totally different. If you don't already know what this is, don't bother to find out. It will just confuse you.)

FURLED BLACK

The message behind the furled black flag is that you have done something bad. If you do it again, or if you do something else bad, you will get a stationary black flag with your car number showing on a number board. The furled black is normally given from the flagging bridge at the start-finish line.

Start-finish may also be the location of the "black flag station" where the flags described below are given. More likely, however, the black flag station will be located somewhere near the last turn before the pit entrance. This allows black-flagged cars to enter the pits without taking an extra lap.

Black Displayed with Car Number

When the black flag is shown with your car number next to it on a chalkboard or pit signal board, you have drawn the personal attention of the Operating Stewards. You have done something bad enough that the Operating Stewards would like to talk to you about it, right now. This is an immediate, large, time penalty. In a race, it amounts to a death sentence. The Stewards, it is said, speak slowly when discussing your transgression and they cover the subject in great depth. (I don't have any firsthand experience, fortunately. You do not want this experience, either.)

Black Displayed with "All" Sign

This signal means that the race has been stopped, at least temporarily, and that all cars are to report to the pits. I have seen it used when a hard rainstorm surprised a track full of cars on slicks. I have also seen it used when it was necessary to protect workers during the clearing of a bad accident.

Normally, a black-all situation includes stationary yellow flags at all corner stations. Thus if you see a couple of yellows on corners, but no incidents, you should expect an "all" at the black flag station.

When the race is restarted following a "black-all," the cars will be re-gridded according to their positions *prior to* the flag being shown. This means that it does you no good to pass anyone on your way to the pits. Settle down, keep your wits about you, and drive carefully. This is a confusing situation, particularly because there are always a few who miss the signal, and confusing situations are always dangerous.

Black with Orange Ball in Center

Fondly referred to by all as "the meatball," this flag is al-

ways displayed with a car number board. It indicates that the officials have detected a mechanical problem with the car and that it poses a danger to its driver and/or to other competitors. The workers do not throw this flag unless the situation is unequivocal. Typical problems include pieces of the car about to come off (such as bodywork or exhausts), streams of oil or water, and engine fires. (If you're driving a mid-engine car, you may well not *know* if there's a fire.) If you get the meatball, take it seriously and proceed to your pits "at reduced speed" per the *GCR*.

Red

The race has been stopped, usually because of a highly dangerous incident somewhere on the track. Stop as quickly as you can without creating an unsafe situation. When you see this flag, do not immediately nail the brakes; others behind you may not react as quickly. Slow down, pull to the side of the track, and stop safely. If you have to pass one or two stopped or slowing cars to accomplish this, no one will criticize you for it. Shut down your engine, but stay in your car until you receive instructions from a worker. It will probably be a while.

Kathy Maleck: "Part of the red flag procedure calls for the corners to display stationary black flags. If you encounter black flags on stations other than the black flag station, it is your indication that the session has been stopped

Here's the meatball. It means that something is seriously wrong with your car. Report to the pits. Note here that the flaggers are quite close to the track. They may not be quite this close during competition, but they will be easy to see.

*Here's the full black flag signal indicating that you have been **very** bad. Report to the pits immediately. Note that this signal is not easy to see. Some track layouts put the flaggers quite a ways from the edge. Nevertheless, it is your responsibility to watch for signals.*

and that there will be a red flag at start-finish. In this situation, you are instructed to stop racing immediately and proceed with extreme caution around the track to your pits or until you see a red flag."

After making the decision to stop the race, the main differentiator (for the operating Steward) between a "red" and a "black-all" situation is whether or not it is safe for cars to continue past the incident to the pits. (Getting everybody together in the pits is obviously preferable from a logistics standpoint.) He or she may choose to restart the race in either case.

CHECKERED

The race or session is over. Proceed around the track for a cool-off lap (unless otherwise instructed by local rules—read the Supps), go into the pits and, from there, back to your paddock spot. On the road from the pits to the paddock, you may encounter a tech worker directing you to the scales or (after a race) to Impound. Obey instructions.

YOUR FIRST LAPS

The feeling of being alone in the car for the first time is probably different for each of us. Sitting in your chair, reading this book, you may not believe that a twinge of fear is involved. It is. But it will disappear when you get busy on the racetrack.

PRE-GRID

Before the session, you should run through a checklist that includes warming up the car. Let it idle long enough to bring the water temperature up to its normal operating range before taking it to the pre-grid.

(In every paddock, you will hear people "warming" their engines from a cold start by repeatedly running them up to redline: vroom...vroom...vroom. These are people who are trying to ruin their bearings. High rpm with cold parts and fluids is not a good combination. Warm *your* engine by letting it sit at a fast idle.)

Charlie Williams: "Always warm up the engine before you go to the grid. It's like running a foot race. You need to warm up before you go flat out. Fire up the engine, *immediately* look to be sure you have oil pressure, then idle it at a medium speed.

"You need to bring up the rpm enough that the oil will splash around onto the parts that are not pressure-oiled: cylinder walls, cams, and tappets. Slow idling is hard on the cam.

"Don't get carried away; an unloaded engine does not like high rpm."

When you get the five-minute warning, get into the car and get strapped in. Start the car soon enough so that the engine water temperature gets up to normal prior to going out.

GOING OUT

When you enter the track, remember that the car is basically cold. Although the water temperature is OK, the oil in the engine, the transmission, and the rear end is cold and needs to be warmed up before it is seriously put to work. The same is true of the brakes and tires.

Spend the first lap warming up the car, not trying to go fast. Pitch it back and forth until you feel the tires heating up. Brake early and long for the first few corners until you feel the brakes beginning to work. Accelerate hard, but shift

500rpm early until the engine oil temperature comes up. (You can tell that the oil is hot when the oil pressure drops into its normal range.)

There are always a few people who go charging out, everything cold, and try to set a lap record. Stay away from them. Their poor judgment probably extends to traffic situations as well. Run your own laps, your way, and don't let their behavior change your plans.

RECONNOITERING

The first lap is also the time to check out the racetrack. Take care to locate the corner stations, off-track hazards, and runoff areas.

Look carefully, too, for evidence of oil-dry or gravel in the corners. (Oil-dry is a gray-beige granular substance used to absorb spills. It appears to be the same stuff as cat litter.) In either case, you will have to be careful until a few laps of traffic have cleared the racing line. In cases where there is *a lot* of oil on the track, you may be verbally warned on the grid or warned with an oil flag. Don't count on this, however.

FIRST LESSON

Once you've carefully surveyed the track, it's time to work on operating the car. Depending on how different your race car is from your street car, this may take a while. Work on getting the feel of the car: the way the brakes work as the pads get to operating temperature, the feel of the tires as they heat. Get used to the noises—racing gearboxes, in particular, are quite noisy.

All the time you're doing this, watch your mirrors carefully. Your first lap will almost certainly be a "no-passing" first session at a school; this is the easiest time to develop your mirror technique. There will almost certainly be a few cars in view, but you won't have to worry about actually being passed. If you have convex mirrors, work especially on depth perception.

Next, begin working on your downshifting and braking. Don't worry about speed; just work on the drill until it begins to feel comfortable to you. Speed in downshifting will come automatically, and you will be hitting the brakes fast enough due to adrenaline alone!

As you become comfortable in the car, shift your attention to driving smoothly: smooth braking, smooth turn-ins, smooth exits. Pick your cornering lines and work on repeating them every lap within inches. Explore the edges of the track with your tires until you develop a good sense of the width of the car. If it feels like things are happening too quickly, shift your eyepoints farther ahead of the car.

That's it! From here on in your career, smoothness is your objective. Everything else is secondary. With smoothness will come consistency, with consistency will come the ability to conduct experiments at the limit, and with the experiments will come the speed.

As you progress through your school, watch your lap times. If they are consistent, you will find that they are also trending downward. If they are erratic, you are trying to go too fast, too soon, and you are not going to be learning much besides how to catch spins. So back off, slow down, and work on smoothness.

Chapter 5

Your First Race

FALSE GRID AND GRID

Get to the false grid early, then relax. Walk around, stand in the shade, whatever. Keep a close eye on the clock, however. If the day's activities are running behind schedule (which is normal), the officials will be trying to flag your group off as quickly as possible. Talk to the grid communicator (with the headset) to see how much track-clearing activity will be required when the current session ends.

Let one of your crew drive the car to the grid; it's a small treat. Have the crew take care of bringing your helmet, the starting battery if you use one, plus some race tape and a few tools. At least one of your crew people should stay with you to help with the belts and to help with any problems. You might want to send one or more of the others to the pits—pit locations are usually first-come, first-served.

You should be in your car about the time you get a 5-minute warning. Get settled in the car, belts fastened and ready to go as soon as you hear the warning. Although in theory the warning indicates that it's 5 minutes until flag-off, in practice it differs. The 5-minute warning means that you

will get a 1-minute warning *sometime in the next 4 minutes.* If the day is behind schedule and the previous session didn't result in a lot of track-clearing activity, the 1-minute warning can come quickly.

The pit communicator, recognizable here by her headset, can give your crew information on what's happening on the track. This is particularly useful when you have gone missing. The grid communicator, similarly equipped, is a good source of information on when your group might be flagged off.

The false grid for a Formula Ford race. The crews are making final psychological adjustments to their drivers before the cars are sent onto the track.

If it's a hot day, you should consider packing your suit with ice. A few handfuls of ice in your front pockets, and some more poured into your crotch area and down your neck after you're seated, will make a *big* difference in your performance. Some drivers pack their suits with a few of the "gel" freeze packs; that's probably fine, but I'm not sure that I would want some unknown gel substance mixed with my blood in the unlikely event of a bad crash.

Don't start your engine too early. Sitting on the false grid will be followed by sitting on the track. If you don't have a radiator fan, this can lead to overheating.

As the 1-minute warning is given, the grid marshal at the front will hold up his arm, fist clenched. He is asking you to do the same to indicate that your engine is running. If your engine is *not* running, make some gesture of desperation that can be seen by the grid marshal *and* by the car behind you.

Almost instantly following the 1-minute warning, you will be waved onto the track. There will be a grid marshal there to signal you to the left or the right. Go where you're told, not where you think you should go based on your grid position. It's quite normal for someone ahead of you to be missing from the grid, causing the left-right order to change.

(Sometimes, a car is missing from the grid because of mechanical problems. More often, though, the car is just late. This is a stupid way to throw away a qualifying position. Don't be stupid. Checklist your car immediately after each session, not immediately before you need to take it to the false grid. Find the problems while you have time to fix them. Yes, that means checklisting the car on Saturday night, before the beer party.)

When the grid is complete, the starter will hold up his arm, fist clenched, and point his furled flag at each driver in turn. Same drill; let him and the drivers behind you know that you are running. Or not.

At this point, the grid will be flagged off for the pace lap.

PACE LAP

The purpose of the pace lap is to get you and the car ready for the race. *You* get ready by watching the track carefully, looking for patches of oil-dry, dirt, or gravel on the track, slippery flags at corners, and so on. Once in a while, there will even be a race car left somewhere off-course after the previous session. Now is the time to assimilate all this information.

Carroll Smith: "In Europe, it's known as the 'reconnaissance lap'—correct nomenclature."

The *car* gets ready for the race by warming up water, oil, and brake pads. Water and oil take care of themselves; you must warm the pads by left-foot braking or making a few

Formula Atlantic grid just about ready to go. The Starter (behind the pace car) is pointing at each driver in turn to make sure all engines are running. The grid worker (at right, in white) is waving the last of the straggler crew members off of the grid. In a few seconds, the Starter will signal the pace car and release the cars. This situation is a bit unusual, as the grid has been formed in the pit area.

The Starter, standing at the front of the grid, releases the pace car and then signals the race cars to go.

Here's another grid, this time Spec Racers, a few seconds later in the release process. The pace car is on its way down the track and the starter is signaling the cars to go, too. Here, the grid is being started on the track itself.

hard applications. When you want to do some hard braking, accelerate first, then brake. This reduces the likelihood that you'll be hit from behind. If you're running racing tires, they need warming as well. Warm them with some hard zig-zagging, watching traffic. Be careful, though, cold tires don't stick. I once saw a "hotdog" driver zag right into a ditch full of water!

(Street rubber warming is problematical. A few years ago, you did not need to warm street tires. In fact, the main concern was overheating them. The current generation of "racing" street rubber does need varying degrees of warming and is less sensitive to overheating. Consult the manufacturer and/or other drivers who are running the same kind of tires.)

The first part of the pace lap is usually fairly fast. Don't worry about staying in picture-perfect grid position during this segment of the lap. But watch for sudden slowdowns ahead. When you must slow suddenly, put your hand in the air (fist closed) to signal those behind you. Watch for raised arms ahead.

The pace car or pole car will slow the grid on the straight before the last corner. This is the time to get into grid position. Check to make sure you're in the right gear, and take a final look at your gauges. Don't forget the gear check. Things are noisy and adrenaline is high; starting in the wrong gear is fairly common. And discouraging.

THE START

The start is the most dangerous moment of the weekend. The cars are crowded together, adrenaline is running high, and every driver is trying to get a better start than the others. This involves getting on the gas somewhat before the green flag is waved.

The danger increases toward the back of the grid, peaking a few rows from the back. The reason that starts are so dangerous is that start-jumping tactics become increasingly blatant as you go back in the grid, farther from the starter's eye. The guys in the back row can get away with almost anything.

Thus, the pack is becoming compressed as the leaders

approach the starter. The front rows are, necessarily, being relatively well behaved. The back rows have been on the gas since the last corner.

The worst case happens when the pack gets a no-start and the leaders do not have the good sense to speed up anyway. Even when the green is thrown, however, the speed differential between the front and the back has to get resolved somehow. Be aware of this, be careful, and good luck!

Carroll Smith: "First, no matter *how bad* the lineup looks, *always* be ready for a green flag when approaching start-finish. And second, watch the starter in the races prior to yours. The good ones are consistent about how they throw the green."

Author comment: "Watching the starter can't hurt, but be aware that they rotate the job on club weekends. Your race may not necessarily be flagged off by the starter you observed so carefully."

You can get a few extra horsepower at the start by using the momentum of your flywheel. Leaving the last turn, push down the clutch, and rev the engine to redline, holding it there with your right foot. Maintain your desired grid position by slightly releasing the clutch, then coasting, repeating the process as necessary. It feels jerky, but that's OK. Do *not* constantly slip the clutch; you'll cook it. When the starter has

The starter will not flag off this race group due to the number of cars being out of position. Note that the second row outside (left side) car is about to overtake the outside pole car, plus there are three cars out of line to the left.

88

made his decision (or you have made yours), release the clutch and nail the gas. The energy stored up in the flywheel will give you a satisfying boost.

THE FIRST TURN

Your principal objective in the first few turns is survival. There is not a lot to be said besides that. Watch your mirrors, make no sudden moves. You can't win a race in the first turn, but you can lose it. It is done every race weekend.

Be especially aware if a fast car has had to start at the back of the grid for some reason. He will be trying frantically to move up to the lead pack before they get away, and he will probably have made an aggressive start. I once had to start at the back and had already passed two rows when the green flag dropped. (The situation here is that, at the back, one has little reason to fear the black flag.)

If the first turn is fairly close to the starter's stand, remember that you won't be going into it as fast as if you had been accelerating since entering the straight. Thus, your first-lap brake point will be farther down the track.

THE REST OF THE RACE

Within a lap or two, the field will begin separating and you will have an idea of how your race will go. The front pack will probably have left without you; the first-lap crashes and spins hopefully will have occurred without your participation.

You will be either running in a pack or running alone. Signals from your crew are especially important when you are running alone. You do not want lap times shown to you on your pit board. Lap times are virtually meaningless. You want your crew to be giving you information on how your position is changing.

If you are gaining on the car (or pack) ahead of you, they should show you lag times (seconds) preceded by a minus sign. Two or three laps will show you the promising trend; some arithmetic will tell you whether you have a hope of catching him, her, or them before the race is over. (For example, if you're 10 seconds behind, gaining 2 seconds per lap, with seven laps to go, you're in reasonable shape. With five laps to go, you'd better hustle.)

If the car or pack behind you is gaining on you, your crew should show you lead times, preceded by a plus sign. Again, project the ominous trend to determine if you are really threatened.

Ideally, a pit board should show both times, but this is rarely done.

In the majority of cases, you will be shown a lap counter from the flagging bridge at start-finish. If yours is the first race of the weekend, take the time to verify (by talking to

The same SR grid, coming around for the second try after the waveoff. This time, they got the green. Some of the same sins are in the process of being committed, though to a somewhat lesser degree.

The grid that got the no-start, as they went past the start-finish line. You can see that the grid is shorter and wider than before. That's due to the higher-speed cars in the back running up into the front cars. Because of this compression, a no-start is a dangerous situation anywhere behind the front row. Beware.

Don't try to win the race in the first turn of the first lap. Things will be crowded and a small mistake can cause big trouble. It appears here that car #41 is about to come down on car #15. Number 15 will probably have to back off a bit. Brian Nooney

If you get to carry a checkered flag around the track for a parade lap, hold it in the middle with most of the cloth wrapped around the stick. It can be damned hard to hold onto in a 50 or 75mph wind. This Super Vee is an ex-pro series car; it runs in SCCA's Formula Atlantic class. Bruce Hanson

a starter or a Steward) that this will be done. Otherwise, just check the bridge during the first race. If you will not be getting a lap count, then you should arrange to get a count from your crew. This is important enough to your race strategy that it should take precedence over position and time signals during the last few laps. Ideally, your pit board will be able to show both laps-remaining (not laps-raced!) and lead or lag time.

Your driving should change depending on whether you are threatening, threatened, or neither. Drive hard when it can affect the result. Remember, though, that there's no point driving at ten-tenths if you have no hope of a reward from it.

When you are running in a pack and cannot get cleanly away, pit wall signals are less important. It is important, however, to understand that *you do not want to be dicing with other members of the pack until the last lap or two.* The reason for this is that dicing slows everybody down. People will catch up to you and you will not catch up to anyone. The number of drivers who do not understand this is astonishing.

Tony Kester: "It amazes me how many drivers would rather fight for sixth place than work with someone to catch the leaders. Two cars, driven wisely, are usually faster than one, and they are definitely faster than a pack of five cars dicing for the lead.

"Sure, you'll help the other guy too, but it's better to be in a seven-car battle for the lead than a two-car scrap over sixth."

A few drafting passes on the straight is not dicing; it is a good technique to speed everyone up. If you are faster on the straight and are running with someone who is slightly faster in the back, be sure to arrange things so that your competitor leads in the back. You'll both go faster.

While running in the pack, study your competition carefully. Brake points, corners where they hold you up a bit, horsepower, everything. Plan your last lap tactics. You can be damned sure they are planning theirs.

Another reason to avoid dicing is that tricks only work once. If you late brake a competitor three laps from the end, you can expect to be blocked on the last lap. And so on.

Lapping backmarkers can be a problem or a blessing. For the race leader, they're primarily a problem. He is the messenger bringing them word that the lead pack is coming. They are not expecting him; he has to push by them as fast as possible. It is not fun for either party.

Getting lucky with the backmarkers is one of the easiest ways to break out of a pack. Watch for opportunities to use the backmarkers as mobile obstacles in the way of your competition.

Early in your career, you are more likely to be getting lapped than you are to be doing the lapping. If you suspect that this will happen, use the qualifying time differentials to estimate the lap when it will begin. For example, if you are 6 seconds off the leader and you expect to be doing 1:20s, you can plan to be passed between lap nine and lap eleven. (Nine laps times 1:20 equals ten laps times 1:14, but he won't be running his qualifying time every lap.) Be ready, watch your mirrors, and make it your objective to be as out-of-the-way as possible. The leader will not be at all polite when he comes by.

Once the leader has come by, you can expect several more impolite encounters. Watch your mirrors, drive smooth

Things like this happen, often on the first turn of the first lap. Here, the driver of the spun Formula Ford is evaluating the evasion skills of his buddies. Jim Casey

These three Formula Vees and the Formula 440 are being held in Impound following their race. The stewards tell the tech guys how many cars to hold; it's usually the top three or four finishers.

and consistent lines, don't do *anything* suddenly, and signal people by wherever possible. Again, point where you want them to go—not where *you're* going. You are not racing with these guys and you are likely to get bunted into the weeds if you behave as if you are.

APRES CHECKERED

The old no-sudden-moves rule applies to the cool-off lap. When you go under the checkered, you can slow down a bit but don't hit the brakes. As you go around on the cool-off lap, wave gratefully to the corner workers. You need them more than they need you.

Remember to keep at least some of your concentration until you get off the racetrack. It's surprisingly easy to get into a corner too fast when you're loafing down the straight and don't feel as if you need to brake. Spinning on the cool-off lap is (1) not uncommon, and (2) highly embarrassing.

In the happy event that you get to carry a checkered flag around the track, be aware that it is damned hard to hold onto in a 30–50mph wind. Don't unfurl it all the way and grab it somewhere in the middle of the stick.

You will usually be weighed immediately after you leave the track. In some classes, the car is weighed without the driver. In others, the weight limit is specified to include the driver. If you get weighed with the car, it doesn't hurt to be drinking from a large jar of Gatorade. Don't forget to have your helmet with you.

At some tracks, they weigh your front wheels and rear wheels separately using one pair of platform scales. In these cases, it also doesn't hurt to stand in the cockpit and subtly shift your weight toward the end of the car being weighed. Don't worry about the corner weights indicated by the track scales. They are always goofy.

If you win (or finish in the top three or four), you will probably be required to leave your car in Impound. Impound is simply a place where the tech inspectors can keep an eye on your car until the Chief Steward tells them that they don't have to do so anymore. Normally, cars are held until the half-hour protest period has expired.

Norma Williams: "Always check the grid results and the posted lap chart as soon as they are available after your race or session. T&S does make errors once in a while and you have only 30 minutes to detect and protest any discrepancies."

MESSING WITH THE CAR

Immediately after your first race, you will be unhappy with your car's performance. This will be true whether it is a pro school car, a rental, or your own equipment.

Here is where driving a pro school car or a rental is a real pedagogical advantage. The car owner will not allow you to begin "improving" the car's performance by changing carburetor jets, alignment, or by beginning a major modification campaign.

Do not do these things to your own car, either.

During your first year, the vast majority of potential improvement is in your personal skills. If you have extra time and money to commit to the racing program, spend it on additional training or on more track time. Do not waste it on the car. You are probably a novice at car preparation as well; you are as likely to slow the car down as you are to speed it up. And you will not be able to tell the difference because your driving performance will be inconsistent enough to mask any small changes in the car's performance.

During your first year, the only sensible improvements for your car are reliability related. If it's not able to give you the track time you need, spend some time fixing it. Otherwise, leave it alone.

Chapter 6

Intermediate Driving Techniques

After you have run a couple of schools and a race or two, you will begin to suspect that it's a bit different out there than you might conclude from reading the SCCA's *General Competition Rules*. It is. Here are some useful things to know, but *don't try to use them* until you've gotten some basic seat time.

THE FLAGS—IN REALITY

One of the major differences between the real world and the *GCR* is in the way drivers react to the flags. The bottom line on flags is that we drivers take chances for ourselves (and increase others' risks) more than we ought to and more than the *GCR* permits.

Before we talk about the flags, let's talk about the Operating Steward and how he or she manages them. The flags are the Steward's only means of communicating with you. In deciding what to tell you, the Steward must consider not only the current situation, but also the fact that things might get worse. This means that the Steward will order the "minimum" flag, not the "maximum." He or she will also try to "reduce" the flag situation quickly, taking a corner from waving yellow to stationary yellow, for example. This is also why stationary yellows and slippery flags are dropped even when the cause is still present.

If you remember the operating Steward's flag management problem, it will help you understand what he or she is telling you.

There's no rule that says you will only get one flag at a time. Here's a slippery flag displayed with a blue one. Often, you will get a yellow or a waving yellow together with the slippery flag.

Now let's talk about the reality of the flags:

YELLOW

The truth is that there is little or no slowing down for yellow flags, whether stationary or waved. The no-passing restriction is observed fairly well, though, because we all know that the Steward also possesses the dreaded black flag.

The reality of drivers' yellow-flag response is the reason that the corners have instituted the unsanctioned "waving yellow, no s#@t!" variation. We all take that one seriously.

Kathy Maleck: "As a long-time worker, I can guarantee you that weakly waved flags don't get the response that arm-breaking yellows do. I have found it interesting that drivers can actually see workers' facial expressions at some stations and will respond to the flags accordingly. We will get theatrical to get our point across.

"You will also see workers using arm motions to slow you down or to direct you around dangerous situations. Pay attention; we're not doing it for exercise! We're motioning to give you a clearer picture of what you can expect around the corner.

"Under FIA procedures, there is a degree of yellow that is higher than the waved yellow. It consists of two waving yellow flags, always backed up by a double standing yellow at the preceding station. The double waving yellow indicates extreme hazard such as almost-complete track blockage. My personal feeling is that additional degree of yellow tells drivers clearly that it is a no s#@t situation and that the procedure should be adopted by SCCA. Stay tuned."

BLUE WITH YELLOW STRIPE

Generally ignored, this is the only flag that a corner worker can throw without instructions from the corner captain. The worker has come to the track to flag; guess which flag gets used? It is not uncommon for you to be in a dice for a whole race, with one corner religiously advising you of your situation each time you come around.

As mentioned previously, however, beginners should take this flag quite seriously. You are going to be getting passed a lot and, regardless of who is theoretically at fault per the *GCR*, you are going to be paying for your own crash damage.

Kathy Maleck: "If a flagger shows the blue more than once to a group that is racing or dicing together, he or she isn't paying attention or doesn't know what the flag is intended to do for you. If you do latch onto a station with an alert blue flagger who knows where you are in the pack,

you can trust him or her to let you know when you may be overtaken, as well as letting others know when you are overtaking.

"When working [as a flagger at] a street race or Formula One, you learn appreciation and respect for the blue flag. You, as the flagger, must be trustworthy. Patrick Tambay told me: 'If we could teach the flaggers one thing it would be that when you are a blue flagger, you belong to the drivers, not to the corner crew. You must learn to concentrate and to talk to the drivers as if you were there with them in the cockpit.'

"It's true; when you concentrate as a flagger you can be trusted and the line of communication to the drivers is open and clear. Unfortunately, it's not always this way. Drivers must get a feel (corner-by-corner) for who is 'just throwing flags' and who has something to tell them."

WHITE

Realistically, the white flag has no perceptible effect on experienced racers.

BLACK

Every month, *Sports Car* prints copies of appeals from drivers who have ignored the black flag and received painful punishment, such as license suspension. Invariably, the Appeals Court upholds the conviction.

If you get a black flag, you might as well obey it. Things will only get worse if you don't.

You should also pay attention to the furled black. Stop doing whatever you did to cause it. Over the past few years there has been a trend toward using the furled black, followed by a Steward's Request for Action after the race. This means that you may be called to explain your behavior to the Stewards of the Meeting and to receive whatever penalty they deem appropriate. The reason for using this method is that black-flagging a driver in a club-length race is effectively a death penalty. If the black is given due to some misunderstanding, there is no reversing its effects.

Finally, be aware that it is possible to get a black-all or a red during the first lap of a race. A bad tangle at the rear of the grid can leave the track blocked. With all of the excitement, tension, and close racing that occurs on the first lap, it's hard to remember to look at the flag stations. Try to do so anyway.

Kathy Maleck: "'The green comes out,...the first lap is under way,...no time for seeing flags now!' Wrong! At Brainerd during a regional race with combined groups of Formula Everything and assorted Sports Racers, we had a start where the front group took off like rabbits in heat. At the back, however, things didn't sort out so neatly—causing a fair amount of carnage at the point where the last turn exits onto the straightaway. The red flag came out immediately, as did black flags on all stations. The lead pack, however, wasn't watching or didn't see and raced all the way around the track [3 miles!] and almost into the incident.

"Try to see through the red mist of first-lap excitement. A green flag at the start is no guarantee that things will stay that way."

YELLOW WITH VERTICAL RED STRIPE

Drivers' reactions to this flag vary. The majority of National-level drivers seem to react by looking carefully at the track surface while keeping their right foot to the floor. Those of us who have crashed as a result of spilled oil tend to lift a bit and get passed by those who do not. The odds favor keeping your foot in it, but the downside is significant.

As you build experience, you will find yourself making judgments about the slippery flag. On a fast qualifying lap or

in the race, you may simply look ahead and keep your foot in it.

If you are in a hurry, look carefully at the track surface for a sheen and at the location and width of the sheen—narrow is more likely to be oil, wide is apt to be coolant. Is it on the racing line or off it? Look far ahead to see if the flag might be for gravel or debris. Look at the cars in the next corner to see if they are having trouble (spinning and crashing into each other, for instance). These observations should give you a clue as to conditions.

Then make your own decision. Early in your career, I'd suggest being conservative in reacting to the slippery flag.

RED

This flag is seen so seldom in actual race situations that driver reaction is unpredictable. This unpredictability is complicated by the fact that the "old" red flag rule called for the cars to proceed to the pits. A major pit incident in the mid-1980s caused the rule to be changed; red-flagged cars were driving right into danger.

When you get the red, realize that the race is over. If it is restarted, the Chief Steward will grid you according to Timing and Scoring's lap chart for the last completed racing lap, not according to whatever positions you try to steal from drivers who have pulled off and stopped. You might as well stop, too.

Tony Kester: "Do *not* immediately slam on the brakes! Remember that there might be someone with his nose stuck up your Hewland who can't even *see* the red flag. Raise your hand, slow down, and pull over when your rear is clear."

CHECKERED

Not a lot to be said here. Unwritten race etiquette says that you do not pass anybody after the checkered. The corner workers and spectators like to know who finished where.

SOMETIMES IT RAINS

Nobody truly likes rain, but it has a great equalizing effect among cars. It is not uncommon for a "slow" car to win

Sometimes it's hard to decide whether it will be raining or dry for the race. Here, the driver has two rains and two drys on the car. This makes some last-minute work inevitable, but cuts the work time in half. His pole-barn parking place is a real luxury in the rain.

Some of our racetracks are dual-purpose facilities, running drag races down the main straight. Be careful of these areas in the rain, they get viciously slippery and the car will spin if you get on the gas too aggressively. This FA car is finding out the hard way, spinning at 80–100mph. He spun another 180 degrees before hitting the wall, tearing off one corner and crunching another.

a rain race because the driver was able to get consistently closer to the edge of the performance cliff without falling off. As a novice driver, I suggest that you pray for a dry school or two. It's inevitable, though, that you will eventually get wet, so here are some tips.

GETTING READY FOR RAIN

Putting air in the rain tires seems to reduce the likelihood that you will actually have to use them. Thus, you want to do it early. The other reason you want to do it early is that there will be a long line at the air hose as the session draws near.

If you're sure it will be raining for your race, you may want to drop your gear ratios a bit, especially first gear. Cornering speeds are much slower in the rain than in the dry. Until you get to the point of wheelspin, shorter gears will help get you off the corners faster. Depending on the track and the weather, top speed may not be much different however, so don't do anything drastic to top gear.

It is also a good idea to unhook the car's sway bars or to set them to full soft. The rationale for this is that the car will not be cornering hard enough to produce significant body roll, so we might as well eliminate the *negative* effect of sway bars: the coupling of left and right side wheels in bumps.

Carroll Smith: "With modern-concept pure racing cars, you don't have to unhook the sway bars. But soften the shocks. Lots! Especially in bump."

The brake bias should be reset to its rain setting, if you have one. In the rain, much less front bias is required because less forward weight transfer occurs under braking.

There are various tricks and magic potions used to eliminate visor and glasses fogging in the rain. None have ever worked for me.

If you're driving an open car and decide to drill some visor holes for ventilation, be aware that the sandblast effects seen on your front bodywork will also occur in miniature inside your helmet. You should somehow prevent the sand from hitting your skin. Drill small holes at a sharp angle, drill them low enough so that the sand hits your balaclava, and so on.

Dry your shoe soles and the car pedals as much as you can before getting into the car. The pedal surfaces should already have been made skid resistant by the car manufacturer or, if they have not done it, by you. You do not want your foot slipping off the brake pedal.

RUNNING IN THE RAIN

Racing in the rain is a series of drag races between the corners. You go as fast as you can, brake as late as you dare, almost stop the car, turn it to point down the next straight, and begin the cycle again.

The normal dry cornering line is usually a bad choice. It's the smoothest part of the track. Just as you want slick tires in the dry and treaded ones in the wet, you want a rougher track in the wet. Even the sand and gravel, enemy in the dry, can be your friend in the wet. Experiment off of your normal lines.

Tony Kester: "When you're walking the track, slide your feet across the pavement, testing the surface. It will be immediately apparent how smooth the track is on the line. Drive on the rest of the track in the rain."

Unless it's pouring, it takes quite a while to really soak a track. It's not immediately necessary to slow down when you spot some raindrops on your visor (or windshield). If you do, in fact, you'll probably be passed by many people. Raindrops are simply a warning that things will be getting slippery.

When it starts to rain, it often doesn't start to rain everywhere on the track. This is important to remember on an inclement day. Watch for slippery (red/yellow) flags, and watch for spinning cars. One of the worst crashes in recent memory occurred at the Runoffs a few years ago when almost the entire GT-1 field encountered a downpour on a section of an otherwise dry track.

When judging how hard it's raining, remember that the amount of rain hitting you depends on your speed. In an even rain, at 150mph on the straight, you're hitting twice as much rain as you are at 75mph in the back. This makes it hard to judge which parts of the track might be wet and slippery and which might still be quite dry.

Be careful of your racing rain tires when it's not that wet; they will overheat and leave you sliding hopelessly. Driving deliberately through the puddles may help a bit. Those on street tires (who only have to choose tread depth) are under a lot less pressure when the sky is ambiguous.

Be careful, too, about driving one pair of wheels (right side or left side) through puddles at high speed, regardless of what kind of tires you have. The lopsided drag will cause the car to turn toward the puddle side, possibly causing a spin. There is a low spot on the main straight at Elkhart that has come close to putting me into the weeds.

Another caution: Many of our racetracks are also used for drag racing. At these tracks, you will find a lot of painted asphalt and a lot of left-over drag rubber at the beginning or the end of the main straight. Both the paint and the rubber get viciously slippery when wet.

UNPLANNED EVENTS

As they say in the Boy Scouts, "Be prepared."

ON THE POLE?

First of all, congratulations! It's unusual for a new driver to be the fastest in his or her group. It may have been pure luck or a small field, but relax and enjoy it anyway.

According to the *GCR*, the pole sitter has the choice of front-row position. In virtually all cases, you want the right-side slot in order to be on the inside at the first corner. As we discussed when we talked about passing, the inside car controls the corner. And you are quite likely to be side-by-side with the outside pole car when you get to that corner.

PACING THE FIELD

It can be a bit intimidating to contemplate the fact that it will be *you* who is leading a pack of twenty to sixty adrenaline-charged lunatics (at least that's how your mother would see it!) to the green flag. In reality, it's not that bad.

When you are parked on the grid, one of the starters will come to you with some instructions. Usually, these are not very illuminating: "Keep it clean, don't go too fast...." You may be tempted to talk to the outside pole driver to agree on how you will handle things. Don't bother; he will assume that you are trying to trick him. And you should be. The racing begins when you can arrange an advantage of any sort, even psychological.

If there is a pace car, it will control the overall speed of the field. Regardless, it is your responsibility to maintain a steady average speed. You can execute a few dart-forward-and-brake maneuvers to heat your brakes, but it is preferable to just left-foot brake against the throttle. If you, as pole car, are driving at an erratic pace, the variation will be amplified farther back in the grid...and the drivers in the back will not be having any fun at all.

As you approach the last turn, slow down slightly (fist in the air!) to allow the grid to form. Watch your mirrors to see this happen, then accelerate slightly through the turn and onto the straight.

GETTING THE GREEN

Except for the fact that you are in front, being on the pole has few advantages. You are immediately under the eyes of the starter and it is difficult to get away with anything. So make the best of it. You can at least use the old revved-up flywheel trick.

GETTING A NO-START

Sometimes the starter will not give you the green. Theoretically, this happens whenever he or she sees that the grid is not "well-formed" per the *GCR*. In practice, this decision is also affected by whether the day's events are running on time or not. There are fewer wave-offs when things are behind schedule.

When the starter decides to give you a no-start, you are supposed to get an exaggerated "no" head shaking from side to side. This is fairly easy to see from the front of the pack, but not from the back.

Tony Kester: "If you're on the front row, never, ever lift until you're *absolutely sure* that the race will *not* be started."

A while back, we talked about the fact that the grid becomes compressed as it approaches the starter's stand. This is because the drivers in back have been on the gas since the last corner and the drivers in front (notably you!) have had to be well-behaved.

In a no-start, it is your responsibility to help sort this out by *accelerating* as you go under the starting bridge. Not enough acceleration that people will think you're racing, but enough acceleration to improve the pack's chances of sorting itself out safely. Do not, under any circumstances, slow down when you get a no-start and you are on the pole.

After the no-start, you simply take the field around the track again. This lap is usually taken faster than the first one, mostly because of the adrenaline factor. You are almost cer-

tain to get a green on the second try (there's a racing schedule to maintain, after all). Everybody in the field knows this, so you had better watch your mirrors at the start. A slight change of your line going down the straight cannot be definitively proved to be a blocking maneuver.

SPINS

Now let's talk about unplanned trouble. There is a definite transition between "I've got it" and "It's got me."

When you have "lost" the car, you immediately have three concerns: not getting hit, not hitting anything, and getting going again safely. These are listed in order of priority. Getting hit is the most dangerous situation, hence the highest priority because there is the energy of *two* cars to be dissipated, not just one.

The standard, and correct, advice in a spin is "both feet out." This means clutch in, to keep the engine running, and brakes locked, to make the trajectory of the car more predictable to those behind you.

If you do not push in the clutch, the engine will probably kill—this tends to compromise objective number three. It is even possible that the engine will be run backwards; no engine builder recommends this.

If you do not lock the brakes, the spin will be a lot more exciting for those behind you. As the four tires individually transition from skidding to sticking, the car will dart in all kinds of thrilling directions. And there will be a smaller chance that they can get around you.

As the spin ends, you will begin to be able to control the car. In the happy event that you are pointed in the general direction of progress, just jam it into first gear and head out with a smile on your face.

More likely, you will be pointed to one side or another or you will be pointed backward, facing traffic. Head for the weeds, as directly and quickly as possible. If the car still has some momentum, let it roll off the track. If you have to drive it off, do so. The more time you spend on the racetrack at zero miles per hour, the more likely it is that you will be hit.

If the car is irretrievably dead and still on the racetrack, take it out of gear so it can be easily pushed and make your exit. Keep the car between you and traffic, and obey the corner workers who have hopefully arrived by now. If you can safely push the car off the track, do so with their help.

OFF-COURSE, CAR ALIVE

When you are off the track with the car running, your objective is to reenter the track without getting hit. You may not immediately realize this, however. You are more likely to feel that your objective is to reenter as quickly as possible. Don't let the adrenaline do your thinking for you. In a practice or qualifying session, reentering quickly is of absolutely no value. In a race, it is of value only if you do not get hit. So in all cases, take it easy.

Sometimes, you will come up a bit short of asphalt at a corner exit and end up running at speed in the dirt or grass along the edge of the track. Reenter the track carefully and slowly. Your car will almost certainly be understeering in the grass and dirt. When that inside front tire hits the asphalt, it will not be understeering anymore; it will bite. If you have the steering wheel cranked over, you will probably dart across the track and either you will end up in the weeds on the other side or you will get hit. Ease the car on gradually.

If you are off-course and stopped, a corner worker will usually appear. The worker will station himself or herself toward the front of your car, but with your car as protection from the racing traffic. Your car is now under the worker's control; you will be held until there is a hole in traffic. The

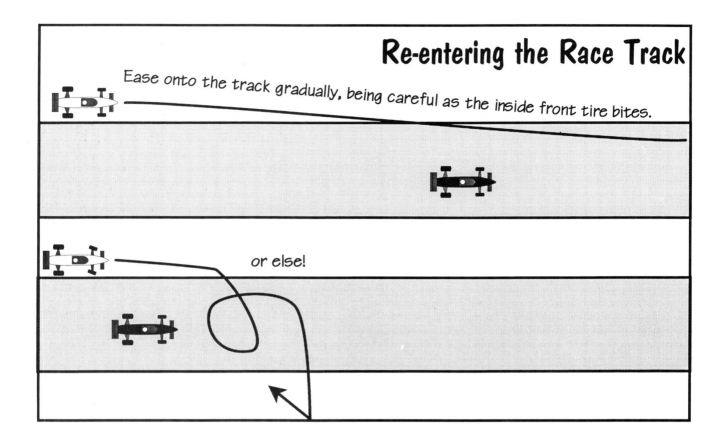

Re-entering the Race Track

Ease onto the track gradually, being careful as the inside front tire bites.

or else!

worker will "stop" you with arms extended, palms facing you.

When there is a hole in traffic coming, the worker will hold you with one hand and point with the other. He or she is pointing at the *last car in the oncoming group.* You are going to be signaled onto the track as this car goes by. Don't

bother to look for the car; the purpose of the pointing is to show you the car's progress. Get ready to go.

(If you must reenter without guidance from a corner worker, be damned careful. Again, remember that getting back on the track and getting hit will not do any good for your finishing position.)

Remember also that your tires will have little traction in the grass and dirt. If your adrenaline-charged right foot immediately goes to the floor, you will probably not go anywhere. The sight of a car sitting on the grass, racing slicks spinning madly, is amusing to everyone but the driver. Also, be careful that you do not fishtail into the corner worker as you enter the track.

When you have been off-course, your tires will probably have picked up some dirt and gravel. In the next corner, these will be miraculously transmuted into ball bearings. Either scrub your tires (gently) before the corner, or take the corner more slowly than normal.

POST-REENTRY DAMAGE ASSESSMENT

As you motor down the track after an excursion into the dirt, be aware that your car may have sustained damage that you don't know about—yet. You may have a leaking tire, a rock may have punched a hole in your oil sump, or you may have damaged a brake line. Do not go charging down the track and into the next corner as if you have never left the racing surface. You may find yourself leaving it again—at more danger to yourself and others, and at greater expense.

After your spin, drive the car cautiously and with your senses turned up to 150% of normal. Feel out the car's handling, watch the gauges carefully, and brake early until you are absolutely certain that the car is not damaged.

Traffic will move over as this Formula Vee reenters the track, but if he catches the track with his left front tire turned too far he will probably end up spinning across the track and getting hit. The tire angle looks OK from here.

At Elkhart a few years ago, a Formula Ford driver took an extensive tour of the tall grass just before the Carousel. He drove back onto the track, through the Carousel, and down the fast back straight to Canada Corner. Going into Canada at 130+mph, he found that both brake master cylinders had been broken off during his off-track excursion. Pedal on the floor, he managed to spin the car and ended up backed into a tire wall. No injuries, but it could have been much worse.

OFF-COURSE, CAR DEAD

If you end up off-course with a dead car, there are two things for you and the corner workers to worry about. First is your personal safety. Just as your car arrived at that particular location, so can another. If you get out of the car, be sure to keep it between yourself and traffic. Resist the temptation to do a damage assessment or, worse, to begin work on the car. The damage assessment can wait and the corner workers won't let you complete repairs anyway.

The second thing to worry about is minimizing the hazard that your car presents to other drivers. If it is dead on the track and immovable, the operating Steward will almost certainly call out a wrecker. More normally, however, it will be off-course. With your help (please), the corner workers will attempt to move it as far out of harm's way as possible. Try to anticipate this as you exit the track. Do not park the car on the shoulder or even in the ditch; drive it as far into the boonies as possible. If you have a lot of planning time (like when you run out of gas because you aren't using a checklist), choose the inside of a turn or a quiet place along a straight.

CRASHES

It is absolutely amazing how much time there is to think about things. This is the consistent experience of drivers who have crashed. Apparently, there is some kind of physiological "overdrive" that kicks in. You will experience it to some degree in spins, but not like you will in a crash.

When it appears that a crash in inevitable, your first action should be to arrange yourself as safely as possible. This means putting both hands at the bottom of the steering wheel and gripping it tightly. It means drawing your feet away from the pedals and tucking your head down.

This is not a good time to be remembering that you left the arm restraints in the trailer because "it's only a practice session." Since 1991, SCCA has required the drivers of open cars to wear arm restraints, but the grid marshals' checking is spotty. My view is that arm restraints are a good idea in all cars. Properly adjusted, you won't be aware of them and they will keep your arms from flailing into the roll bar or, worse, out the side window of a rolling sedan. Both have happened. The window net is not a panacea.

I was once talking to an SSC driver who had just rolled his Rabbit quite spectacularly. He said, "For some reason I had my hands on top of my helmet, like I was trying to hold it on. After the third time that my fingers got pinched, I decided this was not a good idea and grabbed the bottom of the steering wheel like I was supposed to." You really do have time to think through things like that.

As the crash begins to unfold, you often have a small degree of control over what is happening. Here are some of your objectives: (1) You do not want to hit another car in the vicinity of the driver compartment. (2) You probably prefer to hit hard objects while traveling backward; this reduces the chance of injury to your legs and feet, plus the seat and headrest will be available to spread the impact more broadly than the belts can possibly do. This strategy depends, however, on your car. If you are driving a car with a rear-mounted gasoline tank (like many Showroom Stockers), you may wish to hit in some other attitude. (3) You prefer a series of smaller collisions to one big one. As long as you are held in your belts and not otherwise damaged, you are concerned with minimizing the peak g-forces on your body. Thus, you want to dissipate the car's energy over as long a period as possible.

The reason why IndyCar drivers usually walk away from their spectacular-looking crashes is that they are protected by the car's tub while the kinetic energy of the car is slowly reduced by its sliding along the wall and scattering pieces in every direction. It is the sudden stops that injure and kill.

If you arrive at a corner with no brakes, try like hell to spin the car before you leave the racetrack surface. The spin will absorb energy that will otherwise be dissipated much more quickly against whatever you eventually hit. A spin also increases your chances of being able to hit going backward. The only exception to this rule is for the few corners where there are runoff areas with catch fencing and/or catch traps filled with gravel or sand.

By this discussion, I don't mean to imply that you have a broad range of choices while you are crashing. You will, however, have some time to think about what is happening. Use whatever control you can muster to arrange things in your favor.

Tony Kester: "No matter how helpless you feel, don't quit trying to save the car—and your butt!—until the car is actually stopped or until so many pieces have been torn off that the steering wheel and the brake pedal aren't connected to anything anymore. Even after multiple impacts, you can frequently exert some control over the car. Never give up!"

When the crash is over, the corner workers will show up quickly. Shut down the car, take it out of gear, unsnap your belts, and get out if you can. Remember to keep the car between yourself and traffic. If there is any fuel leaking, warn the corner workers.

If you can't get out on your own, trust the corner workers and follow their instructions.

If you're involved in a crash, however minor, you will be required to report to the track medical officials—with your helmet. If you forget it, you or one of your crew will be sent for it. Even if you have no physical injuries, Medical will perform a few simple checks to make sure you're still functional. They will also look over your helmet carefully to ascertain whether you could have suffered a head injury. They may ask you to wait in the quack shack for a while. They are doing all of this in your best interests; cooperate.

Norma Williams: "It's important for you to go to Medical even if you feel OK. If you don't go and something shows up a week or so later, the club's insurance may not cover it."

After your crash, the tech inspectors will probably show up to look over your car. Their intent is to assess the damage and to note it in the car logbook so that your car can be properly re-inspected prior to your next race.

Remember that the next purchaser of your car will be reviewing the car logbook, too. Because of this, you want the logbook entry to be as minimal and as comforting as possible. I suggest that you retain physical possession of the logbook until the tech people have told you exactly what they intend to write. If you do not like their idea, negotiate for less-alarming wording. They will probably acquiesce if you politely explain your reasons.

TIMING ERRORS

Timing errors have decreased with the arrival of computerized timing systems, but they still occur. For this reason, it is important that your crew keep lap times for you during every lap of qualifying. If you are surprised by your grid position, go politely to T&S and ask to talk to the Chief. Show him or her your times, explain why you think that there might have been an error, and ask that the tapes or timing cards be reviewed. Usually, the error is as simple as someone's having circled the wrong "fastest time." You can also offer your crew's lap times in appealing a significant error (for example, they missed your best lap), but your arguments will have to be good. By "good" I mean something like being able to show lap times taken on your car by a competitor, also proving the fast lap.

Tony Kester: "Don't argue about discrepancies of a tenth or two; it's not unusual for your crew to be that far off due to the fact that they are timing a slightly different segment of racetrack than is T&S. Once the race starts, it will all come out in the wash."

If you cannot be polite and calm, you might as well forget about asking T&S to do you a favor.

PROTESTS: AS PLAINTIFF

If you have a gripe against a fellow driver, you can file a protest with the Stewards of the Meeting (SOM). Be extremely careful to observe the protest filing deadline that is applicable. Protests involving a car must be lodged at least 1 hour before the race. Protests involving grid positions, a driver's action, or other race-related issue must be lodged within 30 minutes after specific events (posting of the grid or provisional race results, end of the race, and so on). Out of fairness to other drivers, the Stewards are going to be strict about observing these deadlines.

If there is time, explain your proposed protest to one of the Operating Stewards and seek advice. (The SOMs can't give you advice; it would be prejudicial.) Generally, any operating Steward also has had experience as an SOM. Also, he or she is not as emotionally involved as you are. You may receive encouragement, discouragement, and/or tactical advice. Consider the advice carefully before making your decision. If you *do* expect to file, also ask the Steward where the filing must be made.

Try to use an official protest form if one is available. If not, include all particulars, neatly written, on a reasonably sized and reasonably clean piece of paper. These should include the names, car numbers, and paddock locations of the

Most grid sheets are produced on computer timing systems, minimizing but not totally eliminating the probability of an error.

protester and protestee, a description of the alleged violation, and a recommended list of witnesses. You do not have to get prior permission from your witnesses but, obviously, it is in your best interest to do so.

Be specific in your complaint. Cite the exact paragraph(s) of the *GCR* that apply and state your reasons for asserting a violation. You cannot simply protest "bad driving" or an "illegal engine." You must identify specific actions of a driver that are proscribed by the *GCR* (for example, passing under a waving yellow at Corner 4 during an incident involving car #83 red). You must identify specific engine violations (such as, illegal cam, compression ratio, and/or cylinder head). Yes, I know that it is not fair to expect you to be able to see inside a competitor's engine. Did someone tell you that life was going to be fair?

You will have to pay a nonrefundable protest fee, plus post a teardown bond if you are asking that a competitor's car or engine be examined in some expensive way. The SOMs will determine a suitable teardown bond. If your suspicions are correct, your bond will be returned and the violator will pay the cost of the teardown. If he or she is legal, you pay.

Once you have filed your protest, make sure you understand where and when you are to present yourself to be heard.

PROTESTS: AS THE ACCUSED

As is true in many of life's tribulations, anger is not a productive response to being protested. Save the emotion for later. For now, you should calmly but tenaciously seek all available detail on the protest and on the procedures for resolving it. Nothing good will happen if you refuse to participate, surreptitiously leave the track, or otherwise make yourself unavailable. Most likely, you will lose your racing license.

You will probably want to recommend witnesses to the SOMs. You can also offer other evidence, such as videotapes, lap charts or times, and so forth. Use the time between notification and the hearing to plan your defense. You, too, can seek advice from one of the Operating Stewards. Read your *GCR* carefully, including relevant sections that were *not* cited in the protest.

Then, ride it out. If things go against you, there is always the National Court of Appeals.

ON-TRACK MISCELLANY: GET TO THE GRID EARLY

Under almost all circumstances, you want to be at the front of the grid when it is flagged off for practice and for qualifying. This position has several advantages.

First, planning to roll to the grid early will give you a bit of car and driver preparation cushion in case of a last-minute problem.

Second, the 10–15 minutes spent waiting by and in your car is an opportunity to settle down and to get psychologically ready to implement your plan for the session. (I tend to pace around; I envy those who can sit quietly.) For this reason, you want to be at the grid early even for the race, when your grid position has already been determined.

Finally, being at the front of the grid for a practice session will get you free lessons (and some free drafting) as the faster drivers pass you, while at the same time minimizing the amount of time that you must waste behind slower cars.

Practice and qualifying is first-come, first-served. Thus, to be at the front you just have to get your car onto the pregrid early enough. "Early enough" depends on the weekend. At a laid-back regional, it might be good enough to push or drive down 10 minutes early. In a serious National field, you might have to wait just behind the race group that precedes yours, moving your car into position as they roll onto the racetrack.

If you are among the first cars out for a practice or qual session, you do not normally want to tear hell-bent around the track on the first lap. The car is cold; you should warm it up gradually. Also, and most importantly, hurrying around the track will often cause you to catch the tail end of the grid as it enters the track. The tail end normally consists of the lame, the halt, and the blind—you will catch them eventually, but why throw away several clear laps by rushing around while they are still straggling out? The majority of drivers do not understand this beginning-of-session tactic; unless you are under a full-course yellow, they will come by you, hurrying to catch the backmarkers. Let them.

Be Smooth, Don't Wear Out the Steering

You've probably read many racing books, including this one, that exhort you to be smooth. We've already talked about finesse in braking and not upsetting the car with sudden engine acceleration. The rest of the smoothness is in your steering technique.

Any sudden change in your steering input to the car is an attempt to effect a fast change in velocity, hence you are attempting a large acceleration. (Remember the physics lesson?) Large steering accelerations are not a good idea for a couple of reasons:

First, you are using the car's engine or its kinetic energy to effect the acceleration. This is energy that would otherwise contribute to maintaining or increasing the speed of the car. Thus, don't be jerking the car around on the straightaways. You will be slowing it down.

Second, when you are cornering you are, or should be, at the limit. Large accelerations are simply not available. If you like to jerk the car around in the corners *and* can actually do it, then you're not at the limit and you're already slow. If you *are* at the limit, you will not be changing your steering during a corner except to compensate for upsets to the car.

Bertil Roos: "My steering wheel is, just about 95% of the lap, locked in one position or another, straight or curved. Once I lock in on a radius, the steering wheel must not move. I must be capable of holding it there. I have a firm grip on the steering wheel and my arms do not slacken for a fraction of a second during a practice session or a race."

In the *Drive to Win* video, Gilbert Pednault says that "To go fast on the track, you have to go slow in the cockpit." Going slow in the cockpit includes being gentle with the steering.

On the street, practice using your steering as if you are afraid it will wear out. Practice executing your cornering lines using only one movement of the steering wheel at your turn-in point and one to straighten the car at the exit. If you have to make a correction between the turn-in point and the exit, you have failed the exercise. Try again next corner.

Bedding Brake Pads

This is a lot easier to do than it is to describe.

Brake pad material consists of friction material and a binder to hold the friction material together. The friction material is most commonly asbestos, though alternative materials such as Kevlar are now being used due to asbestos' health hazards. The binder is a proprietary compound that, as manufactured, contains chemicals that will boil out of the brake pad well below the pad's intended operating temperature. These compounds have a lubricating effect between the pad and the disc as they are boiling out. They also have a distinctive smell, which you will learn to recognize.

The objective of "bedding" brake pads is to boil the volatile chemicals out of the pad material before you need maximum stopping power. You will be able to see the results. The edges of bedded pads will show a different color for at least the first 1/8in or so back from the friction surface.

The process of bedding is fairly simple; you go out onto the track and thoroughly heat the brakes without placing too much reliance on them when slowing for corners. You can heat them by left-foot braking down the straights and/or by hard (but early) application in the corners. The latter technique is preferable for a beginner because you will be able to feel them fade, and you will be able to feel when they can be relied upon. As you go through this process, be careful about watching your mirrors. Your fellow competitors will not be expecting your slowness down the straight or your unusual braking points. Wave them by; don't put yourself at risk of being hit from behind.

When you put new pads onto the car, *always* put a "new pads" warning on the dashboard or on the steering wheel hub so that you cannot possibly miss it, no matter how harried you have been prior to rolling onto the track. Just rip a 4in piece of race tape, write "new pads" on it, and stick it in the cockpit. It is no fun at all to arrive at a corner and to find that the brakes don't work. The nature of unbedded pads lulls you, too. They don't feel too bad on the first couple of corners. It is only after they have been thoroughly heated that they go away. Big time.

Once in a while, you will ruin a set of pads due to oil (typically in the rear) or to a brake fluid leak (either end). Sometimes, too, you will just flat run out of pads in the session prior to the race. This is the time to reach into your spares box and get an already-bedded set of pads to put onto the car. Bedding pads on the pace lap is a no-no. (You can't be sure they're bedded before testing them in the first turn of the race. Very dangerous.) If you're desperate, you can try emergency-bedding new pads while driving around the paddock with your left foot on the brake. Try to be unobtrusive about this, though. The Stewards and the paddock marshals will not like it.

Carroll Smith: "If you can get them, use carbon metallic 'black' pads and you won't have to bed pads anymore. They are also the best pads in the world.

"Also, in my experience paddock bedding doesn't work. It only glazes the pads."

Setting Brake Bias

The point of setting brake bias is to get the almost-the-maximum available braking force from the rear tires when the front tires *are* at maximum.

This balancing of front and rear is accomplished using either an adjustable pedal bias bar, or a hydraulic proportioning valve. The bias bar figure illustrates the concept. When the pivot is in the center, each brake cylinder actuation rod gets the same amount of force. When it's off center, the rod *closest to the pivot* is favored. Rough bias is set by selecting master cylinder sizes, fine bias with the balance adjuster.

With a hydraulic bias adjuster, you are setting a maximum hydraulic pressure to the rear brakes. The effect is the same.

The only place to set bias is on the racetrack, ideally on the specific track that you will be racing on. For this reason, you should have cockpit-adjustable bias if the rules permit it.

The procedure is simple, though time consuming if ad-

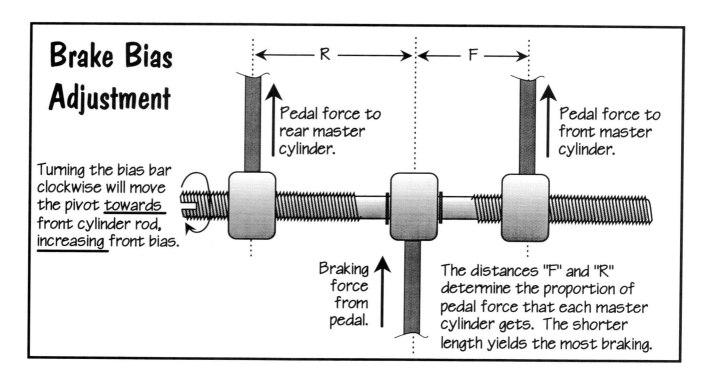

Brake Bias Adjustment

Turning the bias bar clockwise will move the pivot <u>towards</u> front cylinder rod, <u>increasing</u> front bias.

Pedal force to rear master cylinder.

Pedal force to front master cylinder.

Braking force from pedal.

The distances "F" and "R" determine the proportion of pedal force that each master cylinder gets. The shorter length yields the most braking.

justments must be made in the pits. Start with a "safe" baseline where you think the bias is too far forward. Go out and, after your tires are at operating temperature, make a series of straight, hard stops to verify that the fronts are locking first. If you're not sure that this is happening, have one of your crew observe from trackside. (You should, however, be able to

feel it as a slight slackness in the steering wheel—or *see* it, in an open-wheel car.)

From that point, gradually reduce front bias (or increase rear pressure) until you feel the rears locking before the fronts. You'll know it; the car suddenly goes unstable and the rear feels as if it wants to come around. (Or it does actually come around—be careful in traffic.) Then, slowly back off the rear bias (or pressure) until the car is stable in straight-line stops.

With this "trial" bias setting, do a few laps while braking and cornering at normal competition speeds. If there is any hint of rear lockup, reduce rear bias a bit more. When you're comfortable, carefully record the bias setting (twelve turns off full front, two clicks off maximum, whatever).

In the rain, there is a lot less forward weight transfer under braking because the tires just can't generate as much

A Spec Racer brake bias bar, mounted nice and high where it's easy to adjust. The SR rules do not allow cockpit-adjustable bias, but some drivers will temporarily install an adjuster to set the car up during practice. It must be removed for qualifying and the race, though.

The brake bias on this Formula Ford can be adjusted by the driver. Note the cable coming off the right end of the bias bar. It goes to a knob on the dashboard.

force. Because of this, a dry bias setup will give too little pressure to the rear brakes. If you have cockpit-adjustable bias, you have an advantage. You can simply back off the front until you get a little rear lockup, then crank back in a bit. After the session, you can easily go back to your carefully recorded (right?) dry bias setting.

If your bias is pit adjustable, you could conceivably test in the rain to develop a wet-weather setting. I personally do not know anyone (except Carroll Smith, of course) who has gone to this trouble.

In a street car, it's OK for Mr. or Mrs. Average to plow into the car in front; it's not OK for the car to go sideways and leave the lane it's in. To ensure that the former trajectory is accomplished, the factory bias in a street car is going to be set well toward the front. With the brakes of Showroom Stockers being as weak as they are, I suspect that a little optimization inside the bias valve would be productive—also a lot of work, and against the rules.

There are people who will tell you that you can adjust bias by putting the car on stands and using a torque wrench to measure front and rear braking resistance with constant pedal pressure. I have never been able to make the readings repeat. At best, this is an indirect technique suitable for checking and verifying a setting previously developed on the racetrack.

Dennis Eade: "We always set the initial brake bias by steady pressure on the pedal and turning the wheels by hand. The fronts should turn slightly harder than the rears at a constant pedal pressure. This procedure works for me.

"I think it is important to note that brake bias may change from track to track, corner to corner, session to session, and with weather changes."

Carroll Smith: "I set the initial bias the same way as Dennis does. It works for a baseline."

Tony Kester: "Brake bias is a constantly changing thing and is affected by track surfaces, track condition, tire wear, shock adjustments, weight transfer *caused* by braking, and more. It's not unusual to have to readjust it frequently during the course of a weekend."

CHOOSING SHIFT POINTS AND GEAR RATIOS

The objective of this exercise is to maximize the torque being generated at the rear wheels. It's that simple; forget about horsepower and forget about the redline on the tach.

SHIFT POINTS

The torque being generated by an engine at full throttle varies according to rpm. Your engine builder should be able to give you a graph something like the one shown in the figure. If your engine is not being dynoed, then you should try to get at least a "typical" curve for your type of engine.

Ideally, we would always operate the engine at the torque peak. Only in the case of the variable-ratio belt drive can this actually be done. In conventional powertrains, the driver must approximate this optimum by selecting from his range of gears. In *Race Car Engineering and Mechanics*, Paul Van Valkenburgh provides an excellent technical discussion of this subject (see chapter 9), complete with detailed graphs. I'll try to give you the basic theory here.

The gearbox and rear end (or final drive in a front-drive car) are torque multiplication devices. We can neglect the rear end since it's fixed, but the torque multiplication performed in the gearbox is important to shifting. Each time you upshift, you are reducing the torque multiplier between the engine's output and the rear wheels. Hence, you are reducing the maximum amount of thrust that reaches the pavement. As an example, a third gear might have a ratio of

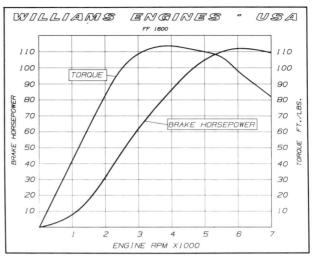

The torque curve of an engine is used to determine gearing and shift points, Williams Engines

1.2:1, thus "multiplying" the engine torque by 120%. A typical fourth is 1:1; thus, no increase.

As you accelerate, then, you want to make your shift when doing so will not cause the torque at the rear wheels to be *decreased*. This means that you must shift sometime *after* the engine's torque peak. Specifically, you shift when the

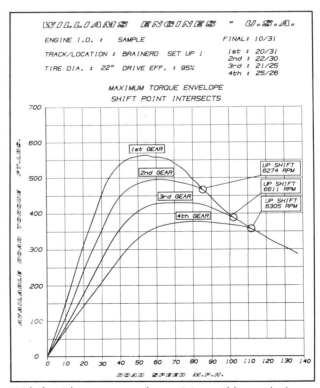

With the right computer software, it is possible to calculate exactly the optimum shift points for a given engine's torque curve and the gearing used at each racetrack. Williams Engines

torque has fallen to the point where the multiplication provided by the lower gear is no longer enough to compensate for the reduction in engine output. Then, you upshift.

To put some numbers on it, with a 1.2:1 third and a 1:1 fourth, you will wait for a 16% drop in torque *if* upshifting at that speed will put you at exactly the torque peak of the engine. Normally, your shift will put you farther back on the torque curve (lower rpm), so you must wait longer to make the upshift. You can think of shifting as a series of traverses of the torque curve, beginning below the peak, accelerating up through the peak and down, then upshifting to begin the traverse again.

It is the business of your engine builder to make sure that the redline is high enough that it does not get in the way of optimum shifting. In some engines, this is not possible. In these cases, the redline is the shift point.

Charlie Williams: "Talk to your engine builder about torque and shift points. The 1600 and 2000cc Ford engines work best between 5800–7000rpm. The 2.0 liter, though, will pull from 5000rpm due to its extra displacement.

"Your engine builder may be able to help you out with customized charts like I have provided in the figure. Here, the computer has done the calculations for a specific engine and gearing setup. As you can see, the optimum shift point is different, depending on the gear you're in."

GEARING

In principle, selecting gears is quite straightforward. First is selected for optimum rpm leaving the slowest corner, and top is selected for optimum rpm at the end of the longest straight. The in-between gears are then spaced accordingly. Carroll Smith and Paul Van Valkenburgh give you the details.

The best way to get your initial gear setup is to talk to people running a similar car and use what they tell you to use. Here are some considerations:

As a beginner, you probably do not have as much horsepower as some of your competition. This may call for a slightly lower top gear to ensure that the engine is operating at, not below, its maximum output point.

The lower the gear, the less it matters whether you optimize the gear selection with the engine torque curve. You simply do not spend much time in the lower gears.

PERFECTION IN SHIFT POINTS AND GEARING

In most club racing cars, perfection in shift points and gearing is probably not too important. Torque curves are broad enough that many combinations will get the job done. A few years ago, I wrote a fairly detailed computer simulation model of acceleration. It considered all the rotational moments of inertia, the various frictional losses, and the aerodynamic drag losses as the car accelerated. I used an actual dyno curve of torque and calibrated the model to on-track data taken in my Swift. The purpose was to determine whether an ultra-expensive F3 clutch was worth buying for its lower rotational moment of inertia. Bottom line: It wasn't. I also learned that optimizing shift points and optimizing gearing produced little benefit. Maybe a tenth of a second in a mile of straight-line acceleration. Gearing, obviously, will be somewhat more important in engines with narrower torque peaks than my FF 1600 engine.

Gearing so that your shift points occur at convenient places is probably more important (especially in the lower gears) than absolute optimization. You do not want to be shifting fifty feet from the end of a short straight. Make your gear a bit longer. You do not want to be shifting in the middle of a high-speed corner, either; it upsets the car. Here,

you can either move the shift point to the beginning of the corner or to the end by selecting a shorter or longer gear. Sometimes, it is easier to "short-shift" at a lower rpm just before the car gets really loaded into the corner.

Paul Van Valkenburgh: "The theory of ratio selection and shift points may be useful in setting up a car for a particular course, but when you get down to the fine points, I think experimentation is probably better. Two big overlooked problems are tachometer accuracy and tachometer lag. You could be off the theoretical 'best' shift point by hundreds of rpm and not know it. Better is to simply go to a drag strip and run against the clocks, trying different shift points in scientifically controlled trials."

Carroll Smith: "Once in the ballpark, I have seldom seen a car get *faster* by changing gears. Easier to drive, yes; faster, no."

MONITORING YOUR CAR'S HEALTH

It's important to watch your gauges. Pick one or two places around the track where you can safely look down, then do it religiously. Watch for trends. Steadily increasing water temperature usually indicates a leak. Steadily increasing oil temperature (or decreasing pressure) can mean you're losing a bearing.

Once or twice a lap is about all you'll have time for, and zero oil pressure can cause you to blow an engine in just a few seconds. What to do? Install an idiot light, preferably with a 30psi racing switch rather than the low-pressure switches used on street cars. If you have a lot of dashboard room, use a big red one-off taillight or clearance light as an indicator. (You can also mount it on the hub of the steering wheel.) If you're cramped for space, a bright electronic-equipment type pilot light installed next to the redline on your tach will get looked at often enough.

MONITORING YOUR PERFORMANCE

You can monitor your performance quite accurately by checking engine rpm at specific reference points around the track. For example, I watch for the point along the pit wall where I make my third-to-fourth shift. The earlier it is, the better I did in the important straight-entry corner. Similarly, bridges, exit roads, and even features of the road surface itself can be used as speed checkpoints.

If you have the equipment and the in-car room, you can learn a lot from on-track videotapes. One slick setup I saw in an IT Porsche 944 included a g-meter display and a tiny brake-light indicator, both visible in the video. It's hard to lie to yourself about "tapping" the brakes when you see the light for 3 solid seconds. The main problem with videotaping is that the feedback is not immediate. It occurs between sessions or between weekends, when you can really study the tape. Consider it to be supplemental monitoring, not a primary tool. Of course, it's great fun as home entertainment.

Bertil Roos: "It's important that you evaluate your performance every time you come off a corner. And what you are specifically evaluating is the degree of difficulty at the exit edge. When you come off the corner under full gas and exactly touch the exit edge—if you have to use up nearly every inch there is—that's fine.

"If you come off a corner and the exit edge is too easy—you have to ease the car out to the edge a little—that means that you are using a too-late apex. Next lap tell yourself to 'turn a touch earlier and get a touch earlier apex.' And when you do that, there will be a little more strain on the exit and you might get it just perfect.

"The same thing goes for the opposite: where you come out of a corner and the exit is too difficult. You might

drop your wheels off or you might have to lift the throttle to stay on the road. That tells you: 'My apex is too early. Next lap, I must turn in a touch later in order to get a little later apex so I don't have the car under such a strain coming out.'

"Work backwards on the corners; get the exit right and then get it right a little earlier and a little earlier and a little earlier until you finally get everything right from the start of the corner."

OIL ON THE TRACK

If there is a serious oil spill during a practice or qualifying session, particularly toward the end of the session, you might as well come in. If you have some pedagogical reason for continuing to run, fine. It will become somewhat more dangerous to be out there, however, and you will not improve your lap times.

A small oil spill on the racing line will be rubbed out in a lap or two. Almost any coolant spill will also disappear quickly. This means that it is worth your while to run a lap or two before deciding whether to stay out or not.

TESTING

If you have the time and the money, you will be tempted to go "testing" early in your career. At this stage, however, you have so little seat time that your ability to develop the car is going to be limited. Your driving won't be consistent enough, your senses won't be developed enough, and you will probably see declining lap times just because you are learning from each lap.

By all means, go testing if you can afford it. Consider it, however, to be driver training and driver testing time. Fool around with brake bias, tire pressures, and other simple variables so that you begin to feel their effects. Tighten and loosen the sway bars. If possible, try springs with a few different rates. At the end of the day, you will be faster. Before adopting any new tweaks, however, take the car back to the morning baseline configuration and see if that's faster, too. It probably will be.

Dennis Eade: "Here are some suggestions on testing:
• **Show up prepared—on time, at the start of testing. Take the best advantage of your available time.**
• **Plan what you want to accomplish during your test day. Try to stick to your plan. Be prepared with an alternate plan if something goes wrong with the original.**
• **Plan your testing to suit your needs. Be honest with yourself. If you need to improve your driving, work on driving—not on the latest suspension tweak.**
• **Record *everything* that you do. It will make it much easier to reconstruct and evaluate your effort when you return home. Draw yourself a course map and keep accurate gear selection, revs (straights, corner entrance and exit) in your records. It is a great evaluation and reference tool.**
• **Do not waste your time. You can eat and talk later. Test time is expensive, so make the most of it.**
• **Learn the signs of driver fatigue, and stop testing when you start making mistakes. It is better to stop testing with a whole car than to continue on with a tired driver and crash the car. There is nothing wrong with going home early if you have accomplished as much as you can."**

IN-CAR COMPUTERS

In Van Valkenburgh's book, you can see that the first generation of on-track monitoring required a truck full of telemetry equipment. Today, electronics miniaturization and costs are at the point where virtually any amateur driver can afford to use computerized monitoring tools.

The concept is to record critical in-car parameters for

In purpose-built race cars, you usually have a choice of gears. Here's another $1,000–$1,500 of your capital equipment costs (if you buy used gears).

review between sessions. If you are doing a lot of car development work, you can easily record more data than you can deal with—everything from suspension link positions to brake and tire temperatures. The most rudimentary systems typically monitor one parameter, either g-force or axle rotation speed.

During 1988, I worked with an axle-speed monitoring device called Tach-Tale. The unit was provided on a rental basis by Tony Kester, and came complete with Tony as a personal coach. The cost per weekend was less than a set of tires, and the benefits were far more permanent.

From reviewing my printouts, I could easily see where I was lifting, where I was getting wheelspin, and where I was inconsistent from lap to lap. Also, just knowing that everything was being recorded had a strong psychological effect. If I screwed up, I would not be able to deny it afterwards—and Tony would know it, too.

One of my most personally valuable experiences was comparing some of my Blackhawk laps to one recorded by Jim Render, who had been CenDiv Formula Ford champion the previous year. (Tony does not normally do this, but he had Jim's permission—Jim does not see me as much of a threat!) The printouts were similar except in Turn 4. I thought I was getting through Turn 4 pretty well; after all, I had 8–9 years of practice, but Jim was 1 full second faster! Well, I went out and found that 1 second and kept it from then on. Same brake point, earlier turn-in. Easy, once you know it can be done.

Skip Barber Racing offers a Computer Car using an instrumented Formula Ford. With their setup, you can record various parameters: speed, brake pedal pressure, throttle position, lateral g-forces, and so on, for later review. An advantage is that they can record the comparison data with an instructor in the car, allowing you to immediately see and correct your errors. A simplified sample of a Computer Car

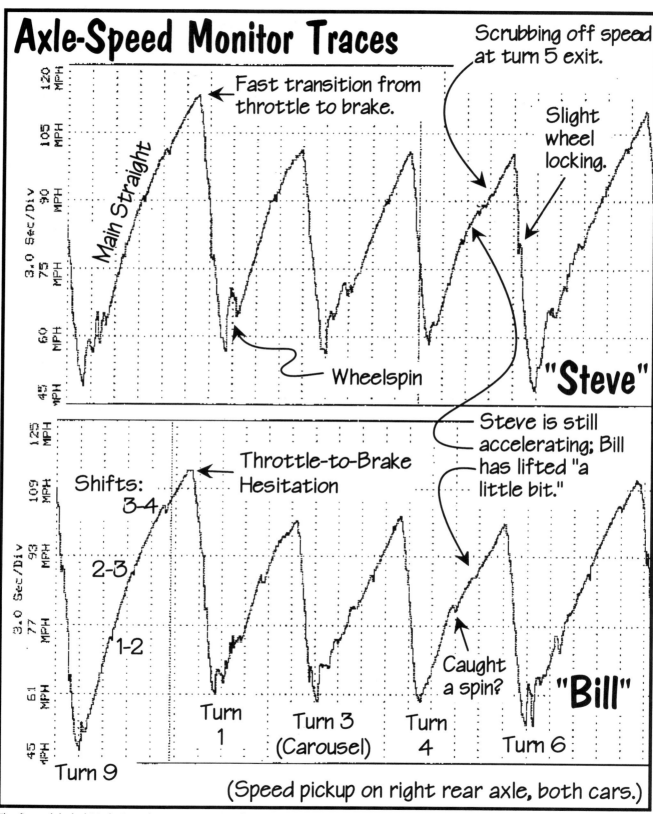

Axle-Speed Monitor Traces

Scrubbing off speed at turn 5 exit.

Fast transition from throttle to brake.

Slight wheel locking.

Main Straight

Wheelspin

"Steve"

Steve is still accelerating; Bill has lifted "a little bit."

Throttle-to-Brake Hesitation

Shifts:
3-4

2-3

1-2

Caught a spin?

"Bill"

Turn 9

Turn 1

Turn 3 (Carousel)

Turn 4

Turn 6

(Speed pickup on right rear axle, both cars.)

The figure labeled "Axle Speed Monitor Traces" shows the wealth of information available from this one simple sensor. In the drawing, I have matched up and annotated actual recordings of laps by two different drivers. The lower lap ("Bill") is about 1/2 second slower than the upper one ("Steve"). There are easy-to-see differences between the drivers; each could learn a few things from the other. Also, you can see that both cars are getting some inside-tire wheelspin coming off the corners. Maybe there would be a benefit to running softer sway bars. (These were Formula Fords with open differentials.)

graph was shown when we talked about driving the corners with full throttle, back in chapter 4.

Competition Data Systems, in Buffalo, New York, offers what is probably the most sophisticated car monitoring system available to amateur racers. Their Commander box will record up to sixteen analog (continuous variable) signals, plus two rpm channels, keeping the data for an entire session. Then, using their Track Master software as shown in the drawing, you can play back the data and examine any point of any lap in detail. With sophistication comes complexity, though (and cost!—figure $5,000 or so). To deal with a system like this, you will probably need to assign a crew member full time to the job of taking care of the computer box, the sensors, and the data recordings.

I would not recommend that you get too carried away with computerization until you have several races' worth of experience. You have to work through the sensory overload period before you can get a benefit from more esoteric information. At that point, though, I suggest that you try to use some type of in-car recording device. If at all possible, use a device that will record an entire half-hour session or race. My first choice measurement would be either engine rpm or axle rpm. (Cornering g-forces are not as good—remember that the trophy is for driving the racetrack, not just the corners.)

Carroll Smith: "There's also a good entry-level product called RaceLog that gives you four channels with sensors for about $2,000.

"Another thing to look at is Bill Mitchell's computer programs. They're good as learning devices, particularly his load transfer program."

Your recordings will allow you to compare individual

An axle speed pickup is normally mounted on the gearbox and activated by a magnet that is somehow mounted to the CV-joint. Each time this glued-on magnet (on the CV-joint) comes around, a pulse is sent from the sensor to the computer. (The cantilevered sensor bracket isn't a real good idea—it is likely to vibrate and fatigue crack at the bend next to the mounting point. I would have mounted it to two of the gearbox side-plate studs.) Peter Kelly, Competition Data Systems

turns from lap to lap, segment timing yourself to identify the good, the bad, and the truly ugly. I'd also suggest trying to work with a partner; comparing two drivers' recordings will allow each to learn from the other. If you can talk a front-runner into recording a tape for you, do it.

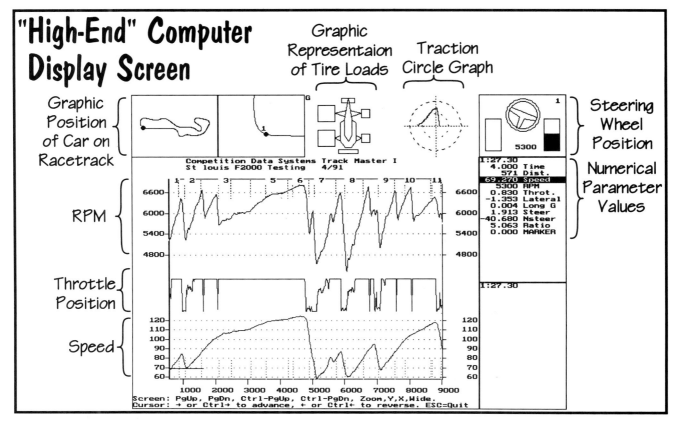

ADVANCED TECHNIQUES, TACTICS, AND TRICKS:
ANALYZING A CORNER

Bertil Roos: "The only way to analyze a corner is to go backwards. Start at the point where the corner is finished. Visualize where you want to finish the turn—that is your goal. You want to come out and hit the exit edge at approximately that point and you want to come off the corner under full gas. That's what you want to accomplish. By keeping the result of the corner in your mind, you can figure out how to do the beginning of the corner.

"Most drivers don't do this. They keep fighting with the first half of the corner, totally forgetting the second half. They probably reason that 'I am going to keep hammering at the first half, and when I finally get the first half decent, that's when I'm going to focus on the second half.' That doesn't work. You will never understand the first half of the corner unless you have a clear picture of how the second half should be taken. As I have already said, if you can't take the corner perfectly, drop the first half. Then focus on doing the second half really well and really fast.

"Decide how you want to finish the corner, then draw a radius backwards into the corner, a radius which represents your car's ability to turn under full gas. Draw the full-power turning radius back into the corner and when it goes by the inside edge, that's the apex. Continue the radius back toward the entrance of the corner. When you come to the entrance, this line is going to intersect your straight approach line.

"Now, if you can come in on your straight approach line, brake down so you can look into the corner and picture this line. If you can hook up with the line, if you can do that on the very entrance, that is the key which allows you crank it in, get off the brake and slam on the gas right from the start.

"If you turn into the corner and end up on the outside of this imaginary line, you cannot take the corner under full gas. You're going to have to do something—back off, make the car turn more sharply later on, or something.

"If you turn in and end up inside this line, then next time you have to remember to stay on the brake a touch longer and make the car turn a little more so you can reach the apex. And once that is done, then you can really be on full gas through and out of the corner."

LINE RECOVERY TECHNIQUE

Although braking while turning spells disaster, application of a mild dose of deceleration can be useful.

When your car is understeering a bit and you are headed wide of the apex, a quick lift and re-application of power will cause the car to turn in nicely. Roos calls this his "line recovery technique" because it allows the car to recover onto the correct racing line.

You have probably seen this turn-in behavior characterized as "dreaded trailing throttle oversteer" in the buff magazines. My guess is that this overused term was originally invented to describe the reprehensible behavior of swing-axle VWs and 356 Porsches. Except in cases where the car goes

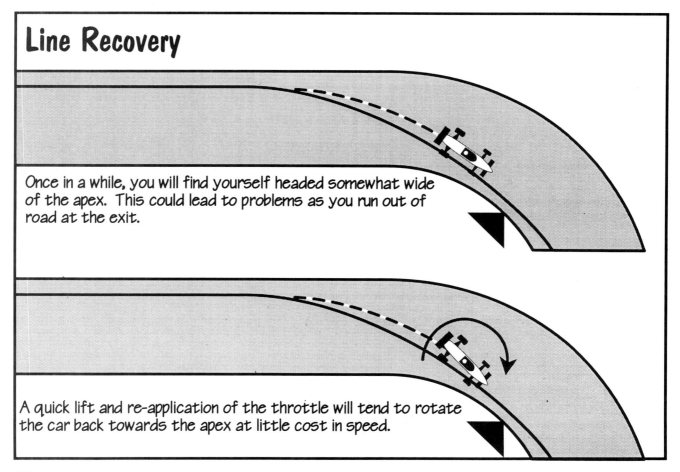

Line Recovery

Once in a while, you will find yourself headed somewhat wide of the apex. This could lead to problems as you run out of road at the exit.

A quick lift and re-application of the throttle will tend to rotate the car back towards the apex at little cost in speed.

crazy, trailing throttle oversteer is a desirable characteristic and should not be "dreaded." If the car does not respond to a lift by turning in, then it is not properly set up.

CONTROLLING SLIP ANGLES

Bertil Roos: "Let's talk about how a driver can control slip angles and change them.

"Think about the situation when you turn into a corner under braking. The braking puts the weight on the front wheels as you turn in, making the car turn better. That means that braking into the corner reduces the slip angles on the front and increases the slip angles on the back.

"If you take the same car with the same settings and you slow down a little earlier, then you turn into the corner under acceleration, the situation changes. You unload the front end and you get more slip in front while at the same time you load the rears and you reduce their slip angles. It's important for race car drivers to know how to change the slip angles to suit different situations.

"A hairpin requires a deep, late turn-in point. When I come up to a hairpin, and I finally decide to turn, I must get the car pointing quickly—so I want a crisp steering response. I want very little slip angle in front and if I can make the rear slip a little more, that's even better—that gets the car pointing quicker. The quicker I can get the car pointing, the quicker I can go off the brake and be on the gas. So, in a hairpin I make sure I enter the corner with smaller slip angles on the front wheels and more on the back wheels."

Carroll Smith: "Here, Bertil's got the cart before the horse. Set up the chassis correctly and you won't have to do this. *And* the car will be faster."

Bertil Roos: "The faster the corner, the more gradual the turn-in; the slower the corner, the deeper and more abrupt the turn-in. When I enter a fast corner, I turn in earlier and more gradually. I don't want the car to turn into a fast corner too abruptly. To prevent this, I change the slip angles so I get more slip in front than I get in the rear. I do that by being on the gas before I turn in. If I am on the gas when I turn in, the nose will be light, the steering will not be responding so crisply, and the rear end will be sticking because the weight is moved to the back.

"George talked a while back about not wanting to have 'the back end hanging out at 150mph.' That's true, that's not what we want. Of course, the aerodynamics are influencing this, but before we screw with the aerodynamics, we must be sure that we have done what we can do with the driver to make the car neutral.

"Again, when you come to a fast corner, you want the car to turn in sluggishly and that is simply accomplished by getting on the gas before you turn in. If it is a very fast corner, you tap the brake, then you hit the gas, and then you turn the steering wheel. Now you have a sluggishly turning car and it should be neutral and the rear end should not let go."

PRE-CORRECTING

When you're going really fast, you can benefit from anticipating some cornering corrections. For example, there is a dip in the Carousel at Road America. When you hit it, the car gets a little loose and tries to come around. If you straighten the car slightly before you hit the dip, you'll be turned back onto your line nicely as you leave it. Much neater than a correction.

GETTING A GOOD START

At the start, experienced drivers have the objective of making the starter think they are behaving according to the *GCR* while, in fact, doing something entirely different. You'll have to do this, too.

The *GCR* says you are to stay in your grid position ("good order") until the flag drops. You do not want to do this. You want to drop back a bit, placing your car about half a car length behind your grid partner. This placement of the car makes it harder for the guy behind you to pass (he's right on your tail unless he dropped back, too), and it makes it easier for you to pass the car ahead.

The *GCR* implies that you do not nail the gas until the green flag is shown. You do not want to do this, either. You

A "Well-Formed" Grid

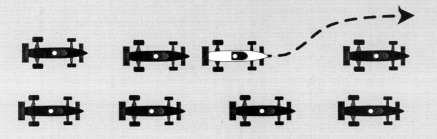

At the start, hang back a bit. It allows you to pull out easily. Also, it makes life difficult for the guy behind you, since it is hard for him to pull out. The key to exploiting this position is to get on the gas a moment before the green appears. (or, at least, a moment before the guy in front decides to nail it!)

Early in the first lap, the pack tends to play "follow the leader." This creates passing opportunities. Note the lone white car coming down the inside. Jim Casey

file. Tony Kester once pointed out to me that this is a pretty good passing opportunity. Each car in the file tends to brake a heartbeat before the driver expects the car in front to brake, leading to earlier and earlier braking. If you are a few cars back, you can move to the inside, brake at the normal point, and pick up two or three positions. Watch your mirrors. Also make sure you don't end up T-boning a car that turns in before you can get up beside it and into the driver's view. (Please review the "crash" drawing back in chapter 3 where we talked about outbraking maneuvers.)

Using Backmarkers

Backmarkers can be a great tool for passing. The general idea is to get beside your opponent as you approach a slower car, then refuse to move over. This forces the other driver to brake unless he can go around on the far side, which is rarely possible. This trick works on the straight or at the entry to turns, but turns are the best because your opponent is usually stuck behind the backmarker through the entire turn.

Poaching the Yellow

The SCCA yellow flag rule prohibits passing between the yellow flag and the incident. This means *from the flag station*, not from the point where you can see the flag. Sometimes, your opposition will relax slightly when a yellow flag appears ahead. This creates an opportunity for you. You must, however, *complete* your pass before you get to the flag. The Stewards are not going to be the least bit understanding, nor are they going to give you the benefit of the doubt.

want to nail the gas just as the starter is making his or her decision to show the flag. You'll speed up, moving back into and through your grid position. When the flag is shown, then you have a speed advantage on the row ahead of you and can move around them on the outside. Be careful, however, that the guy behind you isn't doing the same thing to you.

Carroll Smith: "'Wait for the starter' equals 'Lose three positions.'"

Don't "Follow the Leader"

Entering the first or second slow corner of a race, the pack develops a tendency to "follow the leader" in single

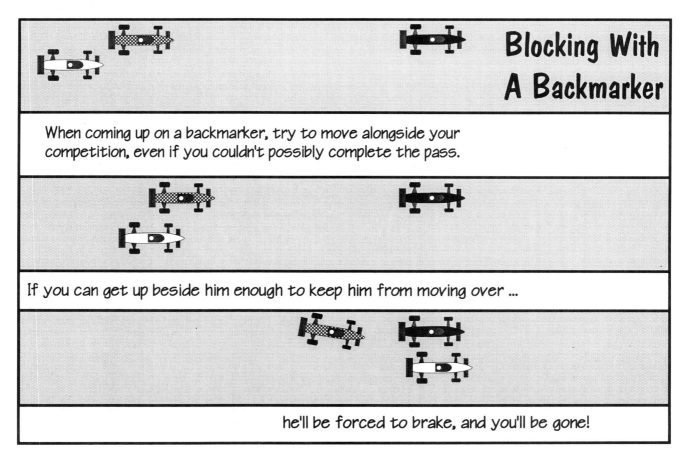

Blocking With A Backmarker

When coming up on a backmarker, try to move alongside your competition, even if you couldn't possibly complete the pass.

If you can get up beside him enough to keep him from moving over ...

he'll be forced to brake, and you'll be gone!

BLOCKING

When an opponent is in position to pass you under braking, there is a subtle blocking line that can be taken to discourage him. Turn slightly before you brake so that the car is headed toward the middle of the corner at the apex. For the critical split-second, your opponent won't know whether you're coming over in front of him or not. You're not, and the line won't slow you down much. This works once per race, per opponent. Don't overdo the maneuver, though, or he'll just go around you on the outside.

DIRTY TRICKS

Tony Kester: "I believe that dirty tricks should be kept to a minimum for various reasons, not the least of which is that they can be used on you. If *you* don't use them, most people won't use them *on you*.

"Blocking, as seen in many classes of racing these days, is way too common and blatant and it shouldn't be allowed. I don't know how to stop it. (Physical violence has worked in some cases, but I wouldn't know personally.)

"If you do encounter problems, deal with them as best you can. Remember that the other driver may be a jerk, but he has a family, too."

Carroll Smith: "If the guy persists, do what you have to do. If he hasn't bred yet, he shouldn't be in the gene pool anyway."

DEALING WITH PROBLEM DRIVERS

Tony Kester: "My favorite trick is the perfect way to deal with a problem driver who kills you down the straight and holds you up in the turns. Frequently these are big-ego, no-talent guys with motors of suspect legality.

"Choose a spot on the track where you can outbrake him and, while under braking, don't pass. Stay directly next to him on the inside and when you get to the corner—turn at the last possible instant. Usually, this will put the other car on the marbles and when its ego-laden driver decides to jump in front of you (instead of backing off), he'll be deposited in the bushes where he belongs.

"Another good trick works for handling the demon late-braker who believes that he can late-brake anyone on the track—and in the process ruin everybody's chance of catching the leaders.

"When he makes his big move (probably at a corner with lots of spectators), hold your braking until well past any sane braking point. Then nail the brakes as hard as the car will allow.

"Mr. Late Braker will try to follow your lead (remember, he can outbrake any driver alive!) and will usually go off the track backwards just as you sail by him at the apex.

"This is one of the few situations where your single-digit salute will be enjoyed by workers and spectators alike."

PRESSURE: GIVING IT AND GETTING IT

If you are following a driver with equal ability and an equally matched car, it can be hard to get by. Try some psychological warfare.

Make yourself big in his mirrors. On the straight, feint some passes. Going into the corners, make some moves that look like you're going to try to outbrake him. Stay close and make sure he knows it. (Be careful, though, not to adopt his lines. Drive your own by using your eyes properly.)

Eventually, you hope that this pressure will cause your intended victim to make a mistake. You also hope to be close enough to capitalize on the mistake. He will often oblige.

If somebody is playing these games with you, your first response should be to ignore it. If he could pass you, he would. Drive your lines, maybe using a slightly modified blocking line where appropriate.

Depending on the race situation (if it's OK that you both slow down, for instance), you might try to give him a little of his own medicine. If you are absolutely certain that the pair of you are not threatened from behind, you could become quite aggressive about blocking. Alternatively, you could create an apparent passing opportunity only to close the door at the last minute. A bit of this, and you might be treated to a mirror-view of your tormentor spinning into the weeds.

Carroll Smith: "To a mature and disciplined racing driver, as opposed to someone who drives racing cars, there is no such thing as pressure from behind."

ADVANCED SHIFTING

Bertil Roos: "If you have a racing transmission, you should not be using the clutch twice. As you come down to the corner, your left foot is on the dead pedal and your right foot has the gas pedal to the floor. Then you hit the brake pedal. (While you hit the brake pedal, it is helpful to have your left foot on the dead pedal because in this initial braking you have to hold yourself back.)

"As your braking begins, you take the gear shift into neutral, but without using the clutch. The gearshift slips easily from whatever gear you want to neutral so long as the gas pedal is off. If you can't get it out of gear, that means your foot is dragging on the gas—that locks the gear in place and you can't get out of it.

"In a street car with synchronizers, it might snag a little to get to neutral. So in street cars, I do a little stab on the clutch to get it to neutral but in a racing transmission, I don't touch the clutch.

"After you set the brake, then your foot goes down on the clutch, you shift into the lower gear, then you go off of the clutch and back onto the dead pedal.

"To do a super-quick downshift you must be really good, especially in smaller Formula cars because they are light, they stop quickly, so you don't have much time to do the downshift.

"So what am I doing in a quick downshift? Let's go over it again. When my brain says brake, three things happen. My foot goes for the brake, my gearshift is kicked to neutral, and when my right foot hits the brake my ankle is already leaned over so my foot simultaneously hits the gas pedal. I hit the brake and the gas pedal at the same time. So the moment I hit the brake, the uprev is starting. I can do this because the gearshift is already in neutral. The engine responds quickly, so the clutch almost immediately comes down and up again.

"If you have a little heavier car, the schoolbook way of doing it is to set the brake first. Shift to neutral, rev up, down with the clutch, into the lower gear, and back on the dead pedal. Continue to the turn-in point and turn, then back on the gas. But if you want to do a quick one, hit the brake and the gas together and have the gearshift in neutral already, then down the clutch and into the lower gear. You can do a very, very quick downshift that way.

"By the way, regarding the double-clutch, the uprev, and so on, the main reason for the uprev in the downshift is to rev up the motor so that when you downshift and you smack it into the lower gear, you can immediately pop the clutch. If you don't rev up the motor enough and you pop the clutch, your rear wheels are going to lock up momentarily and make the car unstable."

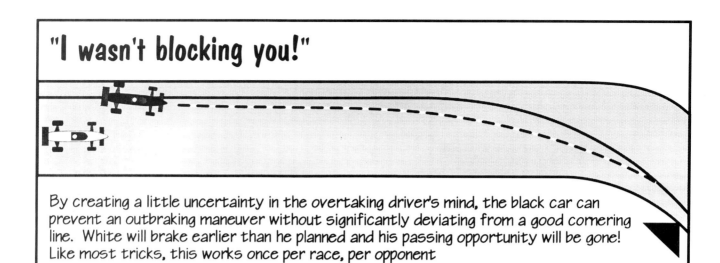

ARE YOU A BAD DRIVER?

Unfortunately, club racing licensing systems are primarily oriented toward *granting* licenses, not *revoking* them. This means that most bad drivers are allowed on the racetrack for as long as they choose to compete.

Thus, every weekend you will find a few truly bad drivers out there. Each seems to have at least a few of the following characteristics.

POOR PREPARATION

Often, the bad drivers come to the track with poorly prepared cars. These cars are usually dirty and unreliable. Their owners are frequently found wandering the paddock, borrowing parts and tools. My guess is that their on-track problems are due at least in part to poorly performing engines and to chassis setups that Fangio himself couldn't drive.

I also suspect that the poor preparation of the cars indicates poor driver preparation as well.

NO MIRRORS

Almost by definition, a poor driver does not use his mirrors. Other drivers are afraid to go around him and he is constantly being surprised as they finally manage to do it. In your first driver school or two, you will be feeling quite overwhelmed by the experience of driving the car. Sensory information is coming at you just too fast. Until you break through this barrier, you will not be good with your mirrors. The problem with bad drivers' mirrors may be that they have never made this step.

INCONSISTENT OR ERRATIC DRIVING

Poor drivers cannot produce consistent lap times. It seems that each encounter with a corner is a fresh and challenging experience, producing new and unpredictable reactions. The issue is that the driver is not *learning* as he circulates the track.

FREQUENT PROXIMITY TO CRASHES

Once in a while, there is a driver that people are just flat out afraid of. This guy is usually in a competitive car, but drives it poorly. He will be slow, erratic, and inattentive to traffic in the corners, but fast down the straight. When he does go off-track, which will happen, he comes zinging back onto the track with total disregard for traffic. This combination of characteristics is a recipe for crashes—by other people.

This type of bad driver will be holding up faster drivers in the tight part of the racetrack: they will be frantically trying to get by him before the entry onto the main straight. (If they don't get by, they are stuck for another slow lap.) Thus, the overtaking drivers will be stretching the risk envelope a bit, just as Crash does something unexpected. Bingo—into the weeds.

I did once succeed in protesting a driver of this type. He ran a Formula C, which was usually grouped with the Formula Fords. After being behind him for two or three first-lap crashes over two years, I finally decided that I didn't want to be scared every time I started a race. That's when I learned that the *GCR* really doesn't prohibit incompetence. Nevertheless, the SOMs knew of the guy, too, and I received some unofficial encouragement to file a protest. He was barred from the race for "incompetent driving" and he left the sport at the end of the season.

DO YOU FIT THE PROFILE?

If, after your first half-dozen races you are not approaching the lap times that your car should be capable of, please reread the above paragraphs thoughtfully.

Are you constantly being surprised by overtaking traffic? Are your lap times varying by a second or more from lap to lap? Have you ever suspected that you've run someone into the weeds? Talk to some of the faster drivers that are usually on the track with you. Ask if you are causing them problems. If you are, they will tell you, but will probably understate things a bit to avoid hurting your feelings. It will be hard on your ego, but try to draw them out. Is it mirrors? Lines?

Then go to work on it. Get your car professionally aligned. Attend a pro school, asking for particularly critical coaching. See if one of your friends will donate some of his track time to working with you. Rent a racetrack for a day of driver testing, and find someone to coach you for the day.

If you're not going to work on your problems, please find another hobby. I do not want to be on a racetrack with you and neither does anybody else.

Chapter 7

Learning in Your Street Car

Before we talk about what *to* do in your street car, let's talk about what *not* to do. Simply and unequivocally: You should not be driving your street car at the limit. In fact, you should not be driving it anywhere near the limit, at any time.

Why not? First, it's dangerous. Driving at the limit means that you are driving without margin for error. Driving on the street, with its inherent unpredictability, and among untrained drivers, is no place to be without margin.

Second, driving at the limit on the street is absolutely useless in developing your racing skills. Unless you are driving a Showroom Stocker, your street car's behavior at its limits bears no relationship to the behavior of your race car. Further, the speeds, corners, and situations encountered on the street bear no relationship to situations encountered in racing, even in Showroom Stock.

If you want to drive fast on the street, scaring your passengers and yourself, that is up to you. Just don't pretend that it is of any relevance to racing.

TRAFFIC AWARENESS

On the racetrack, it is imperative that you know exactly what traffic is around you—without reference to your mirrors. When you have to make a sudden move, there is no time to check. You must *know*.

Once, I relearned this lesson by almost causing a serious accident. Running through a 130mph turn, a friend of mine saw zero oil pressure and shut down his engine. I was behind him and, in the instant I had to make a decision, I could not confidently pull around him because I was not sure that I was clear on the right. I nailed the brakes, but ended up hitting him in the left rear wheel and spinning him across the track. Had there been traffic, this could have resulted in a bad crash, possibly with injuries. Had I been confident that my right side was clear (it was), I could have easily driven around the situation and improved my finishing position besides.

Practice traffic awareness on the street, especially on freeways. At any time, without reference to your mirrors, you should be aware of what cars are around you and know their approximate distances from you.

It isn't that hard. You can train yourself to be conscious of movements in your mirrors, then quickly look at them to catch what is happening. If a brown car was on your right, he is still there unless you have seen him pass or you have seen him move into your rearview mirror. You should not have to check your right side mirror.

"Look where you're going" is as applicable on the street as on the racetrack.

Hold the steering wheel loosely enough that you can feel what it is telling you.

Using Your Eyes

We talked earlier about eye technique. It is as applicable on the street as it is on the racetrack. About 20 years ago, I nearly hit a pedestrian on a dark night. I was making a left turn, looking through the windshield, and suddenly there was a white flash off my left fender. I missed that person but I am convinced that, had I been looking out the driver-side window *looking where I was going*, I would have seen the person and avoided the situation.

So, practice your eye technique on the street until it is automatic. In the beginning, make conscious and exaggerated head movements part of your drill every time you turn. Carefully develop a brake-look-turn habit for every corner. After a while it will become natural and you can begin using more eye movement and less head movement.

How do you know when your eye technique is ingrained and correct? When you start wishing that the car didn't have that damned windshield pillar that gets in your way all the time!

Getting Information from the Car

Most drivers have developed bad habits in their handling of the steering wheel. These habits range from the wrist-draped-on-top-of-the-wheel nitwits to those who tightly grip the steering wheel, elbows bent 90 degrees, while placing their noses within inches of its top.

Start by placing your seat a reasonable distance from the controls. Your feet should be able to operate the pedals without totally extending your legs, and you should be able to grip the top of the steering wheel while still having a slight bend in your elbow. Your seatbelts should be adjusted snugly, if possible (unfortunately, most street car seatbelts do not latch unless the mechanism detects sudden deceleration).

The objective of this position is to allow you to relax in the car while being able to make large steering wheel movements without repositioning your hands.

When you are seated this way you will probably feel somewhat uncomfortable. When you learned to drive, you probably sat fairly far forward so you could "see" where the front of the car was. You have probably been sitting in that position ever since. In fact, you couldn't see the front bumper then and you can't see it now. Now, however, you

do have a much better sense of its location. Because of this, you should be able to get used to your new, improved seating position in a day or two.

The main thing to work on is how you grip the wheel. Most people tend to grip it too tightly in pressure situations and too loosely when cruising down the road,

When you grip too tightly, you cut off the flow of information that comes to you from the car, through the steering. To prove this to yourself, try driving while gripping the wheel with just your fingertips. Find some uneven surfaces to drive on, and drive with a tire on the seam between the concrete curbing and the asphalt roadway. You'll be amazed at what your car tells you.

Now, become conscious of how you hold the wheel in pressure situations like passing cars on two-lane roads, merging into tight freeway situations, and so on. Do you tense up and grip the wheel hard? Break the habit. Ideally, you shouldn't tense at all, but if you must, select some muscles that are not involved with driving the car. Tense those.

It would not surprise me if you spent 6 months learning to stay relaxed in all situations. Why is this important? Because in a racing situation your car will be giving you a lot of information. It will be coming in through your ears, your seat, your feet, and your fingertips. You will be listening to your tires, you will be feeling the car reacting to the track surface, you will be feeling the irregularities in your brake system, and you will be feeling your front tires alternatively washing out and catching. You cannot assimilate this information if you are tense.

On the street, being relaxed is probably less critical than on the racetrack. Nevertheless, if you feel the front wheels beginning to wash out on a rain-soaked freeway ramp, you will be more likely to regain control of the car before it hits a lamppost. Also, if you are able to feel the front tires at the edge of brake lockup, you're more likely to be able to avoid a rear-end collision during rush hour.

OK, what about gripping the steering wheel too loosely? This won't be a problem in your race car (trust me). It's still something to be aware of for safe street driving. Untrained street drivers tend to react to problems by nailing the brakes; your racing experience will make you more prone to steer

Practice precise placement of your tires at the ramp entry, starting on the outside edge.

Clip the inside curb.

around them. You can only do so if your hands are properly placed and gripping the steering wheel *when it's time to react.*

LINES AND PRECISION

We talked earlier about the need for precision on the racetrack. Your tires must be within a few inches of where they should be, all the time.

Precision is an excellent subject for street practice. Practice placing your tires *exactly* where you want them. Is there an irregularity in the pavement? Place a front tire on it and verify your precision by feeling the irregularity through the steering wheel. A discarded soda can? Hit it with a tire; a *rear* tire. You can construct innumerable placement exercises on any trip; think of it as productive entertainment.

Another thing that you can do is to practice driving cornering lines. (No, not at the limit.) Develop the habit of clipping the outside at the entrance to a freeway ramp, a reasonable apex at the center, and an exit at the left edge, merging with traffic at speed. Attempting to do this, especially in unfamiliar corners, will help you hone your judgment for racing situations. In racing, you will have the advantage of repetition in learning corners, but you will be surprised by the variation of lines you must make due to traffic, track conditions, and your own screw-ups!

PASSING

My wife and I frequently drive a 400-mile round-trip on mostly a two-lane highway to get to and from our lake home. The general level of incompetent passing on this highway is a source of constant amazement to me.

Then complete the curve on the outside edge. This is a long, two-turn ramp, so the driver gets to repeat the exercise after the short straight section. Please note that the car in the photos is not rolled over due to cornering forces; it isn't anywhere near the limit. You shouldn't be, either.

It's really simple, just as your high school driving instructor told you. Pretend that you are drafting the car you intend to pass. Start your acceleration well back of the car. As you come up behind him, check your mirrors, then decide whether to pull out and finish the pass or to hit your brakes. If you decide not to pass and you do not have to brake, then you are not doing it right.

Do not jump blindly into the other lane and then mash the gas pedal. On the street, it's dangerous. On the racetrack, it could be suicidal. Also, you will not pass anybody on the racetrack this way. The cars are too equally matched.

SHIFTING

Heel-and-toe downshifting is a good street car exercise. You will be doing your gearbox a kindness, as well as developing the technique into a mindless and automatic habit. The less you have to distract you on the racetrack, the better.

Heel-and-toe is also a useful technique for starting out uphill. If you're in San Francisco, this skill may be of particular value.

BRAKING

It's tough to practice race braking on the street because braking at the limit of adhesion is likely to get you hit from behind. There are a couple of things you can work on, however.

First, discipline yourself to brake only while the car is traveling in a straight line. If you are a typical street driver, you are braking well into curves. For example, you are carrying your brakes a couple of car lengths into freeway exit ramps. This works fine because the car is nowhere near the limit and the tires can provide both braking and cornering thrust.

Think about the exit ramp situation, however, at higher speeds. At some point, the braking-while-turning situation becomes trail braking. This will result in the car's turning in *much* faster than you expect. Beyond trail braking speed, you are in a late or too-late apex situation and applying the brakes will spin the car.

The time that you will learn all of these things is in the rain, at your normal (dry weather) freeway exit speed. The available tire thrust will be reduced to the point where braking during the turn-in phase becomes quite dangerous. Break this habit. It is not good on the street and you don't want to be doing it on the racetrack, anyway.

I have also read a couple of books whose authors suggest that you develop braking control by holding constant pressure from your brake point to the point where you want to stop. If you have to modify (increase or decrease) your initial pedal pressure in order to stop at the correct point, then you have failed the exercise.

I don't know if this exercise actually helps on the racetrack, but at least it's a good amusement. Anything that improves your car control can't be bad.

Carroll Smith: "I think that this is a patently ridiculous idea. On a street car, you must increase pedal pressure (as the pads heat up) to maintain a constant deceleration. On a race car, you must ease up as you lose aerodynamic downforce with decreasing velocity."

Chapter 8

Autocross Solo II Competition

Autocrossing, or Solo II in SCCA parlance, is a great place to begin a racing hobby or career. It will allow you to develop a sense of car control, to experiment with lines through corners, and to experience a harmless spin or two. Costs are low, and specialized equipment is not needed.

(I don't mean to imply that autocrossing is *primarily* a stepping stone to racing; it is also a great sport in itself. There is local, regional, national, and even pro competition. Autocrossing offers competition at a lower level of personal and financial commitment than wheel-to-wheel racing. Try it, you'll like it!)

In this chapter, I'll try to apply some of the previous advice to autocross racing.

WHAT'S AN AUTOCROSS?

An autocross is a low-speed timed competition held on a temporary course, usually on a large parking lot. The layout of the course is determined by the event organizers; typically it is defined by orange traffic pylons and consists of

simple turns, chicanes, and hairpins separated by short straights. The course might consist of ten to fifteen turns altogether.

Cars are grouped into classes according to their potential and they make individual, timed runs rather than competing wheel-to-wheel. Most entrants drive their cars to the event, although there is a constituency that competes in special, trailered autocross cars.

The competition consists of multiple "runs" for each car; four to six is a typical range. Times are posted for all cars and all runs, so it is easy to follow the progress of the competition.

The design of the course is supposed to limit speeds to those experienced "on public roads," and to involve no collision risk beyond possibly hitting a curb. In order to keep things from getting too wild, time penalties are assessed for each pylon that is hit or disturbed. These penalties are large enough (two seconds is typical) that being careful of the pylons is an important driving consideration.

Once in a while, an autocross will be held at a local racetrack. In these cases, speeds are limited by strategically placed chicanes between the normal racing corners. These are typically much higher speed events, although the organizers will deny this to their insurers!

Autocrosses are typically held on Sundays, and run by local sports car clubs. You can make contact with local autocrossers through your SCCA region or, usually, through the salespeople at your local import car parts store. Don't limit yourself to SCCA; most autocrosses are locally organized.

EQUIPMENT

The advantage to autocrossing is that you can use your street car without modifications. I have already stated my views on front-wheel drive, so I will not repeat them. I will suggest, however, that you use a rear-wheel-drive car for autocrossing if you intend to use this type of competition as a stepping stone to club racing.

Usually, a helmet will be the only required piece of safety equipment. Buy a good one (yes, with a Snell SA spec) and get a correct fit. It's unlikely that you will actually bang your head on anything but, if you do, you want maximum protection.

Seatbelts are problematical. Most inertial-latch street car belts do nothing at all to hold you in your seat during cornering. This makes it difficult to drive the car sensitively. Ideally, you should install a set of racing lap and shoulder belts. As an alternative, I have seen a chest-belt gadget sold specifical-

In autocross competition, cars compete based on timed runs. The cars are started at intervals to ensure that they don't interfere with each other. Autocrossing requires the same car control and cornering techniques that are needed in wheel-to-wheel competition. This autocross is set up on a runway apron.

ly for autocross use. You use it to strap yourself to the seat-back. This product will at least keep your upper body in place so you will not have to hold yourself with the steering wheel.

The tire situation in autocrossing is a mess. Manufacturers have recently discovered the sport and are manufacturing racing-type tires with DOT approval on the sidewalls. To really run competitively, you will probably have to use this type of pseudo street tire.

Don't begin this way, however. Just as it is unnecessary to spend lots of money to improve your race car during your first season, so is it unnecessary to spend lots of money on autocross tires. Run your first few events with whatever tires are already on the car. Your objective is to develop as a driver, not to substitute money for skill.

If you can't resist screwing with the car, you can dial in some additional (negative) camber. Extreme settings (more than one degree) are effective in autocrosses because the straights and the runs aren't long enough to overheat the inside edges of the tires. If you drive your autocross car on the street, however, extra camber will cause the inside edges of the tires to wear quickly.

PARKING-LOT AUTOCROSS COURSE

The two main differences between a parking lot autocross course and a road-racing track are size, and the relative importance of cornering speed to lap times.

An autocross course is a miniature road racetrack. It has as many (or more) corners, but it is substantially shorter and is much narrower than a road racing track. Typically, it will be no more than a couple of car widths wide.

The result of this miniaturization is that a relatively high percentage of the driver's time is spent in cornering situations. Thus, smoothness and cornering technique are paramount. The acceleration of the car itself is a smaller part of the equation.

RACE PRACTICE IN A PARKING LOT

There are many aspects of parking lot autocrossing that will develop your racing skills. We'll talk about them in the context of how to attack an autocross circuit, but each is also something you have already read about in a racing context.

WALKING THE COURSE

If walking a racetrack to learn it is a good idea, walking an autocross circuit is mandatory. Instead of several sessions of lapping to learn the course, an autocrosser gets only a few runs, typically all of which are timed. Thus, it is imperative that you walk the course as many times as you can prior to making your runs. Yes, this means that you get to the site of the autocross as early as possible and that you again walk the course during any lunch break.

I'd suggest sketching a rough map of the course on graph paper during your walk. Then, you can observe others' lines on the course and mentally select among them before making your runs.

This preparation will also keep you from getting lost. It's not uncommon to see a driver become confused by all the pylons and go wandering off into the infield. Embarrassing.

While you're walking, study the surface carefully. At the relatively slow speeds of an autocross, even small variations in adhesion become significant. Look for roughness variations due to patches, cracks, and paint stripes. Paint does not provide the same grip as bare asphalt or concrete and, when damp, gets quite slick.

Look, too, for bumps and hollows. You may be able to take advantage of a hollow by tucking a wheel into it during

Autocross pylons create a miniature road racing track, but the lack of natural features makes an autocross course a challenge to learn. It's imperative that you walk the course, as these drivers are doing, prior to running it. Get there early and walk as many laps as you can.

a turn-in. Bumps can upset the car and cause a wheel to temporarily lose traction.

PRECISION

The ability to exactly place your car's tires is critical to fast autocross times. On a road racing course, we may be talking about missing an apex by 6–12in. At an autocross, divide these numbers by three. If you are more than 2in from a pylon, you are wasting a significant part of the corner.

Another thing about road racing is that there's no penalty for dropping an inside tire off the edge of the track. At an autocross, you'll hit one of the inside pylons and receive an instant time penalty sufficient to destroy your run.

Thus if you can become precise enough to succeed in autocrossing, you'll have an advantage on the racetrack.

I don't recommend the Braille method of learning where your wheels are. It's hard to feel the edges of the pylons, and it doesn't help your run times. Instead, work with one or two friends. Observe each other during your runs, taking notes on both inside and outside tire placement in various corners. Draw a rough map of the course and coach each other on where you're wasting space.

This is an area where a portable VCR with a telephoto lens could be of great benefit. Trade off with a friend, taping runs from various angles. Between runs, review the tape and critique yourselves. Here, the miniaturization of the course is a great advantage; you will probably be able to tape yourself in every corner.

As you get more advanced, you'll find yourself "widening" the course by moving outside the imaginary straight line between widely spaced pylons. This technique can be effectively used to make the corners bigger, but it requires superb car placement accuracy.

CORNERING LINES

We talked about the fact that optimizing speed in the corners is not the way to optimize road-racing lap times. This is because most of a racer's time is spent on the gas. This is less true in an autocross; the straights are short and thus less important. As an autocrosser, you will need to put more emphasis on optimum cornering speed.

This doesn't make the cornering lines into easy center-apex problems, however, because autocross corners are gen-

Clipping a pylon costs you at least one second; this Mustang driver has just ruined his run.

During the day, drivers' times are posted, so it's easy to follow the progress of the autocross competition.

erally more complex than road racing corners. A good course designer will have given you diminishing-radius corners, increasing-radius corners, and corners that change width between entry and exit.

As a first step, assume you are *only* interested in optimizing cornering speed. Remember the principle of the center-apex corner and try to adapt it to each corner. Take your sketches of the corners and try to draw a maximum-radius line through them. See where this line ends up relative to the "apex cone." Whether the line looks early or late, it's probably still giving you your best clipping point for the corner.

Next, consider the straight sections. The degree to which they are important depends on your car. If you do not have a lot of horsepower, you cannot afford to lose speed in the corners. Stick with the maximum-radius lines.

If you *do* have horsepower, then consider whether to use slightly later apexes in corners that precede straight sections. (In my Cobra, I tried to turn every autocross circuit into a series of straights, but this was an extreme case because of the car's primitive suspension and colossal horsepower-to-weight ratio.) In a car with decent handling, move your apexes slowly. You can easily lose more time in the corner than you will gain in the short straight that follows.

BRAKING AND TRAIL BRAKING

Recall that when we talked about braking a race car, we said that slow application of the brakes was required only when immediate, hard braking would upset the car.

Autocrossing in a street car, complete with soft suspension and high polar moment of inertia, is an ideal laboratory in which to learn braking control.

Practice brake application before you go to your first autocross. Find an empty parking lot and go at it. Here is where you could use a g-meter-type device to some benefit. Develop your touch until you can achieve maximum deceleration consistently and repeatably without locking either the fronts or the rears.

Develop some sensitivity to brake pad temperature during your braking practice. Cold pads, typical of the beginning of a run, will behave differently than will the hot pads that you use to finish your run.

Once you have mastered brake application, you should begin working on getting off the brakes. The extremely tight corners of a typical autocross circuit are a great training laboratory for trail braking. Explore your car's behavior as you blend the end of your braking with the beginning of your turn-in. This is particularly important to learn if you are dri-

ving a front-wheel-drive car. It may be the only way to get the thing to turn in! Again, you can practice trail braking turn-ins in an empty parking lot.

(People who are solely interested in autocrosses may also wish to perfect their skill at parking-brake turns for the ultimate in quick turn-in. However, this technique is not used much in racing.)

You should be aware of one pitfall in running the low-speed corners of an autocross course. It is easy to overdrive the front tires, causing them to wash out. This can happen almost without notice during a trail braking entry: the front tires are pushed through slip, into skid, and you are left with a hideously understeering car. When this happens, even a normally oversteering car will plow into the pylons. The only cure for it is sensitivity to steering wheel feedback and careful experimentation. Try making your corner entries without trail braking. If this reduces mid-corner push, then you were probably overdoing the entry.

SHIFTING

Your first goal should be to minimize shifting. This may mean holding the engine at redline near the end of a straight in order to avoid shifting. It's worth it; each quick upshift requires a slower downshift.

Next, you should decide whether to double-clutch or not. In almost every case, your downshift will be between two adjacent gears, usually second to first. If you can make this downshift quickly without double-clutching, I suggest that you do it this way. The tiny bit of wear that results from a few autocross runs should not be a problem.

Where the synchro rings are difficult or where it is a two-gear downshift, you will have to double-clutch. The technique is exactly as described in chapter 4. Pay special attention to not wasting clutch pedal travel.

EYE TECHNIQUE

Brake-look-turn and looking where you're going are, if anything, more important on an autocross circuit than they are on a racetrack. Where you're going is probably visible through the driver's side window or through the passenger's side of the windshield. If you're not looking through these pieces of glass before you make your turn-ins, you will not be fast. It's that simple.

RACETRACK AUTOCROSSES

Any time you can spend on the racetrack will be good for you as training. That being said, you should realize that running an autocross course set up on a racetrack is a unique situation. It's neither a "real" autocross nor is it a "real" race event. The extra pylon corners mean that the racing straights lose importance, but the big racing corners offer drivers the opportunity to get into real trouble.

First of all, pay extra attention to your safety preparations. It is quite possible to roll a car during a racetrack autocross. You will probably not go so far as to install a roll cage, but you should at least remove all loose objects from inside the car and trunk. Also, make sure that you have good seatbelts and a good helmet.

I do *not* suggest that you attack a racetrack autocross circuit with street car belts. You will spend all of your time trying to stay in your seat and you will learn little about sensitivity, smoothness, or finesse in car control. Install some real racing belts.

Second, make sure that your car's brakes are in absolutely perfect condition, with high-performance pads and extra cooling installed if possible. The fact that chicanes and other car-slowing arrangements have been set up means that you will be doing more braking during the autocross than you would be during a race. Be ready for it.

Finally, understand that your corner entry speeds will be somewhat slower than they would be in a race situation. This primarily affects your brake points; your turn-in points will probably be no different than they would be at racing

Consistent high finishes on the autocross circuit develop skills that will be useful on the racetrack. And you don't have to have a fancy car to have fun and be competitive in your class. The "169" number on the car probably means that two drivers are running. The other driver will simply remove the "1" and run as car #69. There are suppliers who will sell you magnetic numbers, but white or black liquid shoe polish works fine, too.

speeds. Beyond this, everything previously said about driving at the limit is applicable.

Have fun!

Your approach to an autocross circuit should consider the relative strengths and weaknesses of your car. This Cobra, with a primitive suspension and phenomenal acceleration, requires a different approach than, say, a Lotus which sticks like glue but has only moderate acceleration. The Cobra driver will late-apex to allow earlier throttle-down. The Lotus driver would apex a bit earlier to avoid losing too much speed in the corners.

Chapter 9

Unexciting But Important

TIRES

There is no reason to buy anything but the brand and type of tires that are on most of the winning cars in your class or, at least, on the fastest cars of the type you are driving.

NEW TIRES

A new racing tire is at its stickiest for only one or two heat cycles. The reason for this is that the rubber hardens from heat and age. This unfortunate fact is one of the main reasons for the high cost of racing. We don't wear them out; we just use them up—and fast.

A new street tire, to be fast, must have shallow tread depth. Thus, the fastest street tires are the ones that are shaved to just enough depth that they will survive qualifying and the race. Here we wear them out, but we start the process by throwing away most of the tread rubber on a cutting machine.

Either way, we are talking about one-weekend tires.

Thus, front-runners normally have to buy new tires every weekend. As a novice, you should not be doing this. It is damned expensive and the speed advantage is only temporary. If you have some extra money, spend it on something that will yield more permanent results, like a pro driving school, a test day, or (if you absolutely can't resist spending money on the car) a professionally built engine.

People who are buying new street-type tires every weekend normally have them shaved to the point where they are junk at the end of the race. People who are buying new rac-

Here's the biggest single weekend expense, almost $500 worth of new tires for qualifying.

ing slicks, however, are a source of perfectly good used tires at about 30% of new prices (no typo here—30% of, not 30% off).

So for novices, I suggest buying used racing tires or buying new street tires with minimal shaving. Either way, you should be able to get three or more weekends on a set of tires.

Tony Kester: "Don't buy used racing tires from teams with fast drivers! Buy from big-budget teams with slow drivers—the tires will be barely broken in."

Mixed-condition or mixed-brand tires can be a safety problem. Do not mix brands and do not mix used tires and new ones. A mixture of new and old tires can dangerously upset the handling of the car. I have a friend who (to save money) put two new front tires on his car and left some old ones on the back. Braking into a slow turn, his sticky new tires worked fine, the rears locked up, the car spun, and he got hit to the tune of $2,000 or so in damage.

Mix tire compounds only with trepidation, and never on the same end of the car (front and rear differences can work, but left and right mismatches are to be avoided).

Carroll Smith: "Mixing compounds seldom works anyway."

Never buy tires that are not from the current year's production. These are sometimes offered at bargain prices. The sellers must offer bargains because the tires will be substantially less sticky than even a used set of current-year tires.

WHERE TO BUY NEW TIRES

I suggest that you avoid buying new tires at the racetrack. You will pay list price and you will run a small risk that your tires will not be ready when your session is flagged off. Instead, try to find a local tire dealer who is involved with SCCA racing as a participant or as a sponsor. The dealer will generally be able to order whatever racing tires you need and you will know on Thursday night that you have tires for the weekend. If you are lucky, he may also give you a bit of a discount or may throw in the mounting and balancing. Reciprocate by buying all of your street car tires from him, and by sending your friends to him as well.

TIRE BALANCING

Weights are added to wheels to ensure that the tire-and-wheel center of gravity is exactly on the spinning (axle) axis. This can be adequately done with a "bubble" balancer in most cases. This is the type of balancer usually used by the tire dealers at the racetrack. "Spin" balancing additionally tries to bring the plane of balance parallel to the plane of the wheel's bolt face. Spin balancing has primarily theoretical advantages, but the machines can be successfully operated by idiots—which is not true of bubble balancing.

It is a good idea to check the balance of your tires between weekends. They can become unbalanced from wear and it's silly to waste a session finding out that this has happened to you. Before checking the balance, though, be sure to clean the rocks off of the tread. A wide drywall taping knife is a good tool for this; the edge of your hand is not.

You can often guess which of your four tires is out of balance on the racetrack by paying careful attention to the vibration you feel. If you have an out-of-balance rear, you will feel the vibration primarily in your seat. You will feel a vibrating front more through the steering wheel. The vibration will diminish when the out-of-balance tire is loaded (on the outside) in a turn and increase when it is unloaded. This is not 100% reliable, but it will give you a clue as to which tire to check first.

CAR PREPARATION

If you have read this far without having bought Carroll Smith's *Prepare to Win*, stop now, and go out and buy it. Carroll covers car preparation with a breadth and expertise that is unmatched. The important thing to get from the book is Carroll's philosophy of attention to detail and thoroughness. Don't worry about the fact that you will never have to deal with a Formula 5000 gearbox. Or that you may never have heard of Formula 5000.

Dennis Eade: "No matter what course of action you take in chassis preparation, read Carroll Smith's *Prepare to Win*. Many things will not apply directly to your car; however, it all applies in the overview. This is the preparation primer. Carroll has several other good books out, but I would leave those until later.

"Establish a relationship with your local race shop and parts supplier. These people will be an invaluable source of help and information. The mistakes you are about to make are not new. They have been made before. These people have made them! Learn from them.

"If you can afford to have a race shop prepare your car, choose one that is knowledgeable with the class you are planning to run. A good race shop can advance your learning curve at a rapid pace. They will take over the aggravation of maintaining the chassis. They also can speed your dri-

The Care and Feeding of Your Goodyear Racing Eagles

A proper breaking-in period is necessary for your Goodyear Racing Eagles to perform as they were designed. The procedure requires a few miles of gradual warm-up, three to five miles of hard driving, and then a cooling-down period.

A new tire develops some minor irregularities during shipping and storage. The break-in period reshapes the tire to its intended size and contour for racing, and indicates if the tire/wheel unit has been properly balanced. In addition, dust, oil, and other foreign substances are "scuffed" from the tread surface. The warm-up pace is gradually increased until the driver feels comfortable enough with the tires to go flat out.

Running the next three to five miles as hard as possible completes the internal adjustments to the tire. During this initial hard run, extra internal heat is developed, and the tire may actually overheat if the hard running is continued—a process that can permanently and deleteriously alter the tread compound. A common complaint heard from drivers starting a race on new ("label" or "sticker") tires is that they worked great for a couple of laps and then "went-away" or "gave-up." Running a new tire through and beyond the optimum temperature range may work for a short qualifying effort but is not always a good race strategy.

The best way to cool the tire is to pit. Pitting also provides the opportunity to measure the circumference of each tire hot (see stagger discussion below). If pitting to change or cool the tires is not practical, a couple of slow laps will be of some benefit, at least.

[The following information is specific to the now-defunct Formula Super Vee Pro Series, but should be generally relevant to all Goodyear racing tires.]

Since your FSV Eagles are bias-ply tires, you should pay at least some attention to stagger. The Super Vee group is often not allocated sufficient practice time to spend a lot of it playing around with tire stagger; nonetheless, here are the basics:

Measure and mark all of your "label" tires before you run them.

Sort your label tires into "stagger sets" that best fit the conditions in which you are running. For the occasional "left hand course," try a smaller left rear. Ovals, such as Milwaukee, fall into the "left hand" category and may require as much as 0.4in of stagger. For courses with no particular directional signature, a neutral stagger set-up is usually desirable—the only possible exception being in the case where the longest straightaway is entered and exited in the same direction.

Make a short 1-2 lap run to scuff in your tires and, while they are still hot, remeasure them to check growth.

Small stagger adjustments can be made by varying air pressure: Adding 1 psi will stretch the tire approximately 0.02in in diameter; adding 2 psi stretches the tire 0.05in; 3 psi, 0.08in; and 4-5 psi, 0.1in, which is about the maximum you should attempt to stretch the tire.

As with any other chassis setting or adjustment, you should keep a record of your stagger history at each racetrack.

Given the normally limited amount of practice time available on a race weekend, the best approach is to first set up the car on a good set of used tires. Then break in a new set of tires with a short qualifying attempt, as new tires can be temporarily quicker than used tires. Save this freshly-scuffed set for the race and you should find them quick, reliable, and predictable.

If you have any questions about tires during a race weekend, a Goodyear engineer will be happy to help you.

ving improvement.

"If you cannot afford to have a race shop prepare your chassis, you will still need them for assorted jobs. Befriend them, show up the day they are loading for a race or at the end of a miserable weekend and help them load the trucks, listen to them, help sweep the shop, show up with a couple of cold ones at the end of a hot day at the shop or track, volunteer to be gofer for a big weekend. Pay them when they need it! A few of these little things will go a long way in proper preparation of your race car.

"These people have a wealth of knowledge that you can make good use of. Yes, you will have to pay. However, payment is not always monetary."

After you have absorbed *Prepare to Win*, then you should buy and absorb *Tune to Win*. Again, the philosophy is the key; apply it as appropriate to your level of competition, finances, and expertise.

Unobtanium Parts

Unobtanium is a marvelous engineering material that is used in many racing products. Although you will never see it in its elemental form, it is fairly easy to identify. A product made with unobtanium will be hideously expensive. It will promise substantial performance gain without requiring any driving skill or technical capability on the part of its purchaser.

These performance gains, however, will be qualitative rather than quantitative or, if quantitative, the evidence will be anecdotal.

Unobtanium is used in the manufacture of many proprietary juices offered to the racer for the improvement of his engine and his brakes. It is used in wheels, in specially colored gasolines, and (in especially large quantities) in shock absorbers.

As a novice driver, you should carefully develop your ability to detect products that are made with unobtanium. And you should not buy them.

Just as there is no magic, there is no unobtanium. And

This Taylor Design brake rotor costs $235 (a stock unit is $75), but provides no significant benefit to a novice driver. When you qualify for the Runoffs, you may be ready for this type of hardware.

there are no large performance gains to be had by buying things that are apparently made from it.

Yes, there are tiny gains that can be had for big dollars—carbon-fiber brake discs, for example. As a novice, don't waste your money. When you develop to the point where you are consistently a few tenths of a second off the pole, *then* it may be time for a few judicious purchases of products that could shave the tenths. Tenths, by the way, is what you can expect from your purchases. You don't get seconds by buying them.

Standards

You should have only one standard of preparation: the car should be ready to race when you leave for the racetrack. If it's not, stay home. The racetrack is not the place to be setting valves, fastening the exhaust system so it doesn't fall off, or installing mirrors. (It happens—I once helped out by bolting on a friend's mirrors as his session was being called to the grid. As I recall, he couldn't do it earlier because he put the car on the trailer with the paint still wet!)

Top priority for car readiness has to be safety items and the reliability of safety-related items like suspension elements, brakes, wheels, and tires. Everything connected with the safety of the car should be carefully checked on a schedule that you know will allow time to correct any failures. Depending on the car, this checking may include professional crack-testing (Magnaflux or Zyglo), disassembly of key components, and/or a careful visual check. Unless you have Superman's X-ray vision, a thorough check cannot be done with the wheels on the car.

Performance is a close second priority for preparation time. If you're not trying to achieve your maximum potential, why would you go at all?

Appearance can be third priority. Depending on your tastes, it can be a distant third. Cleaning, however, is safety related. You will not be able to see chassis or suspension cracks under a layer of greasy dirt. Many other things, such as loose electrical wires, seem to show more clearly when they are clean. Also, time spent cleaning can be time spent carefully looking over the car for problems.

Tony Kester: "Your crew, whether paid or not, will especially appreciate a clean car. Don't expect them to crawl underneath it to check something if it's like working on a garbage truck."

Fasteners

Dennis Eade: "If you are not mechanically oriented, the first thing you need to learn is fasteners. *Prepare to Win* does an excellent job of [explaining] fasteners. These fasteners must be installed. Learn about installation.

"Learn about torque! Buy a simple swing-arm torque wrench. Torque every fastener on your race car until you learn the difference between 7lb-ft and 75lb-ft. Learn the differences in bolt sizes and thread pitch. This is the key to holding your race car together.

"Learn about positive locking devices: Loctite, nylocks, lock washers, flat washers, jet nuts. Learn about proper washers. Learn about the wonderful world of chemicals. The adhesives and lubricants currently being marketed are a marvel. Use the best you can buy! To 'cheap out' in your preparation will only cost you later."

Suspension and Chassis Preparation

Between races, this is mostly a safety inspection task. On my cars, I have always marked all (nonsafety-wireable) bolts, nuts, and other turnable objects with paint lines. These lines can be checked at a glance to determine that nothing has moved. In cases where a bolt threads into a blind hole and cannot be safety wired, I paint a horizontal line across the bolt head. My crew knows that any lines that aren't horizontal should be investigated further. (Fastidious marking and safety wiring also communicates a good message to the crew regarding how careful I want *them* to be.)

Paint pens for safety marks can be bought at craft stores. They are sold for fabric painting, and the paint seems to be lacquer. I use a different color each year. This ensures that all the seldom-checked bolts and nuts get checked at least once a season.

If you want to check tightness with a wrench, avoid the temptation to move each nut or bolt a little bit. These "little bits" can soon add up to severe overtorque.

Every chassis has problem areas that are prone to cracking. Learn from others what to look for and you will not find out firsthand, spinning backwards into a wall.

Dennis Eade: "'To finish first you must first finish.' I

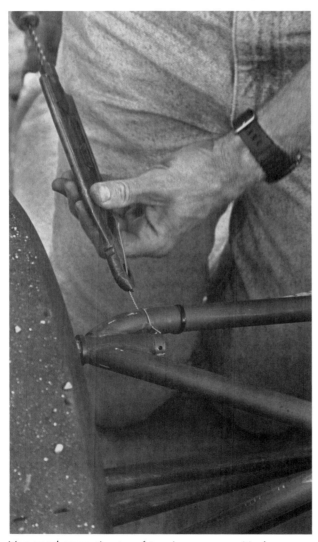

It's a good precaution to safety-wire as many critical fasteners as possible. By wiring the camber adjuster to the A-arm, this mechanic is minimizing the possibility that it will loosen on the racetrack. A pair of safety-wire pliers ($40–$50) is a good investment.

don't know the origin of this quotation, but it's correct! First, the car must be safe and reliable.

"There is only one way to perform maintenance on a race car: using a rigid procedure that is recorded on a check sheet. No one is good enough to work without a recorded procedure. If you need help in designing your initial procedure, a good prep shop will be more than glad to assist you. They probably will even give you copies of their check sheets.

"Basic pre-race and between-session [checks] require a fistful of wrenches, clean rags, brake cleaner, and WD-40. It is a simple procedure. Wipe clean every piece on the car. As you wipe—look and feel. After you have cleaned, a light coat of WD-40 or similar oil will prevent rust and corrosion. It will do wonders to improve the basic looks of your chassis. You are the best inspector you have. Do not neglect this job.

"You'll notice I didn't mention polish. I don't polish. If you have time to polish, you have time to do more important things to make you safer and faster: nut and bolt checking, engine maintenance, alignment, and so on.

"Check the tightness of every fastener. This does not mean you retorque or add torque; just check to see that it is torqued properly. We do this as pre-race maintenance and between sessions. You will be amazed at what you can find before it causes you to DNF. If you have spare time, do a nut and bolt check.

"I do not paint-mark every nut and bolt, as George does. I feel that the paint gives a false sense of security. The nut-and-bolt relationship may not have changed, but the clamped material may have collapsed. Painting also keeps you from cleaning and inspecting as much as is necessary.

"I treat safety wire much as I do paint. Some race car parts need to be wired, however. If they are wired, you need to arrange things so that the fastener head is accessible

Marking things that can loosen makes them easy to check quickly; if the paint line is not horizontal, the bolt has moved. These bolts can't be safety-wired, so it's especially important to check them frequently.

enough to be checked with a wrench.

"Create a rigid procedure for the cleaning and nut-and-bolt procedure. Start at the same point every time. Don't stop until you are at the end of a job. (If you must stop, stop at the front roll hoop or some other clear point where you or someone else can pick up the job and not miss anything.)

Fill out your check sheet religiously! Modify your check sheet to suit your needs and procedures. You must not leave for the track without your check sheet being completed."

VIBRATION

Most of the cars that get parked around the racetrack are victims of some type of vibration-caused failure. Some of these failures are courtesy of the car's designer and some are created by the person who prepared the car. Virtually all of them can be prevented.

Any significant amount of mass that is not somehow constrained *will* move around *a lot* under racing conditions. Things that are close to the engine will be susceptible to engine vibration, things (like brake lines) associated with the wheels will get violently moved up and down by the track surface, and everything in the car will be affected by cornering loads.

Many vibration failures are electrical in nature. Loops of

A cantilever bracket is susceptible to breaking either the bracket or the mounting point. Both the cantilevered oil filter bracket and its mounting point must be solid; here, the engine block provides an adequate mount. A flaw in this setup, though, is that the upside-down filter may drain while the car is standing and delay the engine's oil supply at startup.

wire are left to wave back and forth until the copper fatigues and cracks. Pieces of bodywork or stainless braided hose are left to rub against wires until they are shorted or cut through. Loops of wire or fork-type electrical terminals crawl out from under not-quite-tight terminal nuts.

Another common failure is fatigue cracking of the mounting bracket holding a cantilevered object. For our purposes, cantilevered refers to any object that is attached to the car with its center of gravity left to wave around. Many cantilever mounts (such as oil filter brackets) are made strong to resist cracking. The result of this is generally that the sheet metal to which the bracket is bolted will be the piece that breaks.

Spend some time studying your newly purchased (or rented) car. Identify all situations where wires, hoses, and cantilevered objects can wave back and forth. Add tie-wraps, safety wire, brackets, and so on, as necessary to constrain them. One handy technique for a wire going across a panel is to anchor it with little dabs of silicone rubber gasket goo. (First, clean the panel well with solvent to get the oil off. Then, anchor the wire overnight with masking tape until the goo dries.)

Once all the inadequately anchored objects are taken care of, begin looking for situations where things can rub and chafe against one another. The edge of a fiberglass body panel will, given enough time, saw through a tubular steel brake fluid line. It will cut through an aluminum Halon discharge tube more quickly, and it will do in the insulation on an electrical wire almost instantly. Stainless braided (Aeroquip) hose is equally effective at these tasks.

Whenever you install a new gadget, take care to mount it with two brackets, preferably with the gadget's center of gravity located between them. If you absolutely cannot use more than one bracket, put the bracket at approximately the gadget's c.g.. For example, an ignition coil clamp goes near the center of the coil, not at one end. Two clamps would be better.

Nothing bad will happen if you are excessively careful in anchoring and mounting things. If you are not careful enough, however, you will eventually suffer for it.

ALIGNMENT

For reasons that I do not understand, there is a mystique associated with alignment. People tend to want "pro" alignments—even people with the brains and skill to do it themselves.

Carroll Smith: "If you're prepping your own car and do not feel confident enough to align it—stop. Get your car aligned by someone competent and pay him to teach you how to do it."

To me, a pro alignment has a couple of shortcomings. First, the person doing it does not care as intensely about the car's performance as you do. Second, he is trying to make some small amount of profit while charging you a reasonable price. He may not take all the time that he could or should, not through malice, but simply because of economic reality.

(It is sometimes possible to buy or make special jigs for setting a particular car, like a Spec Racer. A pro with this kind of jigging may well be dramatically faster and significantly more accurate than any amateur. In such a case, I would seriously consider at least a once-a-year full alignment by the pro.)

Dennis Eade: "Chassis alignment is not a black art. It is basic geometry. The black art is *designing* the suspension angles, not *setting* them. Teach yourself a basic understanding of suspension. There is a reason for each of the angles and

Basic Alignment

Tire Camber Setting | True Vertical

Tire camber is the tilt of the tire with respect to true vertical. Normal camber settings are negative values, indicating that the top of the tire is tilted inwards. Typical values are one-half to one degree negative. Large negative camber values improve cornering, but can overheat and wear the inside tire edge on the straights.

Tire toe is effectively a static steering setting. Negative values indicate that the tire is pointed inwards. Normally, negative toe is used to ensure that the tires can't possibly point outwards when the suspension is loaded under braking. Typical values are small (half a degree or less), since toe also creates drag.

A good basic alignment requires setting camber and toe at all four wheels. Of course, solid rear axles have no toe, but pro teams have been known to bend their solid axle housings in hydraulic presses to create some negative camber!

---

measurements.

"You need few special tools to do alignments. A camber gauge (fancy bubble level), a piece of string, and a pair of jack stands will do just fine. It's nice to have digital scales, fancy toe bars, and special alignment jigs, but they are not necessary.

"If you do not understand alignment, have your local race shop do it or teach you how. George is wrong here! Your local race shop *does* care about your alignment. To me, an alignment is as critical a job as an engine rebuild. I can usually make a lot more difference in lap time with a proper alignment than can the latest tweak of the week in the engine. I can also do it much faster than someone at home. I have special tools and I do thousands of alignments. Your local race shop *does* care about your alignment. We need alignments to eat!"

Author comment: "I didn't say that the pro shops didn't care. They care—if they didn't, they would be in some kind of rational business enterprise instead of being in racing. It's just that they probably don't care as intensely as *you* do."

Basic alignment has the simple objective of making sure that all four wheels are pointed where you want them to point, and that they are slanted inward at the top to the degree you wish. Those are the basics: toe and camber. All you need is a good steel rule, a straight string or bar set parallel to the centerline of the car, and a $75 camber gauge.

More elaborate alignment tasks, like setting track and wheelbase and setting bump steer, are also not that hard. Once you have gained some confidence in the basics, you should be doing these tasks yourself as well (at least to the extent that these are adjustable on your car).

For instructions on alignment, read *Prepare to Win* or *Race Car Engineering*.

ENGINE PREPARATION

There are three general categories of racers: those who always use professional engine builders, those who have a pro-built engine but do rebuilds and tuning themselves, and those who are slow. Whichever of the three you are, between-race preparation is about the same.

Charlie Williams: "Generally, if you start with a pro-built engine and you are somewhat mechanically inclined, you should be able to keep up the between-race maintenance yourself.

"We have some customers who are not mechanically inclined. In some cases they have enlisted the help of local people to do engine maintenance such as adjusting valves, checking timing, and R&R of the head to clean the valves. Other customers have me maintain two cylinder heads, which they only have to switch when needed.

"The average club racer will put no more than ten to twenty hours on an engine during a season, then return it for a winter rebuild. Racers with larger budgets, racing every weekend, will own up to three engines. They'll have one in the car, one in the trailer, and one at the engine builder's shop for rebuilding."

Dennis Eade: "I would highly recommend you have a professional engine builder build your engine. He does it all day long. He knows what and how to assemble your engine. Listen to him, believe him, do what he tells you. If you're short on budget, explain that to him. He can help save you time, money, and DNFs.

"Learn how and what maintenance your engine builder

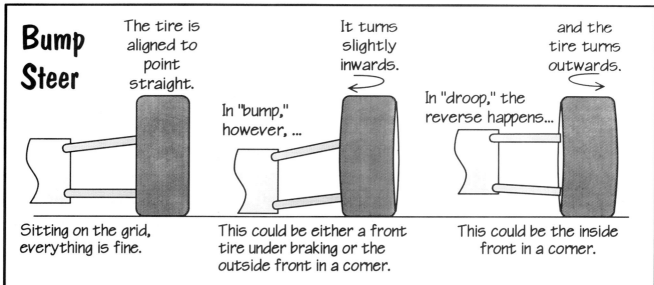

Bump Steer

The tire is aligned to point straight.

In "bump," however, ...

It turns slightly inwards.

In "droop," the reverse happens...

and the tire turns outwards.

Sitting on the grid, everything is fine.

This could be either a front tire under braking or the outside front in a corner.

This could be the inside front in a corner.

The toe-in of each tire is set during alignment with the car at normal ride height. As weight is transferred on the race track, however, the wheel moves up and down relative to the chassis. This motion can produce steering effects, referred to as "Bump Steer" or "Roll Steer." The drawings show a "roll oversteer" characteristic, which will probably make the car hard to control in a corner. The ideal, of course, is to have no steering changes over the normal range of suspension travel.

wants you to perform. **Then do it. A little work here saves a tremendous amount."**

Carroll Smith: "You bet!"

All the externally measurable tuning parameters of the engine should be checked before each race weekend. These include ignition point gap or dwell, ignition timing, carburetor float level, spark plugs and gaps, and valve lash. The throttle should be checked at idle and full-open. (It's embarrassing to find that you're slow because the throttle isn't fully open when the pedal is on the floor.)

As deposits build up in the exhaust passages and on the backs of the intake valves, flow resistance increases and power drops. Depending on the competitiveness of your class and your own level of ambition, you may want to freshen the cylinder head(s) between races. The heads should be stripped, deposits removed with a rotary wire brush in a drill motor, the valves lightly lapped on their seats, and everything cleaned, reassembled, and reinstalled.

If you have chosen to run without an air cleaner (dumb), you can skip the valve lapping. Sand and stones will have made the valve seats look like the surface of the moon, and the craters will not lap out.

It's also a good idea to do a leakdown test (preferably) or a compression check (at least) before each race. Doing so will let you monitor trends and correlate leakdown readings with engine performance. It will also detect a hidden catastrophe before you waste a weekend hauling a bad engine to the track. I once found a loose wrist pin this way; it had worn a groove in the cylinder wall! Had I run the engine another weekend, it almost certainly would have broken first a rod, then the crankshaft and the block. All in about 200 milliseconds.

GEARBOX MAINTENANCE

Dennis Eade: **"Transmissions are sometimes treated as mystical boxes. They are basic, simple, and easy to maintain. Get the manual, have a friend show you through it the first time, or pay your local race shop to show you.**

"Assemble it properly, inspect your gears carefully, use good quality oil (not snake oil with horsepower-creating properties), shift it properly, and it will treat you well."

BODYWORK

I strongly suggest that you learn enough to do at least some of your own paint work. While you may not want to paint a whole production car, you can easily spot-paint damaged areas. Bodywork pieces from purpose-built race cars are usually small enough to deal with easily in the driveway.

Depending on the scope of the job, I use a Sears gun that came with my compressor, a Badger trim and touch-up gun, or an airbrush. Buy any of the many how-to books on bodywork and painting, go to the auto body supply store to get what you need, and sail right in. The sales clerks at the auto body store are reasonably good sources of advice. (The paint companies run training seminars for them.) Except for poisoning yourself, all mistakes are correctable with sandpaper—don't forget to buy a good respirator.

My driveway is my spray booth. I suggest the same for you. Granted, you will get some bugs, dirt, and sand in the paint—at the racetrack, no one will notice. The alternative, painting inside the shop, produces a horrible mess of paint dust on everything. In addition, there's a danger of fire or explosion from the airborne solvent mist.

Stick to a small number of simple colors for your car. "One" is a good, small number. Blended rainbows, airbrush lace, and fancy stripes are great to look at, but are difficult or impossible to spot-repair after an on-track incident. Paint should be acrylic enamel with a hardener, or a polyurethane such as DuPont's Imron.

By choosing your colors carefully, you can economize on paint. Reds, for example, are more expensive than blues. Ask the auto body supply clerks about prices.

Along with teaching yourself to paint, learn to do some rudimentary fiberglass work. It's not hard, and you will need it.

BRAKE BLEEDING

One of the things you will notice in the racing paddock is that a lot of brake bleeding goes on. Much of this is necessary, but much of it is not. There are two reasons to bleed the brakes: first, to replace moisture-loaded fluid with fresh fluid, and second, to get rid of bubbles in the fluid.

It is not necessary to change fluid at the racetrack unless the pedal is going soft when the brakes get hot. This is a symptom of fluid boiling. Change it at home once in a while for good luck, however. From the day you installed it, its boiling point has been declining due to absorption of water. When you do make the change, do not use a pressure bleeder full of old fluid. It will already have absorbed enough water to make the whole exercise pointless. Use brake fluid from small, newly opened containers. If you are replacing fluid due to boiling, consider upgrading the fluid to something like Automotive Products' AP550, too.

If you are getting air in the fluid at the racetrack, it is almost certainly entering the system via a leaking seal on a caliper, a slave cylinder, or a master cylinder. (Each time the pedal is released, a slight vacuum is created in the system. This vacuum will pull air into the system if the seals are not right. A seal can leak air inward without leaking fluid outward; it has to do with the design of the seals.) Rather than simply living with poor brakes and the misery of at-track bleeding, I strongly suggest that you find and fix the sealing problem.

Dennis Eade: "Brake bleeding should be done before leaving for the track and when you have a problem (soft pedal, overheat, or a reason to open the brake system). Use the best brake fluid you can buy. We have had tremendous success with Cartel 570."

AERODYNAMICS

Although even an introductory treatment of race car aerodynamics is beyond the scope of this book, I will give you a few useful facts that I have picked up over the years. At a minimum, they may keep you from wasting time tuning on the wrong things.

The two main considerations in minimizing aerodynamic drag are (1) maintenance of nonturbulent flow over as much of the car's bodywork as possible, and (2) the fact that the main contributor to car drag is the cross-sectional area at the point where flow separates from the car at the rear. It is the low-pressure area *behind* the car that creates the majority of the drag; the drag is *not* created at the front by the nose pushing the air aside.

Carroll Smith: "At least 0.1% of all the racers, pilots, and sailors in the world already realize this!"

The ideal aerodynamic shape for our cars (considering only drag) is a teardrop. A teardrop features a round, blunt nose, smooth flow of air around the sides of the body, then slowly reconvergent rear surfaces to lead the airflow back together without creating turbulence or flow separation. Some Formula Vees (where low drag has been paramount for over 20 years) approximate this shape.

Sharp, pointed noses are not aerodynamically necessary unless you plan to achieve supersonic or near-supersonic speeds. This is why commercial passenger jets don't have pointed noses. (Where a car has front wings, a pointed nose is used to allow maximum wing area. It does not have anything to do with penetration.)

After the rounded nose, the next thing to consider is the cross-sectional area of the car at the flow separation point. Generally, bodywork that tapers more than ten or fifteen degrees relative to the airflow past it will cause the flow to separate and become turbulent. The rear edge of a sedan roof, for example, is a flow separation point. The area behind the rear window and over the trunk is filled with turbulent, low-pressure air. The result is both drag and lift.

Thus, your objective is to keep the air flowing smoothly against the bodywork along the sides of the car and over the roof (if you have a roof). Have you noticed that auto makers have been shifting to flush-mounted glass on street cars? The reason for this is that the bumps and ridges of conventional glass window moldings are great flow separators.

How can you use this information? Well, depending on your class, you may be able to take some small steps to improve drag. At the front, you should make sure that there are no tabs, gaps, or irregularities that cause the airflow to separate. In some Showroom Stock cars, this may mean that you are somewhat more generous with the headlight-protecting

Street-type engines, like this Formula Ford, are fairly reliable. Once in a while, though, one will expire at the racetrack and have to be changed.

Checking the lug nuts is one important item on the between-sessions checklist. Losing a wheel on the racetrack is surprisingly common and does nothing for the car's handling. John Gacioch

race tape than might be absolutely necessary. In a Production or GT car, you may be able to make some subtle modifications to the way you mount your windshield and/or window plexiglass. Fender flares are another area where retaining flow attachment may require some work.

You can easily check for flow separation by taping small pieces of string or yarn on your car, then having a crew member take some pictures as the car passes at speed. Patterns of oil and dirt on the bodywork can provide clues as well. Look for smooth, streamlined flow, where the yarns or oil streaks point generally parallel and toward the rear of the car. Areas of disrupted flow will not show oil streamlines, and the yarn tufts will be hanging down, pointing up, or even pointing back toward the front of the car.

The "spoiler" seen at the rear edge of sedan trunks does not spoil anything at all. In fact, its function is to catch the turbulent air coming down the rear window and to dam it up into a sort of aerodynamic pool over the window and rear deck. The surface of this reservoir becomes a pseudo body surface. The airflow coming over the top of the car is then led smoothly from the edge of the roof and down across the surface of the dammed-up air to the top edge of the spoiler. It does not become separated until this point. The air-damming has the effect of reducing drag *and* reducing lift. Note that downforce is not *created*; the lift due to the turbulent low-pressure area is *eliminated*.

A too-high spoiler, however, can create both downforce and drag. If the rules allow you to have an adjustable spoiler, you are going to have to experiment with its height. Be careful not to trade the secure, comfortable feeling of high rear downforce for the irritation of getting passed by cars with less drag. If you want to be secure and comfortable, I suggest golf or bowling.

As a beginner, you are not likely to be running a car with wings (such as Super Vee, FF 2000, and the like). If you are running such a car, however, the previous comments apply. Lots of wing will make a car solid, comfortable, and slow.

TEAM MANAGEMENT

Like it or not, you will probably be the business manager, the crew chief, and the gofer for your racing team. You might as well realize this and get organized. Doing so will save you money and sleep, plus it will improve your finishing record.

SLACK TIME SCHEDULING

In the language of project management, there is a concept called "slack time." When a given task needs to be accomplished by a deadline and the task itself will take less time than is available, slack time is the balance. Good project management requires starting the task as soon as resources permit, and leaving the slack time to absorb unanticipated problems and delays. Wasting the slack time, then starting the task, is a no-no. Murphy will punish you for it.

This means that you prepare the car on Monday night, not on Thursday night. It means that you checklist the car after the last session on Saturday, not just before the first session on Sunday. Develop this discipline; it increases the likelihood that you will get a good night's sleep on Thursday and that you will make the grid on Sunday morning.

Charlie Williams: "I always crank the engine *right after* a session to make sure that the starter still works and that the engine still runs. This may sound silly, but I have been bitten."

Carroll Smith: "Damned right!"

CHECKLISTS

Checklists are critical. I have five separate lists ranging from making sure everything is aboard the camper and trailer, to a between-session list to make sure all the race car juices are topped off and there's air in the tires. Make up your own, appropriate to your situation and psyche, but make sure all the safety stuff (like lug nuts) is checked every session. It may sound dumb, but wheels come off race cars with astonishing frequency. Running out of gas is also surprisingly common.

The checklist also ought to include thoroughly cleaning the helmet shield and/or the windshield.

On the next four pages, I have provided copies (front and back) of my between-race and between-session checklists. Copyright is waived on these pages; you may copy, adapt, distribute, sell, or use them in your birdcage without legal liability.

CREW

You need some help: at least one person, but two or three is better and more fun. Be appreciative. Buy them Christmas presents, bring them good food and drink. Give them warm, dry places to sleep. Whatever it takes.

Recruiting crew members takes work. You will find that a lot of people are interested in the fact that you are a racer. When they indicate interest, invite them to go along. Make up a small package of hand-out information on club racing, maybe with a picture of your car. Give it to potential crew members and follow up with a phone call. With luck, you'll hook two or three people who will become reliable, repeat helpers.

Invest a little time in training your crew, then encourage the experienced guys to train any recruits that you are lucky enough to snare. Make sure they understand the rules and practices in the pits, how the stopwatches work, and how to signal you with the pit board.

When you have some time during the weekend, take your new crew member(s) out to one or two of the corners and talk about what goes on—brake point, passing, and so on. Also explain the flags. The more interest you can kindle, the more likely you'll hook a regular.

SESSION & CAR LOG ☐-Practice ☐-Qualifying ☐-Race

Date:_____ Track:_____ Time:_____

(Beginning)
Gears : 1____ : 2____ : 3____ : 4____ : Weather:_____ Temp. _____°

Sway Bar Set (Circle 1): Softest 1 2 3 4 5 Stiffest   Cold Tire Press. ____ Front ____ Rear

Lap Times: Car#_____ Car#_____ Car#_____

First Stop

Second Stop

End of Session

Pressures   Temperatures

(End of Session)
Max RPM On Straight _____ Oil Pressure _____ Water Temp _____ Oil Temp _____

Official Weight _____ # minus _____ Gallons in Tank at 6#/gallon = _____ # Without Fuel

Final Sway Bar Setting (Circle 1): Softest 1 2 3 4 5 Stiffest

Beginning Hours : Minutes on Engine ____ : ____ , Added ____ Minutes, Ending Total = ____ : ____

Notes, Changes, To-Do's: _____
_____
_____
_____

PRE-WEEKEND CAR PREPARATION

Race Date:_____   Location: _____

To-Do's: ☐ _____
☐ _____   ☐ _____
☐ _____   ☐ _____
☐ _____   ☐ _____
☐ _____   ☐ _____

CHASSIS FRONT
☐ Front Brakes Bled
☐ Rear Brakes Bled
☐ Clutch Bled
☐ Fluid Levels O.K.

COCKPIT
☐ Throttle Cable O.K.
☐ Idle, Full Open Checked
☐ Electrics Tight
☐ Tach Cable Tight
☐ Tach Calibration is _____
☐ Brake Bias Adjuster Free
☐ Pedals, Bolts O.K.
☐ Steering Free
☐ Rack & Shaft Bolts O.K.
☐ Fire Extinguisher Safety Pin

FRONT CORNERS
Left Right
____ Disc Runout (0.001's)
☐ ☐ Wheel Bearings O.K.
☐ ☐ Hub Bolts Tight
☐ ☐ Pads Used & O.K.
☐ ☐ New Pads Installed
☐ ☐ Calipers Tight, Safetied
☐ ☐ A-Arm Jam Nuts
☐ ☐ Rocker Pivot Bolts
☐ ☐ Steering Jam Nuts
☐ ☐ Upright Lower Nut
☐ ☐ Other Suspension Bolts

REAR CORNERS
Left Right
____ Disc Runout (0.001's)
☐ ☐ Wheel Bearings O.K.
☐ ☐ Hub Nuts Tight
☐ ☐ CV Joints O.K.
☐ ☐ Pads Used & O.K.
☐ ☐ New Pads Installed
☐ ☐ Calipers Tight, Safetied
☐ ☐ Toe-Adjust Jam Nuts
☐ ☐ Rocker Pivot Bolts
☐ ☐ Suspension Bolts

ENGINE LEAKDOWN READINGS:
1____ 2____ 3____ 4____
Readings Done: ☐ Cold ☐ Hot

ENGINE
☐ Oil Pan Bolts Tight
☐ Head Cleaned, Valves Lapped
☐ Oil Filter Inspected
☐ New Filter Installed
☐ Oil Lines O.K.
☐ Water Line Clamps Tight
☐ Water Level O.K.
☐ Water Pump Belt O.K.
☐ Fuel Filters Cleaned
☐ Float Level Correct
☐ Fuel Lines Tight
☐ Throttle and Springs O.K.
☐ Air Filter Cleaned
☐ Starter O.K.
☐ Headers No Cracks
☐ Header Bolts Safetied
☐ Vent Lines O.K.
☐ Prepressure Oil
☐ Run Engine, Check No Leaks
☐ Timing at ____ Degrees
☐ Oil Level O.K.
☐ Intake Valves At ____ (0.001's)
☐ Exhaust Valves At ____
☐ Valve Cover Screws Tight
☐ Plugs Clean and Gapped
☐ Electrics Tight

CHASSIS REAR
☐ Shift Linkage O.K.
☐ Clutch, Brake Lines O.K.
☐ Correct Gears, Shifting O.K.
             Ratios
1)____ : ____ 2)____ : ____
3)____ : ____ 4)____ : ____
☐ Gearbox Filled and Safetied
☐ Rain Light/Brake Lights O.K.

SETUP
☐ Full Alignment Done
☐ Corner Weights Checked
☐ Ride Height Checked
☐ Sway Bars No Preload

MISC. PREP.
☐ Tires Balanced
☐ Numbers O.K.
☐ Bodywork Cleaned
☐ Helmet Cleaned
☐ Suit, Gear Packed
☐ Mirrors Cleaned
☐ Car Battery Charged
☐ Spare Battery Charged
☐ Jump Battery Charged

TO BUY/GET:
☐ New Tires, Mounted & Balanced
☐ Race Gas ____ Gallons
☐ _____
☐ _____
☐ _____
☐ _____
☐ _____
☐ _____
☐ _____
☐ _____

CAR ALIGNMENT RECORD   Date:_____

Front Suspension

		Left	Right
Ride Height	Camber	____	____
_____"	Caster	____	____
	Toe (0.001's)	____	____
Bump Steer	2.25" Droop	____	____
(0.001's.	1.5"	____	____
+ = Toe Out)	0.75"	____	____
	Nominal Ride Height	0	0
	0.75"	____	____
	1.25"	____	____
	2.25" Bump	____	____
	Upper Bump Steer Washers	____"	____" (0.001's)

Sway Bar Diameter _____" Diameter, Set (Circle) Softest 1 2 3 4 5 Stiffest,
Shocks Set _____ Rebound _____ Bump

Rear Suspension

		Left	Right
Ride Height	Camber	____	____
_____"	Caster	____	____
	Toe (0.001's)	____	____
Bump Steer	2.25" Droop	____	____
(0.001's.	1.5"	____	____
+ = Toe Out)	0.75"	____	____
	Nominal Ride Height	0	0
	0.75"	____	____
	1.25"	____	____
	2.25" Bump	____	____

Sway Bar Diameter _____" Diameter, Set (Circle) Softest 1 2 3 4 5 Stiffest,
Shocks Set _____ Rebound _____ Bump

Corner Weights:

Left Front	Right Front
Left Rear	Right Rear

Notes, Changes, To-Do's: _____
_____
_____
_____

PRE-SESSION CAR PREPARATION

Date:_____   Session Time:_____

To-Do's: ☐ _____
☐ _____   ☐ _____
☐ _____   ☐ _____
☐ _____   ☐ _____
☐ _____   ☐ _____
☐ _____   ☐ _____

FLUID LEVELS
☐ Gas Filled to _____; Took _____ Gallons
☐ Oil Level O.K.
☐ Water Level O.K.
☐ Catch Tank Empty
☐ Brake, Clutch Fluid Levels O.K.

CHASSIS
LF RF RR LR
☐ ☐ ☐ ☐ Wheel Nuts at 55#
☐ ☐ ☐ ☐ Axle Nuts No Take-up
☐ ☐ ☐ ☐ Brake Discs No Cracks
☐ ☐ ☐ ☐ Wheel Bearings No Wobble
☐ ☐ ☐ ☐ A-Arm Jam Nuts
☐ ☐ ☐ Rocker Pivot Bolts
☐ ☐ Steering Jam Nuts
☐ ☐ Front Upright Lower Nuts
☐ ☐ ☐ ☐ Other Nuts/Bolts Tight

ENGINE CHECK
☐ Headers No Cracks
☐ Electrics Tight
☐ Plugs O.K.
☐ Run to 200° Water Temp
☐ No Leaks

MISCELLANEOUS
☐ Tires Overpressured
☐ Bodywork Clean
☐ Helmet Visor Clean
☐ Tearoff(s) on Visor

PIT WAGON CONTENTS
☐ Chalkboard
☐ Jump Battery
☐ Umbrella
☐ Air Bottle & Filled
☐ Work Gloves
☐ Helmet
☐ Driver's Gloves
☐ Balaclava
☐ Sunglasses
☐ Pit Tool Box

Grid

☐ **Tires Set _____PSI Front/ _____PSI Rear**
☐ **Pull Fire System Safety Pin**
☐ **Steering Wheel Secure**
☐ **Mirrors Adjusted**

Also, teach your crew how to do at least the at-track maintenance on the car. Sure, you can do all the gear changes by yourself and you can also pull the head off without help. But what happens if both of these things have to be done simultaneously?

Your regular crew members are going to have to belong to the SCCA; it's a requirement. You should pay for your regular crew's memberships; this is a small gesture compared to what you are spending on the race program, anyway.

Norma Williams: "If you're running in SCCA, don't forget to have your crew sign up for crew licenses. This qualifies them for extra insurance."

There needs to be one individual in charge of the car, and it should *not* be you. You are in charge of the driver. The reason you need to have one individual feel responsible is so that everything is sure to get done. If duties are vaguely "everybody's," it is much more likely that something will get overlooked. Crew chief duties can be rotated on a daily basis, but someone needs to have the assignment.

Let the crew take care of the car. That's what they came for. This is easy because you have everything spelled out in your checklist, right? If you do all the work, the crew feels as if you don't trust them, and they don't learn anything.

PADDOCK LOCATION

People have various philosophies on where in the paddock to park the race team. Some go for good views, low-traffic areas, and other factors. I go for convenience. This means close to the water faucet, close to the compressed air, and means close to the water faucet, close to the compressed air, and close to the grid. Better yet is close to the electricity. Carry a 100 foot large-gauge extension cord and a grounded cube tap.

On rain, there are only two paddock philosophies: those who don't worry about it, and those who do. The former can be identified by their occupancy of a large puddle when it does rain. The latter will have taken some pains to locate on high ground.

CANOPIES

You are going to want some kind of cover to work under. It will keep you cool when it's sunny and it will keep you drier (not dry) when it's raining. Blue canopies seem to be the coolest. Light-colored canopies apparently let the infrared get through.

There are all kinds of canopy frames for sale at relatively reasonable prices. If you want to make your own, though, be sure to use 3/4in EMT conduit; the 1/2in is not strong enough to take the wind loads. Plan carefully for drainage. I once saw a beautiful new 16x20ft flat (horizontal) canopy that had collected so much rain that the owner's only option was to cut a drain hole. It took about an hour to empty it, and provided great amusement to the rest of the paddock.

GROUND COVER

It's nice to have the race car parked on something. Especially when you drop a small part.

Your pre-weekend checklist should include verifying that the throttle is fully open when the gas pedal is all the way down. This driver and his crew chief will testify that it is unsatisfying to discover a partially closed throttle after the qualifying session.

When it's "crunch" time, some experienced crew help is essential. This crunched Formula Ford corner had to be changed (and realigned) between morning qualifying and the afternoon race. They got it done easily.

One of the crew's most important contributions is giving you lap times during practice, as shown here, and position information during the race. To improve readability, the pit boards often show only the last two digits (seconds and tenths) of the lap time.

Sometimes, you get to use the pros' paddock area. This Vee driver is comfortably set up on asphalt provided for the IndyCar teams at Elkhart Lake.

Indoor-outdoor carpet and poly tarps are popular ground covers. With all the dirt and oil, however, they can get to be a mess after a few weekends. I buy 12x100ft rolls of black polyethylene film at the lumber yard and cut myself a new ground cover every weekend. Anchor your ground cover using 20-penny nails with fender washers brazed to the heads.

WHERE TO BUY THINGS

As a new driver, you need a lot of information and advice. (In fact, you will find that this continues to be true throughout your career.) You are also likely to get into situations where you need a part or need to have a tire rebalanced at the last minute.

The best sources of information and the only source for gotta-have-it-right-now parts are the racing-oriented businesses in your area. These businesses are almost always run by dedicated, knowledgeable, and helpful people. They are in it for the love of racing, not for the money. There is more money to be made in other business endeavors.

With credit cards and next-day air shipping, it is tempting to price shop the country for supplies and equipment. This is particularly true for big-ticket items like racing suits. With an hour of magazine shopping effort, you can probably save 5% or even 10% over what the object of your desire will cost locally. In fact, you might save 1–2% of your total season budget by shopping in this way—a whole 1–2%!

How much extraordinary effort can you rightfully expect from your local race shop when you are making most of your purchases from far-away suppliers? Zero.

Oh, they will try to be helpful anyway, but you will not deserve it.

Buy from the local shops wherever possible. Even if their stock is not extensive, they can usually order what you need and they will try hard to be price competitive on larger items. If it costs you a few extra dollars, recognize that you are helping them keep the doors open in one of the world's truly marginal enterprises. Your patronage is not charity, it is enlightened self-interest.

BATTERY JUMPER PLUGS

The ubiquitous gray battery jumper plug can be bought from fork-lift truck suppliers or heavy-duty battery suppliers. They are made by Anderson Power Products (no relation) and called 175 amp connectors. Anderson also makes physically smaller plugs with ample power-handling capacity, but they are a bit fragile. The 175 amp plugs are available in several colors, each of which will only mate with another of the same color. No miscegenation.

BUYING BEARINGS AND CV-JOINTS

Do not make the mistake of buying bearings and CV-joints from the manufacturer or importer of a purpose-built race car. Also, don't shy away from replacing them when you suspect problems; they aren't that expensive.

For bearings, call your local bearing-supply company with the dimensions of the bearing you need, plus all the letters and numbers found on it. They will normally be able to supply an exact replacement for under $20.

Most of the CV-joints you will run into are from production cars, usually from the Volkswagen Rabbit. Take the piece to a knowledgeable import parts sales clerk; he or she will probably recognize it. Where the car uses the Rabbit outer CV-joint/axle combination, your bearing-supply company will not recognize the wheel bearing. It, too, is a Rabbit part.

OFF-TRACK MISCELLANY: TOOLS

Carroll Smith has some suggested tool lists in *Prepare to Win*. As usual, his recommendations are overkill, but you cannot go wrong following them. Everything he says about manufacturers is true, except I think Snap-On makes the only really durable Phillips screwdrivers.

For a beginner, I'd suggest a fairly basic set of Sears screwdrivers, combination wrenches, and standard-depth sockets in 1/4, 3/8, and 1/2in drives. You should selectively buy the deep sockets, U-joint sockets, and hex-drives that you need for your car. The big sets are duplicative and contain many (heavy) items that you'll never use. (Despite the opinions of Sears' marketers, you do *not* need same-size deep and flex sockets in every drive size.)

You will also need a torque wrench. I strongly suggest that you bite the bullet and buy a good one, the $150–$200

More normally, your paddock parking will be in the grass or in the dirt. Note that indoor-outdoor carpet has been put under the Spec Racer on the right. A ground cover is a nice thing—especially when you drop a small piece of irreplaceable hardware.

price tag notwithstanding. This is one item where the Sears solution is inadequate. Talk to the itinerant salespeople for Snap-On, Mac, and other tool suppliers, whimper a lot, and maybe you can get a deal. They all seem to sell the same wrench.

Do not go out and buy one of the big thirty-drawer tool chests. They are beautiful when sitting on a rollaway, but you will not be able to lift one filled with tools. Stick to boxes with three or, at most, four rows of drawers. (My four-drawer box weighs about 110lb as it goes into the trailer.) One of these plus a small box to take the stopwatches, tools, and supplies to the pits should provide enough storage space.

Here's the minimalist approach to at-track tools and supplies. You can get by with this for low-maintenance classes like SR and Showroom Stock—assuming you don't have any major problems.

You don't need a huge rollaway at the track; the middle ground in at-track tools and parts is generally best. Medium-sized toolboxes, on some kind of stand or table, are easier to deal with than boxes in the dirt or multi-hundred-pound tool carts. Here, the cars are parked in rental spots under a permanent canopy. More likely, you'll have to bring your own poly tarp canopy and framework.

At the track, try to get your toolboxes to worktable height if possible. An old banquet table works well, as does a smaller homemade table using banquet table legs. One of the trailer ramps held up by rain tires is fine unless you need the tires.

If your toolbox drawers and your storage boxes are labeled in detail, your crew is more likely to put things back.

You do need a pop-rivet gun and a good supply of rivets ranging from 1/8 to 3/16in in a variety of grip lengths. When you're buying race gas at the airport, ask them to show you a cleco pliers and some cleco rivet clamps. These are high on the nice-to-have list.

You also need a supply of solderless crimp-on electrical connectors and the crimping tool. Buy only the ring-type terminals. Rivets and electrical terminals are so much cheaper in quantities of 50 or 100 that it is silly to buy less. You will use them more quickly than you expect.

A battery charger is essential. Buy a size appropriate to your car's battery—many of the small Formula and Sports Racer batteries can only take an ampere or so of charge rate. For a bigger car with a conventional battery, a ten-amp charger is probably about right. Get a charger with an ammeter. This is the only way you can be sure the battery is taking a charge and the easiest way to know when it's done charging.

If you're worried about a battery going flat and needing a quick charge, buy a spare battery rather than trying to haul around one of those Godzilla-sized chargers on wheels.

A pyrometer (tire temp gauge) is high on the nice-to-have list for almost all car classes. As your experience grows, you will find tire temps useful. If you are having problems, the factory tire engineers won't talk to you unless you can give them temps. In addition, a pyrometer is useful for checking oil temp and if you decide to grill a turkey.

The Wayne Mitchell camber gauge is readily available and highly useful on almost any car. Even if you're not yet at the point where you do your own alignment, it is good to compare where things were set before and after that off-course excursion. Dunlop optical toe gauges are beautiful, expensive, and wonderful to work with—a string between jack stands is what most of us use. Better yet is an absolutely straight aluminum beam with spacer bars that hook it up to the car's centerline using pre-drilled holes.

Your stopwatches should have a lap timing mode, giving successive lap times without mental arithmetic. The most convenient kind of watch gives you a new lap time each time you push the "split" button. It is referred to as a "one-push" (per lap) or Taylor-split watch. Two-push watches are more common and entirely acceptable. With these, the split button must be pushed after you copy the reading but before the timed car comes around again.

Ideally, you will have two or three identical watches. Your crew uses one to time you, and the other(s) are used to take sample times on your competition.

You also need a pit signal board. Ron and Jeannie Minor's flip-over Pit-Sig board is a good one available from many sources, but a small chalkboard or a white markerboard works fine too. Stripe your board with colored tape so you can identify it as you flash by along the pit wall.

Everyone needs duct tape in their toolbox. Some race cars seem to be held together with it. Look around at the track to see how many creative ways this stuff can be used. Black and silver are usually available in hardware stores, fancy colors from the race shops. Nylon wire tie wraps are almost as ubiquitous and necessary as duct tape. Buy them in a couple of different lengths in packages of 100.

You'll need a jack and jack stands appropriate to your car. Don't overkill here—you have enough heavy stuff without adding a monster jack and ten-ton stands.

The tongue of an open trailer is a good place to mount a vise. (On a closed trailer, you mount it inside.)

Every spring, put new batteries in your pyrometer and your stopwatches.

TAXES

Amateur racing is a hobby. The IRS understands this and is not interested in giving you a tax deduction for your hobby. If you can bury your expenses in a business, they may not find them or they may permit you to deduct them as long as they are a small fraction of sales, *and* you can argue a business purpose.

For most of us, the best we can hope for is to generate some "hobby income." Hobby income is not taxable as long as it is exceeded by hobby losses. You can generate hobby income by selling parts, canopies, and so on, doing car maintenance work, or doing other money-making jobs that are closely associated with the hobby.

As in most tax situations, you can be aggressive in filing your returns or you can be conservative. If you are going to try to make your hobby deductible, talk to a tax advisor who is experienced in small-business taxation.

OIL-OLOGY

There are many claims made for synthetic oils and for various magic fluids that the vendors would have you add to your oil. The only person I trust for accurate information in these matters is Charlie Williams. Charlie has tried various oils on the dyno and has found no appreciable differences in horsepower.

Generally, people use straight-weight oils. I once heard an interesting argument for multigrade oil, however: Your oil is cool on the first lap of a race, a multigrade will be thinner and will produce less fluid dynamic drag, hence more horsepower at the start.

I have personally used a number of brands, finally settling on Red Line racing oil. I found that this oil left me with the cleanest cylinder heads, specifically leaving little or no deposit on the backs of the valves. This means quicker head

The Dunlop optical toe gauge is easy to use, a feature that is especially appreciated when checking something at the racetrack. The $400+ price tag, though, leaves most of us using more primitive tools. Note the level in the background. Prior to checking camber and caster, the car must be shimmed to be absolutely level. (For toe, don't bother.) Carry a few pieces of 1/8 and 1/4in thick masonite for this purpose. The car is a Sports 2000.

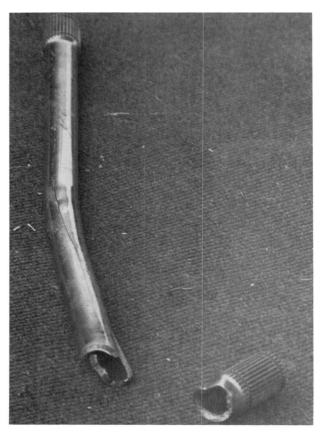

Regular checking of critical components, such as axles, will minimize the probability of something breaking. It can still happen, though. This axle got bent while flailing around after it broke. Note that it's hollow for minimum weight. This has little effect on its strength in torsion.

cleanup between races and, presumably, a little better flow toward the end of a weekend.

Charlie Williams: "Synthetic oil does burn cleaner. If you don't change your oil regularly (each weekend), this is what you should use."

Dennis Eade: "Use the best oil you can buy or get for free. Present-day oils are excellent. We use a multigrade Valvoline synthetic. It is wonderful!

"Multigrade oil is used to lower engine startup wear. Proper oil and proper startup procedure will do more for engine longevity than anything else."

CRACK CHECKING

Depending on your choice of car, there will be anything from a few to many parts that are subject to fatigue cracking from vibration and from intentional or unintentional loads. It will be worth your while to consult others who are more experienced with the chassis you are running. Find out what they have had problems with, what problems they have heard of, and so forth. If possible, also contact the manufacturer or the importer for advice. After a year or two of racing experience, the failure habits of a chassis become generally known around the paddock.

Buy a "dye check" kit from a race shop or a large industrial supplies distributor or industrial hardware store. These kits include spray cans of cleaner, dye, and "developer."

The parts you want to check must be cleaned thoroughly. (The expensive cleaner is fairly interchangeable with lacquer thinner or other handy solvent, so don't be afraid of using it in quantity.) Once the parts are clean, you apply the dye, a low-viscosity red ink, and allow it to soak into the part for a few minutes. The idea is that the dye will crawl into any porosity or cracks. When it has had time to do this, wipe each part clean and apply the developer, a white powder suspended in solvent. When the solvent has evaporated, the part is left with a white coating that is clearly stained by dye crawl-ing back out of any cracks.

If your dye check shows a crack, you have learned something valuable. If it does not, you have learned only that there are probably not any *large* cracks. Parts that are prone to cracking should be checked periodically by a Federal Aviation Administration (FAA) certified shop, using either Zyglo (for nonferrous parts) or Magnaflux (for ferrous parts). On a Formula car or Sports Racer, the critical parts are typically the suspension links, the uprights, and the axles. Axles are worth a periodic check on almost any car; when one breaks and starts flailing around, it can cause major damage. On some cars, a broken axle can cause a wheel to come adrift.

ESSENTIAL FLUIDS

Buy service chemicals like brake cleaner, WD-40, 409, Gunk, and so on, in gallon jugs and use them with hand-pump sprayers bought for $1–$2 at the hardware store. Brake cleaner eats the seals out of these sprayers fairly fast, but doing it this way is still cheaper than buying aerosol cans.

CAR NUMBERS

When you start out as a novice, you will not have a car number that you can call your own. Permanent numbers are assigned by SCCA divisions once you have your National License. These numbers are reserved at each race until the date that Registration closes. The way to minimize novice number hassles is to contact your division's National Number Registrar and pick out an *unassigned* car number, then enter each of your races early and request this number.

Even then, you will have to change numbers at the track occasionally. Make some number templates out of card stock or metal to carry with you. Helvetica bold italic is a good typeface; find a friendly computer jock who will print you a few digits of regulation-size numbers on his laser printer (8 1/2in minimum height, 1 1/2in stroke). Cut them out and transfer the shape to stiff cardboard or thin metal. (Aluminum roof flashing is handy for this; it is thin enough to cut with a scissors. Flashing is also handy at the racetrack and it's easy

Essential fluids should be bought in gallon quantities and put into plastic pump-spray bottles. Not only is it cheaper than aerosol cans, there's little risk of being surprised by an empty bottle at the racetrack.

Early in your career, you will get to change car numbers a lot. If you make up some templates, it will be easy to cut some new numbers at the racetrack. Three or four digits should give you plenty of combinations to choose from.

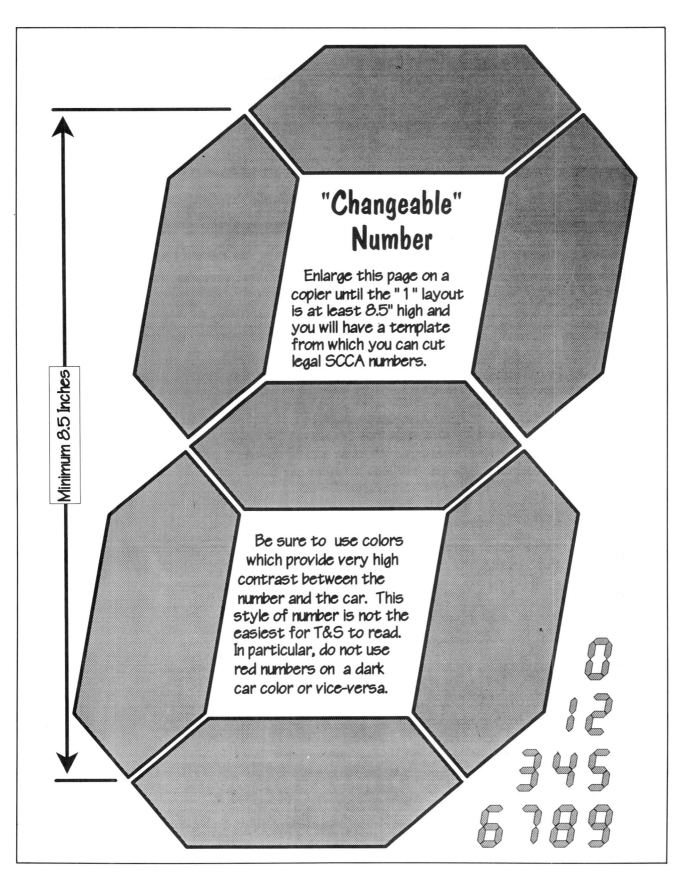

"Changeable" Number

Enlarge this page on a copier until the " 1 " layout is at least 8.5" high and you will have a template from which you can cut legal SCCA numbers.

Be sure to use colors which provide very high contrast between the number and the car. This style of number is not the easiest for T&S to read. In particular, do not use red numbers on a dark car color or vice-versa.

Minimum 8.5 Inches

to carry. Fiberglass repairs can be effected quite neatly by attaching the flashing to the backside of broken fiberglass with a generous quantity of pop rivets.)

The best material for your numbers is truck graphics film, sold by large art supply and sign-painter supply stores. It comes in a variety of bright colors, goes on reliably, and comes off easily when heated with a hair dryer. 3M's brand is called Controltac film.

With a roll of colored film and three or four single-digit templates, you will be in good shape for at-track number changes.

One alternative to template numbers is to put a pair of eights on the car using computer-style "seven-segment" format (see figure). Make them big, contrasty, and bright, as they are somewhat harder to read than conventional numbers. Now, you can make them into anything you want by covering segments with tape that is the same color as your bodywork. This only works, though, if you can match your car color closely with the blockout tape. If you cannot get a match, the numbers will be unreadable at speed. T&S (Timing and Scoring) will not be happy.

Putting Decals on the Car

Don't try to put numbers and stickers onto a dry surface. They will end up crooked and wrinkled. Spray the car surface with water or a household cleaner like 409. Remove the backing paper from the decal and put it on the wetted surface. Slide it around to your heart's content, squeegee most of the water from underneath, and leave it overnight. An hour in the sun seems to work OK, too. Forced drying with a hair dryer or heat gun will produce steam blisters under the decal unless you're a lot more patient than I am.

The heat gun works fine, however, to get them off.

Shrink-Fit Bearings

If you have aluminum hubs that must be heated to get the bearings in and out, there are two approaches. Using an oxyacetylene torch wastes a lot of your time if you are careful (as you should be) about heating the casting slowly and evenly. Instead, just put the casting in your oven at home, set it at 350 degrees Fahrenheit or so, and work on something else for a half hour. This is best done, however, when your wife is gone somewhere.

Charlie Williams: "Amen!"

Norma Williams: "I never leave my oven unguarded during racing season!"

Carroll Smith: "I'm just not brave enough to use my wife's oven any more. Use a propane torch to heat the casting. Also, be sure to cool it in a still air box."

Contacts, Sources, and Driving Schools

GUEST AUTHORS

Several of the people who helped with this book are in the racing business in one way or another. You may find that they can be of help to you, too. Also, I owe them something for their help over the years and, specifically, for their help with this book. I hope this listing is of value both to you and to them.

Danny Collins/Danny Collins Racing School
1626 Albion St.
Denver, CO 80220
(303) 388-3875

To say "Danny Collins Racing School" evokes the wrong image. Danny is more like a private driving coach, available for individual instruction or for custom-designed training sessions with car clubs. I suppose he does actually conduct a formal school from time to time, but it's not his main thing—maybe not even the best forum for his talent and experience. Talk to him, his enthusiasm is infectious and his stories are great. You probably can't come up with a question he hasn't heard before or doesn't have the answer to.

Danny's school staff consists of himself, his wife Carol, and one of those animated little balls of dog fur that looks like a dust mop without a handle. Carol handles the administration, including helping students get their SCCA credentials. The dog entertains the students between sessions. For those who aren't ready to invest in a car, Danny can also connect his postgraduate students with Spec Racer rentals just about anywhere in the United States.

Dennis Eade/Competition Preparations (Comprep)
PO Box 97
Zenda, WI 53195
(414) 275-9806

Comprep is in the top league of race shops running road racing series like the Toyota Formula Atlantics and Olds Pro sports cars. Dennis and his people specialize in full series packages, including complete driver and car development.

Dennis will also do occasional rental deals and one-time projects. For example, Comprep did the development work for Toyota when the pro Atlantic series was switched from Cosworth engines, and Dennis did "a lot of consulting" on the changeover from 2.0 liter Fords to Olds Quad Four engines for the sports car series.

Tony Kester/Datasport
3362 N. 950 West
Michigan City, IN 46360
(219) 872-8977

"Expert racer for hire. Will travel."

Datasport is a consulting service specializing in personalized driver coaching, car setup, test driving, and suspension redesign. Using the TachTale onboard computer and an onboard video camera, Tony is able to provide immediate feedback to a driver as his car is prepared for the next session. Sometimes, Tony will jump into the car and bring back the "how-to" data and video recordings for the driver to review.

Datasport's client list includes tire manufacturers Hoosier and Goodyear, car manufacturers Oldsmobile and Lola, and numerous private racing teams.

Carroll Smith: "Tony's the best driver coach east of the Mississippi!"

Bertil Roos/Bertil Roos Grand Prix Racing School
PO Box 221
Blakeslee, PA 18610
(717) 646-7227

Among life's experiences, Bertil falls into the "interesting character" category. His comments in this book can give you a feeling for what he's like, but nothing beats attending his school to get Bertil straight. Training begins with a student gathering around his desk, which is literally a glass-topped race car, and continues on a specially designed track within the Pocono International Raceway complex. His advice is backed up and illustrated with multiple anecdotes from his extensive international experience, including good stories from his Formula One days.

Carroll Smith/Carroll Smith Consulting
123 Via Landeta
Palos Verdes Estates, CA 90274

You can buy Carroll's books directly from him; he makes more money that way. Send him a check for the current list price of whatever book you want; it'll be shipped UPS the day after your order arrives. As a bonus, when you buy *Carroll Smith's Nuts, Bolts, Fasteners and Plumbing Handbook*, it comes with the "real" title stickered onto the front cover. (Clue: The book is about screws.)

He also does some consulting. Contact him if you're really serious.

Paul Van Valkenburgh
Box 3611-DS
Seal Beach, CA 90740

In addition to the second edition of his frequently referenced *Race Car Engineering and Mechanics* ($18.95 postage paid), Paul also sells a new book about the future technology of auto racing, called *AUTO2010* ($16.95 postage paid). He also does automotive consulting, not just about everyday racing and winning, but more toward research, data taking, and new technologies for secret advantages.

Charlie Williams/Williams Engines
Williams Import Car Service
2701 W. 47th
Shawnee Mission, KS 66205
(913) 262-6300

An article once described Charlie as "resembling a professor who accidentally got grease on his hair while working on his lawn mower." His soft-spoken, patient, and generous style is a long way from what you'd expect from a professional engine builder. My first meeting with him was on the telephone in 1980, when he spent at least a half hour talking to me about a used Williams engine that I was considering buying. He provided free information from his years of experience to a novice whom he'd never met and who hadn't spent one dime at his shop. Charlie's just like that!

One thing about Charlie's operation, which I suggest that you look for wherever you do your racing business, is that the guy making the promises is the guy who does the work.

In addition to doing engine and chassis work on street cars and race cars, Charlie and Norma's shop sells helmets, suits, and most other racing equipment. He also is the sole source for the low-drag piston ring sets which he designed and has made by Hastings, and for Charlie-designed Formula Ford valve springs and locating cups, also specially made for him.

Professional Racing Schools

I have provided summary information on currently approved SCCA schools, plus a few that have been on the approved list in the recent past. "Approved" schools are acceptable as one of the two schools required of novice drivers.

There are undoubtedly good schools that I have missed in this compilation; don't automatically exclude them from your consideration. They can be found through advertisements in buff magazines like *Autoweek, Car and Driver, Racer,* and *Road & Track.*

The information below has been provided by the schools themselves, has been used verbatim, and has not been independently verified. Be sure to inquire about a school's current SCCA approval status. Be cautious, too, about prices—these are 1992 prices and have almost certainly risen by the time you read this book.

Incidentally, I have included the "In-Car Time" figures because people are interested in that. Remember, though, that just motoring around without benefit of classroom time or coaching will be of limited value to you.

Skip Barber Racing School

Route 7
Caanan, CT 06018
(203) 824-0771

Year founded: 1975
Basic racing school cost/duration: $1,850/three days
Racetracks used for training: Bridgehampton, Hawaii Raceway Park, Heartland Park Topeka, Indianapolis Raceway Park, Las Vegas International, Laguna Seca, Lime Rock Park, Mid-Ohio, Moroso, Pocono, Road America, Road Atlanta, Sears Point, Seattle International, Sebring, Watkins Glen, and Willow Springs
In-car time: 8–9 hours
Type of training cars: Mondiale B-1 Formula Ford
Description of school and/or training: Granted, all racing schools are "fun." The Skip Barber objective, however, is to teach the exact skills needed to *race successfully.* We pride ourselves on teaching the initially more difficult, but ultimately more successful, Mark Donohue system (tire-friction circles; determining the line for any track; trail braking). Skip Barber produces winners, because of the quality of the instructors and curriculum, and the quality and amount of seat time.

Fundamental skills that you will master include: double-clutching and heel-and-toeing; threshold braking; trail braking; passing and drafting; and techniques for finding the fastest line. Grads are eligible for IMSA licenses.

Bob Bondurant School of High Performance Driving

Firebird International Raceway
PO Box 51980
Phoenix, AZ 85076
(800) 842-7223/(602) 796-1111
Year founded: 1968
Basic racing school cost/duration: $2,495/four days
Racetrack used for training: Bondurant-designed 1.6 mile road course
In-car time: 22 hours
Types of training cars: Ford Mustang GTs and Formula Fords
Description of school and/or training: Bondurant offers the only purpose-built driver training facility of its kind. Features include a Bob Bondurant-designed 1.6 mile road course, 3.5 acre basic training area, and over 120 specially prepared Ford vehicles.

The basic SCCA course is a four-day Grand Prix Road Racing Course. This course includes two and a half days in the school's race-prepared Ford Mustang GTs, and a day and a half in the open wheel Formula Fords. Instructors ride with the students in the Mustangs, coaching them at every turn. The Bondurant School also offers an Advanced Road Racing course for those who have a current racing license.

Bridgestone Racing School

RR #2
Shannonville, Ontario
Canada K0K 3A0
(613) 969-0334
Year founded: 1992
Basic racing school cost/duration: $1,910US/four days
Racetrack used for training: Shannonville Motorsport Park
In-car time: 12 1/4 hours
Types of training cars: Chevrolet Z28 Camaros, Reynard Formula 2000s
Description of school and/or training: Two-day, four-day, six-day, and seven-day courses are available. All instructors are full-time professionals. Students' safety gear is fully compliant with SCCA standards.

Danny Collins Racing School

1626 Albion St.
Denver, CO 80220
(303) 388-3875

Year founded: 1964
Basic racing school cost/duration: $1,200 in school
car, $500 in your car/two days
Racetrack used for training: Second Creek Raceway,
Denver (designed by Danny)
In-car time: 10 hours
Types of training cars: Quick One Formula Continental
(Ford 2000cc), Spec Racer, or your own car
Description of school and/or training: Utilizing over
thirty years of racing and teaching experience, Danny uses
audio-visual media to reduce classroom time so he can max-
imize student track time. Drivers run counterclockwise one
day, clockwise the second...learning two tracks in two days!
Small classes ensure that Danny can give each student his
personal attention.

Danny uses a sequential program he calls the "4 C's"—
Control, Confidence, Concentration, and Consistency—skills
he believes are essential for eventual success when novices
enter the "real world" of SCCA or Vintage racing. He wants
them to graduate with a mature style and the natural rhythm
of veterans.

Pitarresi Racing School

1940 N. Victory Blvd.
Portland, OR 97217
(503) 285-4449

Year founded: 1986
Basic racing school cost/duration: $1,800/three days
Racetrack used for training: Portland International
In-car time: 15 hours over three days
Type of training cars: Toyota MR-2
Description of school and/or training:

At PMI, they believe that the best place to learn to race
is in a race car, so the school is short on classroom instruction and long on track time. In three days, you'll get
250–300 miles on the track.

After a morning in our Skid Car, you do a course walk
to learn braking landmarks, entry and exit points, and the
elusive "racing line."

With a student-instructor ratio of 2:1, you'll receive personal attention. At the end of each day your instructor will
give you an evaluation, including progress and areas for improvement. The school is recognized by SCCA and IMSA.

Road Atlanta Driver's School

Route 1
Braselton, GA 30517
(404) 967-6143

Year founded: 1971
Basic racing school cost/duration: $1,195/two days
Racetrack used for training: Road Atlanta
In-car time: 11 hours
Type of training cars: Nissan 300ZX
Description of school and/or training:

For those who want to take the first step toward winning
a racing championship, or simply want to experience the ultimate in performance driving, a road racing course at Road
Atlanta offers two benefits unmatched by any other school in
the country: the first is our fleet of new Nissan 300ZX vehicles, specially prepared for road racing conditions. The second is the famous 2.52 mile ribbon of asphalt known as
Road Atlanta!

At our two-day IMSA and SCCA Certified Road Racing
School, you'll learn all about racing, from flags to downshifting, and will develop your skills under the watchful eye of a
seasoned racer.

Bertil Roos Grand Prix Racing School

PO Box 221
Blakeslee, PA 18610
(717) 646-7227

Year founded: 1976
Basic racing school cost/duration: $1,950/three days
Racetrack used for training: Pocono International
Raceway
In-car time: 7 hours, 20 minutes
Types of training cars: Scandia Formula 2000 and
"Slide-cars"
Description of school and/or training: The focus of the
Roos System of Race Driving is on maximizing time spent on
full gas and minimizing time used for braking.

This is the only school that teaches Racing Eye Technique, the most important part of high-speed precision driving. The students also learn line recovery, competitive braking, slide control, straight and curved auto-pilot, visualiza-
tion, spinning without going off the road, passing, quick
down-shifting, and heel and toe.

The school's Formula 2000 race cars are set up to handle neutral, *not* under-steering. Passing is allowed, artificial
rev-limits are never imposed, and students are not liable for
car damage. Approved by SCCA and IMSA.

Russell Racing School

1023 Monterey Highway
Salinas, CA 93908
(408) 372-7223

Year founded: 1957
Basic racing school cost/duration: $1,895/three days
Racetrack used for training: Laguna Seca
In-car time: 15 hours
Type of training cars: Van Dieman FF1600
Description of school and/or training:

The Russell "Techniques of Racing" course is a three-
day school taught in Formula Fords. It covers all aspects of
race driving technique: heel and toe downshifting, threshold
braking, basic car control, racing lines, and shift points.
Heavy emphasis on racing strategy with concentration on
passing under braking and on rolling grid starts. Grads earn
USAC novice competition license.

Stephens Racing

2232 S. Nogales
Tulsa, OK 74107
(918) 583-1136

Year founded: 1989
Basic racing school cost/duration: $1,100/two days
Racetrack used for training: Hallet
In-car time: 7 hours
Type of training cars: Spec Racers
Description of school and/or training: Basic classroom
includes threshold braking, understeer, oversteer, and friction circle theory, along with tire dynamics, flag exercises,
and rules of the road and pits. Video tape review after each
on-track session. The school emphasizes track time—at least
seven 30-minute sessions each day. Graduates qualify for
COMMA (Competition Motorsports Association) license on
completion of two-day school.

Winfield
US Representative: Franam Racing, Inc.
1409 S. Wilshire Dr.
Minnetonka, MN 55343
(612) 541-9461

> **Year founded:** 1962 (Franam-1983)
> **Basic racing school cost/duration:** $2,395 (includes accommodations and meals for six nights)/four days' training
> **Racetrack used for training:** Paul Ricard, France
> **Type of training cars:** Martini Formula Renault, 125hp single-seater with wings, slicks

Description of school and/or training: Franam's introductory courses at Circuit Paul Ricard feature four days of liability-free instruction. Each student is encouraged to take advantage of the safety features offered by this Grand Prix track and to discover his or her natural potential in complete safety. Instruction is in English.

An advanced course held each fall leads to the prestigious Pilote Elf Competition where the fastest pupil earns a sponsored drive in the French Formula Renault Championship. Elf support for an additional five years could bring the total value of this prize to over $1.25 million.

Alumni include Alain Prost and twenty-one other Grand Prix drivers.

Regional Amateur Racing Organizations

Although the Sports Car Club of America is the only national amateur racing organization, grassroots racing is alive and well across the country. Here is a list of some of the regional organizations, together with contact addresses.

These clubs, though usually well established, are primarily volunteer organizations with no paid staff or permanent offices; consequently, the addresses provided may become obsolete. If you have problems making contact, try calling the appropriate racetrack office. They will probably be able to put you in touch with the club.

Arizona Sports Racing Association (AZRA)
c/o Dave Epstein, Race Director
2110 W. Devonshire St.
Mesa, AZ 85201
(602) 844-9677

Founded in 1959, AZRA is based on the "run what you brung" concept—loosely defined groups, all on the track at the same time. The club runs a street group where drivers are restricted to passing only on the straights. They also run two competition groups: open-wheel and closed-wheel. The equipment includes everything from regular SCCA cars to one-offs and kit cars, and an occasional IndyCar. There were 120 entrants at a recent event, including a Spec Racer with a modified fuel-injected engine and slicks! Sometimes large fields are split by engine displacement into an A-group and a B-group, or into Advanced and Novice groups.

The organization does have general safety rules covering driver equipment, belts, roll cage, and so forth. There is no driver licensing, although AZRA normally runs a half-hour driver school before each event. There's no prize money, no points, and no series championship. The idea is simply to go out and have fun driving whatever you want to put onto the racetrack.

AZRA runs both at Firebird International Raceway Park, and at Phoenix International on the road course and the oval. Once in a while they have mounted expeditions to

Willow Springs and to Riverside. There are three to ten events a year, depending on track availability.

Competition Motorsports Association (COMMA)
2232 S. Nogales Ave.
Tulsa, OK 74107
(918) 583-1134

COMMA was formed to organize and conduct motorsports events where safety, fun, and competition are emphasized, with a minimum of expense for the competitor. Except for safety regulations, the rules governing vehicles legal for racing competition are broad enough to allow as many drivers to compete as possible. However, before a driver is allowed to compete, he or she must attend a COMMA racing school or possess a current license or logbook from another recognized track or sanctioning body. Nearly half of the drivers licensed by COMMA do not have a license in another racing organization.

A typical COMMA event includes a rookie session, two practice sessions, a qualifying session, a qualifying race, and a feature race. That's five sessions per day for a $65 entry—pretty good!

Most COMMA events are held at the Hallett Motor Racing Circuit in Tulsa. In 1991, COMMA entered the international arena by sanctioning a Pro Sports Renault race in Chamizal Park of Juarez, Mexico. COMMA has also sanctioned Pro Sports Renault competition in conjunction with the American IndyCar Series. COMMA events feature contingency money, tires, and apparel from various sponsors including CITGO Petroleum and Bridgestone Tires.

Eastern Motor Racing Association (EMRA)
P.O. Box 380
Watermill, NY 11976
516-728-5111 (recording)

For more than twenty years, EMRA has provided exciting, low-budget racing throughout the Northeast. Founded in 1969, EMRA launched its race-sanctioning activities a year later and has been going strong ever since. EMRA's race series generally consists of ten or more sprint races held at major road racing circuits including Bridgehampton, Lime Rock, New Hampshire International, Summit Point, and Watkins Glen.

In addition to club races, EMRA sanctions time trials, endurance racing, and Pro Races for selected classes including Formula Ford and SCCA Spec Racers. EMRA will issue its racing license to holders of other club racing licenses without requiring additional EMRA driver school attendance.

International Conference of Sports Car Clubs (ICSSC)
c/o Tom Busic
6515 Glen Echo Ave.
Gladstone, OR 97027

ICSSC, founded over thirty years ago, is the race sanctioning and organizing arm for a group of sports car clubs in Oregon, Washington, and British Columbia. ICSSC has over 450 licensed drivers, running races at Portland International, Seattle International, and, soon, a new track on Vancouver Island. A typical season includes ten races which form a championship series.

Like other regional clubs, ICSSC emphasizes low-cost racing. For example, ICSSC has strong "stock" classes similar to SCCA Showroom Stock. ICSSC also offers a number of school opportunities for aspiring drivers; the 1992 schedule showed nine "driver training" dates.

Midwestern Council of Sports Car Clubs

c/o Ross Fosbender
147 S. Winston Dr.
Palatine, IL 60067
(708) 359-0204 (recording)

The racing lineage of Midwestern Council extends back to 1930 with the founding of the MG Car Club in Abingdon, England. In the early 1950s, the Midwestern Centre of the Overseas MG Car Club linked chapters in Milwaukee, Kenosha-Racine, Chicago, Rockford, and Detroit to coordinate competition events.

In 1958, The Midwestern Centre expanded to include non-MG clubs and became the Midwestern Council of Sports Car Clubs. Every season since has seen ten to fourteen wheel-to-wheel race events, several driver schools, and recently, racetrack autocrosses, high-speed touring, and vintage events on the council schedule.

Safety has always been paramount with Midwestern, and the combination of thorough driver training, tough Stewarding, sensible competition, and luck has given the group thirty-two seasons of fatality-free racing, with lost-time accidents countable on the fingers of one hand.

While the Midwestern Council's member clubs are headquartered in Illinois and Wisconsin, the group has active participants from Ohio to Nebraska and from Canada to Kentucky. Their primary track is Blackhawk Farms in Rockton, Illinois. Road America is also regularly used.

Race Car Club of America (RCCA)

A. J. Pugliese
166 Elm Street
New Rochelle, NY 10805-2011
(914) 576-7222

RCCA is unique. First, it's a not-for-profit corporation founded and run by "A. J.," who is one of the club's two employees. Second, its concentration is on Formula cars, specifically on several classes of Formula Ford. Classes are determined both by the car itself and by the driver's age and experience. The founding principle of the club was low-cost, spec-tired racing.

The club sanctions races at road tracks and ovals in the Northeast. These include Pocono, Bridgehampton, and Lime Rock Park. A season includes approximately ten race weekends, and numerous class and series trophies are distributed. In addition to Formula car racing, the club sanctions on-track "grand touring" designed to let street car drivers run at speed in a non-race environment.

RCCA membership numbers about 600, with 150 regular driving members.

Waterford Hills Road Racing Club, Inc.

Attn: Cal Cortright, Director of Public Relations
P.O. Box 43105
Detroit, MI 48243

This regional club is *serious!* Their roots go back to 1958 when they built the Waterford Hills Racetrack. They still operate the track, running races on the last full weekend of each month from May to September.

The club sees itself as being complementary to the SCCA. Their goal is to provide a level of competition roughly equivalent to SCCA Regionals, but at a lower cost. They also rent their track to SCCA for driver schools and Regionals.

Their track is the venue for the Meadow Brook Historic Races every year. In addition, it is often rented to manufacturers for testing and photo sessions and it is sometimes rented to racing schools.

Vintage and Historic Racing

This form of club racing is growing in popularity. Essentially, it is a low-pressure form of racing using older, often valuable cars. Passing is usually restricted, and drivers who are involved in metal-to-metal incidents are subject to draconian penalties like one-year license suspensions.

The racing is governed largely by local organizations, each with its own car eligibility, preparation, and driver licensing requirements. Your best sources of information are the two vintage racing magazines:

Vintage Motorsport
1040 S. Florida Ave.
Lakeland, FL 33803
(813) 686-3104

Victory Lane
2460 Park Blvd., #4
Palo Alto, CA 94306
(415) 321-4605

Both magazines publish vintage event calendars and lists of vintage clubs across the country.

You can also get referred to a local club by writing to:

Vintage Motorsports Council
3599 S. Albion
Englewood, CO 80110

Vintage Motorsports Council, or VMC, is a "club of clubs," comprising twenty clubs in the United States and two in Canada. One goal of VMC is rationalization of local rules, with concentration on safety issues. It is unlike SCCA, though. The member clubs make the policies, and the national organization is primarily a forum for communication and coordination. For example, VMC administers a national licensing system which is honored by all its member clubs, and provides nationwide databases on driver infractions, stolen cars, and mechanical failures.

Privately Operated Racing Series

In addition to club and pro racing, there is another kind of racing available to you. This is privately sanctioned racing.

Skip Barber and Jim Russell both run private series, as do others. In each case, the equipment is highly controlled with the objective of making it as equal as possible. Barber owns the cars and handles all preparation for its series. Russell will either sell or rent cars, but still puts rigid controls on the preparation to ensure equality.

In addition to offering arrive-and-drive convenience, these programs offer the developing driver a progression of increasingly tough competition, more sophisticated equipment, and, of course, progressively higher costs. The upper echelons of the Barber and Russell programs offer significant prize money and, sometimes, national television exposure as support races to pro series. The top Barber series, Zerex Pro Saab, is IMSA sanctioned and FIA listed as a full international event.

Private series are not for everybody, but they are a good fit for some drivers. If they sound interesting to you, I'd suggest you contact Barber and Russell for more information. You can probably find other such series in the buff magazines, like *Autoweek, Car and Driver, Racer,* and *Road & Track.*

Other Resources

I have listed a few contacts and sources that may be of value to you. I decided to do this after some hesitation because this kind of list is necessarily unfair to many good people who, for whatever reason, are *not* listed. Please read it with the understanding that these are just some good contacts that have come from my limited experience.

BAT Ltd.
1748 Independence Blvd., Unit G-2
Sarasota, FL 34234
(813)355-0005

The initials originally stood for "British-American Transfer." A good source for English hardware; they bring in air container loads fairly often.

B&F Aircraft
6141 W. 95th St.
Oak Lawn, IL 60453
(312) 422-3220

Aircraft hardware; a good inventory of 4130 tubing suitable for making or repairing space-frame chassis and for sway bars. (Yes, sway bars should be made from tubing, not from solid bar stock.)

Coast Fabrication
17712 Metzler Lane
Huntington Beach, CA 92647
(714) 842-2603

These guys are a good, though narrowly focused, source of AN-series bolts and other aircraft hardware. Unlike most aircraft hardware suppliers, they are racers and can offer advice as well as parts.

Donnybrooke Motor Racing Equipment
319 Lake Hazeltine Dr.
Chaska, MN 55318
(800) 825-2502
(612) 448-1660

Yes, they're friends of mine. Donnybrooke publishes a catalog of universal stuff, plus carries Spec Racer parts and supplies. A good source if you can't buy locally for some reason.

Fast Forward Components
507 Redwood Ave.
Sand City, CA 93955
(408) 899-3636

John Gianelli, who managed the Swift factory for its first couple of years, moved to Fast Forward a few years ago. In addition to being a great source of gossip and advice, he can serve your needs for arcane machined metal bits. Gun-drilled axles, a cute jig to hold the Hewland rear housing while you're changing gears, and so on. Call for a catalog or for help with a special need. Fast Forward is especially strong in Formula Continental and Formula Atlantic hardware.

GrassRoots Motorsports
425 Parque Dr.
Ormond Beach, FL 32174
(904) 673-4148

For a new racer, this magazine is probably more valuable than *Sports Car.* Its roots are in autocrossing, but in the past few years it has expanded its coverage to include classes of interest to new racers, like Improved Touring. According to a recent survey, 40% of the magazine's readers are involved in road racing.

The magazine includes how-to features on project cars, *good* technical articles, and an occasional "School Daze" story based on attendance at a professional racing school. Russell and Bondurant have already been covered; if you are considering one of them, you may wish to buy a back-issue copy of *GrassRoots.*

Industrial Arts Supply
5724 W. 36th St.
Minneapolis, MN 55416
(612) 920-7393

This unusual mail-order business primarily serves high-school industrial arts teachers, providing supplies for student projects. Lots of kitsch plaque molds, and so forth.

Of interest to racers, though, is their broad line of fiberglass supplies—cloth (glass and Kevlar) and mat, polyester and epoxy resins, gel coat, and coloring agents. They also carry two-part foam kits of various densities, both rigid and flexible. Everything is available in quantities from small to large; no need to buy a gallon if you only need a quart. Limited technical consulting is available on the phone, though these people are not racers.

Ron Minor Racing
6511 N. 27th Ave.
Phoenix, AZ
(602) 242-3398

In addition to being nice people, Ron and Jeannie Minor manufacture the ubiquitous Pit-Sig plastic flip-over signal board. Their catalog tends toward things needed by all drivers—safety equipment, tools, pit items, and the like. Another good source if you can't buy locally for some reason.

Demon Tweeks, Ltd.
The High Street
Tattenhall, Nr. Chester
Cheshire CH3 9PX
England
44 829 7065

If you need European hardware or other items, it is sometimes possible to save quite a bit of money by ordering direct. Transatlantic telephone calls are not that expensive, especially when placed early in the morning; England is five hours ahead of Eastern Standard Time and they speak more or less the same language that we do, so calling in orders works nicely. Your supplier will usually be happy to take a Visa card number for payment. The biggest bother is US Customs, but they often pass small packages without asking for duty. On major purchases, I'd suggest calling Customs so you know what you're getting into.

Demon Tweeks is one supplier that I have used, but I suggest you look for other sources by buying newsstand copies of *Autosport* and other English racing magazines. Demon Tweeks sells to both the street car and the racing markets though a large color catalog.

Carroll Smith: "Other good sources include...":
ARP
Automotive Racing Products
250 Quail Ct.
Santa Paula, CA 93060
(800) 826-3045

The best in drivetrain bolts.

Aircraft Spruce & Specialty
201 W. Truslow Ave.
Fullerton, CA 92632
(714) 870-7551
Aircraft hardware and materials.

BRITS
28921 Arnold Dr., F-6
Sonoma, CA 95476
(707) 935-3637
Hewland, Staffs, Webster, AP, Earl's, and other brands.

Pegasus Auto Racing Supplies
2475 S. 179th St.
New Berlin, WI 53146
(414) 782-0880
Just about everything.

Torino Motor Racing
1350-M W. Collins
Orange, CA 92668
(714) 771-1348
Earl's, plus transaxle prep of the highest quality.

Transatlantic Racing Services
5730 Chattahoochee Industrial Park
Cumming, GA 30131
(800) 533-6057/(404) 889-0499
Just about everything.

Publications

As I mentioned in the Introduction, you are not done buying books just because you've bought this one. I have listed some books that I have found helpful. It's not an exhaustive list and, of course, I can't anticipate new publications. Use it as a starting point, not as a prescription.

Racing, The Drivers Handbook by Peter Scott. Northwind, second edition, 1986. Scott's book is an enjoyable introduction to racing. It is a combination of the standard how-to and a sort of stream-of-consciousness description of what racing is really like. Although the how-to is too light for me to recommend this book as basic training, Scott's ability to communicate what it feels like "out there" on the racetrack is unequaled. Read the book for that reason alone.

Driving in Competition by Alan Johnson, CBS Publications, third edition, 1976. Johnson's book, last revised in 1976, is out of date as far as SCCA classes and costs are concerned. The driving advice is, however, still quite good. You should read and understand his categorization of turns as Types 1 (beginning a straight), 2 (ending a straight), and 3 (a turn between turns).

Danny Collins: "[regarding] Alan Johnson's interesting typing of turns—very logical, but misused. The implication is that a driver [in a Type 1 turn] must at all costs sacrifice corner entry speed for exit speed.... You'd be surprised at how much time is *lost* entering a turn (lost elapsed time, never to be regained)."

You should absolutely and positively reject Johnson's advice to turn down your mirrors to avoid being distracted by overtaking traffic. If you have this problem, please switch your interests to gardening or fly-tying. You have no business on a racetrack.

Race Car Engineering and Mechanics by Paul Van Valkenburgh, second edition, 1986, published by the author (PO Box 3611, Seal Beach, CA 90740). This one almost made the "mandatory" list in chapter 1. Be sure to buy it if you are at all interested in the technology of racing. Paul is a professional automotive engineer, and worked with Mark Donohue and Chevrolet during the glory years of the Trans-Am. The book differs from *Prepare to Win* and *Tune to Win* in that they emphasize *doing* things, while Paul emphasizes *understanding* things. The book is an excellent overview of professional racing technology and professional chassis tuning techniques.

Engineer to Win by Carroll Smith, Motorbooks International, 1984; and *Carroll Smith's Nuts, Bolts, Fasteners and Plumbing Handbook* by Carroll Smith, Motorbooks International, 1990. Once you have digested *Prepare to Win* and *Tune to Win*, it is probably time to buy these two. This is especially true if you're interested in the engineering aspects of racing. A nonmechanical racer might find them a bit too technical.

Carroll told us most of what we need to know in his first two books, but some of the subjects do benefit from updating and expansion. *Engineer to Win* is especially good as an update; he brings the reader up to date on, among other things, ground effect technology. *Carroll Smith's Nuts, Bolts, Fasteners and Plumbing Handbook* is both update and expansion.

***Machinery's Handbook, A Reference Book for the Me-
chanical Engineer, Draftsman, Toolmaker, and Machinist*** Industrial Press, Inc. Have you ever noticed the odd-shaped
center drawer in many machinist tool chests? It's for *Machinery's Handbook.* This book, first published in 1917 and revised over twenty times since then, is filled with mechanical
information that's useful to the racer. It includes design formulas for simple structures, strength values for metals, thread
and drill dimensions… too much to list here. If you are or
would like to be an amateur mechanical engineer, you'll
find this book indispensable.

Drive to Win by Mario Andretti and Gilbert Pednault,
Nutmeg Productions, 1988. This is a video, not a book. I
don't know that you need to own it, but viewing it a couple
of times would be a good idea especially if you're going to a
pro school. Much of the tape is devoted to a training session
at Jim Russell of Canada, where Pednault is Chief Instructor.
The tape will give you a good idea of how a pro school op-
erates.

Building a Mini Stock Step by Step by Jean Louis Gene-
bril, Steve Smith Autosports, 1986. If you're a novice driver
thinking about building your own car, this is a good book to
buy. Jean takes you through everything needed to produce a
competitive GT-3 Mustang. It's a big job, as you will see.
The scope of what's required will probably deter you, but
the book will be a help if you decide to go ahead.

The Technique of Motor Racing by Piero Taruffi, Robert
Bentley, Inc., 1958. The more things change, the more they
stay the same. Read this classic. It's a great way to spend an
inspirational evening when, for some reason, you aren't getting dirty working on the car.

The book is not just a nostalgia piece, though. Taruffi
gives you cornering theory and mathematics in more detail
than any book I can think of.

**Tony Kester: "This book is my all-time favorite. No fat
tires, no wings, no ground effects—Taruffi talks about *driving* the car, not just *steering* it."**

Carroll Smith: "Taruffi is my favorite, too!"

Sports Car and Competition Driving by Paul Frère,
Robert Bentley, Inc., 1966. This book, published 25 years
ago, is worth finding for a couple of reasons. First, it comple-
ments Carroll Smith's treatment of vehicle dynamics. This is
physics; nothing really changes. Second, if you are on street
tires and/or in Showroom Stockers, Frère's numbers are surprisingly relevant.

Those of you who are familiar with Frère's name
through *Road & Track* may not be aware of his racing experience. He drove for Ferrari in the 1950s, racing successfully
with the likes of Stirling Moss, Jack Brabham, and Phil Hill.
Most of his race tactics remain relevant, too.

Fluid Dynamic Drag by Sighard F. Hoerner, published
by the author, Hoerner Fluid Dynamics, PO Box 342, Brick
Town, NJ 08723, 1965. As long as we're talking about old
books, you should be aware of this one, self-published by a
former Luftwaffe aerodynamicist. Most of Carroll's discussion
of drag in *Tune to Win* is based on this book.

The book is chock full of real test data and analyses,
largely at air speeds that are relevant to car racing. (The material tends toward data on Bf-109 Messerschmitt fighters!)
It's also great fun to read.

A Brainerd Hot Lap

BY JERRY HANSEN

Hot Laps

When driving Brainerd keep in mind that it is a fast, smooth course with a little faster average speed than Elkhart Lake or Road Atlanta. It's also got plenty of room for run-off.

Turn Two is also taken flat in Can-Am and Atlantic cars, but you must lift a little to set up, and then get back hard on the gas in top gear as you enter this one in SSGT and GT-1 cars. Passing is possible here on the turn's entry during a competitive race.

Turn One, a right-hander at the end of the straight, is slightly banked and taken flat out in a Can-Am, Atlantic, SSGT or GT-2 cars.

Brake hard for Turn Four approximately 200 feet from the corner and take a tight apex, not using all the track on the exit. That way you're in better shape for …

Turn Five, a flat turn which can be taken in second or third, depending upon your car. Use all the track on the exit and shift up one gear.

To get into Turn Three brake medium hard from top gear approximately 300 feet from the corner, shift down to second and clip the apex closely, using all the road on the exit. Shift up to third and move to the right of the track to set up for Turn Four. The entry for this turn is another place to pass during a close race.

Turn Six is dealt with just as was Turn Five, the only difference being that it is dished while Five is flat.

Turns Seven and Eight—a lot of time can be made here on the exit from Eight. I enter Turn Seven tight to the left and I stay to the left, making Turn Eight the major turn and getting good exit speed.

To set up for Turn 10 brake quickly about 300 feet before the corner, get into third and get back on the gas. It's a medium-fast turn, dished at the apex, and in a competitive race is a good place to pass under braking. I use third gear and all the road possible on the exit for good straightaway speeds. The entrance to the pits is just to the left past the exit of this corner. Approach Turn One from the outside.

Turn Nine is flat in either third or fourth, depending upon your car. Use all the road and then some. I went into the ditch here on the exit during the '83 Trans-Am, so remember not to use too much of the and-then-some part.

Jerry Hansen has no less than 26 (!) National Championships to his credit, his most recent being won at the '83 Champion Spark Plug Road Racing Classic in A Sports Racing and GT-1. He has also proven his talent by claiming SCCA professional victories, including five career Trans-Am wins. Jerry is one of the owners of Brainerd International Raceway. Bob Fischer photo.

A Charlotte Hot Lap

A Man Who Knows the Way Shows the Way

by Don Knowles

Bob Fischer

Don Knowles has developed a reputation primarily for racing front wheel drive cars, having won two SSB National Championships in a normally aspirated Saab, as well as having won races in both of the professional front wheel drive series, the Renault Cup and the Rabbit-Bilstein Cup. A winner of the inaugural 24 Hours of Nelson Ledges in a turbo Saab, he won again in 1983 in the Dick Guldstrand Camaro, decidedly a rear wheel drive car. For 1984, he is trying to become a regular in the Champion Spark Plug RS series, racing both the Bill Scott Rabbit GTI and Ford's 7-Eleven Escort at various times. He may even get to the run-offs again, if a hoped for program materializes. Don also received SportsCar® magazine's 1983 Best Feature Story Award for his article entitled "Left-Foot Braking."

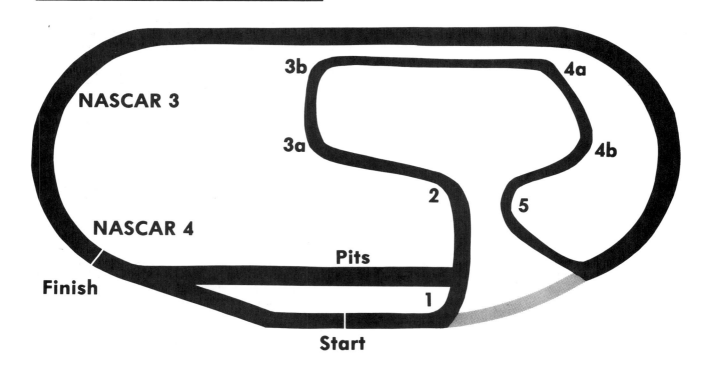

Turn 1

Turn 1 is approached at top speed, the car coming off of NASCAR's Turn 4 bump and through the tri-oval pit straight. Turn 1 is of constant radius and crosses three pavement types: braking is done on the superspeedway straight (which is, by the way, banked 5 degrees); the apex is right before the car moves onto NASCAR's pit road pavement; and the exit leads into the road course pavement. Braking and downshifting, sane drivers do not commit to the turn unless they are sure they can make it, because there is a three foot tall concrete wall abutting the track at the exit. Although the wall is exceptionally well protected by tires, it is still something to be avoided. Drivers inevitably drift right up to the wall, whether absolutely necessary or not. It helps their reputation to end the race with "Charlotte Stripes" on the right side bodywork and it gives the corner workers a chance to practice the proper entry into a foxhole.

Turn 2

Turns 2, 3a, and 3b are run as one segment and provide an excellent opportunity to create a passing opportunity. Exiting Turn 1 right up against the tire wall and following another car, you have several chances to create a pass through the highly cambered Turn 2. The lead car should stay mid-track or to the left exiting Turn 2, so as to be set up properly for the entrance to 3a. If the lead car apexes Turn 2 late so as to stay mid-track or left, the following car can apex early, carrying a few extra miles per hour onto the short chute between Turns 2 and 3a, closing on the lead car. At the last instant before committing to turn 3a, you can: 1) brake late, staying inside of the lead car and taking the 3a apex from him, or 2) move quickly left if the lead car has moved to take a slightly early apex at 3a.

Turns 3a and 3b

The entry for 3a is complicated by a down, then up elevation change in the braking area. Technically, Turns 3a and 3b can be driven either as a double apex or as a decreasing radius single apex. If the lead car early apexes Turn 3a, then the following car can either: 1) take a late apex and try to tuck inside him between 3a and 3b, taking the 3b apex from him; or 2) take a normal apex at 3a, concentrating on maximizing exit speed from the highly cambered 3b. If you mess up 3a, and put a wheel off to the outside of the track between 3a and 3b, hang on for a good ride.

Different racing cars, (for example, a front wheel drive turbo Saab SSA car versus a rearwheel drive Datsun 280Z SSA, or a CP Datsun 280ZX versus a CP Porsche 914), equally prepared and driven, produce excellent racing through this part of Charlotte, because it is almost impossible for the leader to adequately protect the entry to both 3a and 3b and still get optimum exit speed from 3b. The only significant infield straight follows 3b, so exit speed is critical.

Turns 4a and 4b

Following the infield straight is a flat, fast righthand turn (4a), climbing a short hill to a decreasing radius righthander at the crest of the hill (4b). Immediately past the apex of 4a, and with the left side tires still loaded, you lift, rotating the car with trailing throttle, then brake. The apex to 4b is the slowest point on the track, and there are slight bumps at the 4b apex that push you to the left side of the track if you enter too fast. The car should be held at mid-track or to the right as you exit 4b, to get set up for Turn 5. However, to hold the car to the right side of the track past apex 4b requires a pretty slow entry to 4b, so there are a number of available countermoves by other drivers. This is another dicey, thrust and parry segment of the track, like Turns 2, 3a, and 3b.

Turn 5

The last real turn in the infield is Turn 5, a decreasing radius, off-camber lefthander leading onto the NASCAR oval. After passing the apex of 4b, accelerate strongly down a short dip, then lift and turn left as soon as the road begins to rise. You feel the car get heavy and build cornering force and you begin to look around the turn for the late, blind apex. Still accelerating, you begin to arc towards an intersection with an imaginary point. You notice that the front end is beginning a slight push as the track levels out, then loses camber. Lifting momentarily and feeding in a touch more steering, the apex is sighted and, full power now, you drift to the track's edge. Another slight left follows quickly and you bump roughly onto the banked NASCAR turn and shift, shift, shift down the 1.3 mile superspeeding straight.

NASCAR 3 and NASCAR 4

I have found that medium speed cars require no particular driving technique or line through NASCAR 3 and 4. The turns have a large radius (675 feet) and are banked at 24 degrees. Some drivers, however, start in the upper lane, drop to an apex in the bottom lane midway through the turn, then climb out of the turn onto the pit straight. The banking is slightly bumpy and the draft buffets your car a lot. Most passing is done on power, down the backstraight, or by drafting, entering NASCAR 3 or exiting NASCAR 4. Because NASCAR 3 is the last turn before the finish line, this is where you need to have practiced your drafting pass and to know exactly how late you can start your slingshot move and still have it work. Conversely, if you are the lead car, you need to have decided where to place your car so to make the overtaking car climb the track or take the long way around. □

Glossary

Ackerman steering: As a car goes through a corner, the inside wheels travel along a tighter arc than the outside wheels. "Ackerman steering" refers to a steering linkage geometry that turns the inside and outside front wheels to angles that correctly follow the theoretical arcs. In a racing car, of course, high slip angles mean that the front tires are not following the theoretical arcs anyway. Thus, don't worry about it. If you have to know more, Carroll Smith tells you about steering geometry in Chapter 5 of *Tune to Win*.

Aeroquip: Used generically (except by the Aeroquip Corporation and Earl's Supply) to refer to high-pressure hydraulic hose with shiny stainless-steel braided jacketing. Except on brake lines, its pressure capabilities are fantastically beyond anything encountered in racing. It is ubiquitous on race cars, however, because the jacket provides excellent protection from cuts and chafing. In fact, an Aeroquip hose rubbing against a steel frame tube functions as a pretty effective file. If you work with Aeroquip for more than a few minutes, you will inevitably experience the toughness of the stainless braid wire as it punches tiny holes in your fingers.

Refer to *Tune to Win* for instructions on how to cut this type of hose and how to assemble the end-fittings. Assembly is easy to screw up and impossible to check by visual inspection. An assembly error on a brake line can cause the hose to separate from the fitting under pressure. Nothing good will come of this.

Antiroll bar: Steel bar, generally in the shape of a shallow U, which couples the left- and right-side wheels together to resist body roll in corners. If you are tuning your car by changing antiroll bar diameters, you should realize that the stiffness of the bar goes up as the fourth power of the diameter. This means that adding 10% to the bar diameter makes it about 50% stiffer. It also means that hollow bars are as stiff as solid ones. *Machinery's Handbook* gives you the math for this in the "Strength of Materials" section.

Apex: In a corner, the point at which your inside tires clip the inside edge of the track. The "geometric" apex of a corner is halfway around. An "early" apex is one that is made before the geometric apex. A "late" apex is made after the geometric apex.

Apex (correct): The point on a turn where the best driver in your class has his or her inside front tire halfway onto the grass.

Arm, raised: Used in two cases: (1) on the grid to show the starter that your engine is running, and (2) on the track, to show other drivers that you are slowing or stopping.

Back (part of the track): The start-finish line is located on the "front" straight of a racetrack. The balance of the track, especially the tight curves, is referred to as the "back."

Back up: Used in two different contexts: (1) To back up under power in the pits is a no-no. You may be asked about this on your driver school test. (2) To back up a flag is to show a supporting flag one corner station earlier. For example, a stationary yellow may be used to back up a particularly serious waving yellow.

Backmarker: A slow or poorly driven car.

A Hallett Hot Lap

A Man Who Knows the Way Shows the Way

by Anatoly Arutunoff

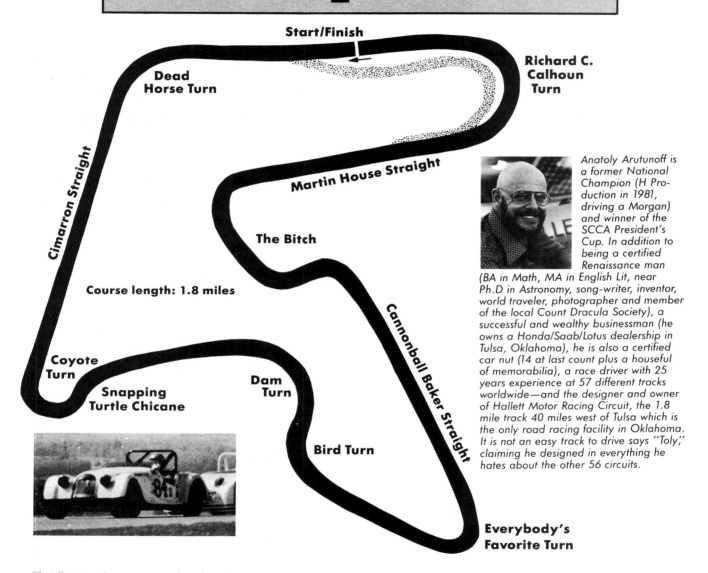

Start/Finish

Dead Horse Turn

Richard C. Calhoun Turn

Cimarron Straight

Martin House Straight

The Bitch

Course length: 1.8 miles

Cannonball Baker Straight

Coyote Turn

Dam Turn

Snapping Turtle Chicane

Bird Turn

Everybody's Favorite Turn

Anatoly Arutunoff is a former National Champion (H Production in 1981, driving a Morgan) and winner of the SCCA President's Cup. In addition to being a certified Renaissance man (BA in Math, MA in English Lit, near Ph.D in Astronomy, song-writer, inventor, world traveler, photographer and member of the local Count Dracula Society), a successful and wealthy businessman (he owns a Honda/Saab/Lotus dealership in Tulsa, Oklahoma), he is also a certified car nut (14 at last count plus a houseful of memorabilia), a race driver with 25 years experience at 57 different tracks worldwide—and the designer and owner of Hallett Motor Racing Circuit, the 1.8 mile track 40 miles west of Tulsa which is the only road racing facility in Oklahoma. It is not an easy track to drive says "Toly," claiming he designed in everything he hates about the other 56 circuits.

☐ Hallett is perhaps an unusual track in that it was laid out to follow the natural land contours and to avoid obstacles; After it was built, the obstacles were removed! We also wanted to keep a bit of tradition, so while the corners and intermediate stations have numbers, I'll use their names instead.

Dead Horse Turn

Running Counterclockwise, Dead Horse Turn is a medium-fast turn of not quite 90 degrees. With its definite crown you need to be well to the inside at the apex—if you try a pass at competitive speed here, you'll discover the outside has a touch of reverse camber.

Coyote Turn

Over the hill (along Cimarron Straight) you go and, as you approach Coyote Turn, a 165 degree left, braking early is necessary due to the downhill approach. The entire turn is slippery, so it's very easy to come charging in at 25mph and miss the apex by a yard! Big cars take this turn differently than slow cars, due to the proximity of the right-hand Snapping Turtle Chicane.

Snapping Turtle Chicane

It's really only half a chicane, but the turtles have gone back to the lake (Veronica Lake) anyway. A rapidly accelerating car takes a very late apex in Coyote, to straighten Snapping Turtle out as much as possible; but a slow car with less cornering power can apex the turn normally and then bend gently to the right immediately afterward. Up the hill we go, setting up for the right-hand Dam Turn.

Dam Turn

The turn is at the brow of the hill, so turning in is complicated by the feeling of the road "falling away" slightly. This turn is effectively apexed at the beginning of the tiny little straight which follows, since the next turn, the left-hand Bird Turn, almost makes these two turns a stretched S.

Bird Turn

Bird Turn falls gently over the brow of the downhill stretch to Everybody's Favorite Turn; there's a bit more grip at the edge of the road on the racing line exiting Bird. However, there wasn't quite enough for Mr. Dunias' Spitfire, which nailed the tires surrounding The Most Beautiful Little Tree on the Property. Unbeknownst to me, maintenance had fully bunkered the lovely tirewall with dirt, which gave Costa a wet red moustache. We've since removed the tree, although we considered putting a sign on it: "Hit this tree and gain National Office."

Everybody's Favorite

I thought I had Everybody's Favorite, a banked, sweeping downhill left, really figured out: A tight line lets you dig into the camber. That still works pretty well on a slow-rotating slug like my Morgan, but Skip Barber's cars and instruction proved to my satisfaction that an apparently late turn-in and moderately late apex is the fastest way through for real race cars. Now we're on a slight upgrade along the .2-mile Cannonball Baker Straight, heading for The Bitch.

The Bitch

An increasingly uphill fast left sets you up for a twitch to the right at the crest of the hill, although a twitch will generally send you gracefully looping downhill to perhaps experience gentle contact with some of our 125,000 tires. The fast uphill sweeping left and twitch right is followed by a down-and-up slowish right-hander, the climbing exit of the turn itself providing a bit of extra bite. Out of The Bitch, move gradually to the right down the quarter-mile Back Straight to set up for the Richard C. Calhoun 170 degree left.

Richard C. Calhoun

This increasing radius, increasingly downhill turn seems to be the most forgiving of them all with regard to exit speed; still, a sharp, late entry and late apex is best for sophisticated machinery. Now it's back onto the .3-mile Founder's Straight, undulating downhill to the Start/Finish line. That's a lap at Hallet. We run some races clockwise, but that's another story; I think it's scarier clockwise. We've even run Standing Start Showroom Stock events—now that's fun! □

Bias, brake: See Lockup, rear brakes.

Black flag station: The flagging station where black flags and "meatballs" are displayed. This station is normally located so that the black-flagged driver can enter the pits without completing another lap. Typically, the black flag station is before the turn that begins the straightaway.

Blocking: Driving a line that is intended to keep an overtaking car from passing. Tolerated (by drivers) only in moderation among equals, and usually only on the last lap. Generally considered, especially by race officials, to be a figment of the overtaking driver's imagination.

Bump: Refers to compression of the car's suspension relative to its normal position, as when hitting a bump. The outside (loaded) suspension "moves into bump" when cornering.

Bump steer: When a tire travels vertically through the range of suspension motion, there is normally some change to the direction it is pointed (toe-in or toe-out). This is a steering input to the car just as surely as is turning the steering wheel. Part of alignment is minimization of bump steer to the extent permitted by the suspension design and the rules of the car class.

Buzz: Verb, "He buzzed the motor." See Overrev.

Camber: (1) A slight transverse slope on a track surface, usually for drainage. Camber that tends to help cornering is usually called a "bank." Camber that tends to toss you into the weeds is called "off-camber." A track with a crown (higher) center has both useful banking and challenging off-camber, depending where you are in a corner. (2) A tire's vertical tilt, measured in degrees, relative to a plane through its center and perpendicular to the ground. Camber settings are normally negative, meaning the tire is tilted inward (toward the car's centerline) at its top.

Car, wide: See Blocking.

CART: Acronym for Championship Automobile Racing Teams. CART is the organization that took over IndyCar racing from United States Automobile Club (USAC) several years ago (and not with USAC's approval). Recently, CART became "IndyCar."

Caster: The tilt, expressed in degrees, of a tire's steering swivel axis relative to the vertical. Don't worry too much about it, it's not important as long as both sides are approximately equal.

Checklist: Tool for success.

Chicane: A "kink" in the track, usually requiring a left-right-left or right-left-right maneuver. Typically, a chicane is an addition to a track that is made in order to slow the cars down. Beloved only by insurance underwriters.

Chief Steward: Official in overall charge of the race weekend. Generally addressed as "sir" or "m'am," even by drivers who would prefer to use another, less respectful form of address.

Chief Steward's Request for Action: The mechanism by which the Operating Stewards "protest" a driver. Handled by the SOMs, just like a protest.

Coil, cooked: The result of discharging your battery by leaving the ignition on overnight with the points closed. Toss it.

Contact patch: The amount of tire that is physically in contact with the track at a given instant. The area of the contact patch is roughly equal to the weight on the tire divided by the tire pressure. As the weight varies during acceleration, cornering, and braking, so does the size of the contact patch.

Contingency: A financial award, usually money or a merchandise credit, paid to a racer who meets certain crite-

A Watkins Glen Hot Lap

A Man Who Knows the Way Shows the Way
by Ken Slagle

Ken Slagle at speed in his Triumph TR8.

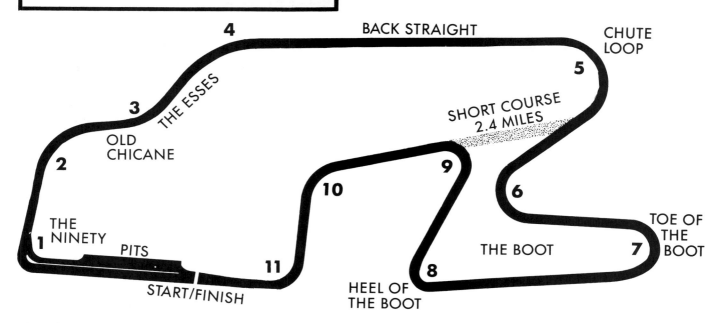

□ Ken Slagle has been competing in SCCA races since 1967, when he attended drivers school (under the tutelage of Bob Tullius) at Marlboro, Md. In the intervening years, he has raced his Triumph 156 national races, with 64 wins and 33 second-place finishes, including national championships in 1975 (FP Spitfire) and 1981 (CP TR8). Ken has been a member of the National Competition Board since 1980, is the secretary of the Road Racing Drivers Club, and is co-driving the Dyson Racing Pontiac Firebird in selected endurance races. Having held lap records at Watkins Glen in four classes (FP, DP, CP, GT1), Ken says Watkins Glen is one of his favorite tracks.

The 3.377-mile long Watkins Glen race course has an interesting combination of various types of corners, elevation and surface changes, guard rails and scenic beauty. The start/finish straight, which passes the pits, is very wide, offering plenty of room for passing (at the start of a race there are generally three or four cars abreast heading for the first turn).

Turn 1

Since Turn 1 is at the end of the second longest straight and is essentially the beginning of the longest straight, it is a key turn to good lap times. Here, as with several other braking areas at the Glen, you're going downhill under heavy braking, necessitating more front brake bias than normal. Good banking and a wide exit make this a third gear turn with a "dive-in/climb out" corner with a somewhat early apex. The real key is getting the car turned in to ensure an apex right at the curbing. Use all the road on the exit, right out to the bumps.

Turn 2

This right-hand sweeper leading up a steep hill, and the following left and right handers, is flat-out, a good place to concentrate on precision and smoothness to avoid scrubbing off too much speed.

Turns 3 and 4

Now that the "Scheckter Chicane" has been eliminated, it is necessary to stay to the inside of the right-hander to be on the proper line up the hill and into the Turn 3 left-hander. Removal of this artificial "hazard" should help safety and improve the course for the driver.

Main Straight

The main straight is slightly uphill for its entire length (over one-half mile) and is quite bumpy, requiring you to be something of a phrenologist to avoid being pitched about or having the car bottom badly. This straight is definitely long enough to find the top speed of most cars (uphill) long before the end. The braking area at the end of the straight, leading into "the loop," is up and over a rise, which (in faster cars) requires considerable braking to be done before the crest of the rise.

Turn 5

Enter the loop (Turn 5) from the left side

of the track and dive downhill into "the chute," hugging the inside of the turn as long as possible. The car will drift out to the left where the transition from the short course to the long course is apparent, at which time you should start easing the car back toward the right side to be on the line for the left-hander (Turn 6) going downhill into "the boot." The braking areas for this turn and the next one are both down steep hills, making it very easy to lock rear brakes with normal brake proportioning.

Turn 6

Turn 6 is an increasing radius, downhill, well banked turn that is much faster than it first appears. It's essential to turn in gradually for a mid to slightly late apex and allow the car to drift toward the curbing on the right as you exit under full power.

Turn 7

Going into the "toe" of the boot (Turn 7), allow for the increased braking distance required by the downhill and start turning toward a mid-turn apex. Two factors affect your speed and line through this turn—first, it is an increasingly uphill turn; second, a pavement patch right on the line, just past the apex, provides much less adhesion than the rest of the track. When the car starts to slide on the patch, have faith that the hill and getting off the patch will "catch" the car.

Turn 8

Up a steep hill you go and into the "heel" of the boot (Turn 8), a 120-degree right-hander that is slightly downhill, requiring a somewhat late apex. The braking area for this turn is another "over-the-crest" situation where if left too late you find the car is "light" when you need to be braking hard (this isn't a problem with "smaller" cars!).

Turn 9

The left-hander leading back onto the "short course" seems to have relatively poor adhesion sometimes, is fairly flat and seems to go forever. A "long" late apex helps so you can get full throttle as early as possible.

Turns 10 and 11

The left and right corners leading onto the start/finish straight are well banked, with wide exits, allowing "normal" approaches and lines.

Racing at the Glen in the rain (as we did in June), points out areas of paving differences even more than driving it in the dry. All you can do is modify your lines to minimize the time you're on the patches, or let the car slide (knowing there's better adhesion at the end of your slide!).

All in all, a very challenging track that is undergoing a fantastic rebirth. With the changes made to date and those promised for the future, it's great that "The Glen Is Back!" □

ria. Typically, a contingency requires that you use the sponsor's product or service, display their advertising stickers on your car, and achieve a minimum finishing position in a race or a series. Often, too, you must preregister with the sponsor to be eligible for the contingency award.

Corner: Refers to a tire, wheel, and associated suspension components, especially on a Formula car. One measure of crash severity is the number of corners destroyed.

Corner station: A location, usually associated with a corner, where the Flagging and Communications workers are located and where the flags are displayed. A corner station always provides physical protection to the workers and, often, provides some sun and rain protection as well. Your first task on a new racetrack is to memorize the locations of the stations and to develop the habit of looking to the *next* station immediately as you exit each corner.

Corner weight: The amount of the car's weight that is carried on a particular tire ("corner"). In road racing, corner weights are normally set equal from left to right. In circle-track racing, adjustment of corner weight ("weight-jacking") is a major element of chassis tuning.

Crashes (proper behavior): Unless it is you, do not slow down to inspect a crash site. If it is serious, it will be there for examination next lap. If it is not, you don't care. You are a driver, not a tourist.

Crew: A species of the genus: saint.

Dead pedal: A dummy pedal, located to the left of the clutch, used as a footrest or for bracing the driver in the cockpit. Common in Sports Racers and older, wide chassis Formula cars. Don't become dependent on using it; your next car may not have one.

Denver: Noun referring to SCCA headquarters, which are actually in Englewood, Colorado. For example, "Denver says...."

Dice: Refers to close racing. Noun: "They had a good dice." Verb: "They diced the whole race."

Differential: The driven wheels of a car cannot be solidly connected because, in turns, the inside tire rotates more slowly than the outside tire. The differential is a gear device that couples the engine torque to the wheels without coupling the wheels to each other.

Differential, limited-slip: A differential that incorporates a clutch system designed to ensure that engine torque is transmitted to both tires, regardless of traction conditions.

Differential, open: A standard differential has the disadvantage that engine torque is transmitted to whichever wheel is turning fastest. Devices that defeat this characteristic ("lockers," limited-slip differentials, and so on) occupy the space between the spider gears of the differential. A standard differential is referred to as an "open" diff because there is nothing in this space.

Dirt: See Sand.

DNF: Results sheet acronym for "Did Not Finish." Often used as a verb ("He DNFed.") To be classed as a finisher, a car must complete half the laps completed by the overall race leader. Beginners who are trying to get credit for every race event are particularly concerned about DNFs, but no driver wants to see the weekend's investment of time, energy, and money documented this way on a results sheet.

DNS: Results sheet acronym for "Did Not Start."

Door car: Car with doors; for example, a Production or GT car. The phrase probably originated as a pejorative with people who believe that "real" race cars do not have doors (or fenders).

Double-clutching: A technique wherein the clutch is

A Portland Hot Lap

A Man Who Knows the Way Shows the Way

by Bob Lobenberg

☐ With two National Championships in Formula Ford (1980 and 1982) and two in Sports 2000 (1982,'83), Bob Lobenberg is quite simply the premier driver in these classes. For 1984 he has been, quite simply, sensational and more than a little unlucky in his rookie year in the Budweiser Trans-Am series driving the STP Son of a Gun! Pontiac Excitement for Joe Huffaker Engineering. His recent showing at Road America, where he outqualified the field and drove away from everybody (only to run out of gas on the last lap) is testament to his smoothness as a pilot. In the recent Trans-Am at Portland tire punctures ruined his chances, and after taking the pole at Watkins Glen a flat tire on the pace lap broke the car's suspension.

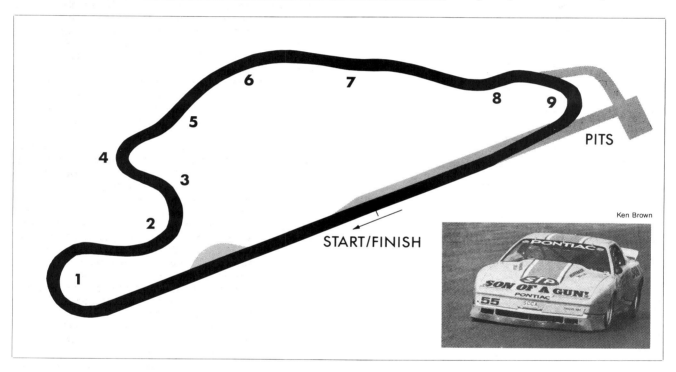

START/FINISH

PITS

Ken Brown

A fast lap at Portland International Raceway may look as if it would be easy because the circuit is flat, without any elevation changes. Not necessarily true. In fact, in order to go really fast at P.I.R. one must have the ability to drive very smoothly, with a lot of rhythm, while keeping the car on the ragged edge. This is true because of the track's layout...a mixture of medium-slow and medium-fast turns. These turns are smooth, but almost always lead into another turn, so one must look further than the end of his/her nose (of the car, of course).

Turn 1

I have raced here for the better part of seven years and still do not feel I have mastered this turn, a medium-fast right-hander. It's hard to judge how deep you can brake for this one.

When you are *too* deep, you'll run out of braking room and have to drive the car virtually off the end of the course onto the grass. This presents a problem if it has just rained or it is early in the morning, because the grass is wet and you will accelerate as soon as you touch the green stuff. However, going off course here is almost a certainty, so when you do, slow everything down, get turned around and head back for the track. The reason I say going off is almost a certainty is because if you are to find the fastest way through Turn 1 you will have to experiment attempting to find the deepest point of braking going in.

Turn 2

Whew! Now that we have got through Turn 1 we must keep the nice drift we generated

working for us in Turn 2. In essense, Turns 1 and 2 are a single turn with a double apex that leads us to Turn 3, a medium-slow right-hander.

Turn 3

At this point we must slow down considerably as compared to Turns 1 and 2. But once again, the rhythm is important here because we are still actually drifting to the left when we have to brake for Turn 3. We have to be delicate so we don't upset the car in its transition from power-on to power-off-and-braking while the car is sliding. Now we turn in for 3, get back on the power for just a second and haul it back down for Turn 4.

Turn 4

A medium-slow speed left-hand sweeper. We

150

must downshift a gear under braking and turn in. Now we modulate the power so we can be deep into the throttle by the time we get approximately two-thirds around this almost carousel-type turn. Exit the turn and squirt-on the power down to Turn 5.

Turn 5.

A slow-speed right-hander of just about 90 degrees. This is a very important turn because it leads onto the back straight. The reason it indirectly leads onto the back straight is because there is a quick left/right esse-turn that you must be lined up for so you can do it without lifting and not disturb your acceleration from Turn 5.

Turn 6

At this point you are sailing around a gradual right-hand sweeper in the "straight" that is taken flat-out no matter what type of machine you are driving. Now things get a little hairier than the proceeding turns, as you are going be traveling at a very high rate of speed by the time you get to the esses at the end of this straight.

Turns 7 & 8

Like the initial turn at P.I.R., you must first determine how fast you can enter this set of turns. The problem is, if you go off here you end up flying over a mound into the air—which will certainly do a lot of damage to your machine by the time it stops flipping over and lands in the infield. Therefore, approach these esses hot, but brake a little early. Downshift to the next lower gear, turn in early, and run up over the berm on the apex of the left-hander. This berm looks as though it will upset the car but, in fact, it is almost all paint and can be treated as if it didn't exist. Now you will have a much straighter line for Turn 8, the next right-hand esse. Try to late apex Turn 8 so you can keep good speed into the last turn of the track, Turn 9.

Turn 9

This is a slow-speed, 90 degree right hand turn and is very important, as it leads onto the longest straight and the start/finish line—where the race is either won or lost. You will approach this turn with some aggression, carrying speed from the esses, but you must brake hard as soon as the car has settled from the previous esses. Once you have slowed the car enough to start the initial turn in, try to make a late apex so you can get right back on the gas for a good shot at the straight. Some cars will tolerate using the berm here, and if so, you can gain a little advantage because you essentially cut down the track length and add more room onto the exit. This means you will be able to get on the gas a little earlier than someone driving a car which gets upset by the berm and must drive around it.

There you have it, a hot lap around Portland. Seems easy, right? Well, let me be the first to say it takes plenty of practice to stay smooth and yet be on the gas hard and early enough to be really fast. All this *must* be done without getting out of shape, because you are drifting through every turn, so any extra sliding — especially sideways — only costs time, and time is what dictates a win or a loss, right?

depressed and released once in shifting the box to neutral, the engine is revved, then the clutch is depressed and released again in shifting into the next gear.

Draft: (1) Verb: To draft a car is to pull up behind it and gain an advantage from the low-pressure air in its wake. (2) Noun: Draft is what the first car gives the second car ("He got some draft," or "I gave him a draft").

Droop: Extension of the car's suspension relative to its normal position, as when dropping off the edge of the track. The inside (unloaded) suspension "moves into droop" when cornering. See also Rebound.

Dry sump: An engine oil system where the oil is pumped from the oil pan and stored in a tank, then returned to the engine through a separate pump. The pump connected to the oil pan is called the "scavenge" pump and the return pump is called the "pressure" pump. These pumps are normally different sections of a single assembly, driven from a common shaft. Multiple scavenge pumps are sometimes used. A dry-sump system has two advantages: (1) the oil tank can be designed to ensure that oil is available to the pressure pump in all high-g cornering and braking situations. This is difficult with a conventional wet-sump system. (2) Because its sump is not required to be an oil tank, the engine can be mounted lower in the chassis, resulting in a lower overall car center of gravity.

Dust clouds, driving through: There are many pilots who race cars. They do not slow their airplanes when they cannot see, neither do they slow their race cars. The rest of us have learned from them or are routinely passed by those who have.

Dye check: Use of a dye penetrant kit to check parts for cracks. Such kits are suitable for quick checking of parts at the racetrack or in the garage. Critical items should be professionally checked at an FAA-certified shop.

Dyno: Short for "dynamometer," an engine test stand instrumented to measure rpm, output torque, and other critical parameters. Always found in serious engine-building shops. A dyno is the best place to check out your newly built engine, even if it involves additional expense. If it is going to come apart, *this* is where you want it to happen.

ET: Elapsed time (taken between two points).

Enterprises: Refers to SCCA Enterprises, a (theoretically) profit-making subsidiary. Enterprises is responsible for the Spec Racer class, née Sports Renault.

Entrant: In pro racing, the "entrant" is usually the race shop that owns the car. In club racing, the entrant and the driver are usually one and the same.

False grid: An area where cars are parked prior to entering the racetrack. Prior to beginning a race, the cars are moved from the false grid area onto the track where they are re-parked to form the "real" grid. For practice and qualifying, this real grid is omitted and the cars do not stop on the track after they are released by the Grid Marshals.

FIA: Acronym for Fédération Internationale de l'Automobile, the United Nations of cars. Of interest to us in its role as sanctioning body for international racing.

First lap (of a session): A good time to warm up the car, locate the oil-dry that has been placed on the track, and identify the real crazies who think it's the race.

Flags, general: For each flag, the *GCR* describes what the officials intend for you to do. You should understand their intentions, regardless of how you intend to respond.

Flag, blue with yellow stripe: Generally ignored, especially by the slug in front of you. This is the only flag that the worker can throw without instructions from the corner cap-

A SUMMIT POINT HOT LAP

A driver who knows the way shows the way

by Bill Scott (edited by Don Knowles)

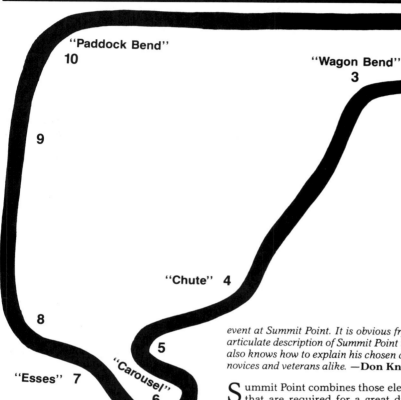

"Paddock Bend" 10

"Wagon Bend" 3

1

2

9

8

"Chute" 4

"Esses" 7

5

"Carousel" 6

Most people know Bill as the owner and president of Summit Point Raceway, as a former U.S. or World Champion in Formula Vee, Formula Ford, and Formula Super Vee. Most also know that, in conjunction with Tom Milner, he has had a role in a number of National Championships for Tom Davey and, most recently, Tom Schwietz. However, few know him as a Yale educated Ph.D. in Geophysics; as an instructor at Yale; as a postdoctoral research fellow at the Carnegie Institute of Washington; as the author or coauthor of a dozen professional journal articles; and as a self-trained horticulturist specializing in fruit trees.

Bill continues to command respect for his driving skills and drove one of the DeAtley Motorsports Corvettes in the 1984 Trans-Am event at Summit Point. It is obvious from his articulate description of Summit Point that he also knows how to explain his chosen craft to novices and veterans alike. —**Don Knowles**

Summit Point combines those elements that are required for a great driver's track — long straight, elevation change, and a good range of corner configurations, i.e. from tight to very fast, sometimes spaced to interfere with the next, sometimes alone. The track is forgiving if you go off, but will bite your lap times if you're inaccurate or rough.

Turn 1 and Turn 2

You will be taking off anywhere from 70 to 100 mph from your speed at the end of the straight, so choice of shut-off point and braking efficiency are key. The entry will be a sharper turn than the exit since the corner is of increasing radius. Choose an apex such that you can be back on the throttle there. The shape of entry or exit lines will be determined by your power and stick. Exit speed, and therefore the earliest application of throttle, is important because the ensuing straight (the slight right kink, Turn 2, is included) is long enough to accrue benefits.

Turn 3 (Wagon Bend)

I've never heard anyone admit to taking this one perfectly. Although in plan view (i.e., an overhead view) it is relatively symmetrical, there are elevation and camber changes that create different conditions throughout. Even the approach, which is flat, is on a slight left bend. Brake lightly, looking for a sensitive, high-speed transition and enter a bit faster than the geometry would indicate. The corner becomes sharply uphill through the apex area, so you'll pick up stick to tighten your line. Keep it tight because at the exit, the hill disappears and the camber goes to negative, making the car step to the right. Maintain momentum throughout.

Turn 4 (Chute) and Turn 5

A very fast downhill right complicated by two dips near the apex. Taken as fast as possible in all except low-powered cars, you won't be able to get back to the right to set up for the left hand Turn 5. Brake as late as possible into Turn 5, emphasizing entry. A tight line with a late apex is my preference to get as early a burst of power before the next turn.

Taking Turn 4 (fast) correctly, with the sacrifice of Turn 5 entry (slow) is doubly advantageous since there is no real straight after Turn 5. If you're a trail-braking advocate, this is the only corner where it might make sense.

Turn 6 (Carousel)

Extremely important, as done well, it will affect your speed all the way to the bridge, three turns and more than a half-mile later. It is a double apex corner. Choose a late enough first apex such that a constant arc will bring you to a well-positioned second apex. Flow and balance are extremely important. Drift car with steady or slightly increasing speed. Take the second apex to position car at right center of track on exit, more towards center for lower powered cars.

Turns 7 and 8 (Esses) and Turn 9

Your exit from the Carousel needs to leave you positioned to take Turn 7 fast enough so you can get back to the left side of the track for the highest possible speed through Turn 8 and onto the second longest straight. This geometry will vary a bit depending on vehicle, but it is extremely important to maintain high momentum and drive in a graceful and fluid manner. Prevent choppy driver inputs into the car, and emphasize sensitive reading of weight transfers. Done correctly, you both get through the Carousel and Esses faster and have a higher speed on the ensuing straight. Turn 9 is a slight kink after Turn 8, and of no importance.

Turn 10 (Paddock Bend)

Not difficult, but extremely important, as it leads onto a 2700-foot straight. Brake lightly on approach to emphasize the high-speed transition. The corner is of slightly decreasing radius, so the apex will be late. Be back on the power well before the apex to get good exit speed. There is enough distance from Turn 10 to the start/finish line that a last lap drafting pass is possible in some cars and classes.

So there it is. Ninety percent of the limit is not hard—98% is excruciatingly tough. There are curbs at all apexes with slopes matched to the tightness of the turns. They aren't advantageous to use, but won't throw the car severely. On the exits to Turns 10, 1 and 3 there are ripples on the outside margin that are definitely to be avoided. The track responds to balance and flow and not well to throwing the car. As will other good circuits, time lost during the race (bad passes, poor starts, poor management of situations, etc.) benefits those with experience at The Point and those who can think while racing.

Track Records			
Class	Time	Speed	Date
FA	1:10.09	102.72	8/14/83
FC	1:14.41	96.75	8/15/84
FF	1:17.15	93.32	8/14/83
ASR	1:17.74	92.62	7/8/84
CSR	1:17.11	93.37	8/14/83
DSR	1:17.59	92.79	8/14/83
S2000	1:18.00	92.31	5/16/82
FV	1:28.22	81.61	6/10/84
F440	1:27.91	81.981	9/1/84
EP	1:24.78	84.92	8/5/84
FP	1:26.08	83.63	8/5/84
GP	1:28.23	81.60	8/14/83
HP	1:28.95	80.94	8/15/82
GT1	1:19.90	90.11	8/14/83
GT2	1:23.40	86.33	8/14/83
GT3	1:22.77	86.98	8/5/84
GT4	1:25.70	84.00	8/5/84
GT5	1:27.99	81.82	8/14/84
GTPinto	1:34.25	76.392	9/1/84
SSGT	1:33.55	76.964	9/3/84
SSA	1:35.86	75.10	8/14/83
SSB	1:37.75	73.66	6/10/84
SSC	1:40.97	71.30	8/5/84
SREN	1:33.20	77.253	9/3/84

tain. The worker has come to the race to wave a flag; guess what he or she will do with this flag?

Flag, green: See Starter.

Flag, red: No one remembers exactly what to do about this flag, but everyone is worried when they see it and will slow down or stop.

Flag, red and yellow: There might be something on the track, it might even be oil. The cars in front of you and behind you will generally not respond to this flag.

Flag, yellow: No passing, slow down. "No passing" is honored; "slow down" is generally ignored, especially by the guy you hope to catch. A stationary flag has no effect on car speeds. Waving yellow rarely affects car speeds. This may not be good, but it is reality. (When they begin jumping up and down while waving the flag, especially if other corner workers are waving their arms, they are *really serious* and you had better slow down.)

Formula car: Literally, a car built to a formula or a set of rules. In practice, a Formula car is a purpose-built race car with fully exposed wheels and tires. Examples include Indy-Cars and Formula One.

Gasoline, track: An overpriced fluid bought only by the foolish, the desperate, and the profligate. Buy in town, or (for higher octane) at the airport instead.

Grass, driving on: Larson's law: "You speed up when you hit the grass." When reentering the track at speed after an excursion into the grass, remember that the slip angle of your trackside front tire will abruptly diminish when it hits the asphalt. That's engineering talk for spinning across the track unless you ease on gradually.

Grid: (1) The place where cars are parked before being flagged off to start the pace lap ("The cars were called to the grid"). (2) The cars themselves ("The grid was in bad shape, but they got the green anyway").

Ground-pounder: Large, noisy car. Typically GT-1.

Homologation: Formal approval, by a sanctioning body, certifying that a car complies with the body's rules for a particular class.

Not only is racetrack gas quite expensive, the hours of availability may not match up well with your time of need. Better to buy ahead of time at the airport.

153

A MOROSO MOTORSPORT PARK HOT LAP

A driver who knows the way shows the way

by Lyn St. James (edited by Don Knowles)

Lyn St. James has been testing and racing at Moroso Motorsport Park for the past 10 years, and it shows. Lyn was regional champion in 1975 and 1976; was the top Woman Kelly American Series driver in 1979, 1981, 1982; has been a Ford motorsport supported driver since 1981; was a Trans-Am series regular in 1983; and is a Camel GT series regular in 1984 in an Argo Ford Cosworth. She manages her own race team; owns and is president of Autodyne, an auto parts company; advises Ford Motor Company on consumer affairs; and authored Lyn St. James' Car Owner's Manual for Women.

M oroso Motorsport Park (formerly Palm Beach International Raceway) is an absolutely flat 2.25-mile circuit located approximately 15 miles west of Palm Beach on the edge of the Florida Everglades. Most of the fill used to build

the track in the late '60s and early '70s was dredged from canals and lakes that surround much of the track itself. Most of the circuit is relatively narrow, about 24-feet in width, except for the back straight, which encompasses part of a very wide drag strip.

The circuit has no really blind corners (as long as the rapidly growing everglades grass is mowed!) and consists of a good mix of fast and slow turns. There are two long straights incorporating the drag strip and a return road, but the circuit has none of the artificial nature of most combination tracks. Learning how to carry as much speed as possible through the connecting turns without burning up your brakes, plus learning how to exit Turns 10 and 6, are the keys to winning races at Moroso.

Turn 1

Turn 1 is not much of a turn and in reality is no more than a flat-out, right-left kink in the front straight-away, even in the fastest of cars. Because Turn 1 is to the right and Turn 2 to the left, it is advisable to choose the outside pole position.

Turns 2A and 2B

Choosing the outside pole puts you on the inside for Turn 2, which is a medium speed, constant radius, 180-degree left-hander. Take this as a double-apex turn, and concentrate on maximizing exit speed from the second apex, which leads onto a 900-foot straight. Both apexes have enough camber to generate good adhesion.

Turns 3 and 4

Hold your car in the middle of the track approaching Turns 3 and 4. These are actually one sweeping, decreasing radius, right-hander with a double apex. Turn 3 can be entered faster than most drivers realize. As the car starts drifting to the left under acceleration you will find improved bite midway through the corner which will allow you to turn in for the second apex. There are "turtles" or bumpers located ¼- and ¾-distance through this sweeping right-hander which accurately locate the two apexes. Good exit speed here is important as it leads to the third longest straight portion of the circuit, so use all the track to the left.

Turns 5 and 6

Turn 5 is a right-hander followed immediately by a little left-hand jog that leads to the very important Turn 6. The section of track from the entrance to Turn 5 to the exit of Turn 6 is my favorite at Moroso. It's the real "rhythm" part of the course. If you do it right, you really know it. You move the car from a right-hand cornering attitude to a left-hand cornering attitude to a right-hand attitude, all the while under acceleration and trying to keep the transitions smooth and positive.

Entering Turn 5 from the extreme left side of the track, a stab of the brakes and a quick twist of the steering wheel gets the car drifting left under acceleration. If done properly, this is a much earlier apex than most drivers realize. A slight jog to the left and then you enter the very important Turn 6, leading onto the back straight. Turn 6 is a very fast right-hander, nicely banked, leading onto the very wide drag strip portion of the track. As the exit is so wide, a medium apex under full throttle is the way to go, using every inch of the track. As you accelerate down the back straight, aim for the timing tower to give you the proper set up to Turn 7.

Turns 7 and 8

Turn 7 is a flat-out left-hander. Clip the apex of Turn 7 and allow the car to drift to the right to set up for Turn 8. Turn 8 is really an "S" turn, a very fast left, then right. Both sides of Turn 8 have been widened by paving with concrete. Although this does not appear to be part of the track, it is quite smooth and should be fully utilized to maximize your speed through this section. Straighten out this section, carrying as much speed as possible to the left side of the track, which is where you want to be for the entry to Turn 9.

Turn 9

Almost immediately after exiting Turn 8 you will be under heavy braking for the entrance to Turn 9, an acute right-hander. Because Turn 9 and the entrance to Turn 10 are so wide most drivers brake too late at 9. The secret here is to get your braking done early and enter Turn 9 under *full* control and hard acceleration. Allow the car to drift out far to the left and set up for a late turn-in for Turn 10.

Turn 10

Turn 10 is a late apex right-hander and leads to the most important section of track, the front straight. Done properly, you should be under constant, hard acceleration in most cars from the entry of Turn 9 all the way through 10 onto the front straight. *Remember,* get the car under control entering Turn 9! You can pick up valuable time here! □

Horsepower: Tony Kester: "If you don't get pulled on the straight, you've got enough." Theoretically, engines can be differentiated by measuring their horsepower on a dyno. In practice, different dynos give different readings, and engine builders claims' may have nothing to do with what they are actually measuring. Charlie Williams will only answer "Adequate" when you ask about your engine's horsepower.

Ice: A good thing to put in your driver's suit before a session on a hot day, and in your drink at the end of the day. Also raced upon in the winter by a particularly demented tribe of northwoods drivers.

Impound: A physically segregated area where cars can be held by Tech pending resolution of rules problems. The top three or four finishers in each race are normally held in Impound until the thirty-minute protest period expires. In F1 racing, impound is referred to as "parc ferme."

IMSA: Acronym for International Motor Sports Association. IMSA sanctions the majority of professional road racing in the United States. There are those who would argue that IMSA "stole" pro racing from SCCA at a point in time when SCCA wasn't as aggressive as it now would like to be. SCCA's pro series are IMSA's primary competitors.

Jacking, weight: Asymmetrical (left-right) adjustment of the weight carried by individual tires of a car. Used principally in circle-track racing, as it makes the handling of the car asymmetric as well.

Kevlar: A strong synthetic fiber that is also fire resistant. Used in driver suits, tire construction, and bulletproof vests. Also used in place of glass fiber for lighter weight or higher strength in "fiberglass" race car body panel construction.

Leakdown: A method of testing piston-ring and valve sealing. The piston is placed at top dead center and the cylinder is pressurized through the spark plug hole via a compressed air line containing a flow restriction (usually a small hole drilled through a metal block-off). Airflow past the rings and valves causes a pressure drop across the restriction. Input pressure (ahead of the restriction) is normally set at 100psi, which creates an irresistible temptation to state the output pressure (past the restriction) as a "percentage leakdown." The flow restriction is not standardized from manufacturer to manufacturer, but it is normally chosen so that a good cylinder will read 90—95psi at the restrictor output. Readings from different leakdown testers cannot be usefully compared.

Lift: Euphemism for getting off the gas when you probably shouldn't be doing so. Also referred to as a "slight lift" or a "confidence lift." Your opponents will be grateful.

Light, idiot: Dashboard light that goes on when your engine oil pressure drops below 30psi. When you save an engine because the light comes on, you will conclude that those without such a light are the idiots.

Locker: A type of limited-slip differential.

Lockup, rear brakes: Frequent cause of spins. When in doubt, adjust your bias a bit heavy on the front. This will not get you into trouble.

Long (referring to gearing): A "longer" gear requires fewer engine revolutions for a given car speed. For example, if you are turning 8500rpm at the end of the straight, putting in a longer gear might reduce rpm to 8000. You might make such a choice to reduce the chance of overrevving the engine if you expect to get into drafting situations.

Loose (as applied to car's handling in a corner): Quick.

Magnaflux: A crack-detection technique used for ferrous parts. To ensure quality, your Magnaflux work should be done by an FAA-certified repair station.

Dave Weitzenhof's racing career is characterized not only by his outstanding a-chievements (four National Championships; six-time winner of the American Formula Ford Association Championship; member of the prestigious Road Racing Driver's Club; winner of both the RRDC Outstanding Performance Award and the SCCA's President's Cup Award), but also by his level of excellence and near dominance through the past dozen years. Others may have achieved similar results for a few years, but few remain as hungry for additional achievement as Dave.

Grattan Raceway is very much a "driver's track" where skill, experience, nerve, and good handling are the key to fast times. It is an outstandingly enjoyable track for drivers with small, agile cars but can be very demanding for those in the larger production classes. The track features many blind-apex and off-camber corners devoid of easily visible entrance markers. Some of Grattan's run-off areas are quite forgiving and some definitely are not. These factors reward driver precision and track knowledge.

Turn 1

This is a very fast 150-degree increasing radius, slightly uphill, right-hand corner which exits the main straight.

The track is fairly wide on the straight and through Turn 1, and quite bumpy on the left in the braking area. A fast lap depends on carrying a lot of speed through this turn, so braking and turn-in should be done smoothly to allow a fast entrance. The apex is early due to the increasing radius and slightly uphill exit which catches the car. Let the car run to the extreme left of the exit to be in position for Turn 2. Run-off in Turn 1 is nearly non-existent at the entrance (dirt bank), but wide and grassy at the exit.

Since this 70-100mph turn follows a 100-150mph straight, it is the best location on the course to attempt a pass, using either the draft or an out-braking maneuver. Markers which can be used for braking and turn-in are the access road and patches in the pavement.

The classic pass entering a corner from a long straight is to pass on the inside entering the corner. This is the typical maneuver attempted in Turn 1. However, because of the characteristics of this corner (bumpy braking area on left, wide track surface, fast and increasing radius) several other techniques may apply. When the usual inside pass is attempted, the car being passed may crowd the passing car to the inside, both to hinder the passer and to avoid the bumps. The passing driver must then beware of loose sand on the inside line which could cause brake locking and a head-on crash into the dirt bank. If this crowding occurs before the corner, the passing driver might then attempt an outside pass by braking later than usual (past the bumps) and trailing the brakes deep into the corner, passing the other car before it can move away from the apex. This can be successful only if the passing car is very stable when cornering under braking or trailing throttle.

Turn 2

This is a medium-speed, slightly downhill 100-degree right-hander. The turn is initial-ly off-camber. This, in combination with the wide, downhill entrance and lack of brake markers makes it somewhat difficult to apex properly. The exit is wide with plenty of run-off. After the exit, position the car to the right to enter Turn 3.

If a car you are attempting to pass tries to block into Turn 2, take a wide entrance and maximize exit speed to enable a pass entering Turn 3.

Turn 3

Immediately after the braking area the track drops abruptly and then turns sharp left, leaving you sliding down the side of a hill. About halfway around, the track goes to positive camber and slightly uphill, which helps catch the car. The entire corner is hidden by the drop-off, so braking and turn-in must be completed before you can see the corner. Passing can be accomplished here by out-braking a competitor on his left, if Turn 2 was done well. Move to the extreme left after the exit to be ready for Turn 4.

Turn 4

This 90-degree right-hander is difficult because it is a blind-apex, very fast (almost flat-out) corner which is over a rise, and reference points are lacking at trackside. Entry from the extreme left and an accurate apex are the keys to this turn.

Turn 5

The braking area for this 80-degree right-hander is very interesting since the faster cars can become airborne just as you would like to start braking. Braking must begin either just before the crest or as the car begins to settle after it. However, there is very little room to get it all together before the turn, so a good technique is to trail the brakes all the way through the turn to get the car slowed down for Turn 6.

Luckily, this is one of the safest areas on the track to go off course. A side benefit to the above technique is that it may enable you to pass entering Turn 6 due to the speed you have carried through Turn 5. Take a very late apex and exit tight to the right (unless you are passing) to set up for Turn 6.

Track diagram labels: 1, 2, 3, 4, 5, 6, 7, 8, 9, 10, 11, 12, "THE BOWL", "THE TOILET BOWL", START-FINISH, PITS

Turn 6

A flat 90-degree left, this slow turn is sacrificed and taken with a very late apex to set up Turn 7.

Turn 7

This is a turn where a lot of time can be lost if you are sloppy. This 90-degree right-hander is off-camber on the outside and apexes on the crest of a hill. Entry to the corner requires the driver to "flick" the car from a left-hand to a right-hand drift with little, if any, braking. If you maintain a tight line with a late apex, the corner is fairly fast. If you enter too fast (or off line) and the car runs wide, adhesion is lost and a lot of time is wasted, not to mention ruining the entrance to Turn 8.

Turn 8 ("The Bowl")

This 100-degree left is very fast despite its tightness because it is well banked. "Tossing" the car sideways into this corner with very little braking works well since the banking will catch the car and help you complete the turn.

Turn 9

A very fast 100-degree right, this turn is taken flat-out in most cars. Placement on the entrance is critical, since the apex and most of the turn are hidden by a long, gentle crest and course markers are hard to find.

Turn 10 ("The Toilet Bowl")

This tight 150-degree right-hander is one of the most difficult to execute. It is slow, off-camber, downhill, decreasing radius, and has a blind apex just over a hump. You are slowing to about 40mph from a top speed of about 100. Even worse, the track goes steeply uphill after the exit, making it very difficult to regain speed lost in the corner. The most effective technique is to brake the car sideways into the turn and then catch it with the throttle at the apex. This is not a good place to pass, since it is too close to Turn 9, and a swamp awaits the errant late-braker.

Turns 11 and 12

The track crests and then immediately turns 45 degrees right. Positioning and timing of the entrance to this corner are extremely critical, since you cannot see Turn 11 or any distinguishing markers until it is too late to react. The exit to this very fast turn is also the entrance to Turn 12, which leads onto the main straight between two earth banks. A "screw-up" in Turn 11 will often result in a crash after the exit of Turn 12, or at the very least, a slow entrance onto the main straight. For safety and to set up the entrance to the off-camber Turn 12, Turn 11 should be taken with just enough braking to permit a very late apex, hugging the right side of the road. Turn 12 should be nearly flat-out if Turn 11 has been executed properly.

That's it, Grattan Raceway: blind apexes, up and down, off-camber, and more. It takes a lot of skill and effort to conquer this track, but like any goal, the harder to achieve, the more satisfying the achievement. □

Marbles, aka rocks, aka gravel: Track lubricant, usually placed off the racing line by Mother Nature. Frequently placed on the racing line by a spinning car. See also Sand, and Flag, red and yellow.

Meatball: Black flag with round, orange center. *This one* you pay attention to.

Meeting, mandatory driver: Usually held at start-finish; they never take attendance and rarely tell you anything useful. "Welcome to our race..." and so on. Introductions of officials you do not care about, and stern admonitions about how to safely enter the racetrack from the pits. Go anyway.

Mirrors: Devices that minimize crashes if used properly. Critical to the well-being of the slower driver.

Money, value of: A noun phrase whose meaning depends on its context. The value of money is measured in quanta; a few quanta are no big deal. In racing, the quantum is $100. In the real world, $10 is a more useful quantum.

Monocoque: Literally, a structure that is both the body of a car and its chassis. True monocoque structures are rarely seen. Modern Formula cars are usually examples of "semi-monocoque" design, wherein the forward half of the car (the "tub") is of monocoque construction, but the engine and transmission comprise the main chassis structure for the back half of the car. Sports racers stretch the definition of monocoque still further, as their tubs are usually covered with separate, nonstructural bodywork sections.

NACA duct: A low-drag air duct, shaped roughly like half of an hourglass, designed in the 1950s under the auspices of the National Advisory Committee on Aeronautics, a bureaucratic ancestor of NASA. NACA ducts are often used to bring cooling air to brakes, rear-mounted oil coolers, and water radiators.

Nuts, lug: Devices that, if not religiously torqued, will cause the wheel to separate from the car on the racetrack. There is at least one wheel in the Elkhart woods that has never been found.

Oil: Normally placed inside your engine by you, and on the outside of your car and on your tearoffs by the guy in front of you. If you have not been smart enough to use tearoffs, it goes on your visor for the duration of the session. Wiping your oily visor with the back of your glove will cause the oil to multiply like wire hangers in a dark closet; the result is an oily glove *and* an oily visor.

Overrev: To run an engine beyond its rpm limit. Over-revving will often result in piston-to-valve contact, which has never been considered to be a good idea.

Paddock: The area of the racetrack grounds where competitors' cars, tow rigs, and (frequently) camping equipment are parked for the weekend. At a spectator race, paddock access is usually restricted to those who have bought special tickets.

Points, finishing: Points counting toward series or geographic championship standings are usually awarded as follows: First Place, 12; Second Place, 9; Third Place, 7; Fourth Place, 6; Fifth Place, 5; Sixth Place, 4; Seventh Place, 3; Eighth Place, 2; and Ninth Place, 1.

Pro event: In club racing parlance, "pro" refers to any event with prize money, no matter how little. Read the fine print.

Protest: Source of entertainment to all but the participants. Procedures are in the *GCR*, which is the reason you carry it in your toolbox.

Push (as applied to car's handling in a corner): (1) Synonym for "understeer." (2) The effect of a poor setup on race car. (3) A normal condition for a Spec Racer.

A LAGUNA SECA
HOT LAP
A driver who knows the way shows the way
by Elliott Forbes-Robinson (edited by Don Knowles)

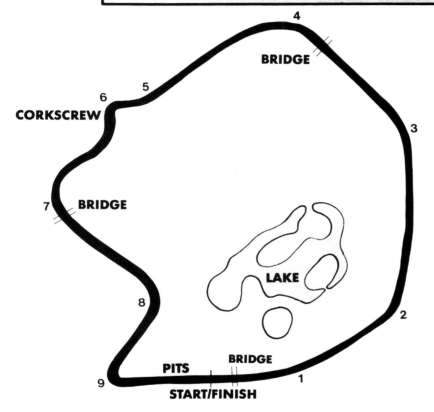

4

BRIDGE

5

6

CORKSCREW

3

7 BRIDGE

LAKE

8

2

BRIDGE

PITS

1

9

START/FINISH

Elliott Forbes-Robinson is a current Trans-Am driver (Somerset Buick Regal) and former T-A series champion (1982) who started his racing career as part of a three-man autocross team in the early '60s, partnered by Don Devendorf and Jerry Barker. It was quite a team, with Devendorf and Barker eventually becoming SCCA National Champions and Forbes-Robinson conquering both the amateur and pro ranks. He has had racing success over a wide range, from SCCA production (National champion in three classes), Super Vee (series champ in 1974), Formula Atlantic, Formula 5000, Can-Am and Trans-Am since 1982.

Turn One

Heading up the gentle hill in front of the pits you pass by the start/finish tower and enter Turn One. This is not much of a turn at all, just a slight bend in the road at the crest of the hill. As you cross the start/finish line, begin to move across to the left side of the track. Stay on the left until after the apex at the top of the hill, then you can let the car move to the right. The track continues turning after the crest and should put you in the braking area for Turn Two. Turn One is taken flat out and is blind, so it is important to watch the flag team for any sign of trouble ahead.

Turns Two and Three

After you crest the hill you enter my favorite part of the course. These are high-speed corners, with Turns Two and Three taken flat-out in top gear for many cars. This section from Turn One to Turn Four can almost be thought of as an effective continuation of the pit straight. If your car must be slowed down for these turns you should brake early and get back on the throttle before turning in. You will want to carry as much speed as possible off these corners. However, in these turns you don't want to have to lift on the exit because your entry speed was *too* high. Lifting at the exit can take off more speed than entering slower. Turn Three is similar to Turn Two, so brake early if necessary and turn in early. Again, it is important to be on the throttle before turning in. Turning in early doesn't send the car off the outside of the track because the turns are banked.

Turn Four

As you approach Turn Four there is a bridge across the track. I use this as a braking marker. In my opinion, if you try to brake late and hard here it will upset the car, so I recommend braking earlier and easier. I find that if full throttle can be attained before the apex, the car pulls more rpm up the hill which follows Turn Four. This is a steep hill, and it is very important to keep the revs and speed up as you exit Turn Four. Keep a close eye on the tach and try to get it as high as possible at the exit.

Turn Five

After coming out of Turn Four on the right side of the road, you will want to slowly move to the left to line up with the braking area as you now approach Laguna Seca's famous Corkscrew. You should have moved over to the middle of the road by the time you're about to crest the hill. Start turning in and braking just before the top. Get the car as straight as you can for braking. When you crest the hill, the car will get light and braking will be less effective, so you will want to lessen pedal pressure in this area.

Turns Six and 6-A (The Corkscrew)

Entering the Turn Six left-hander at the beginning of the Corkscrew, I use a late apex so I will be able to line up for the steep Turn 6-A right-hander at the bottom of the hill. The track is downhill at the exit of 6-A, so the car doesn't stick well, something you should keep in mind as you apply throttle. You will probably have to short shift in the brief distance between the Corkscrew and Turn Seven in order to be in the proper gear.

Turn Seven

This looks like a normal left-hand

sweeper, but it sure doesn't drive like it. Your car will probably turn in fine, understeer in the middle and oversteer at the exit. You will want to enter this corner a little late and hold the car tight to the edge of the track. If you do get understeer at the apex, try entering slower and keeping more throttle on. Enter in a higher gear than would seem correct so you don't have to shift in the corner. Also, since the exit of the turn is downhill, you will gain speed in the turn and the higher gear will be the right choice at the exit. The longest true straight on the circuit follows the exit from Turn Seven.

Turn Eight

Turn Eight is a downhill, banked, right-hander. You should use a late apex here, and be conscious of the fact the exit is not banked like the entry. Thus, the initial part of the turn can be taken faster than the exit. At the exit the outside pavement falls away, so if you use the whole road be ready for this.

Turn Nine

Turn Nine comes up fast if you take Turn Eight well. This is one of the slowest turns on any circuit in the United States. You want to take a late apex and squeeze the throttle carefully, so you don't lose too much time with wheel spin as you exit. It is important to get off this corner with as much speed as possible because of the long straight which follows. If this corner is entered too fast, it will hurt speed on the straight, and remember for many this is all the way to Turn Four. □

─────── **Track Records** ───────

The following information was compiled by Doug Thom, former chief of timing in the SF Region, and Don Wixcell, present SF Region business manager.

CLASS	TIME	DRIVER	DATE
SP	1:10.670	David France	10-28-84
CP	1:11.990	Frank Leary	6-24-79
DP	1:15.380	Greg La Cava	6-24-79
EP	1:16.890	Mac McGarry	10-21-78
FP	1:17.050	Tom McCarthy	6-22-80
GP	1:19.810	Geoff Provo	10-13-79
HP	1:22.100	John Faull	10-10-81
GT1	1:10.550	Frank Emmett	8-12-84
GT2	1:15.170	Roger Edsinger	8-12-84
GT3	1:16.030	Norm DeWitt	6-24-84
GT4	1:17.650	Doug Peterson	6-27-82
GT5	1:18.720	Doug Peterson	8-12-84
SSGT	1:21.850	Luis Sanchez	8-12-84
SSA	1:25.720	Dave Vanek	6-28-81
SSB	1:28.350	Bob Heimann	7-13-80
SSC	1:29.640	Richard Hille	8-12-84
ITA	1:22.000	Sam Stowell	8-12-84
ITB	1:24.550	Lyle Moore	10-28-84
ITC	1:27.590	Ken Murillo	9-3-84
CSR	1:05.180	Tom Foster	9-3-84
DSR	1:06.780	Paul Decker	9-2-84
SP2000	1:08.430	Bob Lobenberg	6-27-82
SR	1:23.510	Jim Black	10-28-84
FA	1:02.380	Steve (Gas) Saleen	6-24-79
FC	1:07.880	Werner Erhard	6-24-79
FF	1:08.180	Steve Bren	6-24-84
CF	1:13.020	Steve Hartgraves	10-28-84
FV	1:18.000	Al Gegaregian	9-2-84
F440	1:17.810	Glen Wild	9-2-84
Rabbit	1:25.800	Karl Hacker	10-21-84
Super V	1:01.120	L. Heimrath Jr.	10-21-84
F5000	58.230	Mario Andretti	10-12-75
Trans-Am	1:08.830	Greg Pickett	10-19-80
CA O2 ltr.	57.470	Danny Sullivan	10-11-81
CA U2 ltr.	1:02.450	Jim Trueman	10-11-81
WCAR FA	1:01.520	Dan Marvin	6-24-84

Race tape: Duct tape, when used by a racer or near a race car. Colored duct tape, when priced high enough, becomes honorary race tape before it is even sold at retail. Race tape is panacea for broken fiberglass. It is also used by the lunatic fringe to cover bodywork cracks and gaps for final aerodynamic streamlining.

RE: Regional Executive, the highest elected official of an SCCA region. Effectively, the RE is the local club president.

Rebound: Refers to extension of the car's suspension relative to its normal position. For some reason, we talk about bump and droop when talking about suspensions. When talking about shock absorbers, it's bump and rebound. Same thing.

Registration: An ordeal, presided over by a mixture of saints (95%) and power-trippers (5%). Fill in all the blanks, be polite. Where "no alcoholic beverages at Registration" applies and you have just completed a long tow, the beer will fit nicely in a pop can.

Rest pedal: See Dead pedal.

Restraints, arm: You could formerly identify open-car drivers who do not mind having their arms broken by the fact that they did not wear arm restraints. They are now mandatory in open cars, still only a good idea in closed cars.

Roll steer: The net steering effect from weight transfer causing the outside suspension to go into bump while the inside suspension moves into droop. See also Bump steer.

Roller: A car (normally for sale) with no engine installed. Depending on the car, this description may not be literal. In many Formula cars and Sports Racers, the engine block is a stressed member. Without it, the front of the car is a physically separate unit, unconnected to the gearbox and rear suspension.

Runoffs: SCCA's national championship event, historically held in October at Road Atlanta. Beginning in 1994, the Runoffs venue has been changed to Mid-Ohio.

Sand: Substance that, when you dip your hot racing tire in it, will exhibit remarkable lubricating powers in the *next corner.*

Scales, official: To be avoided after qualifying, unless they make you go there. Weigh in some other time.

Scrub, tire: Usually used to refer to a tire's running at high slip angles and absorbing (wasting) noticeable amounts of the car's forward momentum. The idea is inexact, however, because a tire is absorbing energy at any slip angle.

Shock absorber: Damping device that keeps the car from oscillating on its springs. Has nothing to do with absorbing shocks. Shock absorbers have two damping characteristics, one for bump (compression) and one for rebound (extension). Adjustments to these settings are sometimes possible, depending on the unit. Consult Carroll Smith or Paul Van Valkenburgh's books for advice.

Short (referring to gearing): A "shorter" gear requires more engine revolutions for a given car speed. For example, if you are turning 5000rpm in a slow corner, putting in a shorter gear might increase rpm to 6000 and put you in a better part of the engine's torque curve.

Signal, passing: Point to where you want the overtaking car to go, not where you plan to go. If the overtaking driver does not approve of your passing etiquette or your use of your mirrors, he will give you another type of distinctive passing signal as he pushes by.

Slip angle: The angle between the direction that the tire is physically pointing and the line it is actually following. This apparent slip is caused by the stretching of the rubber at the contact patch.

A WILLOW SPRINGS HOT LAP

A driver who knows the way shows the way

by John Morton (edited by Don Knowles)

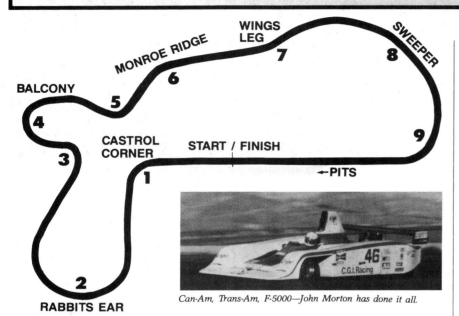

BALCONY · MONROE RIDGE · WINGS LEG · SWEEPER · CASTROL CORNER · START / FINISH · PITS · RABBITS EAR

Can-Am, Trans-Am, F-5000—John Morton has done it all.

In 23 years of racing, John Morton has driven virtually every type of road-racing machine, from tiny production sports cars to prototypes to Indy Cars; and he has accumulated two SCCA National Championships, two Trans-Am 2.5-Liter Championships, and several SCCA Divisional titles.

After attending the Carroll Shelby Driving School in 1962, he began competing in SCCA Nationals in a Lotus Super 7 in 1963. The following year, he co-drove a Cobra prototype with the late Ken Miles at Sebring. Then, in 1968, he won his first SCCA Divisional Championship. He won his second two years later, along with his first National Championship, driving a factory Datsun 240Z.

In 1971, he repeated as National Champion and took his first Trans-Am 2.5-Liter title, qualifying on the pole in every SCCA race. The Trans-Am 2.5-Liter Championship was his again the next year, and he competed in Formula 5000 as well. He continued driving the F5000 series for the next three years—and also kept busy by winning in IMSA's RS and GTU series, moving up to the GT classes in 1977 and winning the GT class in the 24 Hours of Daytona in 1979.

Morton has been a frequent Can-Am competitor since 1977 and has done a great deal of endurance racing in recent years, both in

Europe and America. Last year, he also drove an Indy Car to a ninth-place finish at Long Beach, and was a regular in IMSA's Camel GT Series, competing in the top-level GTP class. He teamed with Yoshimi Katayama and John O'Steen to win Group C2 at Le Mans in one of the BFGoodrich-Mazda Lola T-616s.

W illow Springs has been languishing in the Southern California desert since 1953, which makes it one of the longest surviving road-racing courses in America. The track's layout, which starts on the desert floor and roams into the adjacent foothills, makes it not only challenging to drive, but provides nearly a 100 percent view of the track from any vantage point. Even the sound of a race car in a test session is unobstructed, making it possible for an astute crew chief to evaluate his car and driver's performance with his eyes closed.

Turn 1

Turn One is a rather steeply banked 90-degree left which ends the longest straight. It is a deceivingly fast turn taken in one gear below top in most cars. Late apex and get back on the gas very early (remember it is banked). The right edge of the road is not visible until you pop out of the banking at the exit, making it tricky to use all of the road. This is a very important corner and an excellent place to pass on a late brake.

Turn 2

A short straight precedes Turn Two: a fast 450 foot radius 200-degree right. Some banking and a slight uphill rise aid adhesion until the exit where the banking ends and the road levels out. Most cars like to run slightly inside of the middle of the road, apexing gently about three-quarters of the way into the corner. Spend some time balancing the car for this turn because a large percentage of your time is spent here. Too much understeer and you'll scrub speed and have to lift to apex; too much oversteer and you'll have to ease off the power.

Turn 3

In most cases the same gear is used from Turn One until downshifting for Turn Three—the slowest turn on the track. Braking deep into Three is doubly important; not only can you overtake here, but late braking avoids some bumps early in the braking zone. An uphill well-banked 100-degree corner, Turn Three is again faster than it looks. A late apex and early throttle squirts you up the hill and into the difficult right-hand double apex Turn Four.

Turn 4

Climb the hill and hug the right until the road starts to level. Now allow the car to move to the left side in preparation for a late apex because the turn tightens and heads steeply downhill.

Turn 5

The right-hand jog preceding the left-hand Turn Five complicates the braking zone of Five. No matter how deep you go into Five, the car is still loaded from the jog and traveling steeply downhill. Be willing to forego the perfect line into Five; you can't get to the extreme right if you've gone in really deep. You can make up some of this lost ground by hanging a left front wheel in the dirt at the apex. At the exit the road starts uphill; you'll get some stick here so get on the throttle early.

Turn 6

On the short uphill run to the right-hand Turn Six, don't bother getting to the extreme left before the entry. In a fast car, it is difficult and in a slower car completely unnecessary. In the middle of this fast turn, the road goes from uphill to downhill so you have to deal with an almost complete loss of stick for an instant. Short shift up and apex early to get most of the work done before the car goes light. In a faster car, it may take some time to gain confidence, but lose time here and you'll suffer all the way into Turn Nine.

Turn 7

Seven is no more than a gentle bend in the straight. Stay left for the entry to Eight unless you are trying to block someone's inside line into Eight.

Turn 8

In a fast car right-hand Turn Eight is one of those places where your right foot seems to have better sense than your brain. In most cars it is a no lift corner, but it's kind of scary at first. Enter Eight early and drive around the inside with no pronounced apex. Before the road straightens, let the car drift to the outside of the road. Watch out for the bump, identifiable by a large patch that takes up the inside half of the road. The bump seems to change every year; this year it's not so bad, but when it is an early exit avoid it.

Turn 9

Leaving Eight you just have time to glance at the tach to check your top speed before entering one of the world's worst—Turn Nine. This turn is very hard to get right, but essential for good lap times. It is a top gear turn in most cars, a 90-degree decreasing radius right turn with an exit you can't see until you get there. Enter from the left, but move right slightly in the early part to give yourself some room for error. There is a strong tendency to apex too early because it feels safer. Try to avoid this because you'll have to lift at the exit. Pick a reference that identifies the apex for you. You should be approaching full throttle before the apex in even the fastest car. The exit brings you to the outside of the pit straight and the end of your lap.

Like any difficult track, Willow Springs requires lots of practice. But remember, your crew can see and hear every mistake. □

Willow Springs Lap Records

CLASS	TIME	DRIVER	DATE
ASR	1:18.35	Mike Allen	12/5/76
CSR	1:22.17	Lou Sell	4/8/84
DSR	1:28.32	Jerry Smith	5/4/80
S2000	1:26.34	Rex Ramsey	5/2/82
FA	1:16.39	John Millense	5/2/82
FV	1:38.76	Ray Stephens	5/2/82
FF	1:25.44	Cary Bren	12/4/83
EP	1:36.42	Hardy Prentice	4/8/84
FP	1:37.08	Larry Moulton	5/2/82
GP	1:39.34	Bob Snow	5/4/80
HP	1:42.72	David Bales	10/5/75
GT1	1:28.18	Fred Whitehead	4/8/84
GT2	1:30.84	Robert Reed	4/17/83
GT3	1:34.20	Bruce Short	4/8/84
GT4	1:36.88	Derek McKesson	4/8/84
GT5	1:40.54	Tom Yoshida	12/4/83
SSGT	1:48.58	Bob Brewer	4/17/83
SSA	1:47.00	Lance Stewart	12/4/83)
SSB	1:49.14	Ron McBain	12/4/83
SSC	1:53.09	Max Jones	4/17/83
ITA	1:47.35	Richard Crites	12/4/83
ITB	1:46.99	William Holmes	12/4/83
ITC	1:52.70	Ron Johnson	12/4/83
SP	1:27.91	Richard Wall	12/4/83

Smoke: See Dust.

Solid (as applied to car's handling in a corner): Slow.

SOMs: Acronym for Stewards of the Meeting. The officials charged with adjudicating rules enforcement issues.

Spectators, race: Ego-boosters, sources of annoying questions, and occasional tool thieves. Do not leave your belongings unguarded at a spectator race.

Spin (as participant): If you do not spin occasionally, you are not going fast enough. If you spin off the track and are stopped, your car belongs to the corner workers. Obey their instructions.

Spin (as spectator): If a car spins in front of you and you can't tell where it is going, head directly for it. It will usually be gone when you get there.

Spin out: Spin, as referred to by non-racer.

Sports Racer: Originally Sports Racing cars were limited-production cars nominally intended as prototypes for Production street cars. They were required to have seating for two and to have operating doors. In most examples, the doors and passenger seats quickly became vestigial and finally disappeared. Currently, Sports Racer refers to any purpose-built race car with covered wheels and tires. Examples range from the cars that run at Le Mans to SCCA Spec Racers.

Sprint race: A short race; used in contrast to an endurance race which may run for twenty-four hours. Virtually all club races are sprint races. One major reason is to eliminate the need for dangerous refueling in the pits. Another is the fact that it's hard to get all the classes onto the track in one day, anyway.

Stable (as applied to car's handling in a corner): Slow.

Stagger: Difference in the diameters of a left-right pair of tires. We are talking here about small differences, due to manufacturing tolerances, between tires that are nominally the same size. Stagger is an important aspect of tuning for oval-track cars, especially with limited-slip differentials. On road courses, cars are normally set up with same-size tires, therefore no stagger.

Start, split: In a mixed-class race where there are wide speed disparities, like GT-1—GT5, the grid is sometimes split into two groups, separated by about half the track length, and separately paced. The idea is to let the cars get spread apart a bit before the passing begins. If the first group gets a green flag, guess which color flag the second group will get? Here, an in-car radio would be a real asset.

Starter, bad: Official who throws the green without having noticed that everybody but you is on the gas.

Starter, good: Official who throws the green approximately two seconds after you have nailed the gas. An exceptional starter notices when you have gridded in the back and will throw the flag approximately five seconds after you have nailed the gas.

Stewards: Officials whose jobs no driver bothers to completely understand except (1) when taking driver school written tests, and (2) when involved in a protest. Which is another reason you carry a *GCR* in your toolbox.

Supps: Short for Supplemental Regulations, found in the entry form.

Sway bar: Sway bars have nothing to do with sway. This American misnomer probably originated with the same genius who named the shock absorber. See Antiroll bar.

Tearoffs: Thin plastic overlays for your helmet visor. See also Oil.

Tell-tale: A second tachometer needle that mechanically "remembers" the highest rpm reached by the main needle.

A MID-OHIO HOT LAP

A driver who knows the way shows the way

by Bobby Rahal (edited by Don Knowles)

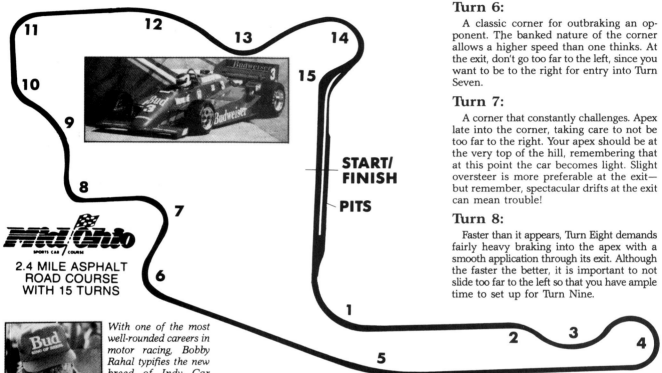

Mid Ohio
SPORTS CAR COURSE

2.4 MILE ASPHALT ROAD COURSE WITH 15 TURNS

START/FINISH

PITS

With one of the most well-rounded careers in motor racing, Bobby Rahal typifies the new breed of Indy Car driver, who climbs to the top by starting on the SCCA's road-racing ladder. The 32-year-old Dublin, Ohio, native was CART's Rookie of the Year in 1982 and last year vaulted into the millionaire's club in career earnings after only 39 Indy Car starts. Rahal began in SCCA Formula Ford competition, winning a Regional Championship in '73. He was awarded the President's Cup in '75, and competed against the likes of Keke Rosberg and Gilles Villeneuve in Formula Atlantic from 1976 to 1978. His performance earned him two F1 rides in '78 on the Walter Wolf team. In 1979 there was a full season of European F2, then SCCA Can-Am in 1980, World Cup Endurance racing in 1981 and finally into Indy Cars in '82, where as a rookie sensation he finished a remarkable second in the PPG Cup Championship. Mid-Ohio is Rahal's "home" track, owned by sponsor Jim Trueman.

Turn 1:

One of the few corners where passing can be done under braking, it is a tricky medium-speed left with adverse camber at the exit. A difficult corner where understeer seems to be the rule, carrying your speed through here is fundamental to a good lap time.

Turns 2 and 3:

A complex of right-left-left corners, it is critical to carry as much speed as possible through the right-hander without missing the apexes of the following lefts. A tight line through the lefts seems to work best so that you're well under control for the entry to the keyhole.

Turn 4:

One of the slowest, yet most important corners at Mid-Ohio. The old adage applies here where the "hurrier you go, the behinder you get." I keep a tight line through the corner and concentrate on the exit as this leads onto the only straightaway of any real consequence.

Turn 5:

Nothing more than a kink in the back straight, it provides no real challenge. Be careful here in passing lapped traffic!

Turn 6:

A classic corner for outbraking an opponent. The banked nature of the corner allows a higher speed than one thinks. At the exit, don't go too far to the left, since you want to be to the right for entry into Turn Seven.

Turn 7:

A corner that constantly challenges. Apex late into the corner, taking care to not be too far to the right. Your apex should be at the very top of the hill, remembering that at this point the car becomes light. Slight oversteer is more preferable at the exit— but remember, spectacular drifts at the exit can mean trouble!

Turn 8:

Faster than it appears, Turn Eight demands fairly heavy braking into the apex with a smooth application through its exit. Although the faster the better, it is important to not slide too far to the left so that you have ample time to set up for Turn Nine.

Turns 9 and 10:

An uphill with a sharply descending right, Turn Nine is one corner where a lot of time can be saved—providing the car follows instructions! Stay to the left up to the crest of the hill and try to straighten out the right-hander as you descend. If you're on the right side going up the hill, the next thing you'll be testing is Mid-Ohio's sand bank!

Turn 11:

Turn 11 is a critical corner as it leads onto Mid-Ohio's second longest straight. Brake hard into the entry, but try to carry your speed with early acceleration up, to, and over the jump. Have the car in a neutral or slight oversteer condition prior to the jump or else!

Turn 12:

Nothing more than a banked bend, but unless the guy you're passing is courteous, it can be difficult to pass. Fast, this bend demands that you stay on the right in order to be in the proper lane for entry into Turn 13.

Turn 13:

Brake late here, but not so late that you overshoot the apex. With adverse camber at the exit, this corner calls for an early apex with smooth constant application of power. Exit well here and you might have a shot at someone on the entry to the Carousel.

Turns 14 and 15:

The Carousel turn or Turn 14, like so many Mid-Ohio turns, emphasizes smoothness—getting power on early and not getting too wide at the exit because you'll want to be set up correctly for the small dip at the exit leading onto the start/finish straight. Once again, the harder you work here, the slower you go.

It sounds like I've turned Mid-Ohio into a series of 15 "critical" turns and I keep repeating about how you go slower when you work harder. It is that way. There aren't really turns that you can afford to slough off and still do a great lap. All racing is a test of smoothness, fluidity of your motions, and a test of your ability to make 100 critical judgment calls per lap.

Most of these judgments are automatic ones, like shifting, braking, a little seesaw on the steering wheel here and there. Some, like passing another car, require extra concentration, as if your powers of concentration haven't been already stretched to their limits.

Mid-Ohio is a classic drivers' circuit. A good driver in a mediocre car can still make a difference. One of the most satisfying circuits, it is probably the most demanding, mentally and physically, of any circuit I have driven. □

——— Mid-Ohio Class Records ———

CLASS	TIME	DRIVER	DATE
EP	1:43.07	David Finch	9/18/83
FP	1:44.88	Bob Griffith	8/2/81
GP	1:47.11	Rick Haynes	7/17/83
HP	1:49.19	Ray Stone	7/15/84
Trans-Am (Pro)	1:35.11	Willy T. Ribbs	7/17/83
GT1	1:38.76	Dennis Cuppy	7/15/84
GT2	1:39.14	Fred Baker	6/29/80
GT3	1:41.02	David Finch	8/2/81
GT4	1:46.61	Russ Theus	8/2/81
GT5	1:47.47	Jack Baumgardner	7/15/84
SSGT	1:55.74	Bob McConnell	9/9/84
SSA	1:59:18	Ron Smaldone	5/9/82
SSB	2:00.00	Bob Sweet	9/9/84
SSC	2:04.08	John Pfetzing	9/9/84
SSC	2:04.08	Harry Gentry	9/9/84
Rabbit (Pro)	1:59.116	Bill Deters	6/28/81
F/Atlantic (Pro)	1:25.92	Whitney Ganz	6/27/82
F/Atlantic	1:28.20	Dan Carmichael	7/18/82
SuperVee (Pro)	1:28.06	Mike Rosen	9/11/83
F/Continental	1:30.02	Jerry Petersen	9/9/84
F/Ford	1:34.75	Howard Katz	7/15/84
F/Vee	1:45.66	Chris Shultz	5/9/82
F/440	1:45.59	Mike Leathers	9/18/83
*Can-Am 5-L	1:22.22	Al Holbert	6/27/82
Can-Am 2-L.	1:25.43	Bertil Roos	6/27/82
ASR	1:30.38	Dale Wise	9/18/83
CSR	1:35.84	Al Zeller	7/15/84
DSR	1:36.32	Jeff Miller	7/15/84
S/2000 (Pro)	1:34.19	Bill O'Connor	7/15/84
S/2000	1:34.20	Larry Campbell	5/9/82
SR	1:51.33	David Finch	9/9/84

*Official Track Record

When you signal for a flat tow, you will not normally get service that is quite this classy. The course marshals will always get you home, though.

Usually reset between sessions. The tell-tale reset button is normally located (by the crew chief or the car's lessor) so that it cannot be reached by the driver.

Temperature, tire: If your tire temperatures are not as high as your opponents are running, you are not driving the car hard enough. There is no other reason.

Time: A noun whose meaning depends on its context. Time is measured in quanta; a few quanta are no big deal. In race car preparation, the quantum is ten hours. In lap times, the quantum is 0.05 second.

Toe: When the steering wheel is centered, the car's front tires are normally set to point slightly inward (toe-in) or outward (toe-out). With independent rear suspension, the rear tires are often given some toe as well.

Tow, flat: A rolling tow behind a car or truck. Also known as "coming in on the rope." If you are in the weeds, you can signal the corner station for a flat tow by holding your arms straight out sideways from your shoulders, making yourself look like a T.

Tow money: Money paid by the organizers of an event to attract entrants who have to tow from some distance. Tow money is available to Runoffs entrants and is occasionally also paid at pro events.

Trailing-throttle oversteer: When you lift, the tail comes out—unless you're driving a terribly understeering car. This characteristic of a well-setup vehicle is often referred to by automotive writers as "dreaded" trailing-throttle oversteer. This superstition is probably rooted in the days of swing-axle rear suspensions, which do have some dreaded characteristics.

Tub: The stiffest and most weight-efficient form of race car chassis is constructed from sheet box sections, bonded together and comprising the cockpit section of the car. This chassis section usually extends from the firewall behind the driver to the front of the footwell and is referred to as the "tub." In SCCA racing, the sheet is normally aluminum and the bonding is by rivets. In the higher echelons of racing, the tub is normally constructed from exotic material such as carbon fiber or Kevlar, and the bonding is by epoxy or other plastic resin. A race car tub might weigh only 80—100 pounds. See also Monocoque.

USAC: Acronym for United States Automobile Club. USAC is the primary sanctioning body for oval-track racing in the United States. If you like to turn left, this is the club for you!

Steve Anderson first raced at Las Vegas International Speedway in 1979, driving an ADF Formula Ford. The North Las Vegas resident currently holds the all-time track record (52.0sec), which he set in 1991 with his Super Production Pontiac Trans Am. A member of both Cal Club and Las Vegas Regions, Anderson holds several regional titles and is the 1977 SCCA AP national champion. The two-time Toyota Super Production champion (1990 and 1991) is leading that series' 1992 points race, competing in selected Tide Trans-Am Tour races, and serving as Las Vegas Region's chief driving instructor for the region's Sept. 19-20 Driving School/Regional at the Las Vegas International Speedway.

Las Vegas International Speedway is a multi-use racing facility located in Las Vegas on Las Vegas Boulevard North, near Nellis Air Force Base, home of the U.S.A.F. Thunderbirds. In fact, it's always a treat to be at the race track when the F-16s are practicing maneuvers overhead.

The desert track opened in 1972, just one year after Stardust Raceway closed, with a round of the NHRA championship. Today, the facility includes a 1.7-mile, eight-turn road course; 3/8-mile, semi-banked asphalt oval; 1/4-mile drag strip; concrete go-kart circuit and a motocross area. The road course recently underwent

HOT LAP

LAS VEGAS
A DRIVER WHO KNOWS THE WAY, SHOWS THE WAY

BY STEVE ANDERSON

improvements, including new pavement, lengthening the course by two-tenths and adding corner curbing.

Thanks to the flat, desert terrain, there is much run-off area. The track itself is also relatively flat and the scenery is scarce, which means it's difficult to develop reference points. Overall, the track is fairly wide in most areas, but the com-

bination of fast and slow turns means **Las Vegas International Speedway** is a challenging course, with little time to relax. The key to LVIS is to develop a rhythm, which hopefully translates into lap times near the one-minute mark.

Turn One

The approach to Turn One is wide and fast. This is a good place to pass; however, it's difficult to find the apex of the turn because the exit is also part of the return road for the drag strip. The key here is a late apex, but pay attention to the changing width of the track surface, as it narrows at the exit of the turn. Smooth and fast is the key. Brake lightly going in and get the chassis set up, then take a late apex and accelerate hard toward Turn Two.

Turn Two

This is a high-speed turn and most race cars are flat-out through this section. The majority of cars will reach their top speeds between Turns Two and Three. Be thinking ahead in this high-speed turn and look for the braking point for Turn Three. If you go off here, be careful of the tire wall on the outside of the turn. In the case of an off-course excursion, lift off the gas gently and steer straight off and then straight onto the track surface. The Super Production cars reach speeds in excess of 170mph in this section.

Turn Three

Turn Three is a slightly decreasing radius, banked turn. Hard-braking is necessary. Diving inside and using a double apex is a good way to pass on the entrance. You can pass on the exit as well with a late apex. The exit of this turn can be tricky and catches drivers off guard. Don't let the car drift out too soon or you may run out of road. Two, maybe three, downshifts may be required.

Turn Four

Considered the most difficult turn on the track, the trick to driving Turn Four correctly is staying in the groove to properly set the car for Turn Five. Don't pick the throttle up too early or you can't get the car over to the left far enough to be set up for Turn Five. A little sacrifice here will be a big gain accelerating through Turns Five, Six and Seven. One downshift going into Turn Four should be sufficient.

Turn Five

There's much time to be gained on the exit of this turn. It's very important to get this apex right. The key here is not to let the car get too wide at the entrance to the turn. Let the car take a set between Turns Four and Five. Get on line and keep it on line with the goal being a late apex on the exit. This is where the sacrifice made in Turn Four will pay off. Throttle steer the car here through Five and then when at the apex, accelerate hard toward Turn

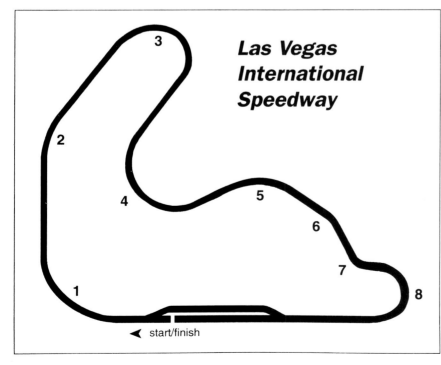

Las Vegas International Speedway

3
2
4
5
6
7
1
8
◄ start/finish

Six. Much time can be gained in this area.

Turn Six

A fast and narrow turn, this is where the access road crosses the track. Get over to the right to prepare for Turn Seven. With the only entrance into the facility crossing the track here, it can be distracting. Look ahead, preparing for the braking point into Turn Seven. A good place to pass if out-braking the competition is an option.

Turn Seven

Combining Turns Six and Seven produces a turn similar to an S-turn. Let the entrance to Turn Seven set the car up for hard braking into Turn Eight. Hard braking will be necessary going into Seven. This is another place where spins occur. Don't throw the car around; use the brakes to set the car up for Turn Eight. Remember, hard braking with two downshifts, maybe three, will be required going into this tight, left-hand turn.

Turn Eight

This slightly banked turn requires a double apex. At the exit onto the front straight, let the car drift out and use all the wide front straight. This is where racers let it all hang out! As the track joins up with the drag strip on the front straight, it is not uncommon to see cars running four-wide as they drag race toward Turn One. This is the real horsepower test.

Turn Eight is a first-gear turn. Drivers usually use all their gears accelerating past the start/finish line. Watch the pit entrance to the right, exiting Turn Eight. Going into the pits, stay low in Turn Eight and keep the car in tight. Slow way down entering the pit lane as it is very short.

Conclusion

LVIS, like other desert race tracks, can be intimidating the first time. Try to get plenty of track time, slowly building up to speed. The most difficult aspect of the track is developing reference points. There aren't any markers to judge distances with the desert terrain as a background. You must develop a guidance system using the pavement changes and locations of the corner worker stations, and then practice by working up to speed gradually, concentrating on always looking ahead until you have developed a keen sense of the appropriate braking and turn-in points for your particular car.

What's special about this track is the combination of fast and tight turns. It's a good test of horsepower as well as braking and handling.

Another major attraction is the track's location—less than 20 minutes from the heart of the gambling capital of the world. Las Vegas International Speedway is a fun change of pace as well as an interesting race track. ■

Warning, one-minute: Sometime soon, they are going to put you on the track.

Warning, five-minute: On the grid, this warning means that sometime in the next five minutes, there will be a one-minute warning.

Weight jacking: See Jacking.

Wing, more/less: The angle of attack of a wing, consequently the downforce and drag. More wing means a higher angle of attack, more downforce, and more drag. "We took a little front wing out of it" means that the wing was reset to a lower (flatter) angle of attack.

Workers (general advice): Be nice to them, for without them we could not race. There is a small minority of workers for whom SCCA is an opportunity to feel powerful by harassing anyone over whom they exercise their temporary authority. One particular Steward and one region's Tech crew come to mind. Console yourself by remembering that you get to race the car. Restrain yourself by remembering that you get to race the car only if you don't get in too much trouble with the power trippers.

Zyglo: A technique that involves using a fluorescent dye penetrant to detect cracks. Used principally for nonferrous parts. (See also Magnaflux and Dye check.) To ensure quality, your critical nonferrous crack-checking work should be Zyglo, done by an FAA-certified repair station.

Bertil Roos began racing in 1967 in a Formula Vee he built himself. Since then he's won scores of races at major tracks in 16 countries, as well as six major championships.

Roos has driven in nearly every kind of competition vehicle: rally cars, ice racers, Formula Vees, Formula Fords, Super Vees, Formulas 2 and 3, Sports Racers, Can-Am cars, Formula Atlantics, Formula 5000, Formula 1 and Indy Cars. He now runs the Bertil Roos School of Motor Racing at Pocono International Raceway.

Don Knowles

HOT LAP

POCONO

A DRIVER WHO KNOWS THE WAY SHOWS THE WAY

BY BERTIL ROOS (edited by Don Knowles)

Pocono International Raceway's 2.8-mile road course combines a six-turn infield with a section of the high-speed oval, making it a real horsepower track. Since a good portion of every lap is spent flat-out in top gear, straight-line speed is most important. Since the infield portion is narrow and twisty, passing is difficult and is best accomplished by drafting on the long straightaways.

Turn One

A lot of passing occurs at the approach to this corner under braking as the cars are funneled from six lanes on the preceding straight to two lanes at the apex. You must start turning gently before braking to angle the car towards the Armco at the outside of the corner. Brake in a straight line—diagonally across the road—right for this point while completing the downshift. When the downshift is completed, continue sufficient braking and, at the right moment, turn and apply full gas. It is critical to clip this apex while under power as it is extremely bumpy here and a freewheeling car will bounce all over the road. Let the car drift to the outside edge, but watch out for the high drop.

Turn Two

Turn Two is a relatively gentle and easy turn as long as you don't apex too early. Clip the apex at the very end of the curbing and let the car drift to the outside edge. Continue along the left edge as you approach the first hairpin.

Hairpin

Speed is high out of Turn Two and there is not enough time to bring the car over to the right. Continue along the left-hand edge and brake straight down to the inside. This looks strange at first, but if you choose a late turn-in point, it works. Point the car up quickly and, once a good angle of attack is created, step on it! Do not let the car drift all the way to the right-hand edge on the exit. If you do, it will then be too hard to bring the car to the left edge and the correct turn-in point for Turn Four. This is critical as Turn Four leads onto a straightaway, and a good entry speed is important.

Turn Four

A fairly straight forward right-hand corner that requires a late apex. There is a strong temptation to turn in too early and, therefore, apex too early. You cannot see the apex from the turn-in point so your eye technique in this corner is critical. Your eyes must continue to glide along the inside edge until you see the apex—a repair spot (tar line) in the pavement. As you exit under full power be sure not to slide off the high edge on the left.

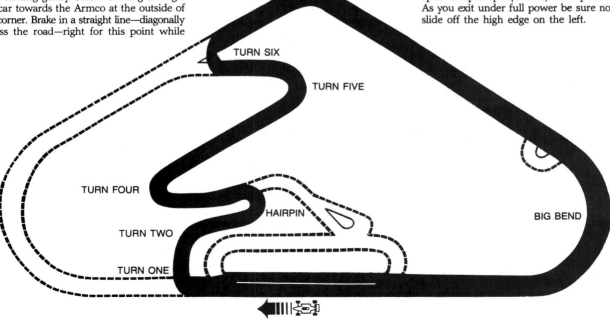

TURN SIX

TURN FIVE

TURN FOUR

HAIRPIN

TURN TWO

BIG BEND

TURN ONE

Turn Five

The approach to Turn Five is probably the best place to pass in the infield. If it is difficult to get the car into the apex from a late turn-in point, it is due to the slight off camber attitude of the corner. Therefore, it is acceptable to turn early and follow the inside a later turn-in point, angle up the car, step on the gas and clip the second dirt spot under full power. Here, it is important to create a good angle of attack very quickly. The sooner a good cornering angle (from the turn-in point through the apex to the exit) is created, the sooner full gas can be applied. You should be able to apply full gas well before the apex and your fastest line.

It is likely a race winner at Pocono will successfully complete a last lap drafting maneuver between Big Bend and the finish line. Experiment during practice to determine where you can start a drafting pass and complete it before the finish line—and not get re-passed.

Drivers at Pocono face a wide variety of challenges, from high speed banked turns to hairpins.

little before clipping the apex. Exiting this corner under full power usually creates a nice drift. When you reach the outside edge, the car should be pointing perfectly toward the turn-in point for the next corner.

Turn Six

This is a very important corner as it will affect your speed all the way down the straight. There are two inside edges that can be confused as apexes. Don't go blasting in and clip the first one, as the car will understeer toward the wall. Instead, take a all the way out of the corner.

Big Bend

This is a constant-radius, 16-degree banked turn leading onto the start/finish straight. There is no specific line in this wide corner, so it is important to find out where your car wants to run. Look at your revs just as you enter the "bowl". Then look at them after you've finished the corner and notice how many RPM's you've lost. Find the line through the bowl where you lose the least amount of revs from entrance to exit—this is

"Hot Lap" Secret

Fine tune your car and improve your driving until you are using either full gas or full brake, nothing in between. Now all your laps at Pocono will be "'Hot Laps." □

Bertil Roos with one of the most unusual—and certainly the fastest—desks in the world.

Hot Lap Directory

CIRCUIT	ISSUE
1984	
Road Atlanta	January
Brainerd	February
Sears Point	March
Lime Rock	April
Riverside	May
Charlotte	June
Hallett	July
Watkins Glen	August
Portland	October
1985	
Nelson Ledges	January
Summit Point	February
Moroso	March
Grattan	April
Road America	May
Laguna Seca	June
Indianapolis Raceway Park	July
Willow Springs	August
St. Louis	September
Mid-Ohio	October

Previous Hot Laps are available for $2.50 each. Write Hot Laps, SportsCar Magazine, 1920-L E. Warner Ave., Santa Ana, CA 92705.

A ST. LOUIS HOT LAP

A driver who knows the way shows the way

by Jim Cook (edited by Don Knowles)

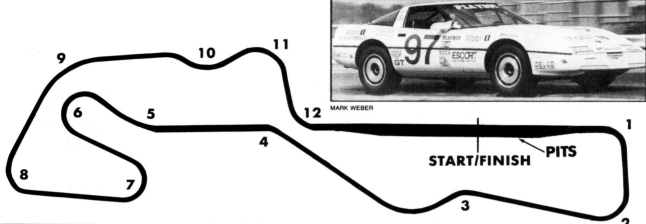

MARK WEBER

START/FINISH   PITS

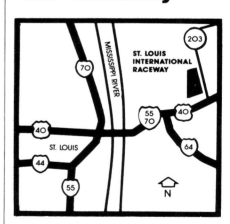

St. Louis International Raceway

As we go to press we regret to report the sudden death of Jim Cook on August 3, 1985, a few weeks after he wrote this description of how to drive St. Louis Raceway. (For full details see FasTrack, page 25). We know Jim would have wanted this printed, and do so in his memory. Jim was the co-owner and a chief driver of the highly successful Morrison-Cook Motorsports team, which is currently the overall leader in the Playboy USEC series. The team has won four of the five events held to date in their Chevrolet Corvettes, and Jim was the co-driver of the winning Corvette in the 24-hour race at St. Louis.

Jim Cook was best known as an endurance driver. In his 21-year career he entered fourteen 24-hour races and won seven of them, including Daytona three times ('73, '80 and '84) and the Quaker State Longest Day at Nelson Ledges twice ('83 and '85). At different times he held 12 IMSA lap records. In addition to his racing career he was also the founder of a successful automotive aftermarket company.

St. Louis is the newest major racing facility in the country, and just beginning its first year of operation. It was built around an existing drag strip and is a 2.2-mile, 12-turn road course. The facility is not yet finished, but promises to be a great one. It features high curbs on the inside of many turns and rippled pavement ("dragon's teeth") on the exit. Some of the curbs and dragon's teeth have not been installed, so temporary markers such as tires or hay bales were in place in the recent SCCA Playboy USEC race. It has some high-speed turns and some difficult braking challenges for both car and driver.

Turn 1:

Turn One is not quite a right angle turn, more like 85 degrees. You approach Turn One blind; that is, you can't see the apex or beyond until after you turn in.

The entrance to Turn One is off the start/finish straight and is one of the two or three best opportunities to overtake another car. But drivers beware, the curbing installed on the apex of the corner is treacherous. It is sharply angled, high and has an abrupt leading end that could tear the suspension off in a hurry. The proper apex is very close to the beginning of the curbing and a relatively small error in turn-in can cause a car to hit the end, with devastating results. The fast line is to enter the corner from the far left of the straight, apex early on the new curb, and exit downstream of the new "dragon's teeth" on the outside of the turn. Because the straight between Turns One and Two is extremely short, the exit speed from Turn One is relatively unimportant. What this means is that you can enter Turn One on the *inside* line (to pass or prevent someone from passing) and not lose a significant amount of time.

The entrance point for Turn One is across the "burnout" area for the drag strip and is rough. If it is raining, the entrance to the turn will be extra slippery, and you should modify your line accordingly. The best traction in the rain would probably be in the middle of the track, between the drag lanes.

Turn 2:

The entrance to Turn Two directly follows the exit of Turn One. The turn is about 100 degrees, is similar to an increasing radius turn, and you should use a slightly late apex because exit speed is important here. Again the curb is high and steep, though the "dragon's teeth" have been placed oddly, since they end before the actual fast-line exit point. The "dragon's teeth" are brutal, and you should make every effort *not* to hit them with the tail out. They can destroy a tire if you drift into them, so you should catch a slide before the exit of the turn. Drive the course in your street car (if you have to) or one of your least favorite rental car agency rent-a-racers (a much better choice), and intentionally drive over the apex curbs and the "dragon's teeth" and you will see what I mean. Stirling Moss particularly likes the Turn One and Turn Two sequence. While Turn Two is not quite flat out, it is close enough that you keep wanting to try it faster.

Turn 3:

Turn Three is really a double turn, a quick left and a sweeping right. This is the beginning of the fastest, most fun part of SLIR. Do this right and you have the basis for a fast lap. The first apex in the turn is in the middle of a "compression," the beginning of a slight rise that loads the suspension and really sticks the car to the ground. Turn left across an early apex and immediately reverse direction to begin a right turn over the top of the rise. The apex of this right-hand sweeper is on the access road into the pits; you have to cross this access road to do the turn correctly. From this point the road falls away, and so does the grip. If you haven't done it right up to now, you are in trouble. In our BFGoodrich-shod Mobil One Corvettes, we can do this corner with just a slight lift at the initial (left-hand) turn-in point and then full throttle in top gear over the crest and down the other side. There is a pavement change just at the point on the exit where your car should reach the left edge of the track. I always glance at the tach (or speedometer) at this change to "grade" myself on how I did the turn (90mph is about right).

Turn 4:

From Turn Three you must cross the track to set up for Turn Four, which is the entrance to an extension of the drag strip (pit straight). Approaching Turn Four, you go up and over a small hill, just tall enough to block your vision of the Turn Four apex, especially at night. You are going fast enough that it can be disconcerting, wondering what is hidden from view on the other side of the hill. Turn Four is a very fast left from a two-lane track onto a four-lane wide straight. The apex is a line of tires, painted white, that can really upset a car if you turned in too soon. The Morrison-Cook SSGT Corvettes can take this with only the slightest lift (to transfer weight onto the front wheels momentarily for the initial turn-in), then it's back to full throttle, still in top gear, well before the apex for the remainder of the turn. This is the second opportunity on this track to set up for a pass. The straight between Turns Four and Five is very wide and there are several approaches to Turn Five.

Turn 5:

Turn Five is a 15-degree right-hand bend that leads directly into the braking area for Turn Six. The fastest line is to cross the straight to the left side so you can approach Turn Five from the left, make a very late apex of Turn Five and take a straight line into the entrance of Turn Six for the latest possible braking. You are braking from top speed into the slowest turn on the course and it is extremely hard to make the braking truly in a straight line. Stirling also likes the challenge of braking from top speed into a slow turn, while turning. However, like Turn One, the time spent between Turn Five and Six is so short the line into Five is not very critical to lap times. This means you can take nearly any line necessary for passing, or not being passed, without losing a lot of time to other competitors.

Turn 6:

This turn seems to last longer than any other turn I can think of. The turn is actually only about 180 degrees, but it seems like a lot more. The apex is very late, around 150 degrees through the turn. The track has temporarily put tires on that portion of the turn, and the apex is about in the middle of the existing tires. It takes tremendous patience to delay applying power long enough to prevent running off the outside.

Turn 7:

Following Turn Six is a short chute leading to a right-hand, 150-degree Turn. After you finally finish Turn Six, cross the track to the left side for the entrance of Turn Seven. This is also a long turn, with a very late apex. The fast line apex is at the very end of the curbing. The pavement at the exit of the turn is full of ripples, which keeps the car from sticking as well as you would expect. Again, a *very* late apex, and this in an important corner for exit speed because of the distance to Turn Eight.

Turn 8:

We called this the "skid pad" turn, because of its constant radius. Because this turn is not yet curbed, there are tires placed around the inside of the turn. The apex (at least for the Playboy race) was the very first tire in a long line. In other words, an early apex. Like Turns Six and Seven, this one is a lot tighter than it first appears, so don't expect it to end too early. Full power can be applied well before the apex, and it's important to get it down as soon as possible, because the exit of Turn Eight leads onto what amounts to a fairly long straight.

Turn 9:

Turn Nine is really just a bend in the straight. If you hug the right side of the turn, you should be able to do the whole thing drifting, but without lifting. Position yourself on the left side of the track after this sweeper for the esses.

Turn 10:

Turn 10 is another compound turn, a right bend followed immediately by a left which leads immediately into the right-hand Turn 11. Braking into Turn 10 requires keeping the car balanced. It is not quite settled from the right-hand Turn Nine and yet you have to take off 30 or 40mph before you turn right into Turn 10 and then immediately turn left. This turn also does not yet have curbs and is dusty (or muddy) because people tend to drive off the track to cut out part of the turn. The entrance is marked by two patches on the pavement on the left side of the track. After pointing the nose of the Corvette in for an early apex, I use the second patch as my braking point. The first apex (for the right-hander) is very early, almost at the beginning of where the track begins to turn. It is also on a slight rise in the road, which prevents seeing the apex of the left turn (right at the top) until you are almost on top of it. Rhythm is the key here. Hug the inside of the right-hand side at the beginning of the turn, then hug the left-hand section until you reach the very short straight into Turn 11.

Turn 11:

This turn is more than 90 degrees and will be taken in second or third gear, depending on your car. The importance of this turn is only to set your car up for the entry to Turn 12 and onto the pit straight. The fast line is to apex the turn at its latest point and white line on the right that leads to the outside of Turn 12. This will provide you the widest line (and therefore the fastest) through Turn 12 onto the straight. However, it is possible to surprise a competitor ahead of you by using an early apex, exiting faster, and reaching the apex of 12 ahead of him and on his left. But this isn't advised unless you are racing, because it will hurt your lap times.

Turn 12:

Turn 12 is a simple 90-degree left-hander onto the pit straight. However, it is one of the most important on the course for a good lap. Exit speed carries all the way down the straight. For that reason, a pass such as I described above should only be used if there is no other way. Entering the corner from the left and sacrificing exit speed will ruin not only the lap you are on but most likely the next one too, since timing is done in the middle of the straight.

The straight is wider than the track between 11 and 12, so therefore make an early apex next to the dirt on the inside of the turn, and then exit as near to the pit guardrail as you dare. The guardrail will most likely be protected by a stack of old

tires, and the exit is blind (due to the end of the guardrail on the left side of the drag strip) until just before you reach the apex. This is a good place to pay attention because of the smorgasbord of problems you can find here. There were several spectacular shunts here during the Playboy race, with cars getting too wide and scattering the tires and themselves around in the paths of other unsuspecting racers just entering the turn.

The start/finish line is far enough down the pit straight that you may be able to pass between the exit of Turn 12 and the start/finish line. This tactic should be attempted during practice to see if it is feasible. □

Hot Lap editor Don Knowles was Jim Cook's teammate and close friend on the Morrison-Cook Motorsports team, and in fact was a co-driver with Cook and Ron Grable in the winning car at St. Louis. Contacted by phone at press time, Don had these few final thoughts on the sudden loss of his friend.

"Right now Jim's death is not real. He had a great sense of humor. There were so many jokes. I keep thinking of Cook and laughing. The sadness and grief is not real yet. He was very tickled he was asked to do a Hot Lap, and I'm glad he got to write one.

"Jim was really pumped up about having done it. I was aware of the level of effort he made. The team was prepping for Lime Rock and Jim was right in the middle of negotiations for 1986 with everyone...but he wrote it himself and sent it in very promptly—the mark of a professional.

"When I received it, I called right away and told him, 'This is the worst piece of s_____ I've ever read.' He knew as soon as I said it the story was alright." —Don Knowles

AN INDIANAPOLIS RACEWAY PARK HOT LAP

A driver who knows the way shows the way

by Dave Finch (edited by Don Knowles)

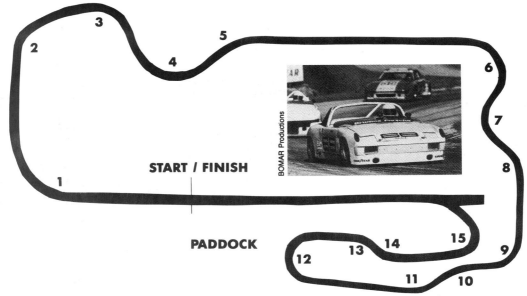

START / FINISH

PADDOCK

BOMAR Productions

David Finch is a consulting engineer and director of the RAE-TECH (Research and Applied Engineering Technology) CORPORATION, located in Ann Arbor, Michigan. RAE-TECH does a major portion of its work for the U.S. automobile manufacturers. Finch became interested in motorsports in 1972, building and racing his own car in '74. Finch has held Lap records on every Central Division road course, in one or more of the following classes; C Production, GT3, E Production, Showroom Stock and Sports Renault. At IRP, Finch held the GT3 record. He still holds multiple records in GT3 and EP at Brainerd and GT3, EP, and Sports Renault at Mid-Ohio. Finch now spends more of his time with development programs and less with behind-the-wheel racing.

''IRP'' is a complete motorsports facility. The 2½-mile, 15-turn road course uses one-half mile of a drag strip as its main straight and surrounds a five-eighths-mile oval track. IRP is owned and operated by the NHRA, who over the past few years has made significant improvements to the facility (including approximately one-half mile of new paving stretching from the beginning of Turn One through the exit of Turn Five, the fastest series of turns. This makes the course both quicker and safer. IRP will test both car and driver with its selection of high, moderate and low speed turn combinations.

Turn One

Enter this sweeping 90-degree right in top gear and from the left edge of the main straight. Depending on your car, it ranges from flat out to heavy braking. Your turn starts just at the end of the guard rail. Precise entry is critical and the apex is a little earlier than one would first assume. Be smooth and on power, pull down to the apex and follow the radius for about 30 ft., adding power, reducing steer angle and drifting out until the left tires just nudge the access road midway between Turns One and Two. Scrub off as little speed as possible; it's hard to regain and must be carried through Turn Two.

Turn Two

Still in top gear you'll enter Turn Two, a right tighter than Turn One and approximately 70 degrees in duration. It's flat out if you dare, but most brake lightly at the entry. As in Turn One, enter a little early to flatten the arc and apex about 20 feet of the grass line starting just before the turn's midpoint. Be on the power keeping the car stable and compensating for scrubbing through the turn's relatively long duration. Your leftward drift ends just in time to enter Turn Three. Be aware that missing the Turn Two entry may cost time through the next four linked turns and onto the back straight.

Turn Three

You have marginally regained lateral stability when it is time to make a braking downshift for the 90-degree right at Turn Three. Some cars scrub enough speed to make braking unnecessary. Most must light brake and come down one gear. With the faster cars, the Turn Two arc combines with the arc of Turn Three. Approximately 75 feet of straight follows Turn Three before entering the first left turn. The car's handling characteristics and speed carried through Turn Two helps determine the line through Turn Three. Now, get a little ahead of yourself and consider Turn Five leading onto the backstraight and the proper position to enter Turn Five. A portion of Turn Four must be sacrificed. Turn Four also helps dictate the Turn Three line. Larger production cars may late apex Turn Three, finishing to the left edge at the Turn Four entrance. The small production cars and formula cars may apex about midway through Turn Three, end the turn earlier and move to enter Four from the track's middle or right. As you can see, Turns Two through Five are linked and an error in any one may cost time through to the end of the backstraight.

Turn Four

The Left of Turn Four must be compromised in both entrance and exit. The main objective is to spend as little time as possible in this turn and finish along the left edge of the track. Entering Turn Four, braking may not be necessary. If the car's line through Turn Three sets up a left side entry to Turn Four, then ride Turn Four's radius. Drift out midway around and pull back tight to the edge in time to get flat and stable for Turn Five. If your Turn Three exit allows a cross back to the right, then start a classic decreasing radius left turn, terminating at the track's left edge. Again, in this series of turns, there are two or three acceptable paths, each requiring an identical amount of time to complete. In every case, much is lost if you are not prepared to enter Turn Five without braking and at the maximum speed for the turn.

Turn Five

Turn Five exits onto the backstraight, the first

good place to pass since the main straight. If by chance the car ahead of you makes an error in the previous series of turns and is slowed for Turn Five, correctly timing your entry to this turn may gain you a significant advantage. By the same note, you may also fall prey to a calculating driver to your rear. Turn Five is a blind 40-degree right, slightly rising to the apex, then dropping slightly off camber and downhill. The apex is late and well-marked by speed bumps. Be as deep in the bumps as your car will tolerate without upsetting its stability. As you exit, use all of the track to absorb your drift. The new paving ends about the point at which you up-shift to top gear. Warning: There is often a step at the left edge of the pavement which can hook a tire; there is also a concrete wall running the full length of the backstraight along the right side. Draw your own conclusions.

Turn Six

Approach Turn Six in top gear. The backstraight is downhill and nearly as fast as the main straight. Turn Six is another compromise due to the short distance between it and Turn Seven. There are distance markers to the left. Braking between the 2 and 1 markers is adequate for most cars. Approach Six from the far left, brake and come down two gears. The pavement allows you to make Turn Six an increasing radius turn; however, this will leave you *out of position for Seven*. As with Turn Four, you must terminate the arc just past the inside radius. There is a series of speed bumps at the normal right apex of this turn. Complete your turn just past these bumps, with the car stable and flat. You are now in position to correctly enter Turn Seven.

Turn Seven

After praising Turns One and Five for being smooth and fast, it's disappointing to inform you that in the next series of five turns, if your tires are on the ground, then most likely so is your chassis. Beware of exhaust systems and other assorted pieces of undercarriage strewn about over this section. The apex of Turn Seven is quickly to your left and marked by a small patch of dirt at the edge of the pavement. Late apex this 90-degree turn. You are now entering the staging lanes of the drag strip and the road course will be marked by colored pylons. If it's your first time on the course, this section is quite confusing. Exit Turn Seven under good power. The car will be bouncing and skipping. Move back to the left in order to miss the worst bump and set up for the right at Turn Eight.

Turn Eight

This turn is 45 degrees to the right and wide. Your line is dependent on the exit of Seven as well as your car's ability to absorb bumps. Late apex Turn Eight, leading onto the short straight. This portion of track is a series of compromises and very dependent on your car's characteristics. The track is wide exiting Eight; therefore, your choice of apex is variable. Use as much of the course as possible in order to reduce the tire scrubbing created by the bumps. The left edge of the course is marked by pylons. You will find that the course tends to widen through the duration of a race. Also be aware that one of those pylons could, at some point, wind up in the middle of your line. Most likely it's the same gear from Six through Eight. If the gear is long, you may be able to carry it to Turn Nine. Otherwise, it's up one gear for 150 feet and back down.

Turn Nine

Important, difficult and perplexing is how I describe Turn Nine. It is the only place to pass between Turns Six and 11. It is also considered the beginning of the straight which lies between Turns 11 and 12. To compound the matter, you enter Turn Nine downhill, off camber, through bumps and blind. If you can't pass cleanly before entering Turn Nine, then you may hurt your lap time all the way to 12. Sometimes you will lose less by holding off a pass until clearing Turn 11. Turn Nine is almost 90 degrees and requires a late apex. If you came up a gear exiting Eight, then you will be braking hard and going back down one gear for Nine. The braking area runs along the pylons and is bumpy. Turn before you see the apex ripples. Pull the car in tight and take as many of the ripples as your car will stand. Be on the power prior to hitting the apex. Use all of the track to complete the turn. You are approaching Turn 10, the beginning of a left/right combination. Your Turn Nine apex should be placed such that you remain on power exiting Nine and can move back slightly to the right for 10.

Turn 10

This turn is only about 30 degrees to the left but full power and bumpy. Your speed through the turn is based on how well you completed Nine. Even though you weave through this section, your ability to pass competitors entering Turn 12 dictates that you consider this turn as part of the upcoming straight. The apex is marked by a patch of dirt at the left edge of the pavement. Get your left front tire onto this patch of dirt, and you will be lined up well for Turn 11.

Turn 11

Turn 11 is a quick 45 degrees to the right. It's bumpy, has a late apex and sees all of the speed you have generated since leaving Nine. The exit puts you to the far left edge with your heart in your throat, especially if driving a high-power car. Turn 11 leads onto the third longest straight and the best opportunity to pass since Turn Six.

Turn 12

If you have an understeering car, Turn 12 is 180 degrees of pure frustration! Otherwise, it's kind of fun. The braking area for 12 is marked. Typical brake points lay between the 2 and 1 markers. A car with excellent slow turn characteristics can double. Trail brake, picking your first apex about 25 degrees into the turn. Get back on the power and allow the car to drift to a mid-track position, halfway through the turn. Lift briefly to increase the rear slip angle and back on the power pulling the car down to the final apex about three-quarters of the way around. Use full power as the car drifts to the left. You will probably raise a little dust as the left rear tire runs partially off the pavement. For the understeering car, enter wide and continue reducing speed. Gradually bring the car to the radius and late apex. Your apex should be placed where it will allow you to carry full throttle out of the turn.

Turns 13 and 14

Turn 13 starts another left/right combination. This is the simplest combination on the course. The apexes are marked by speed bumps. A little nudge of each puts you on the proper line. You can neither pass nor be passed through this set of turns unless by mutual agreement. Upshift to your second highest gear just past 14.

Turn 15

This is your last chance to pass before entering the long start/finish straight. Turn 15 is a 180-degree increasing radius left. It is also the slowest turn but critical for lap time and terminal velocity on the pit straight. Enter from the far right. Brake heavily and come down two gears. About midway through the turn, on the inside, is an extension of pavement which marks the apex. This turn is also very difficult for understeering cars. Be slowed enough to hit the apex. Then, keep pushing the throttle to full open and completion of the turn. Use all of the track by allowing the turn to end along the right side guard rail. Go through the gears, taking every opportunity to pick up the draft of cars already on the straight. □

Track Records		
CLASS	TIME	DATE
EP	1:46.14	10/2/83
FP	1:48.17	9/18/77
GP	1:50.470	4/21/85
HP	1:53.19	9/18/77
ASR	1:25.88	5/04/80
CSR	1:33.660	4/21/85
DSR	1:33.470	4/21/85
S2000	1:36.100	4/21/85
SR	1:52.970	4/21/85
GT1	1:37.747	4/21/85
GT2	1:40.633	4/21/85
GT3	1:41.95	4/22/84
GT4	1:49.419	4/21/85
GT5	1:53.14	7/24/83
SSGT	1:54.466	4/21/85
SSA	1:59.80	7/26/81
SSB	2:02.04	7/24/83
SSC	2:03.893	4/21/85
FA	1:27.35	5/04/80
FC	1:33.16	10/02/83
FF	1:36.395	4/21/85
FV	1:48.340	4/21/85
F440	1:53.18	8/21/83

A ROAD AMERICA HOTLAP

A driver who knows the way shows the way
by Al Holbert (edited by Don Knowles)

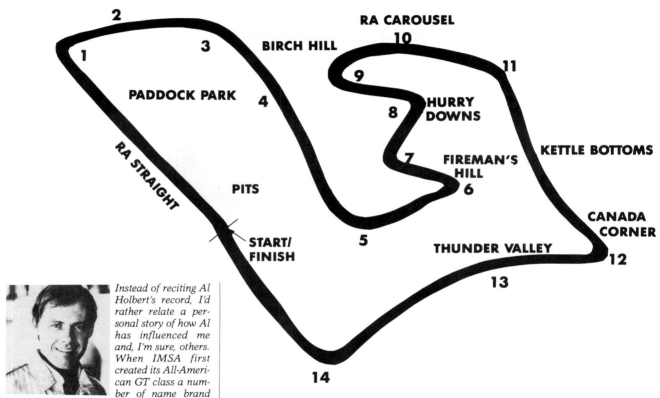

Instead of reciting Al Holbert's record, I'd rather relate a personal story of how Al has influenced me and, I'm sure, others. When IMSA first created its All-American GT class a number of name brand drivers and teams built and raced versions of the Chevrolet Monza. Most broke or had some other failing and they didn't win for a while. Al, meantime, had prepared his own Monza and was entered at Road Atlanta in April, 1976. I asked one of Al's competitors how he expected Al to do in light of the failure of others to win with the Monza. The reply was a flat, unemotional, "He'll win." Surprised by such a confident response, I asked why.

"What sets Al apart is that he tests and develops his car, often simulating an entire race, in order to find out what it takes to win. Then he does it. For example, this race is 100 miles long, and Al was here recently with his car and crew and ran the entire race length at a race pace to see what could keep him from winning."

Sure enough, Al won. From that story, and others like it, I realized there are plenty of guys out there with relatively unlimited bucks who don't win. Those who win work at it, plan it, prepare for it, think about it constantly and

settle for nothing less. That was an important lesson for me to keep in mind through the years and is still a valuable lesson for us all.
—Don Knowles

Although the layout of Road America has been the same since I first raced it 12 years ago, the road surface has changed considerably. There were years that the circuit would be drastically different during the season. It's a smooth circuit, favoring good top speed cars and one that can be very frustrating.

Many of the corners are similar, generally requiring every trick your car knows to eliminate understeer. Yet the key to quick lap times are the four medium-to-fast corners: Turn Seven, the Carousel, the Kink and Turn 13 (under the bridge). Road America

can be very frustrating in that you can beat your brains out mastering all of the approximately 90-degree corners and blow one of the fast ones, and your lap time will just stay the same. Or if you get held up in any turn up to Six, you still will have over two miles to go before you get another shot at a pass. Another generalization is you need to constrain the tendency (induced by wide, smooth braking areas) to rush up to the corner trying to capitalize on every split second of top speed. The important thing about most of Road America's turns is to slow enough, early enough, to get good turn-in and be early on the power. The proverbial "trail braking" is not a rewarding technique at Road America. Road America requires a lot of discipline. Keep in mind the track generally gets better as the weekend (and race) goes on.

Turn One

Turn One is the first test of your "turn-in" and constraint efforts. Because you are ending what sometimes is the quickest straight (depending on the car and the wind), you do want to get in as far as possible. And if you've come onto the start/finish straight well and caught a draft, braking well for Turn One can get you past the guy in front. Turn One is faster (and longer) than all but one of the other similar 90-degree corners. Begin here to establish a rhythm of hard, late, straight-line braking, getting quickly back in the power. In my type car using the three marker for braking and having a tall third or short fourth gear are fundamental for Turn One.

Turns Two and Three

The straight between Turn One and Turn Three has a slight left kink as the road starts a gentle downhill. Turn Three is a tough one. Again, turn-in is critical. The downhill gives a lot of speed into Turn Three, but brake late and plenty. Use all of second, hitting red line almost before the end of the corner, take a slightly late apex (which requires a lot of discipline) and keep it on the road. Generally, the proper fourth gear will get you to red line at the bridge on your way to Turn Five.

Turn Five

The long straight between Turns Three and Five, believe it or not, has some slight kinks that have been used to thwart a pass. After the bridge (Turn Four), the road changes from slightly uphill to slightly downhill. In the braking area for Turn Five (before the "5" marker), the road begins an increasing dive that doesn't flatten out until about the "half a hundred" point. This is a traditional place to pass, but because the road is falling away it can be a real nervous braking area. You just have to grin and bear it. Five is the odd one for gearing, it usually requires a shorter second than any of the other slow ones. Be patient, get it slowed and late apex.

Turns Six and Seven

Squirting well between Five and Six can give you the pass you need in the race. The steep uphill quickly flattens out under the Turn Six bridge and deceives you into braking too late. This is in my mind the most critical of the late-entry, slow-speed, second-gear corners. It's a left that leads to a short flat straight that brings you up to Turn Seven, a quick, starting-to-go-downhill third gear right-hander. Rush up to Seven, lift (and brake slightly—sometimes with the left foot) and quickly flick the wheel right. Now stand on it. This is the first of the four critical medium speed corners mentioned earlier. Concentrate on all of these for quick lap times.

Turn Eight

If you've done Turn Seven right, you'll get into top gear before the slow left Turn Eight. Again, it's downhill heading to "8" and don't wait too long before braking. Turn Eight is a 90 percent left-hander, with a short straight leading to Turn Nine and 10, "The Carousel."

Turns Nine and 10, "The Carousel"

Exit Turn Eight hard, upshift to third, short shift and get into the next to top gear well before the right-hand Carousel. Accelerate hard all the way through Nine to the entrance of the Carousel. Stay about in the middle of the road and then just progressively squeeze the power on all the way through, holding to the inside of the track. You should be flat out exiting the Carousel, even though it tightens up and heads downhill. The last 100 feet of the corner flatten out, so you can get a good bite. Unfortunately, the middle of the Carousel is the bumpiest part of the track.

Turn 11, "The Kink"

Now comes the test—and almost all the improvement (or superiority) in lap time—"The Kink." You'll probably be in top gear and have a tendency to not be in the peak power range of the engine. Be careful, don't brake too hard and too late. Carry speed if you can, late apex (gently) and settle the car by being back on the gas early (i.e. through the corner). It's flat, so you won't get any help from the road loading the car.

Turn 12

Squiggle your way down through Hurry Downs toward Turn 12 and note that if you've done the kink well you may have your highest speed of the lap at the "5" marker. Twelve starts uphill slightly at the beginning. But this turn can make the car a real pusher, requiring a real late apex. It's a second gear turn for most five-speed people.

Turn 13

Uphill toward the bridge is the second toughest challenge and opportunity for good lap time. You'll need to short shift into third and then get into fourth, accelerating hard. Approaching Turn 13, lift and flick the wheel to the left. Be in the power hard under the bridge and use all of the road. If you early apex this one, you'll be in the weeds (excuse me, Road America, grass).

Turn 14

Gradually find your way over to the extreme left of the road. Turn 14 has a long entry and becomes tighter, so apex long and late. Remember, it is greater than 90 degrees, so don't overcharge the entry. This is a toss-up between second and third gears, but do it right, because it's the end of your scored lap and the entry to the longest (and uphill) straightaway.

If you do it right and get into the rhythm, Road America is great fun and one of the prettiest tracks in America. □

Jeff Krosnoff's strong third-place finish in last year's International Formula Atlantic Championship at the new Memphis International Motorsports Park cemented the 23-year-old's reputation as one of America's brightest young talents. It was especially impressive considering he was the first-finishing Ralt driver (in a well-used RT-4/86, behind two Swifts and just ahead of another) and that the Memphis shootout was only his seventh Atlantic race. Krosnoff, who graduated last year from UCLA with a degree in psychology, has also scored victories in the Pro Sports 2000 (in his first start!), in the Formula Russell Pro series, and in the Coors Racetruck Challenge. Currently contesting a full Racetruck season in Spencer Low's Nissan, Krosnoff is embroiled in a tight points battle with Jeep driver Tommy Archer.

Don Knowles
HOT LAP

MEMPHIS

A DRIVER WHO KNOWS THE WAY SHOWS THE WAY
BY JEFF KROSNOFF

O n paper, Memphis International Motorsports Park closely resembles Arizona's Firebird International Raceway. However, the two circuits are quite dissimilar save for the employment of a dragstrip for the main straight and similar (and difficult, at best) passing zones. All other apparent idiosyncracies are purely schematic. Fundamentally, Memphis is a slow track, contrasting very fast sweepers with slow and tight "ems" (at Memphis,

they're called "ems," not "esses"). One of Memphis International's notable attributes is the burnished smoothness of the racing surface. The place is billiard table smooth with virtually no elevation changes.

Turn One

Turn One is a right-hander at the end of the 3,300-foot straight. You are in top gear in any car and running well over 140mph in a Formula Atlantic. Because it is at the end of the straight, it affords the best place on the track to overtake—if you are able to capitalize on the draft. Turn One itself is lightly banked and should be treated as if it were an oval track turn (but in reverse).

Braking into the corner, clipping the **apex** and accelerating out is the slow way. In an Atlantic, I lightly touch the brakes and drop down to fourth, while immediately driving the car from the outside to the inside edge. The key is to carry and maintain **as** much speed as possible into and throughout the corner. At close to full throttle, **pay** particular attention to smoothness. Any sloppiness here will translate into slow lap times. Maintain a low line (about a **half car** width off the edge of the **track**) to **make the** most of the banking as well as to **utilize the** centrifugal force on the **exit.** This means letting the car lead itself over **a slight rise** to the edge of the track. Just **beyond the rise** I grab fifth gear.

Turns Two And Three

Turn Two is a right-hand kink taken flat in top gear. It leads into Turn Three, a left-hand kink, which is also taken flat. At the exit of Turn Three the car becomes neutral. At this point, brake hard for Turn Four, which is the beginning of the Memphis "ems," a very tight and narrow left-right-left-right section.

The "Ems"

The first right-left combination is **not** nearly as critical as the second, which will lead you onto a short backstraight. Therefore it is better to give up these **initial** corners in an effort to be at full throttle as early as possible coming onto the little straight. Enter the initial right in second gear, having already accomplished the majority of the necessary braking in a

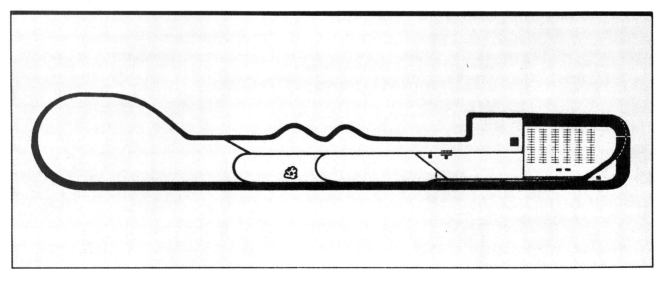

MAC DeMERE

straight line. Then late-apex the left-hander, which sets you up nicely for the secondary combination. Position the car to the left center of the track and turn in late for the next right. Here is where you want to go to full throttle and have the car set so that you do not have to lift. The track falls off at the exit, making the car want to oversteer, especially since you are accelerating. The late line through the right will accommodate perfectly for the off-camber segment and assure a clean line onto the straight.

Depending on personal preference and the type of car, either first or second gear can be used for the "ems." First gear is better for stabbing the throttle—the point and squirt approach—while second gear is more appropriate for a smooth, coaxing throttle. The FIA curbing through this entire section is not only tall, but steep as well. It's well worth the effort to avoid hitting it. Driving over the curbs can drastically upset the balance of the car, not to mention the real possibility of damage.

Turns Five And Six

Coming off the "ems" (grab second gear if you used first) and down the short straight, take third gear to peak power before braking for another tight left-right flick. This braking zone is, perhaps, the only other place to pass outside of the first turn. Gearing down to second after heavy straight-line braking, turn in late for the left-hander, clipping the curb. Position the car to the left center and again get on the power early and exit the right-hander cleanly and near full throttle.

Turns Seven and Eight

Now it's down another short chute to the peak of third gear before entering the "parking lot," Turns Seven and Eight. Brake lightly, drop to second gear and turn in to the right-hand Seven. The apex is about a car width off the guardrail at the base of a small but noticeable bump. This is the pre-

staging area for the dragstrip so it contains a confusing array of white lines, none of which you want to follow. At the top of second, a nice arcing turn will lead you to the outside retaining wall. As you reach the outside wall, breathe the throttle ever so slightly and then stand on it. The car will get out of shape a bit as it traverses the dragstrip launch pad, so it is important to be as straight as possible here. This will minimize the chance of scrubbing off the speed that you must carry down the straight.

Turns Seven and Eight could be handled as if they were a single 180-degree corner. However, I do not recommend it. Turn Eight is the most decisive part of the entire course because it leads onto the main straight and the fast Turns One, Two and Three—a section which accounts for more than half of the circuit's 1.77 miles. If you are slow out of Eight, you will be slow the length of the straight and lose a considerable amount of time. For this reason it is imperative that you concentrate fully on Eight.

I must say that I really enjoy Turn Eight. It is fast and blind. It has walls on both sides of the track, simulating a street circuit to some degree. Coupled with this is a bumpy, car-unsettling surface change from asphalt to concrete. On top of this are strips of rubber laid down by the drag cars, which compound the struggle for traction. All told it makes for a very challenging end to an equally challenging circuit. □

Editor's Note: *Corner station numbers have been used to designate corners at many road circuits. That's why some insignificant kinks become Turn Two or Turn Four, while some notable corners are nameless. However, Memphis is a brand-new circuit and tradition hasn't been established. So, in numbering its turns, we used the numbers given them by racers at last fall's IFAC, not the corner station numbers.*

Photocopies are available for $3 each. Write to Hot Laps, *SportsCar* magazine, 1385, East Warner Ave., Suite C, Tustin, CA 92680. Please allow eight weeks for delivery.

A Sears Point Hot Lap

A Man Who Knows the Way Shows the Way

by Bob Lobenberg

The many elevation changes, camber changes and blind exits of Sears Point make it one of the most demanding circuits in the United States for both driver and chassis.

Turn Two has an uphill entrance with a blind, off-camber exit. All cars must brake hard, down shift, turn-in early and use the berm and off-camber exit to rotate the car. You must be smooth and precise. Using all the road to exit the turn allows you to get right back on the power.

At **Turn 1-A** the Formula Fords, Sports Racers and some sedans can keep the hammer down, grinding through the dog-leg and up the hill. Trans Ams and such must brake relatively hard for the dogleg, then use a short squirt of acceleration up the hill.

Turn Three has a dip at the apex and an uphill exit leading directly to Turn 3-A, a right-hander with an uphill entrance and a downhill blind exit. After braking, you want to enter Turn Three on the far right, getting as late an apex as possible to line up 3-A for another late apex. Again, try to use the berm to help rotate the car and straighten the turn. Stiffly sprung cars may have difficulty doing this here.

Turn Five is flat out, providing the car is set up soft enough to ride over the bump in the middle of the road. If not, the bump hops your car to the left. Exit Turn Five on the far left, then work back to the middle/right as you go up the hill toward the Carrousel.

Turn Six is a decreasing radius, left-hand, downhill turn leading onto a short straight. You enter going uphill, getting very light at the crest, then brake hard and at the last second turn left in the middle of the road. Now wind a constant arc into the apex at the bottom. By now you should be flat down on the gas, and at this point you feel the the car use all its suspension and spit you onto the straight.

Turn Four has a downhill entrance, an off-camber middle and a flat exit. Just when the car really starts to accelerate into the turn you must jump on the brakes, downshift, look for the berm on the right, turn in early and get back on the gas in a hurry to get good exit speed.

For the **Turn Seven** hairpin, the classic Bondurant School line is to enter from the far left and get a late apex. However, the turn can be entered from the middle of the road, using less track, and still get a late apex by using up all the road on the exit. This is a good turn to pass on the inside. Get on the gas ASAP to build up as much speed as possible for the Esses.

Use a late apex for **Turn Eight** to line up for the very difficult Turn 8-A, which has a blind, downhill exit. If you mess up Eight, then 8-A will come up too soon; you'll get an early apex and get off on the dirt going downhill . . . scary! With proper execution you will be carrying a lot of speed and accelerating.

Turn Nine is a flat but extreeeemly bumpy left-hander. Take it from the middle of the road with the latest apex possible so as to exit on the far lets and be set up for Turn 10.

Start/finish is located in the middle of an arc between Turn 12 and Turn One, so in a big, high-powered car it's easy to get loose and out of shape just trying to reach Turn One, as speeds of 125 to 135mph are realistic when completing a lap and crossing start/finish.

The fastest turn on the track, **Turn 10** has a big bump near the entrance which can be used as "rhythm" for your turn-in. The car squats, then comes up and gets light—and that's your cue to turn right. An intimidating turn because of its speed, there is little room for error with no runoff area. You'll know if you take it just right (maybe 20 percent of the time depending on experience) because it feels great and the tach shows the revs you've made.

Accelerating down a short chute brings you to **Turn 11**, a flat, bumpy turn with a movable apex—stacks of tires. Most of the passing is done here. Take the latest apex you can and drag race to the finish line.

With two National Championships in Formula Ford (1980 and 1982) and two in Sports 2000 (1982, '83), Bob Lobenberg is quite simply the premier driver in these classes. For 1984 he is applying his considerable skills to the Trans-Am series, taking over for Elliott Forbes-Robinson to drive Joe Huffaker's Pontiac Trans Am. He unequivocally demonstrated he knows the fast way around Sears Point in the 1983 Camel GT, where he took the pole in the Conte Lola T600 and finished second.

A Lime Rock Hot Lap

A Man Who Knows the Way Shows the Way

by Tom Davey

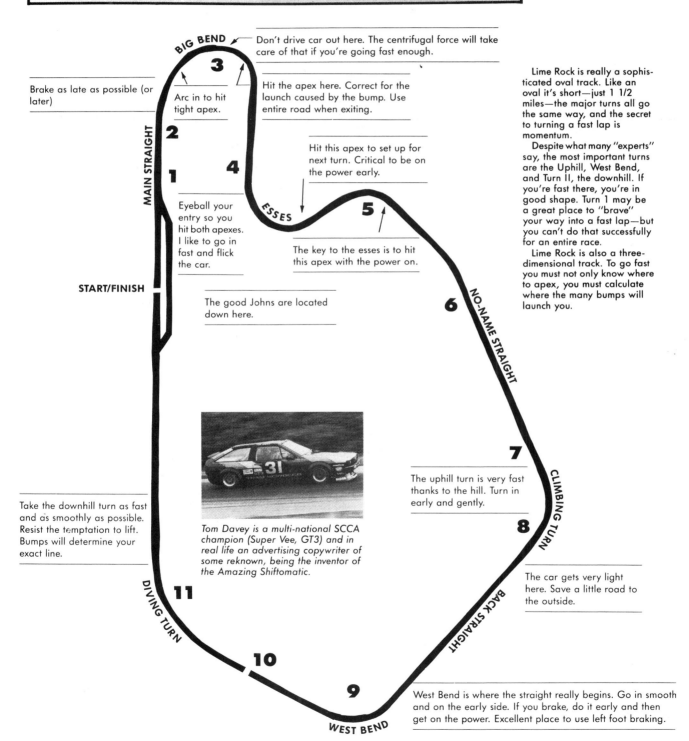

BIG BEND

Don't drive car out here. The centrifugal force will take care of that if you're going fast enough.

Brake as late as possible (or later)

Arc in to hit tight apex.

Hit the apex here. Correct for the launch caused by the bump. Use entire road when exiting.

MAIN STRAIGHT

Hit this apex to set up for next turn. Critical to be on the power early.

ESSES

Eyeball your entry so you hit both apexes. I like to go in fast and flick the car.

The key to the esses is to hit this apex with the power on.

START/FINISH

The good Johns are located down here.

Lime Rock is really a sophisticated oval track. Like an oval it's short—just 1 1/2 miles—the major turns all go the same way, and the secret to turning a fast lap is momentum.

Despite what many "experts" say, the most important turns are the Uphill, West Bend, and Turn II, the downhill. If you're fast there, you're in good shape. Turn 1 may be a great place to "brave" your way into a fast lap—but you can't do that successfully for an entire race.

Lime Rock is also a three-dimensional track. To go fast you must not only know where to apex, you must calculate where the many bumps will launch you.

NO-NAME STRAIGHT

Take the downhill turn as fast and as smoothly as possible. Resist the temptation to lift. Bumps will determine your exact line.

Tom Davey is a multi-national SCCA champion (Super Vee, GT3) and in real life an advertising copywriter of some reknown, being the inventor of the Amazing Shiftomatic.

The uphill turn is very fast thanks to the hill. Turn in early and gently.

CLIMBING TURN

The car gets very light here. Save a little road to the outside.

DIVING TURN

BACK STRAIGHT

West Bend is where the straight really begins. Go in smooth and on the early side. If you brake, do it early and then get on the power. Excellent place to use left foot braking.

WEST BEND

John Powell began his driving career racing at speeds of more than 100mph on the frozen lakes of Quebec. He won a championship his first year out and earned the title "King of the Ice." Powell later moved into professional pavement racing and became chief instructor of Mosport Racing School in 1973.

Don Knowles
HOT LAP

MOSPORT

A DRIVER WHO KNOWS THE WAY SHOWS THE WAY

BY JOHN POWELL
(edited by Don Knowles)

M osport is Canada's premier international race track. It's a challenging circuit with some interesting elevation changes, including a 2,500-ft. straight that is mostly uphill.

There are 10 turns at Mosport; Turns Six and Seven, however, are just kinks on the Andretti Straight.

Turn One

The first corner is a very fast, downhill right-hander. It's taken in top gear; Keke Rosberg says it's flat out in anything, but I've always found mere mortals should gently brake before the turn, especially when learning the circuit. The turn, being such a fast one, has an apex that begins at the end of the speed bumps and continues for 30 feet. Your right side wheels must run on the white line at the apex.

Turn Two

Exiting Turn One on the left side of the road, you have to move all the way back over to the right side of the track to approach Two. Two is a downhill, double apex left-hander that is taken in top gear. Proper entry is the key; turn a fraction too late or enter a meter too wide and Turn Two will become a nightmare. Rosberg says it's flat,

but he was referring to his Atlantic car back in 1975—on a very good day. In 1981, the last time Formula 1 cars were at Mosport, even Ronnie Peterson was on the brakes all the way to the first apex. There's a patch of asphalt just prior to the first apex. Turn gently so the left wheels clip the asphalt patch and then pass over the inside white line at the first apex. The car will drift out into the middle of the turn as you approach the second apex—called Two A—located at the bottom of the hill. You must hit the apex at Two A on the intersection of the two inside white lines and accelerate to the outside of the turn.

In many cars you'll be going as fast or faster here than at the end of the straight. You must then move all the way back to the left of the track to approach Turn Three. Be careful that the pendulum of weight transfer doesn't catch up with you here. Pull the car too violently back to the left for Three and you'll be sorry.

Johnny Rutherford hit the wall at Three so often the last time the Indy Cars came to Mosport in 1979, we thought of dedicating the concrete to him.

Turn Three

Three is a deceptive corner with a decreasing radius turn at the entrance and a slight road camber change at the apex.

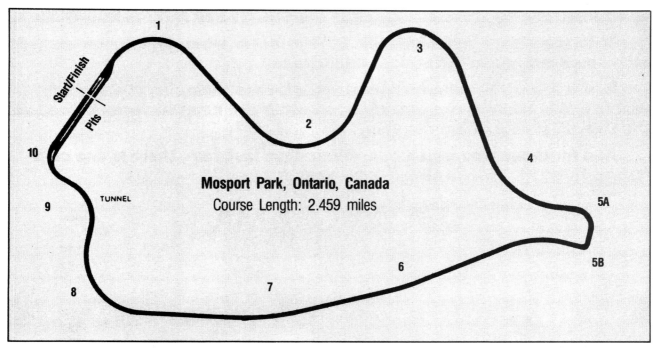

Mosport Park, Ontario, Canada
Course Length: 2.459 miles

Though the Four-Five combo is one of the most difficult, the wall at Three can be disastrous.

Most cars will take Three in third gear, having lost quite a bit of speed while braking for entry.

Hug the speed bumps to the apex, then accelerate out, unwinding the wheel to reach the last one-third of the speed bumps on the left side of the track.

Three is deceptive because it will always make you feel you should have gone faster, but if you rush the turn, the car will understeer. That's a warning. If the car feels really good going into Three, with lots of cornering load and nicely balanced, you'll probably join the Johnny Rutherford club.

Turns Four And Five

Niki Lauda says Mosport's Turn Four-Five section is one of the 10 most difficult cornering sequences in the world. Listen to Lauda. Four is a fast, downhill, late apex lefthander. Five, also known as Moss Corner, is a two-part hairpin. The first part of Five, known as Five A, is an uphill right turn. Five B is a slight downhill right turn. Remember Powell's rule for Four and Five: Carry too much speed through Four and Five A and you'll be spending too much money at the engine shop. That's because exit speed out of Five B is critical to top speed on the Andretti Straight. Carry too much speed in Four and Five A and you'll feel good, but the entry to Five B will be too difficult. A lack of precision out of Five B will spoil your straightline speed.

Use a late apex and top gear for Four, go to third or second for Five A, depending on your gearbox ratios, and third, second or first for Five B. I shouldn't have to tell you that, in the appropriate gear, you'll turn in and balance at peak torque, and then clip the apex and accelerate out to peak power. Don't whine to your engine man about lack of horsepower until you can do Four and Five perfectly.

Turns Six And Seven

These are the kinks on the Andretti Straight. Try to shift on the plateaus and straighten out the kinks. Move to the left of the track for the climb up the last hill and prepare to brake for Eight.

Turns Eight, Nine And 10

Eight, Nine and 10 comprise the Esses at Mosport. Precision through Eight and Nine, which are late apex turns, is essential to doing well in 10. Missed apexes are very costly. Good exit speed out of 10 enables you to carry momentum all the way through One and Two, greatly enhancing lap times. Trail braking can help at Eight, but is a waste of time in Nine and 10. Use up all the road at the exit of 10, and remember that the leader into 10 is usually the winner at the start/finish line. □

Hot Lap Directory

CIRCUIT	ISSUE
1984	
Road Atlanta	January
Brainerd	February
Sears Point	March
Lime Rock	April
Riverside	May
Charlotte	June
Hallett	July
Watkins Glen	August
Portland	October
1985	
Nelson Ledges	January
Summit Point	February
Moroso	March
Grattan	April
Road America	May
Laguna Seca	June
Indianapolis Raceway Park	July
Willow Springs	August
St. Louis	September
Mid-Ohio	October
1986	
Pocono	September
1987	
Pueblo	March
Lake Afton	July

Photocopies of previous Hot Laps are available for $3 each. Write to Hot Laps, SportsCar magazine, 1385 East Warner Ave., Suite C, Tustin, CA 92680. Allow eight weeks for delivery.

John Heinricy put in many testing miles at Firebird Raceway in his role as Chevrolet's project manager for development of the 1984, 1985 and 1986 Corvettes. The 39-year-old engineer has been a racer for only four years, but during that time he has logged a lot of seat time behind the wheels of showroom stock endurance and GTO Corvettes. Driving for the Morrison-Cook Motorsports Escort endurance team in 1987, Heinricy finished third in the SS drivers standings behind the championship-winning Archer brothers.

HOT LAP

FIREBIRD

A DRIVER WHO KNOWS THE WAY SHOWS THE WAY

BY JOHN HEINRICY
(edited by Don Knowles)

Firebird Raceway is a relatively slow and flat track with a good mix of turns, including several challenging interconnected transitions. The main straight (a drag strip) is good for more than 100mph in most cars. It is very much a rhythm track in that there are several sections where the turns are very dependent upon each other. A good example of this is the section from the start of Turn Four to the end of Turn Nine. Even a small mistake can ruin the rhythm of the whole section.

Turn One

Proceeding down the pit straight toward the chicane, I gradually work my way to the left side of the track next to the guardrail. Approaching the chicane there is an access opening through the guardrail on the left side. I use the far side of this access as a precise turn-in marker for the chicane. At this point in a showroom stock Corvette, the car is in fourth gear near peak power. I turn in under full power, lift, begin braking, then quickly progress to limit braking and downshift to third. It's extremely important to do everything here very smoothly. The lift, braking and downshift are all done with the car traveling in an arc. Anything that upsets the balance of the car will destroy the line through the turn, costing a lot of time. If keeping the car balanced is a problem, it's much better to back off earlier and come into the turn a little slower. Less time will be lost.

Continue the initial arc about a car length past the entrance apex and start turning left while still braking. Ignore the first apex and aim for the second apex on the left, achieving full throttle before touching the apex. Now cornering to the left, the car will drift out to the curb on the right at the end of the chicane at the edge of the straight. The exit speed and wide open throttle (WOT) acceleration forces the car almost to the left side of the straight.

You need to cross immediately to the right side of the track to prepare for the lefthander at the end of the drag strip straight.

Turns Two And Three

I treat these two as a single 180-degree decreasing radius turn. I straddle the solid white line down the middle of the straight, avoiding the extra but slick pavement to the right. I continue accelerating about two car lengths past the end of the white line, then turn in slightly and begin braking lightly. Trail braking into this turn is the way to go fast with a Corvette. Trail brake about a third of the way around this turn, tightening up the arc to one car width from the inside. Get off the brakes and use enough throttle to keep the car at the limit of adhesion. Go to WOT as soon as you can see the late apex at the very end of the turn on the inside. A good reference point for the exit of this turn is a patch at the outside edge of the track. If you exit the turn driving across this patch, you've carried good speed through the turn.

I should make a point here about the digital speedometer on the Corvette. It measures changes in speed in smaller increments than the tach and is therefore a better tool for judging exit speeds. A good exit speed from Turn Three is about 75mph.

Turn Four

The straight between Three and Four is

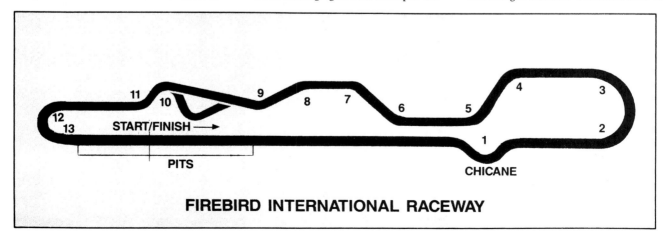

FIREBIRD INTERNATIONAL RACEWAY

The 12-13 combination is the most critical on the circuit as good exit speed pays off all the way down the main straight.

very short. Due to the banking of Turn Four, no braking is required. Still in third gear, lift for the turn, apexing early and staying to the left edge of the track between Four and Five. Turn Four is faster than it first appears, but it is essential to be on the proper line so that the car will be completely settled for the turn-in point for Five. When you see the concrete wall at the outside of Five you'll know why.

Turn Five

Five is a flat, 70-degree right-hander. You should just lift for the turn in or brake lightly if coming in a little hot. Take a late turn in and squeeze the gas to WOT about halfway across the track approaching the apex (which is a very nasty curb you don't want to hit). This should carry you in a nice drift to the exit that is just past the end of the concrete wall (which you also don't want to hit) at the outside edge of the track.

Turn Six

There is virtually no straight between Five and Six. Stay at WOT in third and begin turning in for Six almost immediately. The apex has two very nasty curbs. I apex between them and immediately aim for the apex at Turn Seven, still at WOT.

Turn Seven

There really isn't a *turn* at Seven. The car is going straight and the track just comes out to meet it approaching Turn Eight.

Turn Eight

I lift before passing the Turn Seven apex and begin braking in a straight line on a heading for the outside of the track between Seven and Eight. The braking is light and short, just enough to settle the front of the car, then I begin the left turn, using the throttle to keep the car on the limit. My line is a radius that carries the car to about a car's width from the outside of the track between Seven and Eight, finishes at the apex to Eight (another curb) and keeps me at the left

edge of the track after the Turn Eight apex for Turn Nine and the straight after it.

Turn Nine

It's important to get off Turn Nine smooth and fast to carry maximum speed onto the ensuing straight (the only one since the pit straight). Lift at the Turn Eight apex to prepare for Nine. I don't use the brakes. Turn in late and go to WOT at the Turn Nine apex (another nasty curb). This should carry you in a drift to the exit (which is the nastiest curb of all. Many a wheel has been broken on it!). There's time for one breath on the straight between Nine and 10, but make it a short one.

Turn 10

Move over to the right edge of the track on the straight between Nine and 10. Lift, turn in to a late apex, and go back to WOT on a line headed for the Turn 11 apex.

Turn 11

This turn is taken flat out. There is a slight downhill just past the apex and then an uphill, slightly banked exit. The outside of the turn has a guardrail right at the edge of the track. The exit is just beyond the end of the guardrail. If the entry to 10 is not done well, a drive into the guardrail is a sure bet if you don't back off.

Turns 12 And 13

This combination is the mirror image of Turns Two and Three, except that this one has an increasing rather than a decreasing radius. Immediately after gathering up the car from the Turn 11 exit and moving to the right edge of the pavement, lift and brake hard, aiming for the number four or five staging lane markers for the drag strip. Brake deep, pivot the car to the left and, using the throttle to keep the car at the limit, accelerate onto the main straight using the end of the guardrail on the left side as the apex and the concrete wall on the right side as the exit.

I use third gear for this turn even though the first part of the turn seems slow. Any significant tire spinning can get you in serious trouble due not only to the proximity of the guardrail and concrete walls, but also because there are several surface changes. The staging lanes are asphalt and the straight is concrete. The straight between the apex and the exit crosses both starting lanes of the dragstrip which have lots of rubber laid down. If it's wet, it's like driving across patches of ice. The front straight is long enough to draft past a leading car before taking the checkered flag. □

Hot Lap Directory

CIRCUIT	ISSUE
1984	
Road Atlanta	January
Brainerd	February
Sears Point	March
Lime Rock	April
Riverside	May
Charlotte	June
Hallett	July
Watkins Glen	August
Portland	October
1985	
Nelson Ledges	January
Summit Point	February
Moroso	March
Grattan	April
Road America	May
Laguna Seca	June
Indianapolis Raceway Park	July
Willow Springs	August
St. Louis	September
Mid-Ohio	October
1986	
Pocono	September
1987	
Pueblo	March
Lake Afton	July
1988	
Mosport	February

Photocopies of previous Hot Laps are available for $3.00 each. Write Hot Laps, SportsCar magazine, 1385-C, E. Warner, Tustin, CA 92680. Allow eight weeks for delivery.

Peter Cunningham was picked by Sports-Car's 1988 ''Star Search'' panel as a promising young ''shoe,'' and has proceeded to prove the selection was merited. Among the accomplishments in his racing portfolio are championships of the B Class of the Escort Endurance Championship for both '88 and '89. In addition to his Escort schedule last year, he also competed in the Firestone Firehawk showroom stock series, scoring victories in all three of that championship's categories—a feat never before accomplished in a single season by any one driver. Early last year, Cunningham also recorded his first championship in the International Ice Racing Association championship sprint races.

''P.D.'' as he is fondly referred to by friends, has also tried his hand at autocrossing and PRO Rallying, taking numerous wins and claiming an H Stock National Solo II Championship in the early years of his driving career.

BLACKHAWK FARMS

A DRIVER WHO KNOWS THE WAY SHOWS THE WAY

BY PETER CUNNINGHAM

Blackhawk Farms Raceway is a 1.8-mile, seven-turn road course located just west of Rockton, Ill. The elevation changes are similar to what would be found on a frozen lake, so there are no uphill or downhill sections with which to contend. For years BFR has been an SCCA mainstay for club racing in the CEDiv and, with all its other activities, ranks as one of the busiest tracks in the country.

Although the racing surface is relatively narrow and rather abrasive, the SCCA has begun running professional events there, beginning with last September's Escort Endurance Championship event.

Track owners Raymond and Mike Irwin have made many improvements since purchasing the facility a few years ago, and have promised SCCA several more refinements in the months ahead, making Blackhawk Farms a more enjoyable circuit for competitors and spectators alike. The following lap is being taken with a Team GRR Honda CRX.

Traveling past the pit lane toward Turn One, you are carrying your highest terminal speed. Turn One is a medium-speed, third-gear corner leading onto another sizable straight, so you want to get as good an exit as possible. To do this you must start your braking early enough (the 1.5 marker) to ensure proper velocity by the turn-in point. Take a slightly late apex, getting back on the power as soon as possible. The ''rumble

strips'' at the exit aren't too bad, but you don't want to hit them every lap. Late braking into Turn One is probably the best place to pass on the whole track.

Turn Two is basically a kink to the left. The only thing to remember here is to shorten the distance between One and Three by being smooth.

Turn Three is also known as the Carousel,

a seemingly endless right-hander. Having been in fourth gear since soon after exiting Turn One, you are carrying a good bit of speed once again. This time, you want to try to maintain that speed for as long as possible, giving up a classical entrance into the corner. In fact, don't even bother going all the way over to the left on the approach; instead, try to concentrate on doing the heavy braking in a straight line, and downshift back into third. Then, just before you drive off the outside edge, turn in and start feeding in the throttle, attempting to hit a very late apex two-thirds of the way around the corner. About this time the radius decreases and you find yourself approaching the outside edge again, but don't worry, for the road opens up and you follow the left edge out of the corner hoping you don't have to get out of the throttle. The sooner you can commit to flat-out power at that first apex, the higher your speed at the exit.

After exiting the Carousel, upshift to fourth and ''stroll'' gently to the right side of the road. That's all that's needed on your approach to Turn Four. The entrance to this turn can be intimidating due to a lack of places to go if you gum up, but once comfortable you'll realize how deceptively quick it can be. A good exit is important once

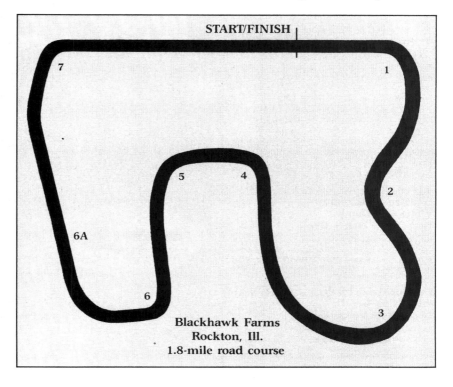

START/FINISH

Blackhawk Farms
Rockton, Ill.
1.8-mile road course

Blackhawk considers the competitors' need to keep their cars clean with this wash bay.

Farm. It is also debatably the most important, as it leads onto another long flat-out section. To do this second gear right-hander properly you must *stop* your car on the way in so you'll be able to do two things: 1) stay on the track at the exit; and 2) get on the power soon enough to guarantee utmost maximum speed at the end of this second longest straight. For some reason, a lot of drivers seem to have trouble being consistent in this corner. It is a somewhat off-camber late-late-apex turn that requires much thought every lap.

Soon after straightening the wheel after Turn Six—or driving back onto the road, as the case may be—you must turn right once again to proceed through another flat-out or near-flat-out bend. Smoothness is the key to preserve the most time.

If you disagree that Turn Six was the most important corner at Blackhawk, then we've found your corner. In any case, Turn Seven is very difficult due to a rather confusing braking zone kink. It is definitely an important corner, as it connects the two longest straightaways on the circuit.

Soon after confronting the kink in fourth gear, begin your braking and downshifting. Strive to keep everything in a straight line so that you finally reach the left side of the road at the turn-in point. Select second gear, and suavely bend the car into a late apex, getting back onto the gas ASAP. This way you can generate that maximum velocity down the 2400ft longest straight. Passing on the way in can be troublesome here, so try instead to feint a pass under braking and hope your opponent runs out of asphalt on the way out. Then it starts all over again □

again, as another fast section follows. Get your braking done early (start at the 2 marker) so you can downshift to third and commit back to the throttle and hit your just-late apex hard. Be careful not to use too much of the road on the exit, though, since there is a drop-off that has bitten more than a few would-be heroes. Passing on the way in can be done, but you will sacrifice terminal speed into Turn Six, so try and be patient.

A short shift into fourth can be done on your approach to Turn Five, but only if you're not comfortable shifting during this flat-out or near-flat-out left-hander. In order to carry as much speed as possible, be sure to use all the road on the way in, then turn in slowly to a late apex which is slightly blind. There is a no passing zone on the way in, but you can set up a late-braking pass for your approach to Turn Six.

Turn Six is the slowest corner on the

Cunningham (42) leads a string of cars through Turn Four, intimidating because of its minimal run-off area, but getting it right pays dividends.

Dennis Macchio has been general manager of the Bridgehampton Race Circuit since 1988, and has provided driving instruction to a variety of clubs and racing organizations. During the 1988 and 1989 seasons he won 11 consecutive Formula Ford races at Bridgehampton, earning the Eastern Motor Racing Association's FF championship both years, and being named EMRA Driver of the Year in '88. He has led the restoration of the circuit that will see it host its first SCCA National in many years during 1992.

Like those famous American racing circuits in Watkins Glen, N.Y., and Elkhart Lake, Wis., the seed for the Bridgehampton Race Circuit was first planted by over-the-public-roads races in the early 1950s. When Long Island's public roads were finally closed to racing, a classic road circuit was built to replace them. Opening in 1957, the 2.85-mile Bridgehampton circuit was characterized by fast sweepers, blind turns and strategically placed elevation changes, and rightly earned a reputation as a real driver's track.

In the '80s, Bridgehampton nearly vanished from view as a variety of

HOT LAP

BRIDGEHAMPTON

A DRIVER WHO KNOWS THE WAY SHOWS THE WAY

BY DENNIS MACCHIO

circumstances tarnished its historic luster, but under the auspices of the New York Region and the track's general manager, Dennis Macchio, the circuit has undergone a substantial upgrading and will return to the SCCA National racing calendar on the weekend of April 25-26.

Complete directions to the track (including alternate routes around New York City) and a listing of discounts available from hotels and motels in the area will be included with the entry forms available from the region's registrar, Lyn Wisbauer, at (516) 665-5635. Workers and spectators can receive a similar packet by calling (718) 849-0171.

The upgrades to the physical plant itself include: significantly expanded runoff areas with new, banded tire walls, new rest rooms with hot showers, and an enlarged paddock area with improved registration facility, newly enclosed tech garage, fuel station and on-site race prep shop. Of particular interest to workers will be the track's new covered corner stations—with benches. Here's how Dennis Macchio gets around.

Turns One and Two

The start-finish line is located approximately midway along Bridgehampton's longest straightaway. At the end of this 3000ft "pit straight" is a downhill right-hand sweeper, followed immediately by another, slightly tighter, right-hand sweeper. The setup for this combination is to stay to the left on the straight and look for a turn-in point just after passing under the bridge. If properly done, both sweepers can be taken flat out in most cars. If it is deemed necessary to lift, it should be done under the bridge. Alternatively, however, there is a point between the two sweepers where the car gets neutral for a moment, and a lift for

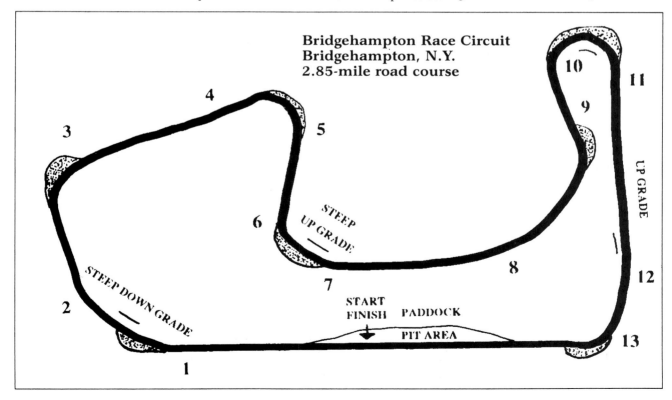

Dennis Macchio has experienced much success at Bridgehampton as both driver and track's general manager.

the second sweeper could be done there. However, as both turns are fast and downhill, it's extremely important to leave the power on once committed to the turn as loss of control in this area seldom results in a "minor" incident.

Turns Three and Four

After a short chute coming out of Turns One and Two, the track flattens out. Turns Three and Four are a fast, right-hand combination usually done as a single-apex, increasing-radius turn. A hard stab on the brakes and a downshift are needed on the approach. The tendency on this corner is to go in too hot and, as a result, lose some exit speed. As the turn is followed by a long straight, the proper strategy is to give away some entry speed and be on the power from the moment of turn-in.

Turn Five

The straight between Four and Five is a quarter-mile long and bumpy. Most track maps don't show it, but the straight fades to the left just before the entry to Five. The braking zone for Five also drops away, and the car is always light there. The hot ticket is to approach from the middle of the straight, angle toward driver's left, brake earlier than appears necessary, trail brake slightly and then get hard on the power. The apex for Five is very late as it is a tight, decreasing-radius turn. It is also blind from the entry point.

Turns Six and Seven

Turns Six and Seven are a combination uphill left-hander that can be taken faster than it initially appears, but proper gear selection is important. Enter the turn from the extreme right and apex early, using the curbing found at the apex. Get the power down early—especially in underpowered cars—as the hill is long and steep. Turn Seven, the second part of this combination, is flat out and should be taken smoothly to carry maximum speed to the top of the hill. The track-out for this turn is at the crest of the hill, and using every bit of roadway is important.

Turn Eight

Between Turns Seven and Eight the track begins to drop off, and bends to the left. Setting up properly for the flat-out left-hand sweeper of Turn Eight is critical as the power must be kept on through this turn. The reward here is being able to extend the period of flat-out acceleration that has been carried down the hill. This is a very fast part of the track where smoothness and precision pay dividends.

Turn Nine

The kink of Eight is followed immediately by Turn Nine, a left-hander that requires a moderate amount of braking and a downshift. The transition between the exit of Eight and the entry to Nine is very short. The trick is first to get the car balanced and then do some very fast footwork. If you can do it, shift without the clutch. If you screw up your footwork here you will run out of braking zone very quickly. If a compromise is necessary, give up the entry to Nine as opposed to jeopardizing Eight.

Turn 10

Turn 10 is a long, right-hand, uphill hairpin that can be done as either a single or double apex. The single apex gives up speed through the first part of the turn, but allows for greater exit speed leading to the long straight that follows. The double apex is useful as a blocking line, especially to maximize a power advantage over a competitor.

Turns 11, 12 and 13

Turn 11 is a modest sweeper that is a turn in name only, but the combination of Turns 12 and 13 that follows is the most important on the circuit as it leads back onto the long straight. Twelve is a flat-out right-hand sweeper. Its strategic importance is that it makes the setup for 13 very difficult since it is uphill and blind. The trick in this combination is to compromise 12 by staying off the apex, which allows for a cleaner, smaller-radius entry into 13. A very quick transition period allows for a stab on the brakes and a downshift entering 13, another fast, uphill right-hander. Thirteen should be early-apexed with the use of a little car rotation and the benefit afforded by the hill. This turn, more than any other, is the key to a fast lap at The Bridge. ∎

Jerry Hinkle has raced numerous production cars over the last 27 years, setting lap records at several road courses, many of which are now defunct. His modern experience is in an EP Lotus 7, winning the NEDiv the last five years, on the pole at the Runoffs in 1990 and finishing second in 1991.

New Hampshire International Speedway has dramatically altered the site of the old Bryar Motorsports Park near Loudon, N.H. Opened in May 1990, it was created as a multi-purpose facility whose centerpiece is the only new superspeedway built since Talladega, Ala., in 1969. Investor Bob Bahre oversees what is now an important venue for SCCA, NASCAR and CART.

A 1.6-mile road course is integrated into the site, using nearly half the 1.06-mile oval. The banking is fairly shallow compared to Pocono or Charlotte, but is substantial enough to allow serious cornering speeds. The "outfield" corners offer great variety in speeds, camber and elevation, while the short "infield" section is entirely flat. Unlike nearly every other SCCA course, it is run counterclockwise, with a predominance of left-handers.

In approaching this course, it is

HOT LAP

NEW HAMPSHIRE

A DRIVER WHO KNOWS THE WAY, SHOWS THE WAY

BY JERRY HINKLE

important for a driver to be willing to explore unconventional lines, particularly if the car has excellent grip and balance. The surface is new, and except for the transitions across the oval, is very wide and smooth. Its first winter brought on no new bumps, and the quality of the construction should make it durable.

The Oval

Entry onto the straight past the grandstands is flat, taken in second gear for a smaller car. A lump in the pavement at the transition to the oval may briefly upset some vehicles. In the rain, the surface tends to collect puddles here, just before the camber changes abruptly. The straight is nearly 1400ft long; the pavement is some 60ft wide, with the turns upward of 75ft wide.

The apparent apex for Turn 12 is near the end of the projecting pit wall. There is a surplus of space available for a wider sweep, with a lot of throttle after the transition across the apron of the oval. Make the car climb the oval at a shallow angle. With a low-powered car, don't be too anxious to eat up momentum; let the car find its way.

As usual, entry onto the longest straight is quite important, as the end of the oval is a real corner that you must accelerate through—thus it is a hybrid, sharing the features of both a corner and a straight. Depending on the thrust available when attempting to accelerate above 100-115mph, you must get all the remaining power to the ground in order to make speed. With a radius of 375ft around the inside of the corner, the 1200ft long straight launches the car out toward the far wall at considerable speed.

The banking absorbs some momentum, but try to continue to accelerate through the corner. Setup here is critical, and gearing needs to be as short as

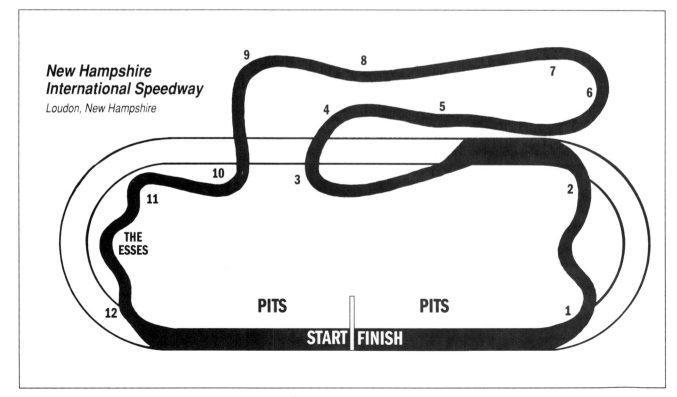

New Hampshire International Speedway

Loudon, New Hampshire

THE ESSES

PITS   PITS

START | FINISH

possible to allow seeking that extra thrust. Feather the throttle if necessary to transit the "stub" of a straight at the exit; but ignore it if you can, since what happens in the corner is most important.

Consider, too, rebiasing weight or altering alignment to achieve more bite in the oval. Don't overlook running higher spring rates on the right side, shifting ballast to the left, increasing ride height slightly and using stagger at both front and rear. Remember that most of the corners are left-handers, and that incorporating some oval track chassis tuning can pay dividends. Tire temperatures may not be revealing, since the esses just preceding the pits will tend to equalize them. The temperatures over the usual Memorial Day SCCA National weekend have been quite warm, so use right side tires that will live through a tough race—you can bet that they are actually running hotter than what temperatures taken in the pits will show.

The SCCA National is traditionally run at a time when the track surface has been thoroughly scrubbed after fall and winter weathering, plus spring's rainstorms. Expect grip to improve throughout the weekend as more rubber is deposited on the surface, especially in Turns One and Two. Be prepared to take advantage of this by varying tire pressures and compounds, or even slight suspension readjustments. If the weekend has been dry, then search for a groove in the oval in morning warmup and in the race itself. Reading and adapting to conditions netted up to two seconds a lap for perceptive drivers during the 1991 National.

Again, let the car find its way exiting Turn Two, where you are at the fastest part of the course. Try not to waste forward momentum by exiting late; the shallowest steering angle scrubs off the least energy. Passage through here is very brief; just allow the car to settle and line up for the braking area into Turn Three.

Turn Three

The roadway begins to narrow rapidly into Turn Three; have the car's direction changed and aligned for a late entry before any heavy braking is done. This is not a place to test high speed directional stability—none of the landscape is soft or flexible, plus the camber changes slightly. A quick transition is made here from the fastest to the slowest part of the course, and is a frequent trap for the impure—it is a great choke point for flow off the oval. It might be exhilarating to charge off the oval at Vmax and bury the car under the noses of the spectators on the inside wall, but conserve the brakes for the next few corners. Early in this sequence there is passing room, but do it decisively, as the track narrows quickly.

Turns Four, Five and Six

Turn Four is blind, as you go over a short crest edged with curbs. Launch out of here with good speed up the hill toward Five. If the car settles quickly over the rise, you can brake very late for Six, which is like a leftover piece of a luge run. A steep, bowl-shaped uphill left, Six will gobble energy at a great rate, so plenty of power is needed to exit quickly. The camber flattens rapidly at the exit, requiring a deft touch with the throttle to preserve the speed gained out of the bowl.

Turns Seven and Eight

As this sequence is blind over another crest at good speed, and gives no good reference until you're through, try for comfortable approaches that help line up the car for an early glimpse of Nine. Stones and sand are commonly strewn on the pavement here from the failed experiments of others, so save attack speed for the corners that really count. Leave a little in reserve to allow altering your line to have the car settled for entry into Turn Nine.

Turn Nine

Seemingly a short, shrinking radius downhill left, this corner tolerates unconventional lines due to its width and smoothness. A stable car can plunge right across the apparent apex while braking hard, then create a much later apex out in the roadway, taking advantage of the space that only becomes visible when you're well into the corner. The camber is more favorable later in the corner, which should encourage you to use more throttle as the car rockets back down to cross over the oval's back straight.

Turn 10

This downhill changes abruptly into a slow, flat 90-degree right that can become greasy. Be prepared to allow some slack here; jumping on the throttle in a slow car can get you loose. Apply the power a few feet later to be under control, building speed and aligned for the esses.

Turns 11 and 12—The Esses

These are flat and grippy, but are bounded by some sharp-edged curbing that will readily cut a tire. Again, experiment—lots of throttle with no twitching can carve a path through the several changes of direction. A car that immediately damps roll transients is a blessing, allowing maximum speed through 12 and on to the banking.

Summary

• Experiment with unconventional lines—this is a three-dimensional track.

• Exploit changing grip conditions—the track's been sitting here all winter.

• Be prepared to alter the chassis setup to make extra speed in the banking and around all the left-handers. ■

Mike Sauce drives a Swift DB-1 Formula Ford around Texas World Speedway as if he owned the place. In his six appearances there in 1992, Sauce has set, then broken the lap record for Formula Ford each time he competed. In the process, he won five races in 1992. Sauce started the 1993 season with a double win at TWS, breaking his own track lap record during a Double National weekend. The Arlington, Texas, based racer was also the '91 and '92 SWDiv FF champion and the 1991 Kimberly Cup recipient. Sauce also set a lap record at Road Atlanta on his way to the Formula Ford pole at the 1992 SCCA Valvoline Runoffs.®

There are two road racing configurations used at the Texas World Speedway (TWS) oval. One course is 1.8-miles long, the other 1.9-miles. Each is driven counterclockwise. The 1.9-mile course eliminates the Turns Eight through 12 complex and exits the infield after the Carousel (Turn Seven), entering the high banking just before the TWS oval Turn Three.

The first three turns of the course are really one left-turn complex positioned at the end of a long straight. On the first lap of this track, it is critical to have your car's tires and brakes up to race temperatures. Turn One is driven flat-out in top gear and Turn Two is flat-out in third gear. If the tires are not warmed up, the car will not stay on the race track. Beware of cool brakes on the first lap. By the time you reach Turn One, you will have covered almost half of the track without really using the brakes, so they will have plenty of time to cool down.

HOT LAP

TEXAS WORLD SPEEDWAY

A DRIVER WHO KNOWS THE WAY SHOWS THE WAY

BY MIKE SAUCE WITH
ANDY ANDERSON

This means that on the first lap, it is difficult to have heated the brakes up enough for the heavy braking you need to do into Turn Three.

You can actually set up for Turn One when you cross the start/finish line on the front straight of the TWS oval. You should be driving down to about a half-car width off of the apron at the start/finish line. Then begin moving slowly up the banking of the oval. Other drivers drive down onto the apron, but I don't think it helps.

Turns One-One A

As you approach the Turn One, One A and Two complex, you want to have gradually climbed up the track's banking to within about a car width of the outside wall. Driving closer to the wall will put you in an area of the track that is dirty with debris.

You want to make a late entry into Turn One. Drive in so that you are making it a long, sweeping corner. This type of line minimizes your scrubbing off speed. You will really load up the suspension as you cross the apron onto the infield road course. Stay on the power as the car settles. You should wind up about 10 feet from the inside dirt/grass of the race track infield in the chute between Turns One and Two. If you want to pass someone in Turn One, you should drive a flatter arc. Turn in early, and you will beat the other driver to the apex. When trying to pass here, you have to keep the other driver on the outside of you until you decide to turn in.

Turn Two

The outside edge of the track is your turn-in point for Turn Two. It will come up as you head for what seems like Houston. It is deceptive, as the track is crowned and you can't actually see the edge of the track or your turn-in point for Turn Two—until it seems like it is too late. When the car is straight, you can brush the brakes and shift down into third gear.

When you run out of pavement, and have to turn in, you are driving the corner correctly. I see a lot of drivers braking hard and early-apexing this turn. Let the turn-in to Turn Two scrub off the speed don't do it with the brakes. You can drive a lot deeper and carry your speed further into this turn than you think you can.

Turn Two is a decreasing radius turn. In Formula Ford you should be flat-out in third gear, pulling 6200 to 6300rpm through the late apex. If you really hustle through here, you can get into fourth gear before you get to Turn Three.

Turn Three

This is a great place for out-braking and passing. You want to set up for the right-hand Turn Three by driving a line to the left side of the track, braking hard and downshifting to second gear. Aim for a late apex, dragging your right front tire across the curbing. Then straighten your line, stay to the right, brake and downshift to first gear for the left-hand Turn Four.

Turn Four

It is not important to get *into* Turn Four fast, but to get *out* of it fast. A lot of drivers will charge into Turn Four, and really upset their line through the following corner sequences. Stay close to

Formula Ford pilot Mike Sauce continues to set lap records at his home track, Texas World Speedway.

the inside curb on the exit of Turn Three, positioning yourself on the right side of the track going into Turn Four. Slow the car down a lot, late apex Turn Four and accelerate straight toward Turn Six. You will only have to give the steering wheel a flick to get through the right-hand Turn Five.

Turns Six-Seven

The left-hand Turn Six is one of those corners where you have to turn in late, then lift to rotate the car to point it for Turn Seven (the Carousel). In Turn Seven, don't use a lot of the race track. You don't want to drive out much farther than the center of the track through the turn. Aim for a very late apex through Turn Seven.

Turns Eight-Nine

Hug the inside curbing on the exit of Turn Seven, up-shift to second gear and aim for a late apex for the left-hand Turn Eight, flat-out in second gear in a Formula Ford. Use all of the track here, all the way out to the right edge. Up-shift to third gear, stay to the right on this "chute" and you're set up for Turn Nine.

Driving Turn Nine in a well set-up Formula Ford can be done flat-out in third gear. It is a mildly late apex corner. You can go through Turn Nine with your foot

flat on the floor, and use a lot of race track. There is a slight banking of the track at the apex (actually something between a bank and a dip).

For the 1.9-mile configuration, as you make the left turn (a new Turn Eight) across the apron and up onto the oval, let the car point up toward the wall. Don't pinch the corner off, or stay low on the oval, it will only scrub off speed. As the oval "catches" you, begin driving a long gentle left turn, using as much of the track as necessary to keep from scrubbing off too much speed. Start a long flattened arc that will carry you down the banking through the short chute between the TWS oval Turns Three and Four. Then gradually unwind the arc, straightening your line on the banking as you enter the main straight. Begin a slow move down across the banking to about a car width off of the inside apron as you cross the start/finish line. Wait a heart beat, then begin your move up the banking and into Turn One.

Turns 10-12

The trickiest part of the track is the Turn 10-12 sequence that returns you back to the oval in the 1.8-mile configuration. Brake and downshift to second gear, clipping the inside (left) curb of Turn 10 (a left hander) for an early apex.

This sets you up for Turn 11, which is much more important than Turn 10. If you were successful in getting through Turn 10—moving all the way to the left side of the track—you can accelerate in almost a straight shot out through Turns 11 and 12 and out onto the oval.

If you drive it just right, you should be shifting into third gear just after you cross the apron onto the oval. Don't worry about carrying what seems to be too much speed through Turns 11 and 12 as the banking of the oval will catch you. When you exit Turn 11, aim the car up the banking. Don't worry about the speed you might lose "climbing up the hill;" you will get it back.

Allow your car to go as far as it wants to go up the banking without turning the steering wheel. Then, as you near the oval wall, start a long sweeping gradual arc (so as not to scrub off much speed) down the banking. Shift into fourth gear when necessary, and end your arc about one car width off of the inside apron at the start/finish line. Driving this arc down the banking will help you pick up as much as 200-300rpm by the time you reach the end of the straight. Just past the start/finish line, begin a gradual climb back up the banking to within a car width of the wall, headed for Turn One. Then the fun begins all over again. ∎

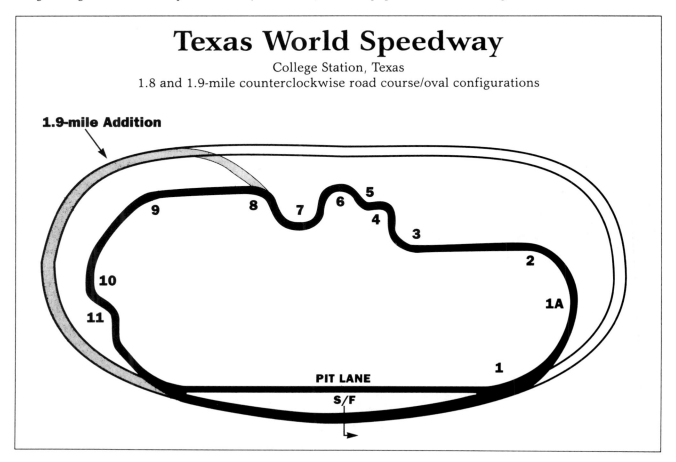

Texas World Speedway

College Station, Texas
1.8 and 1.9-mile counterclockwise road course/oval configurations

1.9-mile Addition

PIT LANE

S/F

Jim Kearney is the 1992 Valvoline Pro Vee champion and was a silver medalist at the Runoffs° in 1991. He now holds the FVee lap record at the newly surfaced Road Atlanta, breaking the mark previously held by Stevan Davis.

The taciturn, unassuming Davis is the 1987 and 1992 FVee National champion who drove such a flawless, blindingly fast race to the title last year; and Road Atlanta· is his home track. He is also now driving in FC and will compete in both classes in the '93 Runoffs. Bill Noble is the grand master, with three FVee National titles captured here, the last in 1990. As you will see, they bring different insights about the best way around this demanding circuit.

HOT LAP
ROAD ATLANTA

THREE DRIVERS WHO KNOW THE WAY, SHOW THE WAY

BY JIM KEARNEY, STEVAN DAVIS AND BILL NOBLE

R oad Atlanta was repaved and significantly widened (to a nearly uniform 40ft) for 1993. The surface is the proverbial billiard table and the curbs are, for the most part, user friendly. The best advice I ever received about Road Atlanta was not to be afraid initially to run six seconds off the pace on a practice day. With its high-speed sweepers and numerous blind apexes, you can't hurry the process of learning this track. You need to develop a sense of timing about the many turns that remain hidden until you are committed.

There are fewer idiosyncrasies to be aware of with the new Road Atlanta, but one critical one needs emphasis: driving the Pit Entry Lane. Although the track has been widened to accommodate it, for much of its length the Pit Entry Lane can be part of some drivers' racing line. Rather than slowing down in preparation to enter the pits, the prudent driver will hustle here to get out of proximity to the racing line. You then need to slow dramatically for the 90-degree turn into the actual pits. For those who haven't driven the new Road Atlanta, practice getting down this pit entry lane at an above average clip. Otherwise, you risk being

clobbered by someone in their racing line (even if they're not supposed to be there) who may not see you in time.

Davis: Everyone always asks me: What is the most important turn at this track? My answer is, no matter what your level of experience, every turn is important. If you want to be fast you can't screw up any turn. You need to treat every turn as if it is the most important turn.

Noble: I think there are two important turns at Road Atlanta: Turn One and The Bridge (Turn 11). Getting these two turns right can make the difference between an ordinary lap and a great lap and that difference can be two seconds.

Turn One

You need to come up with a method whereby you gradually enter this daunting

With the potential for the racing line to get over into the Pit Entry Lane, it is wise not to slow too early when going to the pits.

JOHN SWAIN

turn more quickly. I find it valuable to lift very early at first and work up to turning in under power. You also need to be aware that this is a place where a competitor may be attempting a pass and adjust your turn-in point accordingly.

Davis: Turn One is not any wider than before, except for a two-foot patch of asphalt added where the old pit exit used to be. By the time I reach the patch, I am heading to the apex—even though it seems way too early. The banking that exists at this turn—combined with the hill—contributes to an entrance speed that is seemingly too quick. Faster classes with close-ratio gearboxes will downshift a gear, sometimes as they climb the hill.

Noble: This turn separates the strong from the weak. If you're not scared here, you're going too slow. I drive down the front straight looking for the point at which the left edge turns up the hill. At the point a straight line would run into the grass, I turn in. It seems a bit early, but it works out. I lift off the gas for a beat but I'm working on eliminating that. I am full on the power before I turn in and I pay utmost attention not to scrub off any speed at the entrance, as this kills your exit speed. I drive through the corner using all the track. The key to Road Atlanta is getting back on the power quickly.

Turns Two and Three

As Turn One is now faster with the new paving, it is more important that you move to mid-track as you exit Turn One and climb the hill to Turn Two. Gently move to the left as you crest the hill so that you approach Turn Three with the car "squared up" to the edge of the track. A common mistake is to arrive at Three and still need to move left. Under braking this can upset the car just as you turn in. This area of the track is ripe for first lap accidents as traffic backs up. A large field will accentuate this problem.

Davis: Going up the hill, lower speed cars don't need to apex Turn Two, though it is necessary to do so when I drive the FC car. In most cars, it is just a setup turn for Turn Three. Higher powered cars may drop two gears upon the entrance to Three.

Remember that Turn Three is nearly a 90-degree turn, at least at the point that you turn in. After that it opens up quickly. In pursuit of the ultimate line you can put a front tire on the curbing at the apex, as it is now much lower than it used to be. I try to put some scrub on the car so that the rear tires do not ride over the curb. This is particularly important in a stiffly sprung chassis like an FC car. The penalty in wheel spin and potential loss of control mandates staying off the curb, at least with the rear tires.

Noble: Turns Two and Three are rhythm turns. You can't see Turn Three ahead of time, so you have to select a reference point that enables you to just turn in and jump on the gas. For me, I turn in 2ft past the alligator teeth on the left side exiting Turn Two. Concentrate on your turn-in point for Turn Three and maintain a feel for the rhythm of the flow of a fast lap.

The Esses

Davis: Get the car back over to the left and track the right-hand curbing until you are in line with the next set of curbing on the left. Continue along in a straight line until you need to turn right to set up for Turn Five.

Noble: In a Formula Vee it doesn't matter how you go through the Esses.

Turn Five

This turn is noticeably faster now. A common error here has been to brake too late and enter with the car out of shape. As with Turn Three, it is important to approach this turn with the car squared up to the track edge.

Davis: In most classes you brake and downshift, perhaps twice, to climb the steep hill on exit. In the Vee I use the right side curbing on the entrance as a "bank shot" to turn in. In the FC car I stay away from this, as the curbing tends to pull the car farther away from the track, destroying the line. You can run up on the curbing at the apex, again remembering the proviso to keep the rear tires off the curb if you are in a stiffly sprung chassis. The outside curbing at the track out is less of a threat to upset the car and I often straighten out the line by running up on it before beginning to fade to the left to set up for Turn Six.

Noble: This is a very fast turn. I am not braking for it at all, I just lift and go. You can hit the curb on the inside apex; but if you do, it wants to throw you out over the curb at the track out point. It's important to get a smooth exit of Five. Be on the power early, don't scrub off speed. Don't turn the steering wheel any more than necessary. Relax, don't breathe so hard.

Turn Six

Although this turn is very fast, you have much more to lose here than you have to gain. If you are unstable under braking for Seven, you will pay a penalty for a large portion of the rest of the lap.

Davis: Be sure you check your mirrors as you exit Turn Five before you "think" the car over to the left side of the track. This is a common passing point. You may use the first of the two painted lines at Six as your braking point and begin your turn-in prior to the second line. This heavily banked turn is a lot faster than newcomers believe. The apex curbing here is steep and though it is important to run down to it, you need to stay off it. In the FC car, I downshift to second gear before entering Turn Six to avoid hurrying two downshifts to first gear between Six and Seven.

Noble: Enter Six quickly but don't overdo it, as you have to slow dramatically for Seven anyway. There are two ways to do this turn. One is to brake in a straight line, beginning at the first white stripe and then turn in for the apex under full power. The other is to trail brake, that is, to brake later as you turn, carrying more speed into the turn, at least initially. This second method is harder to control and as exit speeds are comparable between the two techniques, I favor the first.

Turn Seven

Davis: The inside apex curbing at Seven has been lowered significantly and you may want to experiment with putting a tire on it as you apex. A low horsepower-to-weight ratio car will demand as shallow a turn as possible. If your car has significant power you may want to carry the speed of Turn Six for another beat and then initiate your turn-in, although this requires a more abrupt turn. The curbing on exit is OK to run up on, just be sure not to let a tire fall off the outside of it.

Noble: Everybody talks about how significant this turn is, as it is the entrance to a long straight. I don't believe Turn Seven is significant. It is an easy corner and everyone can do it pretty well. The problem that does occur is that everybody tries to overdrive the turn. They make mistakes and lose time. To drive it properly, concentrate on making a nice turn-in and get on the power early.

The Dip

This is one of the scariest places in North America because so much is happening here. In FVee it is not that uncommon for three different drafting trains to run down the hill looking to occupy a single lane at the Dip. You need to maintain a strong sense of the area around each side of your car. You don't want to get off here.

Davis: Like the back straight, you can run just about anywhere, but you don't want to push someone off as you move from side to side. This is critical as you head for the left side curbing, because so much passing occurs here. I let the car drift out a bit wide to the mid-track as I come up the hill.

Turn 11: The Bridge

I need specific reference points to deal with this monster. I use the first painted line to get ready, the second line to brake and the third line to turn in for the automotive equivalent of the bungee jump. You need to stay on the power to keep the car—if not the driver—happy going over the crest.

Davis: This turn looks like a very late apex turn, but it is not as late as it would appear. I use the first painted line to brake and downshift while getting the FC car setup for the change in direction. I apex very close to the bridge abutment to get the maximum runoff area at the exit.

Noble: This turn is about total commitment. You jump back on the power as you turn in and head for the concrete bridge abutment. You find out if you are going to live through it about halfway down the hill. It is not a significant help to your lap time to sweep into the pit lane and it's suicidal to be going out that far, lap after lap.

Turn 12

Davis: As you run down the hill after the Bridge, you will need to swing out left as much as you are allowed in order to make a broad arc down through Turn 12. You may not be permitted to get all or any part of the car into the pit lane. Your turn-in point for Turn 12 is halfway back up the hill, depending upon how much your car might drift. Your car should complete this arc and run straight again right at the start/finish line, directly under the starter's stand. In the FC car, I select fourth gear here.

Noble on Drafting

To get a quick time at Road Atlanta in a FVee, you need both to drive it at 10/10ths and to get a couple of drafts. Ideally, you'll get one down the front straight and another down the back straight. One thing that a lot of people don't remember is that once they have snagged this draft, they will come up on the next corner faster than they are accustomed. You may be entering the turn 2- to 4mph faster than usual. I try to drive the same line as I usually do, but I will enter it a bit early. If I see that I am not going to make it, I scrub off some speed coming out of the apex. ∎

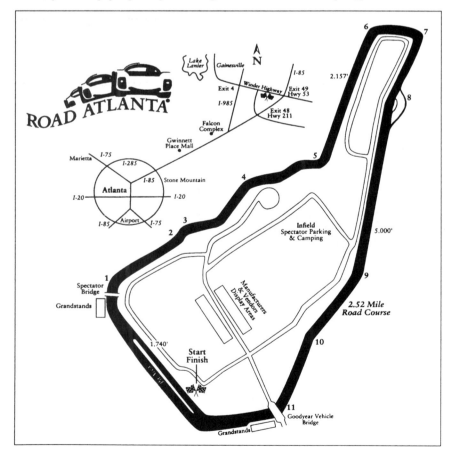

Index